Environmental

Ethics

Environmental

Ethics

An Interactive Introduction

Andrew Kernohan

broadview press

Library and Archives Canada Cataloguing in Publication

Kernohan, Andrew
    Environmental ethics : an interactive introduction / Andrew Kernohan.

Includes bibliographical references and index.
ISBN 978-1-55481-041-3

    1. Environmental ethics. 2. Environmental economics. I. Title.

GE42.K475 2012   179'.1   C2012-904915-8

Broadview Press is an independent, international publishing house, incorporated in 1985.

We welcome comments and suggestions regarding any aspect of our publications — please feel free to contact us at the addresses below or at broadview@broadviewpress.com / www.broadviewpress.com.

North America

Post Office Box 1243
Peterborough, Ontario Canada
K9J 7H5

2215 Kenmore Ave.
Buffalo, New York
USA 14207
tel: (705) 743-8990
fax: (705) 743-8353
customerservice
@broadviewpress.com

UK, Europe, Central Asia, Middle East, Africa, India and Southeast Asia

Eurospan Group
3 Henrietta St., London
WC2E 8LU, UK
tel: 44 (0) 1767 604972
fax: 44 (0) 1767 601640
eurospan
@turpin-distribution.com

Australia and New Zealand

NewSouth Books
c/o TL Distribution
15-23 Helles Ave.
Moorebank, NSW
Australia 2170
tel: (02) 8778 9999
fax: (02) 8778 9944
orders@tldistribution.com.au

Copy-edited by Robert M. Martin

Broadview Press acknowledges the financial support of the Government of Canada through the Canada Book Fund for our publishing activities.

Book design by Michel Vrana

This book is printed on paper containing 100% post-consumer fibre.

Printed in Canada

CONTENTS

ACKNOWLEDGEMENTS

I WOULD LIKE TO THANK ALL THE STUDENTS WHO TOOK MY CLASS ON environmental and agricultural ethics at the Nova Scotia Agricultural College (now the Faculty of Agriculture at Dalhousie University), and who suffered through earlier, less organized versions of this material. I appreciate their patience and their feedback.

Various editors at Broadview Press, Stephen Latta, Jesse Hendrikse, and Greg Janzen, have been very supportive of the project. Nora Ruddock designed the companion website.

Bob Martin from Dalhousie University edited the manuscript for Broadview Press and helped me avoid many errors and infelicities in the presentation. I thank him for his thoroughness, but I take full responsibility for all remaining idiosyncrasies, unwise claims, and contentious interpretations.

Sheldon Wein from Saint Mary's University suggested the initial idea behind the chapter on the Precautionary Principle. Along with his share of the credit comes a share of the responsibility, should our interpretation of the Precautionary Principle prove not to be useful.

My mother-in-law, Marie MacLellan, performed an initial copy edit of the entire manuscript, for which I thank her fondly. My partner, Anne MacLellan, read every chapter still warm from the laser printer, and, along with her encouragement, gave me advice on how to make the material more readable for a non-philosopher.

My thanks to all the above, and to Minou who kept me company during many otherwise lonesome hours at the keyboard.

This book is dedicated to my niece, Mary Xiao Miao Kernohan, in the hope that it will make some contribution to helping her generation make better environmental decisions than my generation has made.

INTRODUCTION

FOR THE READER

THE PURPOSE OF THIS BOOK IS TO GIVE YOU A SET OF CONCEPTUAL TOOLS FOR thinking about ethical issues in environmental policymaking. The book does not set out a code of ethics for environmentalists like the codes of lawyers or psychologists. Its aim, instead, is to provide a flexible ethical toolkit that you can apply in solving environmental problems.

I imagine you, the reader, as a person who will be involved in analyzing and debating environmental policy, as a citizen or as someone with a role in business or government. Perhaps you have studied the biological or environmental sciences, or economics and other social sciences as they apply to the environment, and now you want to see how environmental ethics can give you a useful perspective on environmental problems. You are not necessarily a student of philosophy, and this book requires no prior knowledge of philosophy.

Economics plays a huge role in formulating policy toward the environment. While the science of economics strives to be value-free, economic reasoning unavoidably makes ethical assumptions when applied to environmental policymaking. Not all of these assumptions are environmentally benign. Policymakers must be aware of the ethical assumptions made when economic methods are applied to solving environmental problems. About one third of this book is devoted to the interaction between applied ethics and economics. In my imagination, I see you, the reader, sitting at a committee table arguing with economists about environmental policy, and using the conceptual tools you have learned from this book. None of the economics in this book is above the first-year, introductory level. It is all fully explained, and requires no prior knowledge of economics.

The book will introduce you to around 150 concepts that, depending on your background, will be more or less unfamiliar. Learning the concepts of applied ethics is much like learning a new language. It requires that you see how ethical concepts fit together and interact with one another, and it requires that you practice using and applying these concepts. It is not enough just to memorize the definitions. To acquire the conceptual toolkit that this book offers, you must interact with the material, and you must actively utilize and apply what you have learned. Passively reading the text is not enough. Learning requires establishment of brain patterns, and that happens through repeated interaction with the material in attending lectures, reading the book, and answering questions.

What you have in your hands is only half the book. The other half consists of many hundreds of multiple-choice reading questions that exist on the book's companion website. The questions will reinforce the material in the text and ask you to apply ethical thinking to simple situations. Online reading questions are a pleasant and efficient way of interacting with a text. They allow you to find out if your answers are correct without leafing backward and forward through the pages of a workbook. You have probably answered online questions in your university coursework, and you will face doing online assessments throughout your career. Even if you presently do not like this way of working, you should relax, master the techniques, and learn to enjoy it. You paid for the online questions when you bought this book, so be sure to get your money's worth.

The book divides into twenty-four short, manageable chapters. Each one will take you one-half to three-quarters of an hour to read. You should then spend another half hour or so doing the 30+/- matching, multiple-choice, and multiple response reading questions that go with each chapter. They are fairly easy; you can do them with your book open, and you should expect to get 70–90 per cent of them correct. The matching questions require that you match concepts to their definitions. The multiple-choice questions require you to apply the concepts that you have learned to new situations. The multiple response questions are somewhat more difficult. They function as hints for the study questions in the text, so be sure to use them as such. If you write out, type in, or even dictate answers to the study questions, then these answers will give you a set of notes on the book. The "questions to ponder" ask you to think philosophically about the issues in the text. Think about them or discuss them with friends. They are open-ended, and you could write a PhD thesis on some of them if you so desired. The book's website also contains suggestions for further reading and for relevant online videos that you may enjoy.

When I teach, I repeat everything three times. Therefore, when you meet some rather dry ethical theory in the beginning part of the book, I can guarantee that you will see it again in the context of environmental problems, and again in the analysis of economic solutions to these problems. I think it important that you "see" the conceptual relationships between ethical concepts, so I have broken up the text with diagrams that illustrate these relationships. I was a physicist as an undergraduate, so I like to give simple numerical examples whenever they will be useful, and to summarize these examples in tables and graphs. You should hack your way through these examples in order to understand fully the concepts that they illustrate. The numerical examples require only elementary arithmetical skills, plus a bit of mental effort. You can then forget the details of the examples while retaining your understanding of the concepts involved.

Learning environmental ethics will give you a new conceptual framework for understanding, analyzing, and formulating environmental policy. Here is a metaphor. When ordinary people travel through the countryside, they see the surrounding vegetation as pleasant shades of green and brown. Trained biologists, however, can identify the species of plants that they are seeing, can see why they grow where they do, and can understand the different ecosystems that they support. Their training in the concepts of biology gives them a much deeper understanding of what they are seeing than that of untrained observers. In a similar way, the conceptual tool kit of environmental ethics will enable you to look at environmental problems differently, and give you a deeper understanding of the policies put forward to solve them.

FOR THE INSTRUCTOR

THIS BOOK IS AN INTRODUCTION TO ENVIRONMENTAL ETHICS WITH A PARTICULAR concentration on thinking critically about our society's economic approach to environmental problems. When writing it, I had in mind an audience of readers interested in solutions to environmental problems rather than an audience of specialists in philosophy. It is not a survey of environmental philosophies, so it leaves out many interesting theories, and it simplifies the remainder so that they fit together into a coherent whole. This will help make sense of ethical reasoning to readers for whom this is a first introduction to philosophical thinking. You may find that I have left out or over-simplified your favourite theory, so you are welcome to use the book as an opportunity to show students how to think critically about philosophical texts, and go on from there.

I used to teach environmental ethics by lecturing, leading discussions on an anthology of readings, and assigning my students a couple of essays. Students who were not already accustomed to philosophy often found this lack of structure overwhelming. They seemed to learn a good deal about their essay topics but much less about everything else. To avoid these problems, I developed the more structured approach of this book and its associated multiple-choice reading questions. If your university has an online learning management system, you may be able to set up these questions there; the system will correct the questions and automatically record the results for you. This will enable you to keep track of the progress of your students, even in classes with large enrolments. You can also modify the questions and use them in assessments.

The reading questions, and much else, are available on the book's website. Through the book's website you will find:

- The reading questions set up in an easy-to-use format for direct use by your students on the book's website. If you assign the questions through the book's website, the results will not be reported to your course's computerized gradebook.

- The reading questions in text format. You can read them with your word processor, and can modify the multiple-choice questions to use in paper-based tests and quizzes.
- The reading questions in a format readable by most Learning Management Systems.
- The figures, diagrams, and tables in the book as PowerPoint slides. You can adapt these slides for use in your own lectures as required. This will save you some preparation time if you wish to explain topics covered in the book.
- Suggestions for videos and readings which are openly available on the internet and which supplement the material in the text.

This book presents a highly structured approach to environmental ethics. Neither philosophy as it is actually practised nor the real world of environmental policymaking is so neatly organized. You may wish to supplement the text with readings on practical topics, or to assign theoretical readings using some of the original environmental ethics literature. This will provide resources for discussion or essay assignments. University learning management systems make assigning supplementary readings easy by allowing you to easily reference online material subscribed to by your university's library. For example, in recent years, *Scientific American* has published many interesting articles on environmental problems and their solutions, and it is subscribed to by most university libraries. Many articles from Worldwatch publications, such as the yearly *State of the World*, are freely available for downloading. In my own teaching, which is to an audience of agricultural science students, I have used a book by the agricultural economist Lester Brown, *World on the Edge*. This book can be purchased in paper or can be downloaded free of charge from Brown's website. For a theoretical supplement, the important journal *Environmental Ethics*, has recently put its content online and is now available to libraries, making many classic papers in environmental ethics easily accessible to students.

As is likely obvious, I am very impressed by the pedagogical possibilities opened up by online learning, even in its current state of development. It has the capacity to engage students actively with the educational material and to aid instructors in managing classes with large enrolments. Philosophy instructors, logicians excepted, often lag behind their colleagues in the physical and social sciences in their uptake of online learning resources. I hope that this book, and its online material, will help environmental ethics utilize these new eLearning methods.

Part 1

ETHICAL THEORY

Chapter 1

INTRODUCTION TO ENVIRONMENTAL ETHICS

GOOD ENVIRONMENTAL POLICYMAKING RESTS, METAPHORICALLY, ON THREE PILLARS. The first pillar is environmental science. We need science to identify and understand environmental problems, and we need science to discover possible solutions. For example, we needed science to understand the theory of the greenhouse effect, and we have needed science to measure rising levels of carbon dioxide in the atmosphere, rising global temperatures, and rising levels of species extinction. Now we need science to help us find new, carbon-neutral ways of generating electricity, transporting people, growing food, and preventing deforestation.

The second pillar is environmental economics. We need the help of economics to identify the least costly way of implementing solutions to environmental problems, and to design incentives that will get people to comply with those solutions. Economics helps us to identify the risks involved in adopting a business-as-usual approach to greenhouse gas emissions and to estimate the costs involved in different approaches to mitigating and adapting to climate change. Economics will help us to design regulations, subsidies, carbon taxes, and cap-and-trade systems to minimize these costs within our market-based society.

The third pillar is environmental ethics. Once we have identified environmental problems and discovered the costs of environmental solutions, we need to make final decisions about what we ought to do. We do not make final decisions about environmental policy just based on science and costs. We also consider fairness, justice, respect for rights, human flourishing, and even the flourishing of nonhuman entities and systems. Should global agreements to

FIGURE 1.1: Environmental policy supported by science, economics, and ethics

reduce greenhouse gas emissions assign developing countries the same reduction targets as rich industrialized countries? Are the harms that climate change will do to ecosystems only a problem if they affect human beings, or are they a problem in their own right? These are ethical issues. They are issues about what we *should* do or what it is *permissible* for us to do. Just as the first two pillars rest on the study of scientific theories and economic theories, the third pillar rests on the study of ethical theories.

This chapter introduces the types of ethical theories that apply to environmental issues, and discusses some of the special features of environmental ethics.

Learning Objectives

1. To see the difference between ethical judgments and other normative and factual judgments.
2. To be introduced to the different types of ethical theories.
3. To be introduced to the notion of moral standing in environmental ethics.
4. To understand the distinction between direct and indirect duties to the environment.
5. To understand the difference between intrinsic and instrumental value.

ETHICAL QUESTIONS AND VOCABULARY

Everyone has an intuitive understanding of the force of an ethical judgment. We know what it is that someone is trying to convey when we are told that we ought not to do such-and-such. Ethical judgments have a *normative*—an action-guiding—force. We learned to understand the action-guiding force of ethical judgments when we were children. In fact, we have understood the force of ethical judgments a lot longer than we have understood the judgments of science or economics.

For the most part, we readily recognize ethical judgments when we encounter them. People *ought* to recycle. The government *should* do something about pollution. People have *rights* against the government. Food producers have *duties* to consumers. Wildlife has more *value* than cattle. We recognize ethical judgments and questions because they employ a certain ethical vocabulary of which Table 1.1 gives some examples.

NOUNS	VERBS	ADJECTIVES
rights	*should (and should not)*	*right*
duties	*ought (and ought not)*	*wrong*
obligations	*must (and must not)*	*good*
virtues	*may*	*evil*
vices		*fair*
value		*unjust*

TABLE 1.1: Ethical vocabulary

Whereas scientific statements are purely descriptive, ethical judgments seem to contain both a descriptive and an action-guiding component. "Kicking Rover is wrong" implicitly contains both a description of an action about to be performed on Rover, the dog, and either some sort of imperative, "Don't kick Rover!" or expression of emotion, "How terrible of you to kick Rover!" Though we intuitively understand the action-guiding force of ethical judgments, giving a precise philosophical analysis of it is very difficult.

Identifying ethical judgments can be somewhat confusing because there are cases where judgments that are not ethical appear to use ethical vocabulary. Sometimes we use what appears to be ethical vocabulary when we make predictions such as, "The weatherman says it *should* rain tomorrow." Sometimes we use what appears to be ethical vocabulary when we discuss inferences, as in when we say, "From the fact that A is larger than B and B is larger than C, you *ought* to infer that A is larger than C." Sometimes we use what appears to be ethical vocabulary when we give advice about strategy or tell someone how best to get what he or she wants, as in "In chess, it is *wrong* to get your queen out early."

ETHICS, MORALS, VALUES, AND NORMS

The following terms are almost, but not quite, synonyms: normative judgments, ethical judgments, moral judgments, and value judgments. Normative judgments are the broadest category. Normative judgments include action-guiding judgments both about ethical matters and about reasoning. Norms of rationality tell us how to reason properly and include norms of logic and norms regarding the justification of beliefs based on evidence. A norm of logic tells us to make good inferences: From the statement that all men are mortal, and the statement that Socrates is a man, you *should* infer that Socrates is mortal. A norm of justification for belief tells us to make good inferences in empirical matters: From the rain on the windowpane, you *ought* to infer that it is raining outside, and you *ought not* to infer that it is sunny.

Ethical judgments, in this book, include value judgments and moral judgments. Roughly, value judgments pertain to what is worthwhile, meaningful, or valuable for individuals, whereas moral judgments pertain to how one individual should treat another. The judgment that Alice should get in touch with nature is a value judgment about what would make a good life for Alice. The judgment that it is wrong for Alice to hurt Rover is a moral judgment about how Alice should treat her dog, Rover.

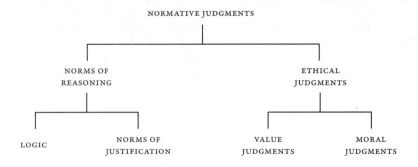

FIGURE 1.2: Normative, ethical, and moral

AREAS OF ETHICS

Environmental ethics is largely concerned with questions of values and morality. These questions arise at the personal level, the relational level, and the policy level. At the personal level, someone might ask, "How should I live a meaningful life?" or "Should I live my life in touch with nature?" At the inter-personal or relational level, someone might ask, "Should I tell a white lie to a friend?" or "Should I put down my pet dog, Rover, when he is suffering from an incurable disease?" At the policy level, we are concerned with questions about what organizations, or governments, or society as a whole should do: Should society help the poor and disadvantaged? Should the department of the environment act to preserve riparian habitats? This book will be mostly concerned with policy questions. It is about environmental ethics for policymakers.

Applying ethics to environmental policymaking requires understanding ethical theories, just as applying science and economics to environmental policymaking requires understanding scientific and economic theories. In order to understand and assess properly a scientific claim such as that the greenhouse effect exists, a person needs to understand a fair amount about the properties of electromagnetic radiation. A person must know that short wavelength visible light from the sun warms the Earth, that the Earth radiates much of this heat energy as longer wavelength infrared radiation, and that molecules of some gases like carbon dioxide, methane, and water vapour differentially absorb infrared radiation and re-radiate part of it back toward the Earth. Fully understanding all of this involves knowing a great deal of physical theory. Similarly, in order to understand and assess an ethical claim, a person needs to know about the ethical theory that is explicitly or implicitly behind the claim. Only in the context of an ethical theory does an ethical judgment have a precise meaning.

ETHICAL THEORIES

An ethical theory is an attempt to systematize our ethical judgments with a small number of principles. There are three different types of ethical theory. We can classify these three approaches, as well as see the special role of environmental ethics, if we look at a typical situation to which an ethical judgment applies. A typical ethical situation involves (1) a moral agent (a person, corporation, or government) performing (2) an action which brings about (3) consequences for some beneficiary or victim who is the (4) recipient of the consequences.

①		②		③		④
Agent	→	*Action*	→	*Consequence*	→	*Recipient*

A moral agent is an entity to which we are prepared to assign praise or blame. Philosophers have asked many interesting questions about just who can be a moral agent that we will not investigate. We know that competent adult human beings are moral agents, as are organizations thereof, whereas cats, dogs, maple trees, and ecosystems are not. However, a big question in environmental ethics is which recipients of beneficial or harmful consequences we should care about from an ethical point of view. This question we will investigate in much more detail.

Depending upon which component of an ethical situation we focus, we generate a different approach to ethics. We can focus on the character of the agent, on the principles that guide the action, or on the benefits and harms of the consequences.

Agent	→	*Action*	→	*Consequence*	→	*Recipient*
Character?		Principles?		Benefits or Harms?		Matters Ethically?

The approach that focuses on the character of the agent assesses the agent's character as either virtuous or vicious, and we will call it VIRTUE ETHICS. The approach that focuses on the principles that guide the action assesses the action as right or wrong according to what duties the action complies with or according to what rights the action respects. We will call this approach DEONTOLOGY, from the Ancient Greek word for duty. The approach that focuses on the consequences of the action assesses the consequences according to how much benefit or harm they produce, and we will call this approach CONSEQUENTIALISM. In each case we have to ask whom or what the consequences affect, and whether or not the entity affected counts from a moral point of view. For example, an organization (agent) might implement a policy (action) that has consequences for an ecosystem. A big question in environmental ethics would be whether that ecosystem is worthy of ethical consideration in the same sort of way as a human being.

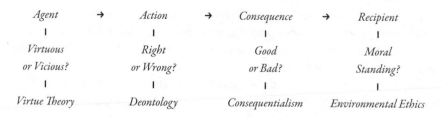

Agent	→	*Action*	→	*Consequence*	→	*Recipient*
Virtuous or Vicious?		*Right or Wrong?*		*Good or Bad?*		*Moral Standing?*
Virtue Theory		Deontology		Consequentialism		Environmental Ethics

The first third of this book will look in more detail at the types of ethical theories generated by the three ethical approaches. The second third of the book will look in much more detail at the question of which entities—humans, animals, plants, or ecosystems—we should consider when we apply ethical theories.

MORAL STANDING

A central question of environmental ethics is who or what counts from an ethical point of view. Which entities do we have to consider for their own sake when we make ethical judgments? Which entities are members of our moral community? Whose interests, besides our own and those of our relatives and friends, should we consider when we are deciding what we ought to do? We will call this the question of moral standing. An entity has MORAL STANDING if we must consider it or its interests for its own sake when we are making an ethical judgment. We call an entity MORALLY CONSIDERABLE if the entity has moral standing. If an entity has moral standing, then we must be virtuous in our behaviour towards it, we must think carefully about our duties toward it, or we must be careful about the consequences of our actions for its health or welfare.

An entity has moral standing only if our ethical concern regarding the entity is for its own sake. For example, human beings have moral standing because we think it is ethically important to respect their interests. We respect their interests, not because doing so is useful to us, but because doing so is good for them. Here is another example concerning the non-human environment. A person might decide not to drain a small wetland on her property because she thinks that it is lovely to look at, that it makes a great bird habitat, and that it will make a great place for her children to play. Another person might decide not to drain a wetland because he thinks that a functioning ecosystem is a good thing in its own right and that it is important to preserve its health and integrity. The second person truly regards the wetland ecosystem as having moral standing, of being morally significant for its own sake, whereas the first person does not. Both persons preserve the ecosystem, but their reasons are ethically different.

The idea of moral standing is analogous to the notion of legal standing. When a judge tries a case in a court of law, not every person or organization has the right to go into the court to make arguments about the case. The judge will allow only those persons or organizations that she regards as affected by the outcome of the trial to present arguments to the court. Such persons or organizations have legal standing in the case. Similarly, we consider only arguments based on the interests of those entities that we regard as having moral standing when we make ethical judgments.

A central question of environmental ethics is whether we should expand our circle of moral concern from ourselves and other people present to us, to people in distant countries, to unborn members of future generations, to animals generally, to all living things including plants, to a concern for endangered species, or to the health of ecosystems.

Figure 1.3 represents pictorially this expansion of our circles of ethical concern. We can think roughly, for example, of an ethical concern for all animals as including an ethical concern for human beings, and an ethical concern for all living things as including an ethical concern for both animals and humans.

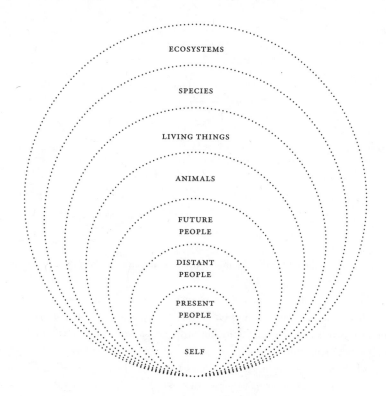

FIGURE 1.3: Expanding circles of ethical concern

ENTITIES POTENTIALLY HAVING MORAL STANDING

The narrowest circle of ethical concern is a circle that includes only one's self and one's own self-interest. Philosophers call the view that only the self has moral standing, "ethical egoism." We will study that view and its weaknesses in another chapter. Most people extend their circle of ethical concern to include people who are special to them, relatives, friends, or fellow members of a community. This concern can grow to cover fellow citizens, people who are in a sense present in both space and time, who share a common geography and who are all currently alive. More demanding is a concern for people who are not geographically present, who live in distant countries, and who are foreign and often very poor. Do people in developing countries have moral standing, and should we have the same sort of concern for their interests that we have for our fellow citizens? Questions about environmental policy are often questions about the effect of environmental degradation on people in the future, people who are not yet born. Should we extend moral standing to future generations, and if so, how? Are we ethically obliged to consider the interests of future generations in our policy-making?

Theories of environmental ethics that assign moral standing to the self, to special people, to present people, to distant people, or to future people we will call anthropocentric. ANTHROPOCENTRIC, or human-centred, views consider only humans, members of the species *Homo sapiens*, to have moral standing. The term "anthropocentric" has the same root

I.	SELF	
2.	SPECIAL PEOPLE	
3.	PRESENT PEOPLE	
4.	DISTANT PEOPLE	
5.	FUTURE PEOPLE	[anthropocentric] ↑

....

6.	ANIMALS	[zoocentric] ↑	[non-anthropocentric] ↓

....

7.	LIVING THINGS	[biocentric] ↑

....

8.	NATURAL OBJECTS	[individualistic] ↑

....

9.	SPECIES	[holistic] ↓

....

10.	ECOSYSTEMS	[ecocentric]

FIGURE 1.4: Theories of moral standing arranged in increasing order of inclusiveness

as the term "anthropology," which is the science of human beings. We must be careful to distinguish it from the term, "anthropomorphic," which is to attribute human behaviour to a nonhuman entity, and from the term, "anthropogenic," which is to attribute causation by humans to a phenomenon.

We label NON-ANTHROPOCENTRIC views that extend moral standing to nonhuman entities—to animals, plants, or ecosystems. Animal rights or animal welfare views that extend moral standing to all animals, we will call ZOOCENTRIC by analogy to zoology, the scientific study of animals. Theories of environmental ethics that extend moral standing to all living things, including plants, we will call BIOCENTRIC by analogy to biology, the scientific study of living things. Finally, theories of environmental ethics that extend moral standing to ecosystems we will call ECOCENTRIC by analogy to ecology, the scientific study of ecosystems.

Theories of environmental ethics that are concerned with the moral standing of everything from the self through animals and plants to natural, though nonliving, objects are concerned with individual entities. We will call INDIVIDUALISTIC those theories of moral standing that are concerned only with individual entities. Species, and particularly ecosystems, are not individual entities. The notion of a species is an abstract classification taken from the science of biology. An ecosystem is a highly organized collection of both living and nonliving entities that is, in some sense, more than just the sum of its parts. What is important about an ecosystem is the ecosystem as a whole, the way it organizes itself into a food chain or the way that energy flows through it. We will call HOLISTIC those theories of moral standing that are concerned with organized wholes composed of individual entities. Figure 1.4 summarizes these distinctions.

DIRECT AND INDIRECT DUTIES TO NONHUMANS

The notion of an entity having moral standing relates to two other important distinctions in environmental ethics, that between direct and indirect duties, and that between intrinsic and instrumental value. An INDIRECT DUTY is a duty regarding a non-human entity that an agent owes to a person. Suppose that Bob owes Alice a duty not to burn down her forest. This is an indirect duty regarding the forest because Bob owes the duty to Alice. Bob does not owe a duty directly to the forest itself. If Bob owes a duty to Alice not to kick her dog, Rover, then he owes the duty to Alice and not to Rover. He has a duty to Alice not to harm her property and only an indirect duty regarding Rover.

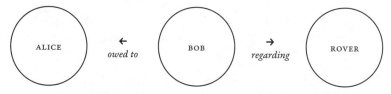

FIGURE 1.5: Bob has an indirect duty regarding Rover but owed to Alice

On the other hand, a DIRECT DUTY is a duty regarding a non-human entity that an agent owes to that non-human entity itself. For example, Bob might have a direct duty to the forest ecosystem not to burn it or he might have a direct duty to the dog, Rover, not to kick him.

FIGURE 1.6: Bob has a direct duty regarding Rover and owed to Rover

There is a connection between direct duties and moral standing. In order for a moral agent to owe a direct duty to a nonhuman entity, a nonhuman entity must possess moral standing. Indirect duties do not presuppose the moral standing of the nonhuman world. Both types of duty can protect the environment. If Bob does not burn the forest because of his duty to its owner, Alice, or if Bob does not burn the forest because he believes he has a duty to the forest ecosystem, the result is the same, the forest is preserved. However, the indirect duty view offers less protection to the forest than does the direct duty view. We can imagine a situation where Alice asks Bob to burn her forest. In this situation, Bob is relieved of his duty to Alice, and Bob's indirect duty to the forest no longer protects it. On the other hand, if Bob has a direct duty to the forest ecosystem, then despite Alice's request, he still has a duty not to harm the forest. In general, an ethical theory that assigns moral standing to nonhuman entities in the environment will offer the environment stronger protection than will an anthropocentric theory.

INTRINSIC AND INSTRUMENTAL VALUE

Another important distinction in environmental ethics is the distinction between instrumental and intrinsic value. A state of the affairs is INSTRUMENTALLY VALUABLE if it brings about or causes another state of affairs that is valuable. A state of affairs is INTRINSICALLY VALUABLE if it is valuable for its own sake and not because of some other state of affairs that it can bring about. For example, a $100 bill is not intrinsically valuable. It is not valuable for its own sake; it is just a dirty piece of paper. However, we could use it to bring about a state of affairs that is valuable for its own sake, such as buying a good dinner, or purchasing and preserving a piece of the Amazon rainforest.

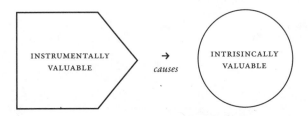

FIGURE 1.7: Something is instrumentally valuable because it ultimately brings about something that is intrinsically valuable or valuable for its own sake

We can always say what something that is instrumentally good is good for. Thus, ice cream is good for eating, exercise is good for health, and a beautiful symphony is good for the aesthetic pleasure of listening to it. In all these cases, what makes something good is what it is good for, or how it affects people. People value it because of what it does. When people value money instrumentally for the pleasure it buys them, they do not get the pleasure because they value money. Instead, they value money because it buys them pleasure. However, something like species diversity, which is valued intrinsically, is not valued because it is good for anything. People think of it as good in and of itself. The pleasure people get from contemplating its existence or preservation is not what it is good for. This pleasure is not what makes it good. If people get pleasure from species diversity, then they get that pleasure because they value it. They do not value it because it gives them pleasure.

The anthropocentric view is that animals, plants, endangered species, and ecosystems are not intrinsically valuable. They are only valuable because we can use them to bring about good consequences for human beings. The anthropocentric view is that the environment has merely instrumental value. Only satisfying the interests of human beings has intrinsic value. Because the environment has instrumental value, the anthropocentric viewpoint will still offer a fair amount of protection to the environment. However, when the preservation of nonhuman entities in the environment comes into conflict with the needs of human beings, then the anthropocentric view will always sacrifice the interests of the environment. Hence, an important question in environmental ethics is whether the nonhuman environment has intrinsic or instrumental value.

SUMMARY

1. Ethical judgments are both descriptive and action guiding.
2. Ethical theories organize and systematize ethical judgments.

3. The three main types of ethical theory concentrate on (1) the character of the agent, (2) the principles that the agent should obey, and (3) the consequences of the action.

4. We will call these three types of ethical theories virtue theory, deontology, and consequentialism.

5. Actions produce good or bad consequences for some beneficiary or victim. One of the main questions of environmental ethics is the moral status of this recipient, especially when the recipient is a nonhuman entity. An entity has moral standing just in case we must consider it for its own sake when we make ethical judgments.

6. Environmental ethics considers the potential moral standing of people in distant countries, of future generations, of animals, of living things generally, of species, and of ecosystems.

7. Anthropocentric views of moral standing assign moral standing only to human beings. Non-anthropocentric views assign moral standing to nonhuman entities in the environment. Theories that include both animals and humans are zoocentric. Theories that include all living things including plants and animals are biocentric. Theories that include ecosystems are ecocentric.

8. Agents can owe direct duties only to entities with moral standing. Anthropocentric views of moral standing permit only indirect duties, duties owed by a moral agent concerning a nonhuman environmental object, but owed to another human.

9. Anthropocentric views of moral standing claim that the nonhuman environment is only instrumentally valuable. Its value depends on whether it is a useful resource for human beings. The anthropocentric view claims that the nonhuman environment is not intrinsically valuable, not valuable for its own sake, and that policymakers may sacrifice the environment when its preservation comes into conflict with human interests.

ONLINE READING QUESTIONS

The book's website contains reading questions on this chapter. Working through these questions will help you understand, remember, and apply important concepts from the chapter. Some of the questions supply useful hints for the study questions.

Using the text and hints from the online reading questions, write out, type, dictate to your computer, or at least formulate in your head answers to the following questions.

1. Explain the difference between saying that it is wrong to keep hens in battery cages and saying that it is wrong to draw another card in Blackjack when you have a count of 17 in your hand.
2. Clearly explain the concept of moral standing, and say why it is an important concept in environmental ethics.
3. Explain, using examples different from the ones in the text, what the difference is between direct and indirect obligations to the non-human world.
4. Explain, with examples, the difference between something having intrinsic value and something having instrumental value.
5. What is the difference between an anthropocentric and a non-anthropocentric view of moral standing?

QUESTIONS TO PONDER

Spend a few minutes thinking about the following questions, or, better yet, discuss them with fellow readers of this book.

1. Surely, it is enough to know the science behind an environmental problem and how to fix it economically in order to preserve the environment. Why do we need to know any environmental ethics?
2. We have learned all we need to know about how we ought to behave from our parents, our schools, our religions, and from our life experience. Why do we need to know anything about boring ethical theories?
3. Only human beings and organized collections of human beings like business corporations can be held morally accountable. Animals and ecosystems, on the other hand, are not moral agents. Should it not be the case, then, that only those who can be held morally responsible should have moral standing?
4. We can do a perfectly good job protecting the environment if we consider only the consequences of decisions for present and future generations of human beings. Why should we worry about the intrinsic value of the nonhuman environment?

Chapter 2

METAETHICS

THOUGH WE HAVE BEEN FAMILIAR WITH ETHICAL JUDGMENTS FROM THE TIME WE were children, we can still be mystified about their nature. On the surface, an ethical judgment, such as the statement that increasing fossil fuel consumption is wrong, seems similar to the scientific judgment that increasing fossil fuel consumption will lead to faster climate change. Both seem to be intended as descriptions of the way the world is, both are either true or false, both are judgments about which there can be argument and disagreement, and both are judgments upon whose truth (or falsity) we seek to agree. Ethical judgments, like scientific judgments, are agreement-seeking.

Yet there is an important difference. By itself, a scientific judgment tells us nothing about the attitude of the person who makes it or about that person's intentions to affect the hearer's behaviour. An ethical judgment, on the other hand, does tell us something about the attitudes of the person who makes it and the intended effect. People sincerely making the judgment that increasing fossil fuel consumption is wrong are angry about the increasing consumption of fossil fuels, perhaps feel guilt at their own consumption, and intend that their audiences should share their disapproval of the situation. Their judgment about the increasing consumption of fossil fuels provides them with motivation to cut their own consumption, to argue with others, to seek the agreement of others, and perhaps to take political action. They likely base their ethical judgment that increasing fossil fuel consumption is wrong on their acceptance of the scientific judgment that increased fossil fuel consumption will speed up climate change, but their ethical judgment goes beyond the scientific judgment in that it motivates them to action. Ethical judgments, unlike scientific judgments, are action-guiding.

Reconciling the agreement-seeking and action-guiding aspects of ethical judgments is a major philosophical puzzle that we will not be able to resolve here. However, failing to attend to both aspects of ethical judgments can lead to problems. Forgetting that ethical judgments are action-guiding can lead someone to try deriving ethical judgments from purely scientific ones. Forgetting that ethical judgments are agreement-seeking can lead someone to believe that ethical judgments are merely relative.

Learning Objectives

1. To become familiar with the various approaches to the nature of ethical judgments.
2. To understand the action-guiding and agreement-seeking aspects of ethical judgments.
3. To understand the fact/value distinction and the principle that "ought" implies "can."
4. To survey the strengths and weaknesses of ethical relativism.

THREE BRANCHES OF ETHICS

There are three ways that people study ethics. They study (1) Descriptive Ethics, (2) Normative Ethics, or (3) Metaethics.

DESCRIPTIVE ETHICS is a branch of sociology whose goal is to describe the ethical beliefs of a community or culture. For example, a survey might conclude that 76% of North Americans are opposed to clear-cutting the Amazon rainforest. In itself, this is a factual description of the beliefs of North Americans, and offers no guide to how anyone should act. (After all, 76% of North Americans might be wrong about this.) It might be useful information for someone plotting an advertising campaign or a political action, but it in no way tells us what to do. None of this book is about descriptive ethics.

NORMATIVE ETHICS, on the other hand, does try to discover what actions we should take. It identifies, justifies, and applies ethical judgments to the world we live in. After studying and thinking about the topic, someone might conclude that people should stop clear-cutting the Amazon rainforest because we should all try to preserve resources for future generations. By a process of reasoning and argument, he would try to get others to agree with his judgment. His ethical judgment would motivate him to act to preserve the rainforest. Most of this book, starting with the next chapter, is about normative ethics. This chapter, however, will be about metaethics.

METAETHICS studies the meaning of ethical judgments. It tries to formulate a theory of the nature of ethical judgments that incorporates both of their important aspects, that they are action-guiding and that they are agreement-seeking. For example, one possible meta-ethical theory is that an ethical judgment such as that clear-cutting the Amazon rainforest is wrong is really a disguised command: "Do not clear-cut the Amazon rain forest!" Another possible metaethical theory might hold that this ethical judgment is simply a declarative sentence whose truth can be decided by reflection, debate, and reasoned argument. A third possible theory is that this ethical judgment is an assertion whose truth is relative to a particular cultural community.

APPROACHES IN METAETHICS

We can make a fairly complete categorization of the various approaches that philosophers have taken in metaethics as follows. We can use this categorization to assign labels to our own views on the nature of ethical judgments.

ETHICAL NIHILISM is the view that there is no such thing as right or wrong. Ethical judgments are meaningless and have no force. Ethics does not bind people's actions because there is no such thing.

ETHICAL SKEPTICISM is the view that actions may be either right or wrong, but that we can never know which is which. This is not such as strongly a negative view as nihilism because it allows that there is such a thing as morality. However, it claims that ethics is not much use because we can never know what its dictates are.

ETHICAL UNIVERSALISM is the view that if an action is right, then it is right for everyone in a similar situation, and if an action is wrong, then it is wrong for everyone. The same ethics applies to all moral agents. The denial of this view is ETHICAL RELATIVISM, which is the view that whether an action is right or wrong is relative to the cultural membership of the person making a judgment on it.

ETHICAL EXPRESSIVISM is the view that to say an action is right or wrong is to express an attitude toward that action. (A related view, ETHICAL PRESCRIPTIVISM, holds that to say an action is right or wrong is to express a command to do it or not to do it.) Such an expression of attitude or command is neither true nor false. For example, the ethical judgment that the US should do more to prevent climate change means something like, "Hoorah for the US doing more to prevent climate change!" The ethical judgment that people should not drive gas-guzzling SUVs means something like, "Boo on people who drive an SUV!" Ethical argument is then about whether the attitude of approval or disapproval is appropriate. ETHICAL COGNITIVISM, on the other hand, is the view that to say an action is right or wrong is to assert a belief about it. Such an assertion can be either true or false, and is something about which people can argue and debate.

STRENGTHS AND WEAKNESSES OF EXPRESSIVISM AND COGNITIVISM

The strength of expressivism is that it easily explains why ethical judgments have action-guiding force. Either the attitudes that are expressed or the commands that are prescribed can motivate people. The weakness of expressivism is that it cannot easily explain how people seek agreement in their ethical judgments. Seeking agreement requires argument and debate, argument and debate require logical reasoning, and expressivism has difficulty accounting for logical reasoning about ethical judgments. Valid logical reasoning requires that the ethical

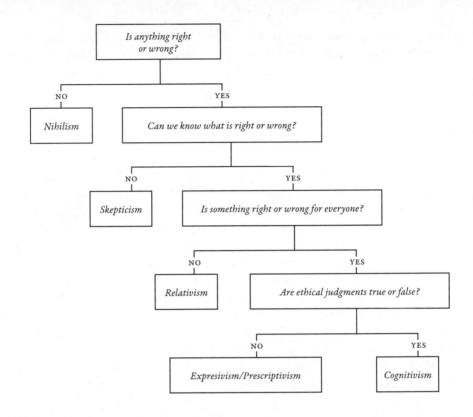

FIGURE 2.1: Decision tree on the nature of ethics

judgment that is the conclusion of an argument acquire its truth from the ethical judgments that are the premises of that argument. Expressivism, however, holds that ethical judgments are not the sorts of things which can be true (or false either) because either they are expressions of an attitude or issuances of a command. Because ethical premises, being ethical judgments, are not the sort of thing that can be true, there is no truth for logical reasoning to transfer to the conclusion of the argument. For example, the following ethical argument is valid, and might feature in a discussion between people seeking agreement on a controversial ethical question:

1. If people should not drive SUVs, then Charles should not drive an SUV.
2. People should not drive SUVs.
3. Therefore, Charles should not drive an SUV.

The argument is an instance of the valid inference pattern that logicians call "*modus ponens.*" Yet if the ethical judgment that people should not drive SUVs were, as simple expressivism would claim, just a disguised way of booing people who drive SUVs, then the above inference no longer works:

ENVIRONMENTAL ETHICS

1*. If "Boo!" to people driving SUVs, then "Boo!" to Charles driving an SUV.
2*. "Boo!" to people driving SUVs.
3*. Therefore, "Boo!" to Charles driving an SUV.

This latter set of three sentences is not a valid argument because its component clauses are not assertions of belief that can be true or false. It is difficult to see how we can use merely expressing attitudes or issuing commands in attempts to reach agreement about ethical questions.

The strength of cognitivism is that it explains how people can seek agreement about ethical judgments. If ethical judgments are assertions of beliefs that can be true or false, then we can use them to construct arguments just like any factual assertions. The weakness of cognitivism is that it has trouble explaining the action-guiding aspect of ethical judgments. Assertions of ethical belief, like assertions of belief about the natural world, are motivationally inert.

Pictorially, we can think of factual beliefs as squares containing a lot of cognitive content —that is, beliefs which are either true or false—and about which people seek agreement through argument and debate. The squares, however, offer no guidance regarding how to act, so they have no arrow indicating what to do. We can think of expressions of emotion or commands as being very thin arrows pointing the direction to take, but with little cognitive content to disagree about. Finally, we can think of ethical judgments as fat arrows with both content and an arrow to guide action.

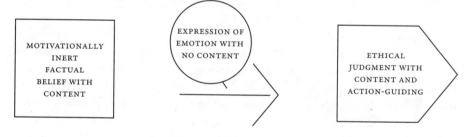

FIGURE 2.2: Factual beliefs, expressions of emotion, and ethical judgments

There are many philosophical theories about, but no one accepted solution to, the problem of reconciling the two aspects, action-guiding and agreement-seeking, of ethical judgments.

"OUGHT" IMPLIES "CAN"

One important consequence of the fact that ethical judgments are both action-guiding and agreement-seeking is that moral agents cannot be morally obligated to perform actions that they are, by their very nature, unable to perform. A human being cannot be morally obligated to do something that is humanly impossible like, for example, flying from one spot to another with no mechanical aids. This is because of the action-guiding feature of ethical judgments. There is no point to ethical judgments that guide people to perform actions that they are incapable of performing. Consequently, if the conclusion of a chain of ethical reasoning is the ethical requirement to perform an action that people cannot perform, then something is wrong with the argument. The ethical requirement is too demanding.

A person cannot be morally obligated to perform an action or bring about a consequence if he is physically unable to do so. It is impossible for someone to bring about world peace or prevent world hunger all by himself, so he is not obligated to do so, nor should he feel guilty about this. It is, however, possible for him to *contribute to* bringing about peace or to aid the hungry, so he may well have moral obligations to contribute or donate, and it may be legitimate for his conscience to trouble him if he does not.

We should apply the principle that "ought" implies "can" with care. For example, people and businesses sometimes complain that they cannot be obliged to reduce their use of fossil fuels because the hardships of doing so would be too demanding; they would be unable to heat their houses, or drive to work, or compete in the global economy. We must scrutinize claims about what is too demanding carefully and skeptically.

THE FACT/VALUE DISTINCTION

Another important consequence of the action-guiding and agreement-seeking aspects of ethical judgments is that we can never derive an ethical conclusion from purely factual premises. We can never successfully argue for an ethical judgment based on purely descriptive, factual, empirical, scientific, or what economists call "positive" statements. To produce an ethical judgment as its conclusion, an argument must contain one or more ethical principles that are derived from some ethical theory. The reason is that factual statements are motivationally inert. They do not have action-guiding force. Therefore, it is not possible for the ethical judgment, which is the conclusion of the argument, to acquire its action-guiding force from any of the premises. For example, we cannot move from the factual premise that keeping hens in what are called "battery cages" causes them pain and discomfort straight to the ethical conclusion that egg farmers should not keep hens in battery cages. We also need an ethical premise, such as that causing pain to either animals or humans is wrong. This is a premise that is derived from some ethical theory, in this case a theory called "Utilitarianism." The ethical theory, in conjunction with the factual premise, provides guidance to action.

The eighteenth-century English philosopher David Hume described in *A Treatise of Human Nature* the fallacy of moving from purely factual premises to an ethical conclusion in the following passage:

> In every system of morality, which I have hitherto met with, I have always
> remarked, that the author proceeds for some time in the ordinary way of rea-
> soning, and establishes the being of a God, or makes observations concerning
> human affairs; when of a sudden I am surprized to find, that instead of the usual
> copulations of propositions, is, and is not, I meet with no proposition that is
> not connected with an ought, or an ought not. This change is imperceptible; but
> is, however, of the last consequence. For as this ought, or ought not, expresses
> some new relation or affirmation, it is necessary that it should be observed and
> explained; and at the same time that a reason should be given, for what seems

altogether inconceivable, how this new relation can be a deduction from others, which are entirely different from it. But as authors do not commonly use this precaution, I shall presume to recommend it to the readers; and am persuaded, that this small attention would subvert all the vulgar systems of morality....
(Hume 1740: Book III, Part I, Section I)

Hume's observation of the fallacy of deriving an "ought" from an "is" is sometimes picturesquely called "Hume's Guillotine" because it can sever an ethical conclusion from an argument consisting of purely scientific or factual premises. It is also called the FACT/VALUE DISTINCTION because it insists on a rigid distinction between questions of fact and questions of ethical value. As well, it is sometimes called the IS/OUGHT GAP because of the logical gap between factual is-statements and ethical ought-statements. Finally, it is sometimes called the NATURALISTIC FALLACY because it calls attention to the fallacy of deriving ethical judgments from statements about the natural world.

Because the factual statements of environmental science and of positive economics are motivationally inert, we cannot derive any ethical conclusions about how to act from them alone. We must supplement factual premises with ethical premises in order to argue for ethical judgments. The ethical premises needed to add the required action-guiding component are generally ethical theories of the virtue-theoretic, deontological, or consequentialist types introduced in the last chapter. We will begin to look at these different types of normative ethical theories in more detail starting in the next chapter.

ETHICAL RELATIVISM AND ITS ATTRACTIONS

One view about the nature of ethics, or metaethics, that many people find attractive is ethical relativism, which is the view that what actions are right or wrong for a person is relative to the culture to which that person belongs. As a matter of anthropological fact, different cultures do have different views on what to eat, on how to eat it, on how to dress, on how to greet others, on duties to kin, on how to express respect, on how and with whom to have sex, on what attitudes to take in certain situations and how to express these attitudes, on how and whether to worship a god or gods, and on the nature of life after death. Different cultures have different worldviews, different conceptual frameworks for interpreting the world. Cultural diversity exists. In addition, it seems, different cultures appear to accept radically different ethical systems.

In the recent past, economically and militarily powerful Western European and North American cultures have often been guilty of forcing their own cultural and religious beliefs on other cultures. This sort of ethnocentrism has appeared wrong to many liberal and progressive people. These people have embraced principles of toleration with regard to other cultures. Cultivating the virtue of toleration has made ethical relativism attractive. Just as we should respect the divergent worldviews of other cultures, so we should respect the different ethical systems of these cultures. Some people have thought that the best way to respect the different ethical systems of other cultures is to allow that certain actions might be right for them while wrong for us, and vice versa.

Reflection on the existence of cultural diversity makes ethical relativism more attractive. Different cultures do follow different moral systems. Therefore, it seems to follow that it is ethically permissible for different cultures to be guided by different moral systems. For some people, skepticism regarding the universality of truth in general strengthens this attraction. It seems to some people that the truth of all claims, scientific and religious as well as ethical, is relative to the culture of whoever is making them, and that ethical relativism follows from the relativism of truth in general.

WEAKNESSES OF ETHICAL RELATIVISM

Ethical relativism, however, is less attractive than it might first appear. It has conceptual weaknesses of which someone who is attracted to the view should be aware. For one, defending the virtue of toleration that attracts us to ethical relativism is difficult within an ethical relativist framework. Toleration of the customs of others is virtue in a progressive, liberal culture, but it may be a vice in an intolerant, fundamentalist culture. The ethical relativist cannot say that toleration is a virtue universally, but only that it is a virtue for her and fellow members of her liberal culture.

Suppose we agree that toleration is a virtue and ethnocentrism is a vice. The best way to show respect for the ethical judgments of others is not necessarily to uncritically accept their views—to see their ethical views as true for them but false for us. Such a failure to engage with the ethical judgments of others can be disrespectful. Failure to engage with the ethical views of others does not take their views seriously and can even express contempt for their views. Engagement with the views of others, allowing their ethical views to challenge our own, is important to our own moral development. Dismissing the ethical views of other cultures as merely relative is a way of avoiding letting those views challenge our own.

The toleration argument only goes so far. There is a big difference between believing that a different style of dress is morally permissible and believing that, for example, female genital mutilation is morally permissible. Some views about what is ethically permissible are just too ghastly to let pass without contesting them. To avoid contesting such views is to fail to take our own morality seriously and to fail to respect our own moral integrity. We are forced to seek agreement with others regarding the morality of terrible practices.

We should also note that the argument from cultural diversity could easily fall afoul of Hume's Guillotine. From the fact that different cultures are guided by different moral systems, it does not immediately and easily follow that it is ethically permissible for different cultures to be guided by different moral systems. Such an argument jumps the is/ought gap that Hume pointed out. We need to supplement the argument with an ethical premise, and the best candidate would be a principle of toleration. The toleration principle would say that every culture *should* see the moral systems of all other cultures as permissible. This, however, is a universal ethical principle applying to all cultures, and an ethical relativist cannot defend such a principle within her own framework.

The general relativism about truth that attracts some people to ethical relativism is also difficult to justify. Suppose Charles believes that all truth is relative, and Donna does not. Is the principle that all truth is relative itself universally true (true-for-everyone) or just true-for-Charles? If Charles says that it is universally true, then Charles is contradicting himself. If he says it is only true-for-him, then he cannot justify why Donna should believe it. Ethical relativism makes it impossible for people to seek agreement about ethical matters, while relativism about truth in general destroys the possibility of any agreement seeking.

According to ethical relativism, what actions are right, wrong, or permissible for a person depends on that person's cultural membership, and on what ethical principles that person's culture accepts. However, a person's cultural membership is not always clear. A person is often a member of different cultural groups simultaneously, and when the principles accepted by these different cultural groups conflict, the person has no ethical guide to action. For example, consider a US citizen of Jain background. Eating meat is generally accepted as morally permissible in American culture, but is regarded as morally wrong in Jainism. Which principles is an American of Jain descent obliged to follow? He is a member of both cultures, but their conflicting ethical principles give him no guide to action. Ethical relativism, in situations of multiple cultural memberships, cannot provide ethical judgments that are action-guiding.

In situations where cultural membership is clear, where people are members of one dominant culture, it hard to see how it can ever be even morally permissible for a person to criticize or reform her own culture. Ethical relativism defines what is right, wrong, or permissible for a member of the culture as what is accepted by the culture. Any other ethical judgments, proposed by a member of the culture as a critique of accepted practices are just false by definition. How, for example, can an ethical relativist, who is a member of a consumerist culture, agitate for reducing fossil fuel consumption when the ethical permissibility of unlimited fossil fuel consumption is the accepted cultural norm? Ethical relativism can easily support cultural conservatism, whereas the role of philosophy is to examine generally accepted ethical beliefs critically.

The diversity of moral systems between different cultures may be less extreme than it seems at first sight. Different cultures may actually agree on ethical principles, but when they apply them in reasoning, they also use factual assumptions drawn from their cultures' different worldviews, and they may come up with contradictory ethical judgments and action recommendations. For example, suppose we were to meet a tribe of people who judged it ethically right for children to kill their parents just as soon as their child-rearing work was finished. This would appear awful to us, in violation of principles of respect for parents and respect for human life in general. Suppose, however, that we then learned that, in this culture's worldview, people live endlessly after death at the age they were when they died. It is important to people sharing this culturally specific, but deeply held, conceptual framework to enter life after death before they become elderly or infirm. Thus, children who kill their parents as painlessly as possible are actually showing them love and respect. Though their particular ethical judgments seem very wrong to us, we actually share with them the ethical principles on which the judgments are based. What we do not share is their worldview and their factual beliefs about life after death. We must distinguish between ethical principles and their application in deciding just how much cultural diversity there is in moral beliefs.

Ethical relativism is a threat to environmental ethics. Many environmental problems are global and thus require cross-cultural solutions. Suppose, for the sake of argument, that what is ethically permissible is relative to what a particular culture generally accepts as ethically permissible. Suppose that it is a fair description of North American culture that the heavy per capita use of fossil fuel resources and the associated high per capita emissions of carbon dioxide are ethically permissible. Suppose that it is a fair description of Swedish culture that such high per capita levels of fossil fuel use and emission production are not ethically permissible, and instead are something requiring action. Are we really to say that it is permissible to burn a lot of oil in North America but not in Sweden? How can North Americans who are worried about climate change criticize their culture as gluttonous if majority opinion defines what is ethically permissible in that culture? How can we see Swedes and North Americans as disagreeing about anything? What motivation do they have to seek agreement on new protocols for greenhouse gas emissions? By glossing over ethical disagreements between cultural groups, ethical relativism fails to respect the agreement-seeking aspect of ethical judgments.

SUMMARY

1. Philosophical discussion of the nature of ethical judgments is called "metaethics."
2. Ethical judgments resemble factual judgments in having cognitive content and being potentially true or false. We discuss them, argue about them, and try to resolve disagreements. Ethical judgments are agreement-seeking.
3. Ethical judgments resemble exhortations, expressions of emotion, and commands in their ability to motivate people to act in certain ways. Ethical judgments are action-guiding.
4. The range of possible positions regarding the nature of ethical judgments includes the view that they are meaningless (nihilism), that they can never be known (skepticism), that they are relative to the maker's culture (relativism), that they are assertions of belief which can be true or false (cognitivism), and that they are expressions of the maker's attitudes (expressivism or prescriptivism).
5. Cognitivism can explain how and why people seek agreement regarding ethical judgments, but has difficulty explaining why they are motivating and action-guiding.
6. Expressivism and prescriptivism can easily explain why ethical judgments guide action, but has difficulty explaining how it is possible to reason about them in the pursuit of interpersonal agreement.
7. Because ethical judgments are action-guiding, it follows that people cannot be morally required to do actions that they are unable to do. "Ought" implies "can."
8. Because ethical judgments are action-guiding, they cannot be derived solely from factual judgments such as scientific judgments or the judgments of positive economics. Hume's Guillotine is a dramatic name for the fallacy of deriving an "ought" from an "is" or a value from a fact. An ethical premise, usually an ethical theory, is also required.

9. Ethical relativism, the view that what is right, wrong, or permissible for a person is determined by the accepted ethical norms of the person's culture, is attractive as an expression of tolerance and the avoidance of ethnocentrism.

10. Ethical relativism, by making it too easy to agree to disagree, fails to do justice to the agreement-seeking aspect of ethical judgments. It encourages a sort of intellectual laziness that leads adherents not to allow their own moral views to be challenged and not to respect their own moral integrity.

ONLINE READING QUESTIONS

The book's website contains reading questions on this chapter. Working through these questions will help you understand, remember, and apply important concepts from the chapter. Some of the questions supply useful hints for the study questions.

STUDY QUESTIONS

Using the text and hints from the online reading questions, write out, type, dictate to your computer, or at least formulate in your head answers to the following questions.

1. Explain clearly why ethical judgments cannot be deduced from scientific or empirical statements. Employ Hume's Guillotine.
2. Describe the argument from the premise of cultural diversity to the conclusion that ethical relativism is correct. What is a main weakness of this argument?
3. Describe the argument from the premise of the ethical importance of toleration to the conclusion that ethical relativism is correct. What is a main weakness of this argument?
4. Why does being an ethical relativist make it difficult for someone to criticize the ethics of her own culture?
5. Describe how two cultures that apparently differ in their moral principles might actually have similar moral principles and differ only in how they apply them.

QUESTIONS TO PONDER

Spend a few minutes thinking about the following questions, or, better yet, discuss them with fellow readers of this book.

1. What is your view of the meaning of ethical statements? Which of the metaethical views in the text best fits your view?

2. Can ethical judgments be identified with legal judgments? Is being immoral the same as being illegal? Can civil disobedience ever be ethically required? Why or why not?

3. All around us we see evidence of ethical disagreement. People disagree about the morality of abortion, gay and lesbian sex, eating meat, carbon taxes, and so on. Is it really true that ethical judgments are agreement-seeking?

4. Watch the Sam Harris video, "Science Can Answer Moral Questions," at http://www.ted.com/talks/sam_harris_science_can_show_what_s_right.html. Should we understand him to be saying that science, by itself, can supply ethical principles, or to be saying that a secular, scientific worldview will result in different ethical judgments than will a religious worldview?

5. Consider the view that ethics is relative to individuals themselves and not to the cultures of which they are members. Everyone can legitimately have different ethical principles that are true for them though not necessarily for anyone else. What are the strengths and weaknesses of this view?

Chapter 3

ETHICAL
ANALYSIS

ENVIRONMENTAL POLICIES MAKE RECOMMENDATIONS FOR ACTION AND GIVE reasons for those recommendations. The ethical analysis of environmental policy requires examining these reasons and recommendations using the conceptual tools of normative ethics. We need to see the policy through the lens, as it were, of ethical theory. Giving an ethical analysis of an environmental policy recommendation, or writing environmental policy in an ethically informed way, requires six steps:

1. Recognize the ethical claims that the policy recommendation makes.
2. Identify the ethical reasons explicitly or implicitly given.
3. Classify these reasons according to the ethical theories that the recommendation assumes.
4. Investigate who or what the recommendation assumes to have moral standing.
5. Reflect critically on the strengths and weaknesses of these assumptions.
6. Decide which policy to adopt or recommend.

To make this process of ethical analysis more concrete, we will look at an imaginary and highly simplified policy regarding the logging of the Amazon rain forest. Suppose the Brazilian government is considering a policy statement recommending that it make clear-cutting in the

Amazon rain forest illegal. The policy statement gives the following reasons for that recommendation: Clear-cutting will result in the suffering and death of many of the animals who live in the rain forest. Clear-cutting will adversely affect the hunting territories of indigenous forest-dwelling people. Clear-cutting will destroy whole forest ecosystems. Clear-cutting will result in the extinction of animal and plant species whose genetic material is essential to future drugs. The reasons mentioned are each a fact or a prediction based on scientific evidence and observation. The policy, however, makes a recommendation for action, and so takes us across the is/ought gap. An argument from how the world is to how it ought to be is only valid if it contains ethical premises. Therefore, ethical analysis must identify the often implicit ethical assumptions of environmental policy. Ethical analysis looks at the implicit assumptions that move the policy from a study of biological and anthropological facts to a set of recommendations for action. The policy we are looking at assumes that it is wrong to cause animals to suffer, wrong to harm indigenous people, wrong to destroy ecosystems, wrong to deprive future generations of useful drugs, and therefore right to stop clear-cutting the Amazon rain forest. We need ethical theory, however, to see more clearly how these ethical judgments can be justified and to assess whether or not they are good reasons for the recommended actions.

Learning Objectives

1. To understand the components of the ethical analysis of an environmental policy.
2. To begin classifying the reasons that are either explicit or implicit in environmental policy.
3. To begin learning some of the types of theories appealed to by different ethical approaches.

1. RECOGNIZE ETHICAL CLAIMS

Explicit ethical judgments employ an ethical vocabulary of words like "must," "ought," and "duty." The imaginary policy document that we are considering might say, "The Brazilian government must...." More likely though, the ethical judgment will be disguised as a recommendation for action, "We recommend that the Brazilian government...." If the government itself authors the document, then it may make a commitment to action such as "The Brazilian government will...."

We have to be careful, though, because sometimes policy recommendations are strategic rather than ethical. For example, the above policy statement might be based, not on ethics, but on a desire on the part of the Brazilian government to satisfy environmental organizations whose criticisms are costing Brazil foreign tourists and foreign trade. In this case, the recommendation would be a conditional one, "If the government wishes to avoid criticism, then it should...." The apparently ethical term "should" signals a strategic, not an ethical, recommendation. (For the record, philosophers call such strategic recommendations, "hypothetical imperatives," because they are based on the hypothesis that the agent wants some outcome. Ethical recommendations which are independent of what the agent wants, philosophers call "categorical imperatives.") The ethical analysis of strategic policy turns from analysis of the detailed reasoning within the policy statement to analysis of the ethical justification, or lack thereof, for the strategy itself.

2. IDENTIFY ETHICAL REASONS

The second step in an ethical analysis of environmental policy is to identify the ethical reasons offered for the policy recommendations. To do this, we start with the facts, observations, and evidence offered in the statement and look for the ethical reasons that underlie them. Since philosophers do not write most policy statements, the policy will not usually explicitly state these ethical reasons. We will have to interpret the implicitly assumed ethical judgments, and, if the ethical assumptions are not obvious, we may have to consider several possibilities that are compatible with the policy statement. In the Amazon rain forest example, the stated reasons for the recommendation to stop clear-cutting were:

A) Clear-cutting will result in the suffering and death of many of the animals who live in the rainforest.
B) Clear-cutting will adversely affect the hunting territories of indigenous forest-dwelling people.
C) Clear-cutting will destroy whole forest ecosystems.
D) Clear-cutting will result in the extinction of animal and plant species whose genetic material is essential to future drugs.

Behind these observations are principles drawn from ethical theories that turn inert facts into reasons for action that support an overall recommendation for action. Behind the first is a principle such as:

A*) People should not cause suffering to animals.

Behind the second might be a concern for the happiness of indigenous people, a concern for the rights of indigenous people, a concern for injustices committed against indigenous people, or any combination of these concerns. If nothing is explicit in the policy statement, an ethical analysis should consider all three reasons. Suppose, however, that there is further textual evidence in the policy statement for the concern:

B*) People should not violate the ancestral rights of indigenous people.

Behind the third observation is the ethical reason:

C*) People should not cause the destruction of ecosystems.

Finally, behind the fourth observation is a concern for the welfare of people who will need these drugs in the future:

d*) People should not cause harm to the interests of future generations.

The underlying ethical structure of the policy is starting to emerge. This implicit structure takes the policy from observations and predictions about the world to recommendations for action.

3. CLASSIFY REASONS ACCORDING TO TYPE OF ETHICAL THEORY BEING ASSUMED

In the first chapter, we looked at a way to begin classifying ethical approaches according to the component of an ethical situation on which they focused. We will begin refining these broad approaches into a classification of the types of ethical theories. Once we have classified the reasons offered for an environmental policy recommendation, we will have a framework for thinking about them critically. In what follows, we will take a very preliminary first look at the varieties of ethical theories in order to see how the process of ethical analysis works. We will return to these ethical theories in more detail in later chapters.

The sort of state of affairs about which we form ethical judgments is typically one where some moral agent (a person, organization, or government) performs an action that causes consequences for some recipient (beneficiary or victim) of those consequences.

Agent	→	Action	→	Consequence	→	Recipient
Virtue/Vice Approach		Deontology Approach		Consequential Approach		Moral Standing

The VIRTUE/VICE APPROACH makes moral judgments based on the character of the agent. For example, it assesses character according to the virtues of benevolence, thoughtfulness, courage, fairness, and so on, or according to the vices of selfishness, thoughtlessness, cowardice, and so on.

The DEONTOLOGICAL APPROACH makes moral judgments based on intrinsic features of the act. Theories of the deontological type worry about what principle the agent is following, what duty the agent is obeying, what rights the agent is respecting, and whether the agent is treating recipients according to principles of justice.

The CONSEQUENTIALIST APPROACH makes moral judgments based on features of the consequences. Theories of the consequentialist type are concerned about the outcome of an action, for example, about how much pleasure (or pain) it creates (or prevents), or about the balance of benefits over costs that it produces.

One large task of Environmental Ethics is to make judgments of moral standing based on features of the recipient. For example, a theory might conclude that animals have moral standing because they can feel pleasure and pain.

The following chart gives a broad, initial view of how we categorize these different approaches to ethics. When we apply any of the approaches, environmental ethics reminds us that we should sort out to which of the affected human and non-human entities we should give ethical consideration.

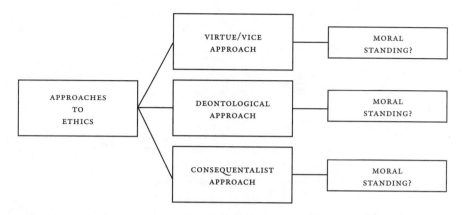

FIGURE 3.1: Chart summarizing the three main approaches to ethics

The virtue/vice approach tells people to work on their character to rid themselves of bad or vicious habits and acquire virtuous attitudes, dispositions, and character traits. The virtue/vice approach does not lend itself easily to making recommendations for specific environmental actions, but it is useful in environmental ethics when we wish to talk about changing people's attitudes and habits in fundamental ways in order to implement new "green virtues." If the VIRTUE/VICE APPROACH has a rule of action, then it would say that each agent ought to act so as to emulate the decisions of a virtuous person.

The DEONTOLOGICAL APPROACH, in its most general formulation, says that each agent ought to act so as to obey the moral principles governing that type of act. It comes in several varieties:

In DIVINE COMMAND THEORIES, the moral principles that the agent should obey are the commands of God. An example is the set of duties imposed by God in the ten commandments of the Jewish and Christian bible. Our principle concern in this book will be with those particular divine commands that have not had an "environmentally friendly" impact such as the command in *Genesis* to be fruitful and multiply, and to conquer the earth and its fish, birds, and mammals.

In RIGHTS-BASED THEORIES, the moral principles that the agent should obey involve respecting the moral rights of ethically considerable recipients. Two interesting examples in environmental ethics are the interaction between respecting the property rights of others and protecting the environment and the question of respecting the moral rights of animals.

In JUSTICE-BASED THEORIES, the moral principles that the agent should obey concern treating all morally considerable recipients with fairness. We should give each morally considerable recipient what he, she, or it deserves, and treat each morally considerable recipient equally. Environmental policies often impose benefits and burdens on different people, and it is important that policies distribute these benefits and burdens justly.

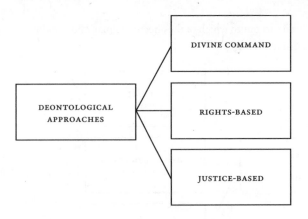

FIGURE 3.2: A taxonomy of ethical theories within the deontological approach

The CONSEQUENTIALIST APPROACH is concerned with the causal consequences of actions and, in its most general formulation, says that each agent ought to cause intrinsic value for recipients with moral standing. For example, one type of consequentialist theory says that each agent ought to bring about the largest possible total amount of pleasure for all conscious beings.

If only the Self is a recipient with moral standing, then we have ETHICAL EGOISM, which is the view that each agent ought to cause maximum intrinsic value for him or herself. Each agent should act in his or her own narrow self-interest. Because each person's only obligation is to cause the best consequences for him or herself, ethical egoists have difficulty cooperating. As we shall see in the next chapter, ethical egoists are prone to the dilemmas of cooperative action. Thus, ethical egoism often evolves into CONTRACTARIANISM, the view that ethics is a state-enforced social contract that forces cooperation between ethical egoists, for the eventual benefit of each.

If we extend moral standing to recipients beyond the self, then we get other forms of consequentialism. According to consequentialist views, each agent ought to cause states of affairs with intrinsic value. That agents should cause intrinsic value is what makes this theory consequentialist. What they should cause is ultimately states of affairs with intrinsic, not instrumental, value, that is, states of affairs that are valuable for their own sake. Most descriptions of the consequentialist approach go on to add that the agent should cause maximum aggregated intrinsic value. The intrinsic value is aggregated, or added up, for all of the morally considerable recipients. This formulation assumes that intrinsic value is somehow measurable. This formulation also assumes that if something is good or valuable, then more of it is better. We should therefore maximize aggregated intrinsic value.

Consequentialist theories come in two main varieties, depending on the type of things that the theory claims have intrinsic value. SUBJECTIVE CONSEQUENTIALISM or UTILITARIANISM says that the intrinsic value which we should maximize pertains to the mental states of recipients. "Subjectivity" here refers to the internal psychological states of the beneficiary, mental states of which only that beneficiary is aware. OBJECTIVE CONSE-QUENTIALISM, on the other hand, holds that the intrinsic value which we should maximize pertains to features of recipients other than their mental states. For example, a consequentialist theory that says to maximize pleasure would be subjective, whereas one that says to maximize scientific knowledge and artistic achievement would be objective.

There are two main varieties of subjective, or mental-state, consequentialism. One is HEDONISTIC UTILITARIANISM. According to this type of theory, each agent ought to cause the maximum balance of pleasure over pain. In its simple form, hedonistic utilitarianism assumes that the only states of affairs with intrinsic value are the pleasurable mental states of entities with moral standing. A more complex form of hedonistic utilitarianism distinguishes between different types of enjoyment and suffering, and sees some forms of enjoyment as being of more value than others. One environmental implication of this view is that we should not consider the interests of entities without mental states, like ecosystems, in ethical thinking. Another potential environmental implication is that all entities that can feel pleasure and pain, including all complex animals, do have moral standing.

The other variety of subjective consequentialism is desire-satisfaction or PREFERENCE-SATISFACTION UTILITARIANISM. According to this type of theory, each agent ought to act to bring about the maximum amount of satisfied desires or preferences of recipients with moral standing. The difference is that hedonistic utilitarianism is concerned with mental sensations, like feelings of pain and pleasure, whereas preference-satisfaction utilitarianism is concerned with complex psychological attitudes of desiring and wanting that people direct toward changing the world. Versions of preference-satisfaction utilitarianism underlie much of the economic approach to the environment—topics like cost-benefit analyses and external costs—that we will examine in much more detail later. Understanding the distinctions between the various varieties of preference-satisfaction utilitarianism, and becoming familiar with their strengths and weaknesses is essential to environmental ethics.

Objective consequentialism, where the intrinsic value that we ought to maximize pertains to features other than mental states, comes in three varieties. Because objective consequentialism relies on features other than psychological states, it can potentially apply to entities like plants and ecosystems that do not have an inner, mental life.

In the COMMON GOOD APPROACH, each agent ought to act so as to contribute to the betterment of the community as a whole. The good of a community is here something more than the sum of the goods of its members, and in fact may even conflict with the individual goods of its members. We will utilize this approach when we discuss the moral standing of ecosystems.

In the TELEOLOGICAL APPROACH, each agent ought to act so as to best enable the natural functioning of recipients with moral standing. Sometimes we equate an entity's natural functioning with its natural purpose, though we must be careful not to see such purposes as psychological. We will utilize this approach in discussing the moral standing of living things that have no mental life, such as plants.

According to the DISPOSITIONAL APPROACH, each agent ought to act so as to best satisfy the wants that people would have if they were fully informed and were reasoning rationally. The wants that people would have if they were fully rational may well be different from the wants that people actually do have in their present, less than fully rational, state. This approach is concerned with hypothetical desires and preferences and not with actual mental states. Therefore, it is not really a fully subjective view like preference-satisfaction utilitarianism, which tells us to satisfy the actual wants of people, their wants as we find them, not the wants they would have if they knew more or reasoned more clearly. This approach provides us with a critical perspective on subjective desire-satisfaction utilitarianism.

Figure 3.3 classifies the forms of consequentialism that we have looked at so far, and we can combine it with previous taxonomies to give a picture of the ethical landscape. Our taxonomy of types of ethical theories has grown quite large, and it will become still more detailed in future chapters. We have classified ethical reasons in a preliminary way to show how the process of ethical analysis works. We will return to these theories in later chapters and explain them in more detail. For now, it is enough just to introduce them.

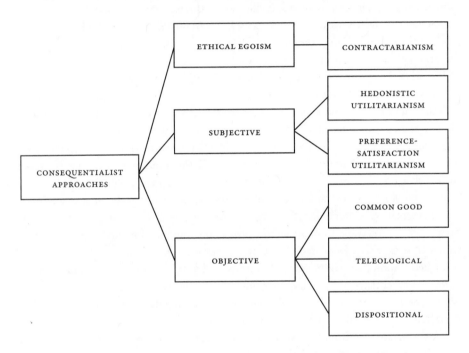

FIGURE 3.3: A taxonomy of ethical theories within the consequentialist approach

4. INVESTIGATE WHO HAS MORAL STANDING

The fourth step in analyzing or formulating environmental policy in an ethically informed way is to investigate who or what should have moral standing in the reasoning. The first chapter introduced the issue of moral standing. We can think of environmental ethics as trying to answer the question of how far our ethical concern should extend. Should we extend moral consideration only to our selves, or to our selves plus nearby people, or to all of those plus distant or future people? Should we adopt a non-anthropocentric view of moral standing and extend ethical consideration to animals, to all living things, or even to species and ecosystems? Putting this together with the sorts of ethical theories just canvassed, we can construct a table of possible configurations of ethical theory and moral standing.

	NEARBY PEOPLE	DISTANT PEOPLE	FUTURE PEOPLE	ANIMALS	LIVING THINGS	SPECIES & ECOSYSTEMS
Character-based						
Virtue ethics						
Deontological						
Divine command						
Rights		B*				
Justice						
Consequentialist						
Hedonistic utilitarianism				A*		
Preference utilitarianism	(E*)		D*			
Common good						C*
Teleological						
Dispositional						

TABLE 3.1: Some possible configurations of ethical theory and moral standing

Table 3.1 is a conceptual grid that we can impose on the reasons and recommendations of environmental policy. It provides us with a way of classifying and interpreting the implicit ethical reasoning involved in policy work.

If we return to our example of Brazilian government policy toward the logging of the Amazon rain forest, we can see how to fit its reasoning into this conceptual grid. The policy gave four reasons for its recommendation:

A) Clear-cutting will result in the suffering and death of many of the animals who live in the rain forest.
B) Clear-cutting will adversely affect the hunting territories of indigenous forest-dwelling people.
C) Clear-cutting will destroy whole forest ecosystems.
D) Clear-cutting will result in the extinction of animal and plant species whose genetic material is essential to future drugs.

We saw how these factual obaservations and predictions depended on corresponding ethical reasons to get their action-guiding force.

A*) People should not cause suffering to animals.
B*) People should not violate the ancestral rights of indigenous people.
C*) People should not cause the destruction of ecosystems.
D*) People should not cause harm to the interests of future generations.

If we add some reasonable hypotheses about the basis of the moral standpoints just listed, we can place them on the grid of Table 3.1, as shown. The ethical theory behind A* comes from the consequentialist approach and is a form of hedonistic utilitarianism which considers animals to have moral standing, and place it in the grid of Table 3.1 as shown. The ethical theory behind B* is drawn from the deontological approach and is a rights-based theory. It extends moral standing to people outside mainstream Brazilian society, so extends moral standing to distant people. The ethical theory behind C* is consequentialist, but of the objective type since ecosystems do not have a mental life. Ecosystems have a common good that is different from the goods of the plants, animals, and habitat of which they are comprised, so the ethical theory behind C* is a common or community good theory extending moral consideration to ecosystems. Finally, behind D* is a consequentialist theory of the desire or preference-satisfaction type that considers future generations to have moral standing.

Familiarity with ethical theories and theories of moral standing allows us to locate the ethical reasoning involved in environmental policymaking in a conceptual framework that reveals the ethical assumptions behind its recommendations. Locating policy reasoning in the conceptual space of environmental ethics enables us to assess its strengths and weaknesses efficiently.

5. REFLECT CRITICALLY ON THE STRENGTHS AND WEAKNESSES OF THE ETHICAL ASSUMPTIONS

One weakness in ethical reasoning that we should look for is neglect of reasons that go against policy recommendations. For example, a factor that our example of a policy statement on clear-cutting the Amazon rain forest did not consider was that to stop logging the rain forest will create unemployment for many Brazilian forestry workers. This point (E) is an argument against the policy recommendation that we should also consider. The policy's reasoning should either rebut the point or argue that other considerations outweigh it. Behind this contrary reason is a consequentialist theory of the preference-satisfaction utilitarian sub-type that assumes only the moral standing of nearby Brazilians (shown in Table 3.1 as E*). Abstract theories of moral standing become relevant here. If moral standing is narrowly anthropocentric and confined only to nearby people, then the contrary point will outweigh all the other reasons advanced earlier. If distant people, future people, animals, and ecosystems are not morally considerable, then only the reasoning based on jobs for present Brazilians will have any ethical force. Arguments based purely on the economic costs and benefits of an environmental policy often assume that only nearby people—market participants—need to be considered ethically.

Each type of ethical theory and theory of moral standing has a particular set of strengths and weaknesses that we will look at in future chapters. Once we have classified the ethical reasoning behind a policy recommendation we can start to see to what degree we can depend on that reasoning. Understanding the strengths and weaknesses of each reason is also very useful when we must weigh contrary reasons against one another.

6. DECIDE WHICH POLICY TO ADOPT OR RECOMMEND

Once we have sorted out all the ethical reasons relevant to the situation under consideration, figured out presuppositions of moral standing, classified these reasons according to the various ethical theories, and thought about the strengths and weaknesses of these ethical theories, we are ready to decide what policy to recommend or oppose. It would be a mistake here to expect environmental ethics always to give a definitive answer regarding what is the best policy option. The situation, and the ethical reasons that are relevant to it, may be just too complicated to permit a definitive answer. Suppose we are considering four policy options: (1) Increased Logging, (2) Business-as-Usual, (3) Sustainable Logging, and (4) No Logging. It could be that our ethical analysis gives us good reason to reject options (1) and (2), but cannot tell us whether option (3) or (4) is the ethically superior one. Perhaps the ethical considerations favouring (3) are roughly equal to the considerations favouring (4). This is still progress. We are able to move forward with a (perhaps equivocal) recommendation that eliminates the ethically inferior options. We can make our recommendation with confidence that we have been appropriately careful not to miss any contrary ethical considerations. We will have performed our ethical due diligence.

This chapter has introduced an almost overwhelming flood of new concepts, some of which may not yet be clear. Future chapters will return to this material, making it more easily understood, and expanding on its relevance to critical reflection on environmental policy.

SUMMARY

1. The first step in an ethical analysis of environmental policy is to recognize which aspects of its reasoning and recommendations involve action-guiding, ethical judgments.

2. The second step is to identify what ethical reasons implicitly support a policy's recommendations.

3. The third step is to classify these ethical reasons according to the type of ethical theory that they are assuming.

4. There are three broad types of ethical theory: the virtue/vice approach, the deontological approach, and the consequentialist approach.

5. Deontological approaches include justice-based theories, rights-based theories, and divine command theories.

6. Consequentialist approaches include mental-state-based, subjective versions and non-mental-state-based, objective versions. Subjective versions come in two varieties: sensation-based hedonistic utilitarianism, and desire-based preference-satisfaction utilitarianism. Objective versions come in three varieties: a natural purpose-based teleological type, a community-based common good type, and a dispositional type that appeals to what people would desire if they were fully rational. Ethical egoism is a type of consequentialism that considers only the self to have moral standing.

7. The fourth step in an ethical analysis is to investigate which entities the ethical reasoning assumes to have moral standing.

8. The fifth step is to think critically about the ethical reasoning that is now explicit. This step considers the strengths and weaknesses of the various ethical theories and theories of moral standing that the reasoning employs.

9. Finally, the last step is to make a policy recommendation that has eliminated the ethically inferior options.

The book's website contains reading questions on this chapter. Working through these questions will help you understand, remember, and apply important concepts from the chapter. Some of the questions supply useful hints for the study questions.

STUDY QUESTIONS

Using the text and hints from the online reading questions, write out, type, dictate to your computer, or at least formulate in your head answers to the following questions.

1. "It was very careless of you to let your campfire escape and burn down the forest." Explain what type of ethical reason is being given here, and what entities are assumed to have moral standing.
2. "You ought not to burn the forest because doing so will painfully burn all the baby animals." Explain what type of ethical reason is being given here, and what entities are assumed to have moral standing.
3. "You ought not to burn the forest because doing so will destroy other people's private property." Explain what type of ethical reason is being given here, and what entities are assumed to have moral standing.
4. "You ought not to burn the forest because doing so will destroy the last remaining habitat of the endangered spotted owl." Explain what type of ethical reason is being given here, and what entities are assumed to have moral standing.
5. Explain the difference between the consequentialist and the deontological approaches to ethics.
6. Explain the difference between subjective and objective consequentialism.

QUESTIONS TO PONDER

Spend a few minutes thinking about the following questions, or, better yet, discuss them with fellow readers of this book.

1. Someone says, "You shouldn't kick my dog." He gives as reasons that dogs feel pain, that kicking dogs is cruel, that his dog has a right not to be kicked, and that you should not injure his property. What ethical reasons is he offering, to what ethical theories do these reasons appeal, and what claim about moral standing does each reason make?
2. An author recommends that people in industrialized, developed countries cut 80% of their greenhouse gas emissions by the year 2030, and makes the

following points: Climate change will cause the oceans to rise and flood low lying areas in Bangladesh, Vietnam, and Florida. Industrialized countries have experienced most of the benefits of burning fossil fuels, whereas developing countries will experience most of the bad effects. Climate change will cause the extinction of useful species which cannot migrate northward fast enough as their habitat changes. Mitigation of climate change will cost all countries about 2% of their GDP per year starting now. The author herself lives in a place where the climate will actually improve as the earth heats up. What ethical theories and what theories of moral standing do these points presuppose? How can the author, on balance, recommend cutting emissions?

3. Not all policy reasons fit neatly into the conceptual framework offered in the text. Suppose the Brazilian rain forest policy also made the following points: Clear-cutting the Amazon rain forest is wasteful. Clear-cutting the Amazon rain forest will result in the extinction of many utterly useless species of plants and animals. How would you classify these reasons in terms of ethical theories and of assumptions about moral standing?

Chapter 4

ETHICAL

EGOISM

ENVIRONMENTAL PROBLEMS NEARLY ALWAYS ARISE BECAUSE PEOPLE ACT ONLY IN their own narrow self-interest and neglect the effects of their actions on the rest of the planet. One ethical theory, ethical egoism, says that this way of acting is the way that people should behave. ETHICAL EGOISM is the theory that people should always act in their own self-interest, that they are morally obligated to do what is best for themselves. If ethical egoism were the correct moral theory, then there would be no such thing as environmental ethics. We will start our survey of ethical theories with an examination of the weaknesses of ethical egoism.

Few people profess to be ethical egoists in the stark form defined above. Most of those who believe in looking out only for themselves, especially the ones who have become very rich in doing so, believe in a constrained form of ethical egoism. In this form, the enforcement of private property rights and the enforcement of commercial contracts coercively restrict the pursuit of self-interest. CONTRACTARIANISM is the theory that ethics is a coercively enforced social contract between ethical egoists. It is relevant to the ethical analysis of the economic approach to the environment.

Though it is uncommon for individuals to behave as ethical egoists, it is very common for governments to behave like ethical egoists in their interactions with the governments of other countries. Many environmental issues are global, not national, and when national governments attempt to decide on joint environmental policies, with each negotiating team working purely for its own national interest, their interactions are subject to the problems of cooperation that are the weakness of simple ethical egoism. We will examine a simple problem of cooperation for ethical egoists, the prisoner's dilemma. The prisoner's dilemma helps explain why, for example, the US and China have difficulty reaching an agreement on decreasing greenhouse gas emissions.

Our world is no longer one of isolated hunter-gathering clans, but instead is one of large urban populations living close together in intricate systems of specialization and division of labour. Making such a system work requires cooperation and collective action, and ethical egoists are not good at cooperating. Solving major environmental problems will require collective action on the part of us all. The prisoner's dilemma illustrates, in miniature, how difficult it is to get people to cooperate in collective action. What is a clever action for an individual may be a very stupid action from the point of view of the long-term interests of society.

Learning Objectives

1. To understand ethical egoism and its connection to psychological egoism, an empirical theory.
2. To understand some of the weaknesses of ethical egoism as an ethical theory.
3. In particular, to understand why ethical egoists have difficulty cooperating.
4. Especially, to understand the prisoner's dilemma, a very powerful conceptual tool.
5. To understand contractarianism as a response to ethical egoism's cooperation difficulties.

ETHICAL EGOISM—ONLY THE SELF HAS MORAL STANDING

Ethical egoism does not fit within the virtue/vice approach because it is not concerned with the character of the agent. Nor does it fit within the deontological approach because ethical egoism is not a divine command, is not concerned with the rights of the recipient, and is not concerned with justice or fairness. Ethical egoism fits within the consequentialist approach, the view that agents ought to cause maximum aggregate intrinsic value. The ethical egoist does not have to worry about aggregating (or adding up) the intrinsic value caused for different recipients, because he needs to worry about causing maximum value for only one recipient, himself.

We could interpret ethical egoism as a form of objective consequentialism, where the value or good that we maximize is not directly a mental state. We could imagine an ethical egoist who was concerned with maximizing his own natural functioning, or with maximizing his self-interest conceived of, not as what he actually finds himself wanting, but as what he would want if he were perfectly informed and totally rational in his reasoning. It is less easy to imagine a type of ethical egoism where the ethical egoist identifies his self-interests with the common good, though we will mention a possibility below.

We more commonly think of ethical egoism as a form of subjective consequentialism, where the value of the good that we maximize is directly concerned with mental states. An ethical egoist is likely to be concerned with maximizing his own pleasure, or with best satisfying his own desires and preferences.

Turning from the dimension of moral theory to the dimension of moral standing, we see immediately that ethical egoism does not naturally concern itself with the fate of ecosystems, species, living things generally, animals, future people, distant people, or even nearby people. However, there is an interesting possibility. Ethical egoism is about the moral obligation to promote the interests of the self, but there is dispute over the nature of the self. A person's self plausibly consists in that with which she psychologically identifies, and that could include her immediate family or her whole community. For example, parents often identify with the interests of their children and treat their children's interests as their own, even sometimes to an extreme degree. One important environmental philosophy that we will consider in more detail in a later chapter, deep ecology, claims that we can and should seek identification with the whole planetary ecosystem. Then a deep ecologist acting in her own self-interest will thereby act in the planet's best interest. In the rest of this chapter, however, we will be concerned with ethical egoists who are obligated to promote their own narrow self-interest.

ETHICAL EGOISM AND PSYCHOLOGICAL EGOISM

It is important to distinguish ethical egoism, which is the *ethical* theory that people always *ought* to act to maximize to their own narrow self-interest, from PSYCHOLOGICAL EGOISM, which is the *empirical* theory that people always *do* act to maximize to their own narrow self-interest. Psychological egoism is a plausible scientific hypothesis that we test by experiment in a psychology laboratory rather than by reason and debate in a philosophy seminar room.

It is also important not to understand psychological egoism in a way that makes it true by definition. One way this could happen is if we reflect that, because we have to be motivated to perform any action, there is a sense in which we must want to do any action that we perform. If we take acting in our self-interest to mean just acting as we want to do, then we only ever act in our self-interest. To avoid psychological egoism being true by definition, we must look at the origins of our motivations. If, for example, our ethical judgments do motivate us, and if these ethical judgments are based on wanting to respect human rights, then it would be odd to say that we are motivated by self-interest. Another way psychological egoism could become true by definition is if we carelessly allow the notion of self-interest to become so wide that our wanting to help our family and neighbours, or doing what we think is morally right, all become "self-interest." (This sort of thinking may be what the "expansion of the self" we just talked about involves.)

Ethical egoism is not the same as ethical relativism. Ethical relativism is a metaethical theory about the nature of morality, whereas ethical egoism is a normative ethical theory about what an agent is obligated to do. The form of ethical relativism that is most easily confused with ethical egoism is the form that takes the truth of ethical judgments to be relative to the individual making the judgment. An individual ethical relativist might claim that his doing what is best for him is morally right for himself, even if not so for others. However, he could equally well have claimed that his emulating the actions of Mahatma Gandhi is morally right for himself, though not for others. Nothing about ethical relativism forces its proponents to be selfish or ethical egoists.

Ethical egoism can occur in two versions, strong and weak. STRONG ETHICAL EGOISM is the theory that it is always *morally required* that people should act to maximize their own self-interest. WEAK ETHICAL EGOISM is the theory that it is always *morally permissible* for people to act to maximize their own self-interest. The trouble with weak ethical egoism is that it permits everything, since it is also morally permissible not to act in one's own self-interest. If every act is permitted and no act is required, then weak ethical egoism is not really a moral theory.

ATTRACTIONS OF ETHICAL EGOISM

One attraction of ethical egoism is that it, together with psychological egoism, explains why ethical judgments are action-guiding. According to the empirical theory of psychological egoism, people *are* always motivated to pursue their own narrow self-interest. According to the ethical theory of ethical egoism, people *ought to* pursue their own narrow self-interest. So it follows that people are always motivated to do what they ought to do, and the judgments of ethical egoism are action-guiding.

Another attraction for ethical egoism is that, it is claimed, in a free-market economy, if people are ethical egoists then this will lead to the maximum balance of benefits over costs for everyone in the economy. This argument is based on Adam Smith's famous metaphor of the "invisible hand." In *The Wealth of Nations*, Smith pointed out that, in a market economy, we expect people to be acting only in their own self-interest. He wrote that, "It is not from the benevolence of the butcher, the brewer, or the baker, that we expect our dinner, but from their regard to their own interest. We address ourselves, not to their humanity but to their self-love, and never talk to them of our own necessities but of their advantages" (Smith 1776: Book I, Chapter II, Paragraph 2.2). However, this is not a problem, because if people behave as ethical egoists, then this will end up working in everyone's best interests. In another famous passage, Smith wrote,

> ... by directing that industry in such a manner as its produce may be of the greatest value, he intends only his own gain, and he is in this, as in many other cases, led by an invisible hand to promote an end which was no part of his intention. Nor is it always the worse for the society that it was no part of it. By pursuing his own interest he frequently promotes that of the society more effectually than when he really intends to promote it. (Book IV, Chapter II, Paragraph 2.9)

We will return to the invisible hand in later chapters because the invisible hand does its job only under certain crucial assumptions and environmental problems frequently violate these assumptions.

First, we should note that ethical egoism does not follow from psychological egoism as a direct argument. The following argument is fallacious:

1. It *is* the case that people always maximize their own self-interest.
2. Therefore, it *ought* to be the case that people always maximize their own self-interest.

Any such argument falls afoul of Hume's Guillotine, neglects the fact/value distinction, crosses the is/ought gap, and commits the naturalistic fallacy by attempting to derive an ethical "ought" statement from a factual "is" statement.

The "invisible hand" argument is not as strong an argument for ethical egoism as it might seem. Firstly, it is actually a utilitarian justification for ethical egoism. It is based on the claim that self-interested behaviour is justified, not because it is in the interest of the agent, but because it promotes the interest of all members of society. A better interpretation of Smith's argument is that self-interested behaviour is justified indirectly because it contributes to causing the maximum aggregate desire-satisfaction for all participants in the market economy. As an indirect utilitarian argument, it presupposes that all people have moral standing. We will have a brief look at the economic argument for Smith's claim later. Secondly, the argument is not that a society of pure ethical egoists will maximize aggregate satisfaction, but is instead that a society of *constrained* ethical egoists will do so. The constraints are that egoists obey the rules of a market economy, that they respect private property without stealing from one another, and that they keep contracts by paying each other what they owe. We will see below that this contractarian assumption has to be added to ethical egoism; the assumption is not built into egoism itself.

Another weakness of ethical egoism is what is called the "paradox of egoism." Some valuable consequences, like friendship, are not available to people who always act to maximize their own narrow self-interest. Friendship requires that people sometimes put the interests of their friends ahead of their own. Ethical egoists, however, ought to betray their friends whenever betrayal is in their own narrow self-interest. Thus, ethical egoists cannot have friends and so cannot maximize good consequences for themselves. In a sense, ethical egoism is self-defeating.

Since the various approaches to ethical theory each developed partly in response to weaknesses in the others, it is often useful to look for weaknesses in an ethical theory by considering it from the perspective of other approaches. We will apply this technique frequently. The considered intuitions that support other approaches to ethics often go against ethical egoism. From the point of view of the virtue theorist, the ethical egoist has the vices of self-centredness and selfishness. From the point of view of the deontologist, the ethical egoist is too ready to sacrifice the rights of others. For example, the ethical egoist ought to keep other humans as slaves if doing so would make him more comfortable. From the point of view of the utilitarian, the ethical egoist is too reluctant to put himself out for the benefit of others.

For example, the ethical egoist ought not to press a button to end world poverty if doing so would cause him the least inconvenience.

From the point of view of theories of moral standing, we must be able to point to some feature of ethically considerable recipients that justifies their having moral standing. For example, animal welfare theories point to SENTIENCE, the capacity to feel sensations of pain and pleasure, as a feature that the more complex animals share with humans. Sentience is an important, morally relevant, feature. Hedonistic utilitarians often give moral standing to animals that possess the feature of sentience when they are maximizing the total balance of pleasure over pain. In contrast, an ethical egoist can point to no morally relevant feature of himself that justifies his having moral standing while other humans do not. Pointing to his unique driver's license number, for example, is simply morally arbitrary. The ethical egoist has no morally relevant feature that differentiates him from other human beings. Any non-arbitrary feature that he has will be possessed by other, similar human beings and will justify them having moral standing too. There are no morally relevant differences between him and other humans.

Most of the good things that humans enjoy are the product of specialization, the division of labour, and cooperation. We can produce together much more than the simple sum of what we can produce working alone. Ethical egoists, however, cannot enjoy the gains from cooperation because they have difficulty cooperating. We can design situations, called "prisoner's dilemmas," where the ethical approach of ethical egoists will oblige them to cheat, even though they would maximize their self-interest by cooperating. We can illustrate this by describing a simple game.

GAME THEORY AND THE PRISONER'S DILEMMA

Mike and Nancy are two egoists each planning to build a cottage on a small lake. It is cheaper for each of them to dispose of their wastewater in the lake than to build a septic system. If one of them were to put wastewater in the lake, then the lake would be fine, but if they both were to do it, then the lake would become smelly and unpleasant. The best individual outcome for each of them is if the other builds a septic system and they do not. The best overall outcome is if they cooperate and both build septic systems. The worst outcome is if they both cheat and put all the wastewater in the lake. Mike and Nancy make their decisions on the same day. What will happen?

The best way to understand the problem of cooperation inherent in this situation is to represent it using the abstract techniques of game theory. A simple game has three basic elements:

1. The players.
2. The player's available strategies.
3. Each player's payoff for each possible combination of strategies.

A PAYOFF MATRIX is a table that shows each player's payoff for every possible combination of strategies. Table 4.1 shows a payoff matrix for the situation faced by Mike and Nancy.

		MIKE	
		Cheat	*Cooperate*
NANCY	*Cheat*	5 5	2 15
	Cooperate	15 2	10 10

TABLE 4.1: Payoff matrix for a prisoner's dilemma

The two players are Mike and Nancy. Their strategies are either to cheat or to cooperate. They each decide on their strategies independently, without knowledge of what the other has actually decided to do. They each make their choice of strategy based on reasoning about what the other might do. We represent Nancy's two available strategies by rows in the payoff matrix, while Mike's strategies are columns. The payoff matrix is Table 4.1. We show the payoffs in the cells of the table. Mike's payoffs are in the upper right of each cell while Nancy's are in the lower left. For example, if Nancy's strategy is to cooperate with Mike and Mike's strategy is to cooperate with Nancy, then Mike will receive 10 as shown in the upper right of the lower right cell. The payoff units are arbitrary. They could be dollars, or units of pleasure, or utiles, the abstract units of value used by utilitarians. We can see that each player is better off with both cooperating rather than with both cheating. If they both cooperate, then they will each get 10, as shown by the intersection of the cooperation strategies in the lower right cell, whereas if they both cheat, then they will each get only 5. Unfortunately, Mike and Nancy are ethical egoists who believe that they ought always to maximize their own payoff. On this assumption, we can demonstrate that they will end up both cheating and thus fail to maximize their self-interest.

REASONING THROUGH A SIMPLE GAME

Some people can see intuitively what will happen in these games, while others must reason them through. To reason through a simple game, the technique is to look at each player's best strategic response to each of the other player's available strategies. So we first ask: if Nancy's strategy were to cheat, then what should Mike do? In Table 4.2, Nancy's strategy of cheating is represented by the top row of the payoff matrix. For clarity, we will eliminate her other strategy.

		MIKE	
		Cheat	*Cooperate*
NANCY	*Cheat*	✓ 5 5	2 15

TABLE 4.2: What should Mike do if Nancy's strategy were to cheat?

Ethical Egoism

The answer to our question is that he should cheat because his payoff for cheating is 5 which is greater than his payoff for cooperating which is 2. We will put a checkmark beside this payoff of 5 to record his strategic response.

Next we ask: if Nancy's strategy were to cooperate, then what should Mike do? In Table 4.3, Nancy's strategy of cooperating is represented by the bottom row of the payoff matrix. For clarity, we will eliminate her cheating strategy.

		MIKE	
		Cheat	Cooperate
NANCY	Cheat		
	Cooperate	✓ 15 2	10 10

TABLE 4.3: What should Mike do if Nancy's strategy were to cooperate?

The answer to our question is that he should cheat because 15 is greater than 10. We will record this with a checkmark beside 15.

Now we can ask what Mike should do. In this game there is an answer that is independent of the other player's strategy. To see this put Tables 4.2 and 4.3 together again into Table 4.4.

		MIKE	
		Cheat	Cooperate
NANCY	Cheat	✓ 5 5	2 15
	Cooperate	✓ 15 2	10 10

TABLE 4.4: Mike should cheat no matter what strategy Nancy chooses

The answer is that Mike should cheat no matter what strategy Nancy chooses. All of his checkmarks are in his cheat strategy column. If Nancy cheats, then his best strategy is to cheat; if she cooperates, then his best strategic response is still to cheat. Mike has a dominant strategy, which is always to cheat. A DOMINANT STRATEGY is a strategy that yields a higher payoff regardless of the strategy chosen by the other player. A dominant strategy happens in our representation when all of a player's checkmarks are in the same row or column. Without knowing what Nancy actually does, Mike is able to reason out what he should do.

Now we can move more quickly and ask what Nancy should do. In Table 4.5, if we look in the column where Mike cheats, then we can see that Nancy should cheat because her payoff of 5 for cheating is higher than her payoff of 2 for cooperating. We put a checkmark by her 5 in the cheat/cheat cell. In the column where Mike cooperates, Nancy is still at an advantage to cheat because 15 is greater than 10. We put a checkmark by her 15 in that cell. Therefore,

Nancy should cheat, no matter what strategy Mike employs. Nancy, *qua* ethical egoist, also has a dominant strategy, which is to cheat.

		MIKE	
		Cheat	*Cooperate*
NANCY	*Cheat*	5 5 ✓	2 15 ✓
	Cooperate	15 2	10 10

TABLE 4.5: Nancy should cheat no matter what strategy Mike chooses

Now we can see that, in a situation like this, where each player's incentives are always to maximize their own payoff, each player will reason that he or she should cheat no matter what his or her opponent does. If we collect all the checkmarks in Table 4.6, then we can see that their self-interested reasoning will put them into the upper left, cheat/cheat cell of the payoff matrix.

		MIKE	
		Cheat	*Cooperate*
NANCY	*Cheat*	✓ 5 5 ✓	2 15 ✓
	Cooperate	✓ 15 2	10 10

TABLE 4.6: Equilibrium in a prisoner's dilemma

The game has what game theorists call a "NASH EQUILIBRIUM" because there is a combination of strategies (cheat, cheat) such that each player's strategy is the best he or she can choose given the other player's strategies. A Nash equilibrium occurs when there is a cell in which the payoffs of both players are checked.

CONCLUSION OF THIS COOPERATION DILEMMA

The two players, following the rule of ethical egoism always to maximize narrow self-interest, will both decide to cheat. In doing so, they will receive the payoffs in the upper left corner of the payoff matrix, that is, 5 each. If they were not ethical egoists, they could have followed a rule to cooperate, and received the higher payoffs in the lower right corner, that is, 10 each. A game is called a PRISONER'S DILEMMA when both players have dominant strategies that, when played, result in an equilibrium with payoffs smaller than if each had played another strategy. The term, "prisoner's dilemma," comes from the original formulation of the problem with two prisoners interrogated separately by the police and given incentives to "squeal" on one another. The original prisoner's dilemma is illustrated in the reading questions for this chapter.

Not every payoff matrix will result in a prisoner's dilemma. But some will, and that is what causes the dilemma for egoists. Not just ethical egoists can get into this dilemma, psychological egoists can also. The dilemma is particularly acute for ethical egoists whose ethical judgments guide them to maximize their own self-interest and then find that their ethical reasoning brings them into a situation that does not maximize their self-interest. We can also predict that psychological egoists will end up failing to cooperate and thus failing to do as well as they could do. In answer to the question regarding the ethical egoist cottage owners that began this section, we can now see that their ethical reasoning will bring both of them to discharge their wastewater into the little lake, resulting in a less than optimum situation from both their points of view (and from the point of view of the environment too).

CONTRACTARIANISM

In the seventeenth century, Thomas Hobbes realized that ethical egoists would always cheat on one another and that life for a society of ethical egoists would be "nasty, brutish, and short" because of the war of all against all.

> Whatsoever therefore is consequent to a time of Warre, where every man is Enemy to every man; the same is consequent to the time, wherein men live without other security, than what their own strength, and their own invention shall furnish them withall. In such condition, there is no place for Industry; because the fruit thereof is uncertain; and consequently no Culture of the Earth; no Navigation, nor use of the commodities that may be imported by Sea; no commodious Building; no Instruments of moving, and removing such things as require much force; no Knowledge of the face of the Earth; no account of Time; no Arts; no Letters; no Society; and which is worst of all, continuall feare, and danger of violent death; And the life of man, solitary, poore, nasty, brutish, and short. (Hobbes 1651: Chapter 13)

He proposed that ethical egoists should make a social contract to establish a state with the coercive power to punish cheating. State punishment would then give cheating a lower payoff than cooperating. We can model this situation for Mike and Nancy if we imagine the state fining each of them 6 units whenever they cheat (or put wastewater in the lake), as shown in Table 4.7.

		MIKE	
		Cheat	Cooperate
NANCY	Cheat	$5-6 = -1$ $5-6 = -1$	✓ 2 $15-6=9$
	Cooperate	$15-6=9$ 2 ✓	✓ 10 10 ✓

TABLE 4.7: State coercion and the former prisoner's dilemma

With the state's intervention, the payoffs have changed and the egoists will reason to a different conclusion. If Nancy were to cheat, then Mike should cooperate because 2 is better than −1. If Nancy were to cooperate, then Mike should cooperate because 10 is better than 9. So Mike has a dominant strategy, which is always to cooperate. Likewise, Nancy should also always cooperate. With the intervention of the coercive power of the state, the two egoists can reason their way to the best joint outcome of 10 units each in the lower right cell.

CONTRACTARIANISM is the theory that ethics is a state enforced social contract among ethical egoists. This would allow ethical egoists to achieve the benefits of cooperation. Ethical egoists take this to entail a minimal state, sometimes called a "night watchman state," with powers limited to enforcing contracts, protecting private property, and establishing a free-market economy.

WEAKNESSES OF THE CONTRACTARIAN APPROACH

We can see many of the weaknesses of the contractarian theory if we examine it from the perspective of the other ethical approaches we have considered. First, from a virtue theory perspective, contractarianism would create a free-market society that encourages highly competitive, self-interested behaviour, and would thus foster the vices of greed, ruthlessness, and selfishness. (Of course, these character traits would not bother a committed ethical egoist.)

Second, though a contractarian society is to the mutual advantage of those who are able to cooperate, contractarianism says nothing about those who, for reasons of physical or mental handicap, are unable to participate in the marketplace. From a rights-based perspective, a contractarian society will not respect the rights of the handicapped to a decent life. Limiting the role of the state to the protection of private property and the enforcement of contracts will allow the development of extremes of wealth and poverty. From a justice-based perspective, such an unequal distribution of benefits and burdens may seem unfair.

Third, though Adam Smith's invisible hand will maximize the economic production of a contractarian market economy, it will do so only under certain conditions. One condition is that economic activity does not create pollution that falls on persons who do not participate in that activity. Since pollution is a common by-product of economic activity, a contractarian market society will often not maximize economic well-being, as the invisible hand approach requires. We will return to this point in much more detail in later chapters.

Fourth, in a contractarian framework the only entities that have moral standing are the various selves who form a social contract to respect each other's property rights. This is problematic from a moral standing perspective because it leaves out many human and nonhuman entities without further argument. Contractarian obligations only extend to people in the society that has the social contract. Therefore, contractarians have no obligations to distant people. For example, on this view citizens of industrialized countries would have no duties of foreign aid toward hungry people in poor countries. Nor would contractarians have obligations to future generations since they cannot form a contract with people who do not yet exist. Contractarians cannot have obligations to animals (or species, or ecosystems) because they are unable to enter into contracts with humans.

Finally, the contractarian approach to ethics keeps some of the weaknesses of the ethical egoist approach on which it is based. For example, though it is possible for contractarian ethical egoists to cooperate, they still cannot form friendships. Since ethical egoists always ought to cheat when they think that they can get away with it, a contractarian arrangement will always be unstable. The contractors will always cheat when they think state punishment is avoidable. This contrasts with non-egoists who will not cheat because they have internalized a set of other-regarding ethical values.

SUMMARY

1. Ethical egoism is a form of subjective consequentialism in which only the self has moral standing. It is an ethical theory that says each agent should maximize his or her own narrow self-interest.

2. Psychological egoism is the empirical theory that people always do act in their own narrow self-interest.

3. The attractions of ethical egoism are that it explains why people are motivated to do what they believe is right, and that, under certain conditions, Adam Smith's invisible hand will cause egoists to maximize economic production.

4. The weaknesses of ethical egoism include not following from psychological egoism because of the is/ought gap, maximizing net benefits only under pollution-free conditions, encouraging selfishness, permitting the violation of the rights of others, and discouraging aid to the needy. Paradoxically, ethical egoists may not be able to maximize their own self-interest because they will be unable to make friends without betraying them.

5. One huge weakness of ethical egoism is that ethical egoists will be unable to cooperate in many circumstances because their ethical beliefs will oblige them to cheat. We can illustrate this with the prisoner's dilemma game, where two players will each reason that they should cheat in order to maximize their own self-interest, yet their cheating will result in an outcome that is worse for each of them than the outcome where they both cooperate.

6. One way for egoists to solve their cooperation dilemma is to create a state that enables economic cooperation by coercively enforcing property rights and contracts. This contractarian solution will create cooperation in prisoner's dilemma situations by punishing cheating. However, it will still encourage both selfishness and injustice, while neither giving ethical consideration to distant and future people outside the social contract, nor giving ethical consideration to animals, plants, and ecosystems which are unable to enter any contract.

The book's website contains reading questions on this chapter. Working through these questions will help you understand, remember, and apply important concepts from the chapter. Some of the questions supply useful hints for the study questions.

STUDY QUESTIONS

Using the text and hints from the online reading questions, write out, type, dictate to your computer, or at least formulate in your head answers to the following questions.

1. Explain the difference between psychological egoism and ethical egoism. Why is the former not a sound argument for the latter?
2. Explain, with an example, the paradox of ethical egoism.
3. Explain why ethical egoists have difficulty cooperating and why this difficulty appears to make ethical egoism self-defeating.
4. Describe Contractarianism and explain why it might be a solution to ethical egoism's difficulties with cooperation.
5. Describe what you think are important difficulties for Contractarianism.

QUESTIONS TO PONDER

Spend a few minutes thinking about the following questions, or, better yet, discuss them with fellow readers of this book.

1. Is ethical egoism an ethical theory that everyone can consistently follow? Can it be a universal rule of conduct, or will it result in cases where it calls the same action both right and wrong?
2. Is psychological egoism a true empirical theory of human nature?
3. China and the US are considering implementing a new version of the Kyoto Protocol on greenhouse gas emissions. If both countries implement the agreement, then they will each gain $10 billion on their GNP. If they both ignore the agreement, then they will each lose $5 billion. If the US implements and China ignores, then China will gain $15 billion while the US will lose $15 billion. If China implements and the US ignores, then the US will gain $20 billion while China will lose $10 billion. Set up a payoff table for this "game" and show whether it is a prisoner's dilemma.
4. How does the prisoner's dilemma help us understand both the creation of large-scale environmental problems and the lack of collective action toward their solution?
5. Could a contractarian, night-watchman state survive for very long if everyone were truly an ethical or psychological egoist?

Chapter 5

UTILITARIANISM

UTILITARIAN ETHICAL THEORIES ARE SUBJECTIVE CONSEQUENTIALIST—THEY LOOK to the consequences of an action or policy for the mental lives of those whom it affects. Utilitarian theories claim that the right action, or the best policy, is the one that creates the maximum happiness, welfare, pleasure, or desire-satisfaction for all those who have moral standing. In this chapter, we will look at the strengths and weaknesses of different forms of utilitarian ethical theories.

Philosophers have been thinking about ethical issues for thousands of years, but have developed utilitarian approaches only in the last several centuries. In the modern world, the utilitarian approach to ethics is very influential. Utilitarian reasoning implicitly underlies much of the economic approach to environmental policy. According to utilitarians, we ought to maximize the aggregated amount of satisfied wants. Money gets people what they want. If people have more monetary income, then they can get more of what they want most. Some utilitarians conclude that economic policy should always maximize a nation's total income in the present, and create maximum economic growth in the future. Unfortunately, as experience has shown, unrestricted economic growth frequently leads to environmental destruction. The interpretation of utilitarian ethical theory and the examination of its problems are essential to environmental ethics.

1. To understand that other ethical theories are possible only if psychological egoism is false.
2. To understand the most popular modern ethical theory, utilitarianism.
3. To understand the strengths and weaknesses of both hedonistic and preference utilitarianism.
4. To begin to understand the different varieties of utilitarian theories.

IS MORALITY POSSIBLE?

Utilitarianism requires that we are ethically obliged to maximize everyone's welfare, not just our own. Psychological egoism is the empirical theory that people always act in their own self-interest and act to maximize only their own welfare. The principle that "ought" implies "can" says that people are not ethically obliged to do what they are not able to do. If psychological egoism is a true theory of human nature, then utilitarianism cannot work as an ethical theory because it obliges people to work for the welfare of others.

Is psychological egoism true? We can answer from our own experience. One telling example is the almost universal tendency of people to leave a tip in an out-of-town restaurant. People might tip out of self-interest at a restaurant that they were planning to revisit so as to ensure better service, but they have no self-interested reason to leave a tip at a restaurant that they will never visit again. More scientifically, we can point to the evolution of KINSHIP SELECTION, where people have altruistic tendencies toward relatives who carry the same genes. We can also point to the evolution of RECIPROCAL ALTRUISM in human populations, where people will be willing to bear a cost for others if they think that they will receive a benefit back in the future. This, just by itself, points to ethical egoism, but reciprocal altruism in humans depends on the evolution of certain emotional tendencies, for example trust, friendship, guilt, shame, anger, and indignation that enable reciprocal cooperation. These tendencies lead us to further other people's interests just because we want to, and not because we expect something in return. Humans have thus developed the ability to act for reasons other than maximizing their own narrow self-interest.

An interesting example of non-self-interested behaviour is the ULTIMATUM GAME, a little piece of behavioural economics that has been tested many times across many cultures. Here is how a sample game involving three people—Referee, Proposer, and Decider—works:

1. Referee gives some money, say $10, to Proposer.
2. Proposer may offer any amount $X, between $1 and $10, to Decider, with Proposer keeping the balance of $(10 − X).
3. If Decider accepts the offer, then Decider gets to keep $X and Proposer gets to keep $(10 − X).
4. If Decider rejects the offer, then they each get nothing.

Empirical research shows that most games result in a roughly 50/50 split, or proposals and acceptances of $5 each. However, from the narrow self-interest point of view, Decider should accept any offer of more than $0, since that will leave Decider better off than refusing the offer. Similarly, if Proposer really thought that Decider was a rational psychological egoist, then Proposer would offer only $1 and keep $9 for herself. Proposer would either feel guilty at offering less than half the windfall, or predict that Decider will be offended at being offered less than half and that Decider will refuse the offer in order to punish Proposer. The outcome of this very simple game is more evidence that psychological egoism is a false empirical theory.

UTILITARIANISM

We classify ethical theories according to the components of ethical judgments: An agent or agents perform some action that has consequences for entities with moral standing. Virtue ethics worries about the character of agents, deontology worries about the principles governing the action, and consequentialism worries about the results of the action. Consequentialism is the ethical theory that each agent ought to cause maximum aggregated intrinsic value for all recipients with moral standing. Ethical egoism is the theory that only the self has moral standing, so we should each maximize intrinsic value for ourselves. If we extend moral standing to recipients beyond the self, then we have standard consequentialism.

Objective consequentialist theories claim that the intrinsic value which we ought to maximize pertains to features of the world other than the actual mental states of recipients. Subjective consequentialist, or utilitarian, theories claim that the intrinsic value which we ought to maximize pertains to the actual mental states of recipients. According to utilitarianism, an action or policy is the right one if, and only if,

(1) it causes
(2) the maximum
(3) aggregate
(4) amount of utility.

Clause (1) makes utilitarianism consequentialist. Clause (2) makes explicit the assumption that if something is intrinsically valuable, then more of it is better. Clause (3) says that we must add up intrinsic value across all those beings with moral standing. Clause (4) contains the odd term, "utility." UTILITY is an abstract measure of quantity and intensity for whatever mental states a utilitarian thinks we should aggregate and maximize. Actions are instrumentally valuable insofar as they cause utility.

Utilitarian reasoning works like this. Suppose a utilitarian is deciding between policy A and policy B that will affect three people. Implementing policy A will cause utilities of 30 for Eve, 40 for Farouk, and 50 for George. The consequence of implementing policy B will be utilities of 20 for Eve, 20 for Farouk, and 90 for George. Adding up, or aggregating, the utility of each policy gives a total of 120 for policy A and 130 for policy B, as shown in Table 5.1. According to utilitarian reasoning, we should implement policy B because doing so causes the maximum aggregate amount of utility.

	EVE	FAROUK	GEORGE	AGGREGATE	MAXIMIZE?
Policy A	30	40	50	30+40+50=120	No
Policy B	20	20	90	20+20+90=130	Yes

TABLE 5.1: Example of utilitarian reasoning

Hedonistic utilitarians claim that the source of utility is mental sensations like pleasure, enjoyment, or the absence of pain. Sensations are internal, psychological feelings or experiences brought about by stimulation of the sense organs. John Stuart Mill (1806–76), a nineteenth-century English philosopher and economist, described utilitarianism as follows:

> The creed which accepts as the foundation of morals, Utility, or the Greatest Happiness Principle, holds that actions are right in proportion as they tend to promote happiness, wrong as they tend to produce the reverse of happiness. By happiness is intended pleasure, and the absence of pain; by unhappiness, pain, and the privation of pleasure.... But these supplementary explanations do not affect the theory of life on which this theory of morality is grounded—namely, that pleasure, and freedom from pain, are the only things desirable as ends; and that all desirable things (which are as numerous in the utilitarian as in any other scheme) are desirable either for the pleasure inherent in themselves, or as means to the promotion of pleasure and the prevention of pain. (1863: Chapter 2)

HEDONISTIC UTILITARIANISM is the ethical theory that each agent ought to cause the maximum balance of pleasure over pain for recipients with moral standing.

Preference-satisfaction utilitarians claim that the source of utility is the satisfaction of wants or desires, which are different types of psychological states from sensations. Desires and wants are psychological states that are directed on what it is that is desired or wished for, and which are satisfied when that thing is obtained. There are many other sorts of things that are desired beside pleasure and the absence of pain. PREFERENCE-SATISFACTION UTILI-TARIANISM is the ethical theory that each agent ought to act to bring about the maximum amount of satisfied desires and wants of recipients with moral standing. Figure 5.1 reviews our classification of ethical theories and shows how these two varieties of utilitarianism fit in our taxonomy.

ATTRACTIONS OF UTILITARIANISM

In nineteenth-century England, utilitarianism was a democratic, progressive, even radical doctrine. It claimed that the happiness of all people was equally important, whether they were aristocratic landowners and wealthy industrialists or factory workers and household servants. Utilitarianism calls for equal considerations of interests in the sense that, when utilitarians add up everyone's utility, they weight the utility of each person by the same factor. As Jeremy Bentham (1748–1832), the first person to formulate a utilitarian theory, put it, each person was to count for one and no person was to count for more than one. Utilitarianism

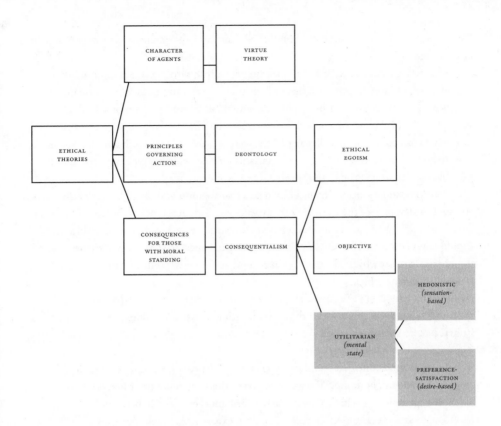

FIGURE 5.1: Classification of utilitarian ethical theories

·is not classist, sexist, or racist. Many people believe that animals can feel sensations of pain and pleasure. One attraction of hedonistic utilitarianism is that it offers a way to extend moral standing to animals. We simply count the pains and pleasures of animals in our utility calculations.

A second attraction of utilitarianism is that it promises to yield a decision in every case. We just have to add up the utilities of the consequences of all the possible acts and pick the act that maximizes aggregate utility. Equal totals are possible, but infrequent. This attraction depends on our ability to compare, measure, and aggregate utility. If we cannot do these things, then we will not be able to generate clear decisions.

SOME WEAKNESSES OF HEDONISTIC UTILITARIANISM

Simple hedonistic utilitarianism has received much criticism since it was first formulated. Some of the most important criticisms are the following:

1. COMPARISON PROBLEMS. Utilitarianism requires that we compare the pains and pleasures of different people in order to aggregate the pains and pleasures. How, for example, can we compare the intensity of one person's pleasure in reading a novel with another person's pleasure in eating a hamburger?

2. MEASUREMENT PROBLEMS. How do we measure the intensity of someone's pain or pleasure?

3. QUALITY OF PLEASURES. Are all pleasures equally important, or are some, like reading a good novel, of more importance than others, such as watching cartoons? Bentham argued that playing the pub game of push-pin was as valuable as reading poetry, if both gave the same pleasure. Mill famously replied, "It is better to be a human being dissatisfied than a pig satisfied; better to be Socrates dissatisfied than a fool satisfied" (1863: Chapter 2). Again, we have to go beyond simple hedonistic utilitarianism to say why one type of pleasure is more valuable than another, though they both have the same intensity.

4. SADISTIC PLEASURES. The utilitarian says that we must add the pleasures of the sadist and subtract the pain of the victim in order to judge sadistic acts morally. But should we even count sadistic pleasure in our utilitarian calculations? If we decide, quite reasonably, that we should never count sadistic pleasures, then we have to appeal to some ethical theory beyond utilitarianism to say why. Having to appeal beyond utilitarianism indicates that utilitarianism is not the ultimate ethical theory.

5. VIRTUAL REALITY. We can design thought-experiments to show that sensations, feelings, and experiences are not the things with ultimate intrinsic value. A great example is Robert Nozick's Experience Machine:

> Imagine a machine that could give you any experience (or sequence of experiences) you might desire. When connected to this experience machine, you have the experience of writing a great poem or bringing about world peace or loving someone and being loved in return. You can experience the felt pleasures of these things, how they feel "from the inside." You can program your experience for tomorrow, or this week, or this year, or even for the rest of your life. If your imagination is impoverished, you can use the library of suggestions extracted from biographies and enhanced by novelists and psychologists. You can live your fondest dreams "from the inside." Would you choose to do this for the rest of your life? If not, why not? (Nozick 1989: 104–05)

If we would not choose to hook ourselves up to the experience machine, then we do not really believe that only pleasurable experience has intrinsic value.

6. ACCUMULATIVE CONSEQUENCES. Sometimes an individual action may cause no pain, and hence be permissible, but when many people perform the same action, the consequences can be very bad. Consider Derek Parfit's Harmless Torturers problem: The victim is hooked up to a torture machine. The machine has a dial with 1000 clicks. Turning the dial by one click causes an imperceptible addition to the victim's pain. Turning the dial by 1000 clicks causes the victim excruciating pain. 1000 people each turn the dial by one click. Each person causes no addition to perceptible pain. Therefore, each person does nothing wrong. However, the victim experiences extreme pain (Parfit 1984: 80).

One way round the Harmless Torturers problem is to distinguish between people deciding which act to do and people deciding which rule to follow. If each agent should perform only acts that do not increase subjective pain, and if turning the dial one click causes no additional feeling of pain, then each agent may turn the dial one click. However, if each agent should follow the *rule* which would result in minimum aggregate pain, and if everyone's following the rule, "Do not turn the dial one click," causes less pain than everyone's following the rule, "Turn the dial one click," then agents may not turn the dial even one click. This is analogous to the familiar consideration in everyday ethical thinking: "What if everyone did that?"

Accumulative consequences are very important in environmental ethics. For example, each person driving a car will cause little harm to the environment. Yet, when hundreds of millions of people do so, they will contribute to climate change. We will return frequently to this type of problem.

SOME WEAKNESSES OF PREFERENCE-SATISFACTION UTILITARIANISM

To preference-satisfaction utilitarians, the only consequence with intrinsic value is the satisfaction of desires and wants. They believe that happiness and welfare are a matter of fulfilling preferences, and this is the only source of utility. An act or policy is the right one if, and only if, (1) it causes (2) the maximum (3) aggregate amount of (4) preference satisfaction. In order to aggregate and maximize the satisfied preferences of many different people, we have to be able to compare and measure the intensity of the preferences of different people. The problem of how to do this is the first of several problems for preference-satisfaction utilitarianism.

1. COMPARISON AND MEASUREMENT PROBLEMS. How do we compare intensity of preference between two people? How do we measure the intensity of preferences for one person? One response to the difficulties of comparing preferences between persons is to look to what people reveal by their choices, and not to try to measure what is going on inside a person's head. By examining their behaviour, we can tell that a person prefers outcome A to outcome B, or that he prefers B to A, or that he is indifferent between A and B. For example, by watching what a person does in a restaurant, we can see whether he prefers a spinach salad to lettuce salad, a lettuce salad to a spinach salad, or does not care which he gets. Such observations produce what mathematicians call an "ordinal" ranking of preferences. An ordinal ranking tells us that one outcome is preferred to another, but it does not say by how much. Welfare economics often uses an ordinal ranking of preferences and the concept of a person being indifferent between two outcomes.

A cardinal ranking of preferences not only tells us that outcome A is preferred to outcome B, but also tells us by how much. It puts preferences on a scale that we can identify as a measure of the utility brought about by their satisfaction. The most common method of making a cardinal ranking of preferences is to ask how much each person is willing to pay to have her preference satisfied. Environmental economists use willingness to pay (WTP) to measure utility in cost-benefit analyses. In a cost-benefit analysis, economists assign monetary values to all the expected positive and negative consequences of each policy option, and then the option is chosen which has the highest sum of monetary values. Willingness to pay as a measure of the intensity of preferences has many drawbacks, which we will study later in more detail. For example, does a billionaire stamp collector who is willing to pay $1000 for a rare stamp really want it more intensely than a working class stamp collector who can only afford $50? Does everything have a dollar value? Can we put a price on friendship, health, or clean air?

John von Neumann and Oscar Morgenstern invented another method for converting ordinal rankings of preferences into cardinal measures of utility in the 1940s. To apply the method, we first identify the worst possible outcome for a person, say total poverty and destitution, and assign it a utility of zero utiles, where a "utile" is a unit of utility. Then we identify the best possible outcome for a person, say being healthy, wealthy, and wise, and arbitrarily assign it a utility of one hundred utiles. This is like calling the freezing point of water o degrees and the boiling point of water 100 degrees on the Centigrade scale. We then construct a sort of lottery in which the prize is getting the best possible outcome. Normal lottery tickets all have the same set price, and all have a small but equal probability of winning the prize. Our lottery tickets are different. They each have different probabilities of winning the best outcome and they have no set price. Tickets with higher percentage chances of winning the best outcome are, of course, more valuable than tickets with lower percentage chances. Suppose we want to measure how much utility someone would get from receiving a new laptop computer. We ask her to compare receiving lottery tickets to receiving the new laptop. We will find that she will prefer the laptop to lottery tickets with a small chance of winning the best outcome, but prefer tickets with a high chance of winning the best outcome to the laptop. The point at which she is indifferent between the laptop and a lottery ticket with a particular chance of winning is a measure, on a scale of o to 100, of the intensity of her preference for the laptop. Table 5.2 gives an example where the utility of the laptop turns out to be 30 utiles.

Per cent chance of best outcome	10 %	20%	30%	40%	50%	70%	90%
Prefers laptop to ticket?	yes	yes	indifferent	no	no	no	no

TABLE 5.2: Measuring the utility of a laptop computer

If we gave her the same choices between a new car and these odd lottery tickets, then we might find that she was indifferent between the car and a lottery ticket with a 38% of winning the best outcome. We could then say not only that she prefers a new car to a new laptop, but also that she would get 38 utiles of utility from a new car and 30 utiles from a new laptop. This procedure suggests that we may be more successful in measuring degrees of preference satisfaction than of measuring intensities of pain and pleasure.

2. KNOWLEDGE PROBLEMS. Besides measurement problems, applying a utilitarian ethical theory also requires more knowledge of the world than we are likely to have. It must answer questions like the following: What are all the consequences of an action or policy? How far into the future must we look? How can we know the consequences for future generations? What do we do when we can only assign probabilities to different consequences, and how do we determine these probabilities? What happens if it is too difficult for people to calculate the utilities of all the possible consequences of their actions?

3. DEONTOLOGICAL PROBLEMS. It is always profitable to examine an ethical theory from the perspective of other ethical approaches. Thinking about utilitarianism from a deontological perspective, we ask whether all preferences, as a matter of principle, should be worthy of

satisfaction. Should we include in our utility calculations, for example, the preferences of sadists to hurt others? From a deontological perspective, we can also see cases where maximizing aggregate utility will violate the rights of people. Consider the Transplant Case. In a certain hospital, five people will die without a transplant operation. Each of them would prefer to live. One needs a heart, two each need a lung, and two each need a kidney. Into the operating room comes an unsuspecting person with one healthy heart, two healthy lungs, and two healthy kidneys. The surgeon removes the organs from the unsuspecting person and transplants them into the five needy people, thereby maximizing the aggregate lives saved, by saving five lives but losing one. The surgeon maximizes aggregate utility by satisfying the preferences of five people, but violates the rights of the unsuspecting victim. We can easily construct cases where maximizing utility goes against our intuition that we should not violate the rights of other people.

4. VIRTUE ETHICS PROBLEMS: We can imagine situations where an agent can maximize aggregate utility by being less than virtuous, for example, by being dishonest, or by sacrificing his or her integrity. An example is the Kidnap Case, invented by the English philosopher Bernard Williams. Terrorists capture George and twenty companions. The leader of the terrorists makes George the following proposition: "If you shoot just one of your friends, I will let the others go free. If you do not, then I will kill them all." From the utilitarian point of view, George should shoot one rather than allow all twenty to be killed. However, this would seriously violate his moral integrity, which is an important virtue.

5. MORAL STANDING PROBLEMS. Environmental ethics suggests the question of whose preferences we should take into account. Should we consider satisfying the preferences of distant people, future people, or animals? What should we do about non-human entities like plants and ecosystems that do not have preferences to satisfy? Perhaps preference-satisfaction utilitarianism is seriously incomplete because it cannot easily accommodate the moral standing of entities that cannot have wants, desires, and preferences.

6. ADAPTIVE PREFERENCES. People's preferences are not fixed. Education, advertising, propaganda, and cultural change can all alter preferences. We could maximize people's preference satisfaction by getting them to want fewer things, or want things less, or to prefer things that are easily provided. Should utilitarianism require adapting people's preferences to what they have now, rather than trying to give them what they now prefer but do not have? The contemporary philosopher and economist, Amartya Sen, has pointed out that very poor people have generally adapted their expectations to their impoverished circumstances, and that any theory which took their preferences as given in a utility calculation would be deeply unfair.

7. ACCUMULATIVE CONSEQUENCES. Preference-satisfaction utilitarianism also faces the problem of accumulative consequences, as in non-point source pollution caused by many harmless actions. For example, people prefer to have nice lawns in public parks. One person walking across the grass will not injure it, but if many people walk on the grass, then this will turn the grass to mud. One solution is for everyone to obey the rule, "Keep off the grass." This rule, however, does not maximize preference satisfaction because utility would be maximized if some people, a number less than the threshold of harm, get to walk on the grass, as they would prefer to do. It is not clear how to design the best rule.

If we apply utilitarianism indirectly, then we may avoid some of the above problems. DIRECT UTILITARIANISM treats utilitarianism as a *decision procedure*. It judges each act according to a calculation of the utilities it causes. INDIRECT UTILITARIANISM treats utilitarianism as a *standard of rightness* for the application of the tools of non-utilitarian ethical theories. It advocates obedience to principles, respect for rights, inculcation of virtues, or any other ethical tool that is useful to maximize aggregate utility. One form of direct utilitarianism is ACT UTILITARIANISM, which uses maximizing utility as a decision procedure for each action. One form of indirect utilitarianism is RULE UTILITARIANISM, which uses utilitarianism as a standard of rightness for which rules people should follow and which types of action they should perform.

Indirect utilitarianism offers a way around some of the weaknesses of direct utilitarianism. It might advocate respect for rights on the grounds that enforcing rights will maximize utility by reducing feelings of anxiety and insecurity. So applying utilitarianism indirectly to justify the right to life of all persons may avoid the Transplant Case by reducing the anxiety of surgical patients. Indirect utilitarianism might advocate the inculcation of certain virtues, like moral integrity, on the grounds that overall people will be thus made better off. This might enable it to avoid the Kidnap Case. By laying down rules and principles for people to follow, it may alleviate knowledge problems by making unnecessary the huge calculations needed for each individual decision. Indirect utilitarianism's use of rules and principles from the deontologist's toolbox may enable it to avoid problems like the Harmless Torturers, where harms accumulate.

One distinction between varieties of utilitarian theories is that between TOTAL UTILITARIANISM, which maximizes the aggregate utility added up for everyone, and AVERAGE UTILITARIANISM, which maximizes the aggregate utility per person. The difference is akin to the difference between measuring the economic status of a country by using its total Gross Domestic Product (GDP) or by using its average or *per capita* GDP. This distinction is important when we are dealing with policies that will affect the size of the population. If the population stays the same, then total and average utilitarianism will recommend the same decision. Their recommendations will diverge when population size changes. Environmental policy is heavily entwined with population policy, so we will return to this topic in a later chapter.

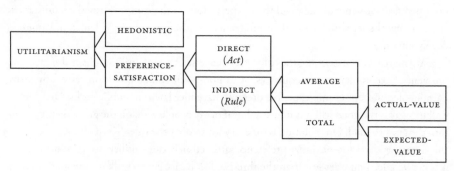

FIGURE 5.2: Taxonomy of utilitarian ethical theories

Another important distinction between ways of interpreting utilitarianism is whether we should employ ACTUAL-VALUE UTILITARIANISM, which judges an agent's action after-the-fact based on the utility the action actually produces, or employ EXPECTED-VALUE UTILITARIANISM, which judges an agent's action based on the utility and on the probability that this utility will result. Expected-value utilitarianism leads to the question of how moral agents should handle risk. How should they proceed in situations where they cannot know for sure what will happen but can only know probabilities of consequences? The usual procedure is to use probabilities and utilities to make expected-value calculations. The expected value of a consequence is the utility it will produce multiplied by the probability that it will occur. For example, suppose that an agent believes that policy option A has a 20% chance of producing 50 utiles and an 80% chance of causing 100 utiles, whereas policy option B has a 30% chance of producing 40 utiles and an 70% chance of causing 120 utiles. What should the agent do?

Probabilities are measured on a scale from 0 to 1, so a 20% chance of producing 50 utiles is equivalent to a probability of .2 of producing 50 utiles. Converting percentage chances to probabilities, the agent should make the following expected-value calculation:

Expected value of A = .2 × 50 + .8 × 100 = 90 utiles.
Expected value of B = .3 × 40 + .7 × 120 = 96 utiles.

Option B's expected value of 96 utiles is higher than option A's expected value of 90 utiles. Therefore, the agent should implement policy option B. Since economists often do not know for sure the consequences of environmental policies, this style of reasoning is important in environmental cost-benefit analyses.

SUMMARY

1. Utilitarian ethical theories hold that we should maximize everyone's happiness or utility, not just our own.
2. Utilitarianism is possible because psychological egoism is not universally true, as is shown by our own observations, anthropological theory, and behavioural economics experiments like the Ultimatum Game.
3. Hedonistic utilitarianism holds that we should maximize everyone's pleasurable feelings and experiences while minimizing their painful sensations.
4. Preference-satisfaction utilitarianism holds that we should maximize the satisfaction of people's strongest wants and desires. Environmental economics measures the strength of people's preference for something by their willingness to pay for it.
5. Difficult problems for hedonistic utilitarianism include dealing with comparing and measuring pains and pleasures, accounting for the quality of different pleasures, sadistic pleasure, dealing with the Experience Machine, and accounting for accumulative consequences as in the case of the Harmless Torturers.

6. Difficult problems for preference-satisfaction utilitarianism include knowing the consequences of actions and policies, measuring the utilities of consequences, dealing with rights violations such as in the Transplant Case, preserving virtues like moral integrity in the Kidnap Case, accounting for the moral standing of non-human entities, saying why we should satisfy preferences rather than adapting people's preferences to what they have, and accounting for accumulative consequences in cases such as non-point source pollution.

7. Indirect utilitarianism uses utilitarian reasoning as a justificatory standard for applying the tools of other ethical theories such as respect for rights, the inculcation of virtues, and obedience to rules. It may avoid some of the problems of direct and act utilitarianism.

8. To deal with environmental policies that affect the size of populations, utilitarians must decide whether to maximize total or average utility.

9. To deal with cases where we know only the risks or probabilities of different outcomes, utilitarianism will choose the policy whose outcome will maximize total expected value. The expected value of an outcome is the utility of an outcome multiplied by the probability that it will happen.

ONLINE READING QUESTIONS

The book's website contains reading questions on this chapter. Working through these questions will help you understand, remember, and apply important concepts from the chapter. Some of the questions supply useful hints for the study questions.

STUDY QUESTIONS

Using the text and hints from the online reading questions, write out, type, dictate to your computer, or at least formulate in your head answers to the following questions.

1. Explain the significance of the Ultimatum Game for the truth of psychological egoism.

2. Explain how hedonistic utilitarianism and preference-satisfaction utilitarianism differ in their understanding of the source and nature of utility.

3. Why does Derek Parfit's case of the Harmless Torturers create a problem for act-utilitarianism but not for rule-utilitarianism?

4. Why does the existence of sadists, persons who take pleasure in inflicting pain on others, create a problem for hedonistic utilitarianism?

5. Why does the difficulty with comparing and measuring different people's degrees of preference satisfaction create a problem for preference-satisfaction utilitarianism?

6. Explain how the Transplant Case shows a conflict between the deontological/rights-based approach and the utilitarian approach to ethics.
7. Population policy A will result in a world population of 9 billion with a per capita utility of 100 utiles. Population policy B will result in a population of 12 billion with a per capita utility of 90 utiles. Explain how average utilitarianism and total utilitarianism will differ in their assessment of these two policies regarding future generations.
8. Explain why indirect utilitarianism offers a way around some of the weaknesses of direct utilitarianism.

QUESTIONS TO PONDER

Spend a few minutes thinking about the following questions, or, better yet, discuss them with fellow readers of this book.

1. Will utilitarians ever be successful in defining utility, measuring it, and comparing it between people?
2. Can we extend preference-satisfaction utilitarianism to recognize the moral standing of animals, of plants, or of ecosystems?
3. House cats often torture mice. Are cats wrong to do this from a utilitarian perspective? Why or why not? Should a utilitarian rescue the mice?
4. No sign on the lawn means everyone will walk on the lawn and ruin it. A keep-off-the-grass sign means no one will get to enjoy walking on the lawn, and will thus fail to maximize utility. Is it possible for utilitarians to design a rule that is fair to everyone and that maximizes utility? Will the rule become so complicated that it will effectively become a sophisticated act utilitarian decision procedure?
5. Is there any way to take an accumulative harm, such as the non-point source pollution involved in greenhouse gas emissions, and turn it into a point-source harm by assigning a portion of responsibility for the harm to each individual person?
6. Indirect utilitarianism uses utilitarian reasoning to justify applying other ethical theories to situations. Is indirect utilitarianism vacuous? Does it just say to use whatever ethical theory works best?
7. One problem for utilitarianism is that it is too difficult for people to calculate the utilities of all the possible consequences of their actions. Can a utilitarian reply to this objection that this just shows that utilitarianism is right: it does not answer questions that everyone would feel have no good answer?

Chapter 6

VIRTUE ETHICS

AS WE SAW IN THE LAST CHAPTER, UTILITARIAN ETHICAL THEORIES FORM A FAMILY of subjective consequentialist theories telling us to maximize the production of certain mental states—sensations of pleasure or satisfied desires—in entities with moral standing. This approach limits moral standing to those entities that can have such psychological states. Utilitarian ethical theories apply most naturally to human beings and perhaps to complex animals that have mental lives. Plants, natural objects, species and ecosystems, however, do not have mental lives. Utilitarian ethical theories fit with anthropocentric or zoocentric theories of moral standing, but do not easily work with biocentric or ecocentric theories of moral standing.

So it is worth looking at objective consequentialist theories. These ethical theories tell us to cause states of affairs other than subjective mental states. As we will see, dispositional theories allow us to attribute intrinsic value to non-human aspects of the environment, common good theories can extend to environmental communities or ecosystems, and teleological theories can extend to entities like plants or ecosystems that appear to have natural purposes or modes of flourishing. Each type of theory also has its weaknesses, and these weaknesses extend to the environmental version of the theory.

Human flourishing is not a subjective matter of having enjoyable mental states, but an objective matter of living a human life well; so this notion has appealed to some objective consequentialists as an appropriate general description of intrinsic value.

It also can lead to a non-consequentialist virtue ethics. Virtue ethicists believe that the way to lead a human life well, the way for a human being to flourish, is to cultivate virtues (character traits) like fairness and benevolence while avoiding vices like selfishness and greed. Possessing a virtue does not *cause* a human life to flourish; possessing a virtue is part of a flourishing human life. Virtues do not result in human flourishing: they constitute it. A virtue ethic can become an environmental ethic if we come to see that human life can flourish only in a healthy environment. To preserve a healthy environment, human beings will need to cultivate "green" virtues, like habits of reducing, reusing, and recycling. Virtue ethicists point out that communities are essential to teaching and reinforcing virtues in their members. Environmentalists will argue for creating new, green communities that teach and reinforce green virtues. Virtue ethics reminds us that good environmental policy must include more than rules, regulations, and cost-benefit analyses. It must also include education for practical wisdom, attitude change, and habit development.

Learning Objectives

1. To understand the varieties of objective consequentialism and start to see their application to environmental ethics.
2. To understand virtue ethics and its role in implementing environmental policy.
3. To understand the view that virtues are learned, internalized, and reinforced in communities, and the role of communities in implementing environmental policy.

OBJECTIVE CONSEQUENTIALISM

Consequentialism is the ethical approach that tells us to cause the maximum amount of intrinsic value aggregated across all those with moral standing. Objective consequentialism is an approach which says that the intrinsic value which ought to be maximized pertains to features of recipients other than their mental states. Three interesting varieties of objective consequentialism are the following:

1. DISPOSITIONAL THEORIES, or informed-preference theories, say that each agent ought to act so as to best satisfy the wants that people would have if they were fully informed and were reasoning rationally.
2. COMMON GOOD THEORIES say that each agent ought to act so as to contribute to the betterment of the community as a whole.
3. TELEOLOGICAL THEORIES say that each agent ought to act so as to best fulfill the natural purposes of recipients with moral standing.

1. DISPOSITIONAL THEORIES OF VALUE

Suppose Harriet wants to order a chicken salad sandwich at a restaurant. A chicken salad sandwich would satisfy her food preference. Unbeknownst to Harriet, the chicken salad

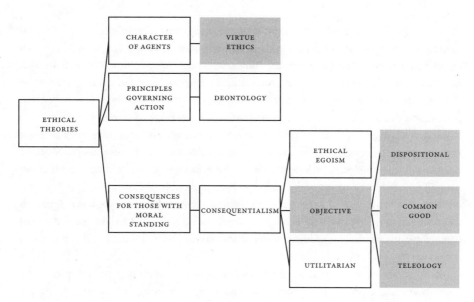

FIGURE 6.1: Taxonomy of the ethical theories discussed in this chapter

is contaminated with salmonella bacteria and would make her sick. What Harriet would prefer for her lunch, if she were fully informed and reasoning properly, is some other food item. What Harriet actually prefers is the chicken salad. According to the simple utilitarian preference-satisfaction theory of value, what is intrinsically valuable for Harriet is to have her actual preference satisfied. This seems wrong. How can getting a contaminated sandwich be intrinsically valuable for her? What is valuable for her is to get what she would want if she were fully informed. What is really good for her is some other food choice.

Dispositional, or informed-preference, theories say that what is intrinsically valuable is satisfying the preferences which people would have if they were fully informed and made no mistakes in their reasoning. The dispositional approach appears to be a form of subjective consequentialism since it talks of informed wants or preferences, but it is not. The preferences that a person would be disposed to have, if he or she were fully informed and rational, are not always the same as the preferences the person actually has. Therefore, we are not talking about satisfying actual, existing mental states, but about satisfying dispositional, hypothetical, or counterfactual mental states.

The informed-preference approach and the actual-preference approach differ from the point of view of metaethics. An actual-preference view fits most readily with an expressivist theory of value. On this account, for a person to say that something is valuable is for him to express his want, desire, or preference for it. The advantage of this account is that we can see immediately that value is action-guiding. People are motivated to pursue what they want, desire, or prefer. The disadvantage is that value, on this account, is not agreement-seeking. A person who expresses his preference for some good does not seek the agreement of others.

An informed-preference view fits most readily with a cognitivist theory of value. On this account, for a person to say that something is valuable is for him to assert his belief that he would be disposed to want, desire, or prefer it if he were fully informed and reasoning rationally. The advantage of this account is that value is agreement-guiding. That he would prefer something if he were fully informed is an assertion which is either true or false, which can be reasoned about, and which he can discuss with other people. However, his belief that he would prefer something if he were fully rational is not always action-guiding. It could be that, despite his belief, he actually wants something else. People are often weak-willed and prone not to want what they know is good for them. Addicts are an extreme example.

Because actual preferences are action-guiding, but not agreement-seeking, they are most naturally treated through calculations of intensity, perhaps as revealed in a market economy. Because informed preferences are agreement-seeking, but not action-guiding, they are most naturally treated in a context of discussion, debate, and public deliberation. One powerful criticism of a market-based approach to the environment is that a market-based approach treats all environmental values as consumer preferences, and fails to allow for the role of democratic deliberation regarding environmental values. We will return to this point in a later chapter.

An advantage of the dispositional approach is it allows us to say, for example, that a business-as-usual approach to climate change is wrong even though it is what most people want. We can argue that if people were fully informed about the dangers of climate change, then they would not want to support business-as-usual. In a similar way, the dispositional approach allows us to argue that a wilderness area that no one ever visits, and which no one actually wants, is still intrinsically valuable because people who were fully informed about it would want to preserve it. On the dispositional, informed-preference approach, we can argue that the wilderness area is valuable, even though no one is willing to pay to preserve it. Thus, the informed-preference approach allows the environmental policymaker to argue with the economic utilitarian who thinks that we should satisfy actual preferences as revealed by willingness-to-pay in the marketplace.

A weakness of this approach is that it could become paternalistic. We "philosopher kings" may be tempted to unnecessarily dismiss the opinions of regular people, and think we know better than they do what is good for them. The cure for paternalism is a strong commitment to democratic debate and public deliberation.

2. COMMON GOOD THEORIES

Common Good theories say that agents ought to contribute to the betterment of the community as a whole. Here the community as a whole is something other than just the sum of its individual parts. If we identify the good of the community as the aggregate good of all the members of the community, then the common good theory would be a version of utilitarianism. We are familiar with the idea that a whole may be different from its parts or even the sum of its parts. For example, the individual members of a community, the people who are its parts, all have psychological states, whereas the community itself does not have psychological states. We must distinguish the common good from the total utility of the community. Even though achieving the common good may benefit individuals, this is not its aim, and sometimes it will not do so. In the common good approach, the good of the community can trump any and all individual goods or aggregations thereof.

Working to increase a country's Gross Domestic Product (GDP) would count as working to increase the sum of each individual citizen's economic good. Working to increase the world's respect for a country would count as working for the common good of all its citizens. The common good of the citizens of a country consists in having the country's political institutions and systems of social cooperation functioning in a healthy way. This will benefit citizens, but in a different way from maximizing the sum of their individual goods.

The common good of a community also includes the community's having a healthy environment to sustain itself. Therefore, the common good approach does permit the development of an anthropocentric environmental ethic.

Structurally, the common good approach is also compatible with the extension of moral standing to ecosystems, if we conceive of them as living communities. Such a non-anthropocentric extension would be a holistic, as opposed to an individualistic, conception of the good. We will return to this point when we look at ecocentric accounts of moral standing.

One problem for the community-good approach is that its central notion may seem mysterious. Increasing the intrinsic good for individual members of a community has an obvious appeal; but what could be the value to anyone of a so-called good that does not benefit individuals? For this reason, the incentives of community members may differ from their moral obligations. Community members may be happy to accept the benefits of community membership, but be reluctant to contribute to conserving and bettering the community, its institutions, and its environment, when this is unrelated to good results for them or particular other community members. Even if they value these community goods, they may be tempted to free-ride on the contributions of others, knowing that the contributions of others will keep the community healthy.

Another weakness is apparent from the moral standing perspective. Restricting moral standing to one's community (and its members) leaves out other communities and individuals.

A third weakness of the common good approach is apparent from both the rights perspective and the utilitarian perspective. For the good of the whole community, the common good approach is prone to accept violations of rights, and reductions in the welfare of individuals. For example, in the nineteenth century, loyal subjects died for the good of the British Empire. In the twentieth century, the fascists in Nazi Germany sacrificed millions of people for what they saw as the health and glory of the so-called Third Reich. The common good approach does not have the resources necessary to protect the rights of individual members of the community. Later we will see how this can lead to a conflict between holistic, ecocentric ethical theories and individualistic, animal rights theories. Utilitarians also find the common good approach objectionable, in that it holds that the needs of the community, not those of real individual people, are the basis of ethics.

3. TELEOLOGICAL THEORIES

One plausible theory about the development of human intelligence is that it evolved, not to aid our interaction with the natural world, but to aid our interaction with other people. In order to interact either cooperatively or exploitatively with people in large groups, humans needed to understand the purposes and plans of other humans. A simple illustration of these strategic interactions is a game like the prisoner's dilemma. Keeping track of favours given, favours received, lies heard, lies told, promises made, promises received, and so on requires a hefty intelligence. Given this framework, the obvious way for humans to understand the non-human world around them is to see animals, plants, and natural objects as also having purposes and strategies. Humans could understand the purpose of a tree as trying to grow taller to get more sunlight than its neighbours do. They could understand the function of flowering plants as trying to set seed in order to reproduce. They could understand seeds as having the potential to become plants. They could understand what it is for a plant to flourish. They could even understand volcanoes and thunderstorms in terms of the whims and purposes of the gods and goddesses who inhabited the sky and the mountains.

A teleological conceptual framework understands everything in terms of its natural purpose, its potential, or its function. The term "teleological" comes from "*telos*" meaning "function" or "purpose" in Ancient Greek. The teleological conceptual framework immediately suggests an ethic. What is *good for* a plant is whatever enables it to flourish and fulfill its potential or natural purpose. It is easy to take this non-moral conception of the good and moralize it. A consequentialist teleological ethic says that an agent's action is a good one when the action's consequences enable some entity with moral standing to fulfill its natural purpose, or actualize its potential. An action is right when its consequences are good for some entity with moral standing.

For example, people sometimes argue that because Darwinian evolutionary theory is about the survival of the fittest, the natural purpose of a living thing is to survive. Therefore, moral agents ought to promote the survival of living things. For another example, some people argue that people should actualize their potential. The distinctive natural activity of humans is thinking, and education develops this capacity. Therefore, moral agents should ensure that people should get as much education as possible. Other people disagree about the nature of human potential, and argue that, instead, it is a spiritual potential, the capacity for a blissful consciousness in oneness with the world. Consequentially humans should spend their lives meditating in pursuit of this spiritual state. All of these examples, plausible or not, exhibit teleological reasoning about what is valuable.

The attraction of the teleological conceptual framework for environmental ethics is that teleological reasoning allows the extension of moral standing to entities that have natural purposes. It allows moral consideration of non-human, non-animal, and holistic entities that do not feel pain and pleasure, do not have preferences, and cannot make rational, autonomous decisions about what they want to do. Teleological reasoning can assign intrinsic value to any thing that has a natural activity, purpose, potential, or function.

Despite this attraction, the teleological approach to value has weaknesses. For one, teleological reasoning about value appears to violate the fact/value distinction. Even if it is true that the natural purpose of living things *is* to survive and reproduce, it does not follow that the survival and reproduction of living things *ought* to be promoted. Such an argument crosses the is/ought gap without the required ethical premise. Teleological arguments can confuse the non-moral sense of something being *good for* an entity with the moral sense of some state of affairs being a good one. Even if it is good for (non-moral) HIV to find a new host, it does not follow that it is good (moral) that people pass on HIV to others.

The teleological approach to biology is now out of date. Teleological explanations have given way to evolutionary and molecular biology explanations. At one time, it was an advance in knowledge when doctors discovered that the function of the brain was to think, as opposed to being an organ for cooling the body. But that advance did not take medicine very far. Now to understand the brain, scientists study its anatomy, physiology, and molecular biology. It is sometimes useful to talk of the function of different parts of the brain. For example, it is useful to know that one function of the frontal cortex is the regulation of emotion, but the real work of understanding this emotional regulation goes on when scientists study the molecular biology of the neural pathways that are involved. To people living in a world of tools and machines designed to fulfill the (mental) purposes of human beings, the teleological conceptual framework is normal and everyday. Nonetheless, it is no longer the basis of scientific understanding.

VIRTUE ETHICS

The notion of flourishing also plays a role in virtue ethics, though in a very different way from its role in teleological consequentialism. In teleological consequentialism, a moral agent is required to cause good consequences, where good consequences are ones that are good for the flourishing of morally considerable beneficiaries. We picture this in Figure 6.2.

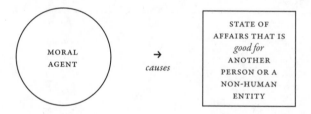

FIGURE 6.2: Teleological consequentialism: agent causes what is good for another

In virtue ethics, the moral agent is required to become a flourishing person. To flourish, she needs a good character. Having a good character means possessing good character traits. Possessing good character traits means possessing strong virtues. In virtue ethics, the virtues are morally required not because they cause people to flourish, but because possessing virtues is part of what it means to flourish. We can illustrate this pictorially in Figure 6.3.

In virtue ethics, a flourishing person is also thought to be a happy person. The notion of happiness operating in virtue ethics, however, is very different from the notion of happiness employed by utilitarianism. Utilitarianism employs a psychological or subjective notion of happiness; happiness consists in experiencing pleasure and avoiding pain, or in having all one's desires satisfied. Virtue ethics employs a non-psychological or objective notion of happiness. Happiness consists in flourishing, in being a good specimen of humanity, in living the life that a person would want if that person were fully informed and rational, which is not necessarily the life that she actually does want. In utilitarianism, the person living a life can assess the happiness of her life from the inside. In virtue ethics, we assess the happiness of a

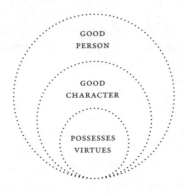

FIGURE 6.3: Virtue ethics: good agent has good character because she possesses virtues

life from the outside. Other people can look at how the person's life is going and see whether she is flourishing as a human being.

Virtue ethics looks at features of the agent (his or her character) in order to make ethical judgments. A good character is one with strong virtues and no vices. A virtue or a vice is a character trait, a set of stable dispositions to act in certain ways. Table 6.1 contains some examples of virtues and vices.

VIRTUES	VICES
Honesty	Dishonesty
Courage	Cowardice
Compassion	Insensitivity
Generosity	Selfishness
Loyalty	Disloyalty
Integrity	Sleaziness
Fairness	Unfairness
Self-control	Self-indulgence
Prudence	Short-sightedness

TABLE 6.1: Examples of virtues and vices

Insofar as there is a rule of action in virtue ethics, it would be that each agent ought to act so as to emulate the decisions of a virtuous agent. Following this rule, however, requires a great deal of good judgment. Being virtuous is different from just following rules, obeying duties, respecting rights, or acting according to principle, as in the deontological approach. Being virtuous is also different from properly calculating the nature and value of the consequences of actions, as in the utilitarian approach. There are no hard and fast rules in virtue ethics; instead, virtue ethics demands good judgment and practical wisdom from its practitioners. For example, virtues and vices often differ in degree. Cowardice is a deficiency in bravery whereas recklessness is an over-abundance of bravery. It requires wisdom to see where bravery ends, and cowardice or recklessness begins. Virtues sometimes conflict. It can require wisdom to see when to be kind to a friend and when to be honest. To implement the virtue of benevolence, a person must have an excellent understanding of the needs of others. It requires wisdom to apply the virtues

From the perspectives of the deontological and utilitarian approaches, this appeal to wisdom and this lack of defined rules renders virtue ethics imprecise. This lack of clarity regarding what an agent should do, in turn, makes virtue ethics difficult to assess philosophically. When we critically reflect on ethical theories that do give clear guidance, we can sometimes show that this guidance is at odds with our ethical intuition, and thus show that the theory in question needs modification. For example, when we applied hedonistic utilitarianism in the case of the Experience Machine, we could see that hedonistic utilitarianism implied that we should hook ourselves up to the machine. This seemed clearly wrong, and suggested that another form of utilitarianism, preference-satisfaction utilitarianism, might be a better theory. However, it is difficult to see how we could derive an implication from virtue ethics that was contrary to our ethical intuitions. Any such implication would merely indicate a deficiency in practical wisdom in our application of the virtues to the ethical problem. So virtue ethics becomes rather empty of substantial content, saying only that someone who is wise enough will always do the ethically correct action. If virtue ethics is to have interesting content, it will be in the independent description of what it is to be wise.

One attraction of virtue ethics is that it can easily become an environmental ethic. The virtues are character traits that are part of what it is to lead a flourishing human life. Human life can only flourish in a healthy environment. Therefore, character traits that promote the preservation of a healthy environment for human beings are virtues. Habits of reducing, reusing, and recycling are character traits that preserve the environment, and thus are, "green virtues." Other examples of character traits that are useful in preserving the environment and preventing pollution are the cultivation of simple tastes, a vegetarian diet, a disinclination to travel by air, and a thriftiness with respect to electrical power usage. Similarly, there are green vices such as a tendency to litter, the wasteful use of electricity, and so on. Such green character traits do not have special names like the traditional virtues of honesty, courage, compassion, and so on in Table 6.1, but perhaps they will acquire names in the future. The environmental ethic constituted by the green virtues would be an anthropocentric ethic, since its concern is the development of virtues necessary to human flourishing.

We can also imagine the development of a non-anthropocentric environmental ethic if we shift our concern from the flourishing of humans to the flourishing of life in general. This would give us a biocentric virtue ethic that called for the inculcation of those character traits needed to promote the flourishing of all living things. (However, as noted above, we do not want to praise the flourishing of HIV.) Similarly, an ecocentric virtue ethic would require character traits that promote the flourishing of ecosystems. We will examine the possibilities for a non-anthropocentric virtue ethics in later chapters.

DERIVATIVE VIRTUES

In virtue ethics, character traits are justified as being virtues because their possession is part of what it is to flourish as a human being. The virtues of virtue ethics do not derive from some ethical theory outside of virtue ethics itself. They are non-derivative virtues. However, we can also conceive of derivative virtues, character traits that are justified because they help an agent fulfil the requirements of some other type of ethical theory. For example, there are the civic virtues that are justified within an objective consequentialist theory of the common good: A virtuous citizen is one who advances the common good.

One important example of derivative virtues is their use by indirect utilitarianism. We saw in the last chapter that we could apply utilitarianism directly as a decision procedure every time that we had to decide what action was the right one. To apply utilitarianism directly, a moral agent must add up the costs and benefits of each possible action and choose the action that maximizes the total utility for everyone who is affected. This makes every decision very complicated, perhaps beyond the calculating capacity of human beings. It also leads to some counter-intuitive recommendations, as in the Transplant Case. One way around these problems is to apply utilitarian reasoning indirectly by using it, not as a decision procedure in each case, but as a way of justifying non-utilitarian ethical tools like rules, duties, and moral rights. Indirect utilitarianism's standard for the rightness of non-utilitarian ethical tools can also apply to the virtues. The indirect utilitarian standard of rightness might justify teaching certain virtues instead of using utilitarianism as a case-by-case decision procedure. For example, teaching people the virtues of generosity and compassion may help them perform actions that maximize everyone's well-being better than teaching them how to calculate utilities.

Similarly, various derivative virtues can be justified from the perspective of other types of ethical theory. Fairness could be a justice-based, deontological virtue because it helped its possessors make the world more just. Scrupulousness could be a rights-based deontological virtue because it helps its possessors respect the rights of others. Prudence could be an ethical egoist virtue because it helps ethical egoists act in their own long-term interest.

VIRTUES AND COMMUNITY

A development of virtue ethics is the idea that certain types of community should be preserved and/or expanded because membership in these communities inculcates important virtues. A person is born with a certain temperament, and the determination of this temperament has a strong genetic component. A person's personality is formed by the interaction of her temperament with her familial and social environments in her childhood and adolescence. Though temperament and personality traits make the acquisition of certain virtues and vices either easier or more difficult, virtues (and vices) are acquired by explicit or implicit education in the community to which a person belongs. Character traits are taught explicitly during formal and informal education in a community. Character traits are also learned implicitly, or internalized, from membership in the culture of a community. Character traits are reinforced by approval and disapproval from other community members. Thus, one type of community will be better than another is at teaching, inculcating, and enforcing a particular set of virtues.

Different ethical viewpoints will lead to the promotion of different types of community. Conservatives will argue for preserving communities that strengthen the virtues of the past.

Environmentalists will argue for creating new communities that teach, inculcate, and psychologically enforce green virtues. Even if we should find virtue ethics unsatisfactory as a basis for environmental ethics, the teaching of environmentally virtuous character traits and the role of community membership in this sort of moral education are important policy tools for us to keep in mind.

SUMMARY

1. Objective consequentialist theories look for the source of intrinsic value in states of the world that are not mental states like pleasure or desire satisfaction.

2. Dispositional theories of value say that states of affairs are valuable if they would be wanted by persons who were fully informed and reasoning rationally, whether or not the persons actually want those states of affairs. Dispositional theories can say that environmental situations are valuable even if no one actually wants them, but can be paternalistic if not applied carefully.

3. Common good theories of value say that the good of a community is more than the sum of the subjective goods of the individuals who are its parts. By promoting the good of the whole, common good theories risk sacrificing the interests of individual members of the community and allowing the violation of individual rights.

4. Teleological theories of value tell us to promote the flourishing and potential of entities that have natural (not mental) purposes. Teleological theories extend easily to all living things, but depend on an out-of-date scientific conceptual framework.

5. Virtue ethics sees the possession of certain character traits (virtues) as part of human flourishing and others (vices) as preventing it. Being a virtuous person requires wisdom both in balancing the virtues and in seeing what the virtues require in particular cases. Utilitarians and deontologists criticize this lack of precision in the application of virtue ethics.

6. We can extend virtue ethics to the environment because human flourishing depends on maintaining a healthy environment.

7. Virtue ethicists stress the importance of virtue education within a community.

ONLINE READING QUESTIONS

The book's website contains reading questions on this chapter. Working through these questions will help you understand, remember, and apply important concepts from the chapter. Some of the questions supply useful hints for the study questions.

Using the text and hints from the online reading questions, write out, type, dictate to your computer, or at least formulate in your head answers to the following questions.

1. Describe the common good approach to ethics. Why is it consequentialist? What is its major weakness?
2. Describe the teleological version of objective consequentialism. What do you see as its major weakness?
3. Distinguish between derivative and non-derivative virtues. Give an example of the former.
4. How might virtue theory be employed by environmentalists?
5. What is the significance of the community to ethics?

QUESTIONS TO PONDER

Spend a few minutes thinking about the following questions, or, better yet, discuss them with fellow readers of this book.

1. Suppose all life, and all moral agents, became extinct in the universe. Would anything still be intrinsically valuable according to utilitarian theories of value? According to teleological theories of value? According to dispositional theories of value?
2. Do common good theories of value and those that concentrate on the importance of community in the ethical life amount to the same thing? How would you distinguish between them?
3. We can discuss, argue about, and seek agreement on whether an action is brave or cowardly. We are also motivated to be brave and not to be cowardly. Can virtue theory contribute to resolving the agreement-seeking/action-guiding dichotomy in metaethics?
4. Are the calculations of utilitarianism and the rights and duties of deontology really as precise and clear in their application as they are advertised? Do we also need practical wisdom to be effective utilitarians or respecters of rights?
5. Make a more complete list of green virtues and environmental vices than given in the text. Can this list form the basis of an adequate environmental ethics?
6. Possession of the virtues, and avoidance of the vices, is said by virtue ethicists to be a necessary part of leading a flourishing or objectively happy human life. Think this through for some of the virtues and vices. Is the general statement true? Consider that bravery can get a person killed.
7. The preference-satisfaction theorist might reply to the Harriet-objection in the text by pointing out that one of her actual subjective preferences is not

to get sick, so eating that sandwich would actually considerably lower her aggregate subjective preference satisfaction. Can the preference-satisfaction theory of value always avoid missing information problems by appealing to other, more general, preferences?

Chapter 7

RIGHTS

DEONTOLOGICAL ETHICAL THEORIES HOLD THAT THERE ARE PRINCIPLES OF ACTION which moral agents must follow regardless of the consequences. Rights-based ethical theories are one of the main types of deontological ethical theories. An action that does not respect rights is immoral even when it results in higher overall welfare. Using a metaphor taken from card games, we can say that rights considerations trump utility considerations.

In the Magna Carta of 1215, English aristocrats forcibly gave themselves certain rights by imposing duties on King John not to interfere with their activities. During the Enlightenment era, philosophers like John Locke argued that everyone had moral rights simply because of their nature as human beings. Moral rights are the birthright of commoners as well as aristocrats. The English Bill of Rights of 1689 legally recognized the moral rights of male, property-owning, non-aristocrats. The United States Bill of Rights of 1789 (the first ten amendments to the US Constitution) recognized the rights of male citizens of European descent. The Thirteenth Amendment in 1865 recognized the rights of citizens of African descent not to be enslaved. The Nineteenth Amendment in 1920 recognized the equal rights of women. The right against involuntary servitude, the right to vote, the right to freedom of expression, and the right to freedom from unjustified search and seizure have played a pivotal role in the development of modern democratic societies. In environmental ethics, one question is whether this process should continue with the legal recognition of the rights of animals.

If animal nature is relevantly similar to human nature, then we should extend moral rights to animals. Environmental economists should look out for potential rights violations in the results of their cost-benefit analyses. In many aspects of environmental ethics, however, rights-based ethical theories do not play the pivotal role that they have played in political theory. Environmental ethics is interested in sustainability and the interests of future generations. As we will see in a later chapter, applying moral rights to unborn people involves conceptual difficulties. As we will see in this chapter, much of the pollution that we need rights to protect us from is not caused by determinate individuals. Instead it accumulates from the individually harmless activities of many people. This makes it difficult to draw the connection between our right not to be polluted and their duty to cease their independently harmless activities. The modern world faces many global problems, such as climate change, which are the accumulative consequences of activities that would be harmless in isolation. Contemporary environmental ethics must find ethical tools to deal with such problems.

Learning Objectives

1. To understand the varieties of deontological theories.
2. To understand the relationship of rights and duties.
3. To understand Kant's theory of rights and see its relevance to discussions of animal rights.
4. To understand the varieties of rights and the justifications for them.
5. To understand the notion of an accumulative harm.

THE DEONTOLOGICAL APPROACH

We classify types of ethical theories according to their application to situations about which we must make an ethical judgment. A typical situation consists in an agent implementing a policy that has consequences for some beneficiaries or victims. Virtue ethics concentrates on the character of the agent, the consequentialist approach concentrates on the nature of the consequences, environmental ethics is particularly interested in the moral standing of the recipients, and the deontological approach is interested in the principles or moral rules that the agent should follow.

The DEONTOLOGICAL APPROACH holds that each agent ought to act in obedience to the moral principles governing that type of act. The term "deontology" comes from the Ancient Greek word, "*deon*," meaning "duty." Deontology is the study of duties just as biology is the study of living things. The rights-based approach to ethics is deontological because one person's moral right implies another person's moral duty.

One sort of deontological approach is the DIVINE COMMAND THEORY, in which an agent's duties are the commands of God. For example, in the Jewish and Christian Bible, God gave the Ten Commandments to Moses in order to impose duties of right action on the Israelites. Divine command theories work best in monotheistic religions like Christianity and Islam. In a polytheistic religion like that of the Ancient Greeks, where the purposes of the various gods often conflicted, it would have been difficult to determine which commands humans should take to be their duties. Philosophically, divine command theories require us to consider arguments for the existence of God and details of the interpretation of God's will that would take us far from environmental policy. So we will look only at secular ethical theories.

The deontological approach also includes JUSTICE-BASED THEORIES, where the moral principles that an agent should obey concern treating all morally considerable recipients fairly. For example, one theory of justice is that each morally considerable recipient should get what he, she, or it deserves. Another says that we should treat all morally considerable recipients equally. We will look at justice-based theories more closely in the next chapter.

Thirdly, the deontological approach includes RIGHTS-BASED THEORIES, where the duties of a moral agent are to respect the moral rights of all morally considerable recipients. This might include the duty to respect the property rights of others or the duty to respect the rights of animals.

In the deontological approach, an action is judged not by its consequences, but by the intention of the agent. In turn, an intention is judged by the principle that is being followed or the duty that is being obeyed. For example, we can imagine someone who intends not to cheat, and does not do so, because she believes in the principle, "It is always wrong to cheat, no matter how good the consequences." It is important here to distinguish between:

1. An action that someone performs.
2. An event that happens to that person.

If we suppose that Ira raises the gun, takes aim at Jane, pulls the trigger, and kills Jane, then this is an *action* by Ira because Ira *intends* to shoot Jane. If we suppose instead that Karl overpowers Ira, puts the gun in Ira's hand, points Ira's hand and the gun at Jane, pushes Ira's trigger finger, and kills Jane, then this is an event that happens to Ira. Ira has no *intention* to shoot Jane. An INTENTION is a goal or plan that guides an action. An action is a behavioural event intentionally chosen and performed by an agent.

One attraction of the deontological approach is that it avoids the inadequate knowledge objection to utilitarianism. Because of the principle that "ought" implies "can," we are morally responsible only for what we can foresee and control. We cannot know all the consequences of our actions, or control all the consequences of our action. Thus, defenders of the deontological approach argue, it cannot be the consequences of our actions that are morally important. However, we can control what principles we intend to act on. What are morally important, therefore, are the principles on which we act, or the duties that we follow, not the consequences of our actions.

RIGHTS AND DUTIES

A moral right is a morally justified claim on others. So the possession by one person of a moral right creates a duty in others to respect that right, a duty that is correlated to that right. If Ben has a *right* that Alice do X, then Alice has a CORRELATIVE DUTY to do X that she owes to Ben.

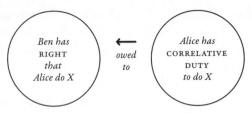

FIGURE 7.1: Ben has right against Alice, and Alice has correlative duty owed to Ben

Correspondingly, if Alice owes Ben a duty to do X, then Ben has a right that Alice do X. Correlative duties are direct duties in a sense that we looked at in the first chapter.

By contrast, an indirect duty is a duty regarding some other entity that is owed to a third party. For example, suppose Charles has an indirect duty regarding Donna's dog, Rover, not to kick Rover. Here, Charles owes a duty to Donna not to kick Donna's dog, Rover. In this case, Donna has a right against Charles but Rover does not. If, on the other hand, Charles has a direct duty to Rover not to kick Rover, then Rover does have a right against Charles.

The correlative duty of a right is always a direct duty. Notice that in the framework, Agent → Action → Consequence → Recipient, it is the agent who owes the duty, and it is the recipient who bears the right. Duties are often justified by justifying their correlated right. For example, Eve has a duty not to hit Frank because Frank has a right to personal security. Or, George has a duty not to steal Harriet's laptop because Harriet has a right to her private property.

JUSTIFYING RIGHTS

Like the virtues, rights can have derivative or non-derivative justifications. A derivative justification of moral rights assigns moral rights as the conclusion of an ethical theory that is not itself rights-based. One important example, which we have discussed before, is the indirect utilitarian justification of rights. A system of rights is justified because in produces the greatest utility for everyone. For example, indirect utilitarianism would justify the assignment of a right of life to all hospital patients in the Transplant Case. In the Transplant Case, five patients are each awaiting the heart, lung, or kidney needed to save their lives. These organs could all be provided by the death of one innocent victim. Direct utilitarianism would require the transplant operations because the satisfaction of the preferences to live of the five dying patients would outweigh the preference of the one innocent victim. However, an indirect utilitarian would argue that the anxiety and distrust created by permitting such practices would stop anyone ever going to the hospital. An indirect utilitarian would assign a right to life to all hospital patients, a right that cannot be trumped by considerations of maximizing welfare, because a right to life would maximize welfare in the long run. This derivative moral right would override or trump considerations of maximizing preference satisfaction when the surgeon made her decisions.

Another derivative justification for the assignment of moral rights is justice-based. A system of rights is justified because it is the best way to treat everyone fairly, or to treat everyone as equals. We will look at justice-based assignments of rights in the next chapter.

Moral rights are justified non-derivatively by treating them as natural rights. According to the doctrine of NATURAL RIGHTS, rights-bearers have rights because they have certain natural features. These natural features are held to be inherently valuable and thus requiring protection by moral rights. Ethicists have suggested two types of inherently valuable natural features that might justify possession of moral rights: interests and the will.

The WILL THEORY points to how the holder of a right has the power either to insist that others follow their correlative duties, or not to insist that they do, according to the right-holder's will on the matter. For example, Alice's promise to Ben that Alice will drive him to the airport creates a right: Ben's right that Alice give him that drive. According to the will theory, it is a right because Ben can choose whether or not to claim that right. At Ben's discretion, Ben can choose to require Alice to give him that drive, in performance of her promise, or Ben can choose to relieve Alice of her promise and allow Alice not to drive him. In the limited matter of whether or not to give him that drive, Alice is morally subject to Ben's will.

One weakness of will theory is that there are important moral rights the claiming of which is not at the discretion of the right-holder. Some rights are inalienable—that is, incapable of being surrendered—such as the right not to be enslaved. People are no longer allowed to sell themselves into slavery, even if they would choose to do so. Another weakness stems from the underlying natural feature that the will theory holds to be inherently valuable. This is the rights-bearer's capacity to make competent, rational choices, a feature called AUTONOMY. If potential rights-bearers did not have this capacity, then there would be no point in using rights to secure their discretion over the duties of others. However, some persons, whom we think to possess moral rights, do not possess autonomy. Small children, mentally incompetent adults, and people who are alive, but in a coma, have rights that should be respected, yet do not have the capacity for making autonomous choices. From the point of view of attempts to extend moral standing to the non-human environment, autonomy is a feature of adult human beings not possessed by animals, plants, and ecosystems. So the will theory is not easily compatible with the extension of moral rights to the non-human world.

The second theory of natural rights, the INTEREST THEORY, holds that the inherently valuable natural feature that justifies possession of a moral right is the interests of the right-holder. A right is justified because its possession is to the benefit or advantage of the right-holder. Interests can be either subjective or objective, where the distinction is analogous to the distinction between subjective and objective consequentialism.

The more commonly accepted form of the interest theory of rights takes interests to be subjective or psychological. In the SUBJECTIVE INTERESTS approach to justifying natural rights, the natural feature that justifies a right is the mental benefits (e.g., pleasure, satisfied desire) that the rights-bearer will experience. One problem that arises is determining which interests lead to rights and which do not. Someone's interest in continuing to live is an important interest that justifies a right to life. Someone's interest in having oatmeal for breakfast rather than cream of wheat is a trivial interest that does not justify a right to oatmeal. Somewhere we have to draw a distinction between those interests that are urgent enough to justify rights, and those that are not. One criticism of the language of rights is the way rights proliferate; people enthusiastically assert their rights to all sorts of things. To sort out which interests lead to real rights and which do not we need a criterion of importance for subjective interests. Not all interests lead to rights. If rights are to trump considerations of utility, we need a way to tell which interests should be considered in utility calculations and which interests are important enough that their protection should serve as a limitation on how we maximize social utility. Subjective interests are features of human beings and arguably of other animals. The subjective-interests justification of moral rights opens the question of whether animals can have rights.

In the OBJECTIVE INTERESTS approach to justifying natural rights, the inherently valuable feature that justifies rights is the non-mental benefit that will accrue to the rights-bearer. Examples of such non-psychological advantages are the fulfillment of natural purposes or the preservation of functional integrity. Such teleological accounts of objective interests suffer from the general weaknesses of the teleological approach canvassed in the last chapter. However, since they are interests that human beings, animals, and possibly plants and ecosystems all share, the objective interests approach potentially permits non-human entities like plants and ecosystems to have moral rights. Figure 7.2 shows the above distinctions between ways of justifying rights. Derivative rights appear in two ways, first, classified under rights-based theories and, second, classified under the indirect utilitarian and justice-based approaches that justify them.

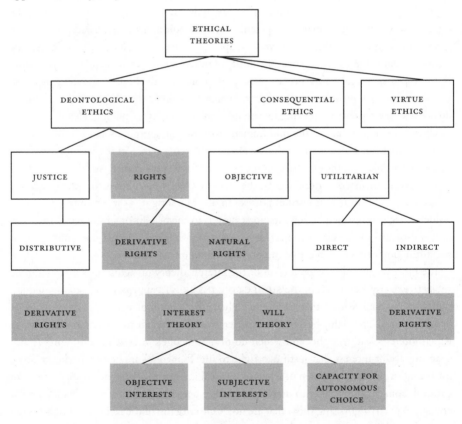

FIGURE 7.2: Taxonomy of rights-based theories

ENVIRONMENTAL ETHICS

In the history of philosophy, perhaps the most important justification of a rights-based approach to ethics comes from the German philosopher, Immanuel Kant (1724–1804). Kant concluded that only beings who can choose principles according to reason can be moral agents. Only autonomous, rational beings are moral agents. And he concluded that true moral principles must respect the rational autonomy (dignity) of moral agents. He captured these ideas in his famous version of a categorical imperative. A categorical imperative is a moral principle of action that does not depend on anyone's wants or desires (for example, "don't tell lies"), whereas a hypothetical imperative is a strategic principle of action that will help someone get what he wants (for example, "if you want to get the advantages of others' trust, don't tell lies.")

Kant's first formulation of his general categorical imperative, the one that is supposed to sum all categorical imperatives up, is, "Act only on those principles that you can at the same time will to become universal laws of nature." For example, a person can tell a lie when convenient only if she can intend that everyone may lie when convenient. But if everyone tells lies whenever it is convenient, then the assertion of facts in conversation will become impossible. So she cannot will that telling lies when convenient become a universal law of nature, and so it is a wrong form of action. It is important to distinguish this from a rule-utilitarian justification. A rule utilitarian would argue that if everyone told lies, then we would all be worse off as a result. In contrast, Kant argues that if everyone told lies, then conversation would become impossible.

Kant's second formulation of his categorical imperative is, "Act so as to treat humanity, whether in your own person or in that of any other, in every case as an end and never as merely a means only." So we should never enslave another person, nor in any way interfere with their autonomy or dignity. Lying to people interferes with their autonomy by manipulating the information on which they base their decisions. A corollary of this formulation is that the best way to treat a moral agent as an end-in-herself is to respect her rights. The natural feature picked here is that of being a rational, autonomous, moral agent. To have rights, the recipient must have the same features as the agent.

The Kantian approach to ethics has several weaknesses that we should note. The first is specific to its grounding in the natural feature of autonomy. Considerations of moral standing suggest that the Kantian natural rights theory may be too restrictive. Only autonomous rational agents have rights, so only they are considered by his rights-based theory, and so only they have moral standing. Kant's view assigns no rights or moral standing to infants and children, to the cognitively or emotionally disadvantaged, or to the irreversibly comatose. Nor does it make room for animal rights or for the moral standing of animals.

From the consequentialist point of view, natural rights based theories are overly stringent and absolutist. An often cited example is the case of the Truth-teller and the Axe Murderer. Karl's roommate, Jane, is in her room. An axe murderer comes to the door and asks Karl if she is home. Karl believes that he has a duty to always tell the truth to others, no matter what the consequences. Karl believes that the axe murderer has a right to hear the truth from him.

Karl tells the axe murder that Jane is in, and believes that, since his intentions were good, he should not be morally condemned for the ensuing bloodshed.

From the virtue ethics point of view, natural rights theories require people to have characters that are overly rigid and show little wisdom. The above case illustrates this.

TYPES OF RIGHTS

One important distinction between types of rights is that between legal and moral rights. LEGAL RIGHTS are rights that people have that are justified according to legal standards. MORAL RIGHTS are rights that people have that are justified by moral standards. A system of legal standards can be justified or criticized from the ethical point of view. Environmentalists will criticize the existing property rights of a factory to discharge pollutants. Activists who believe in the moral rights of animals will criticize the lack of legal rights to protect animals from abusive medical experimentation.

Another distinction is that between specific and general rights. A SPECIFIC RIGHT is one whose correlative duty only falls on a determinate person or group. A paradigm example is a contractual right. Someone's loan contract with the bank gives her a duty to pay the bank a certain amount of money, and the bank a right that she repay the money. The bank's contractual right, however, gives no one other than her a duty to repay that money. A GENERAL RIGHT is a right whose correlative duty falls on everyone. For example, someone's right to personal security means that everyone else has a duty not to hurt him.

A third distinction is that between negative and positive rights. A NEGATIVE RIGHT imposes a duty on everyone else not to interfere with the right holder's activities. It gives the right bearer a liberty or freedom from the interference of others. Examples include freedom of expression and freedom of association, which give people freedom from the interference of the government. Negative rights, freedoms, and liberties protect entities with moral standing from interference by others, but they have limits. These limits are set by the Harm Principle, first formulated by John Stuart Mill in his book, *On Liberty* (1859). The HARM PRINCIPLE says that people (or the government) are permitted to interfere with someone's freedom, liberty, or exercise of their rights only in order to prevent harm to others. For example, people have a negative right to freedom of movement. This freedom is not absolute or unlimited. The right to freedom of movement may be limited to prevent people from hurting others, as in the saying, "Your freedom to move your fist stops one inch from my nose."

A POSITIVE RIGHT imposes a duty on others to assist the right bearer is some way. Examples include the right to welfare assistance, the right to unemployment insurance payments, the right to an education, and, in many countries, the right to medical care. The existence of positive moral rights is more controversial than the existence of negative rights. A weakness of positive rights is their indeterminacy regarding on whom their correlative duties fall. While it is usually evident on whom negative rights impose the duty not to interfere, it is less obvious on whom positive rights impose duties to assist. Who has the duty to satisfy the right to an education? Parents? Society? If the latter, how much of the duty lies on each member of society? The usual solution is to say that the positive right imposes a duty on the state to provide the education. The state must then find a just way to spread the cost of providing education across all its citizens.

RIGHTS AND ACCUMULATIVE HARMS

Many important sources of environmental damage are accumulative in their effect. An ACCU-MULATIVE HARM is a type of harm such that individual acts are not harmful, but when many individuals perform the acts, they accumulate into a serious harm to others. Accumulative harms have the same structure as the case of the Harmless Torturers. Each act of turning the dial by one click causes only an imperceptible increase in pain. But when 1000 people each turn the dial one click, it causes great harm to the victim. The individual acts are not them-selves harmful, but the accumulative consequence is. One person crossing the lawn will do it no harm, but many people crossing it will. One driver will make not change the climate, but billions of drivers will.

The type of activity that causes accumulative harms is typically non-point source pollution. POINT SOURCE POLLUTION happens when we can easily identify determinate individuals whose activity is causing the harm done by the pollution. For example, it may be easy to iden-tify a particular factory as the source of noxious fumes. NON-POINT SOURCE POLLUTION happens when we cannot identify determinate individuals whose activity is causing the pol-lution. For example, the smog in a large city is not easily imputed to individual drivers. A few drips from the oil pan of one car in a large parking lot may lead to no environmental damage, but a few drips from each of thousands of cars may lead to damaging run-off. Point source pollution is an individual harm, whereas non-point source pollution is an accumulative harm. Figure 7.3 attempts to picture this idea.

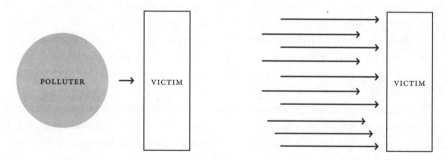

FIGURE 7.3: Left: point source pollution; Right: non-point source pollution

The types of pollutants that lead to accumulative harms typically stay in the environment for long periods. Some pollutants do their damage immediately after emission, and then go away because they are assimilated by the environment. Noise pollution is an example. Other pollutants, like ozone-depleting CFC molecules or climate-changing methane molecules, stay in the atmosphere for years contributing to an accumulative harm. Once the flow of pollutants passes a certain threshold, the Earth can no longer assimilate them, and the stock of pollutant in the environment begins to rise and remain high. In the graph on the left of Figure 7.4, large individual flows of a pollutant happen at different times, but the total stock of the pollutant spikes and returns to zero after the emission is over. In the graph on the right of Figure 7.4, small emissions result in no increase in the stock of pollutant in the environment until the environment's ability to assimilate the pollutant is overwhelmed. When this threshold is past, the stock of pollutants in the environment begins to rise, and stays above zero even when individual small emissions cease. Because these pollutants are long-lived, tracing the connection between future damage and past emissions becomes scientifically impossible.

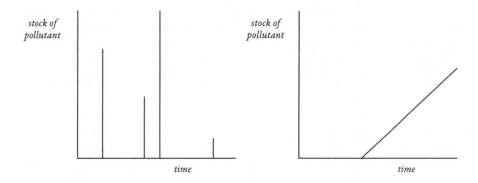

FIGURE 7.4: Left: Large individual emissions that do not accumulate;
Right: Small individual emissions that accumulate once the threshold for assimilation is passed

As well, the accumulative harms of many important forms of environmental damage are global in their effect. Because climate change affects the climate of the whole planet, the harms of climate change will not be confined to the industrialized countries which emitted most of the greenhouse gases. Harm will also fall on people in southern countries who have historically emitted very little. Though it might be relatively easy to trace the connection between an individual upstream polluter and individual downstream victims in the same locality, the geographic spread of many accumulative pollutants makes such tracing virtually impossible.

Moral rights are of little help in protecting people from accumulative environmental harms, like non-point source pollution, for two reasons: Firstly, the structure of a moral right is such that one person's right not to be polluted places a correlative moral duty on all other agents not to pollute. The agents who owe these correlative duties are those agents whose actions, if performed, would interfere with the right holder's interest not to be polluted. In cases where harms are accumulative, however, there are no such agents. Each agent can legitimately claim that his or her activities do not interfere with the right-holder in any way. If any of the agents stopped their activities, the violation of the supposed right against pollution would still occur. Analogously, each individual harmless torturer can claim that her turning of the dial has no effect and does not breach her duty not to hurt the victim, and thus does not violate the victim's right not to be tortured. Each walker on the lawn can claim that his walking does no injury to the lawn and thus does not violate anyone's right to conserved parkland. Each driver may claim that his driving will have no effect on the climate and so does not violate the rights

ENVIRONMENTAL ETHICS

of anyone harmed by climate change. Because of their structure, moral rights cannot protect people from accumulative interferences. (Kernohan 1995: 250–52)

Secondly, the Harm Principle does not work well to limit individual rights when we try to apply it to non-point source pollution and other accumulative harms. In rights-based theories, each individual's freedom to do an activity stops only when that activity causes harm to other people. In the case of accumulative harms, no individual is doing any harm by herself, so no individual should have her liberty limited to prevent accumulative harms. Each individual car driver can claim that his or her driving is doing no harm, so her freedom to drive her car may not be limited to protect others from the effects of global warming. Not only do the rights of pollution victims not impose a duty to stop polluting, but polluters may also claim that any attempt to stop their polluting activities is an infringement of their liberty not justified by the Harm Principle.

The above two points are weaknesses of the rights-based approach to environmental ethics and of the Harm Principle. They show that the rights based approach needs further development if it is to be useful in pollution problems in environmental ethics.

SUMMARY

1. The deontological approach to ethics emphasizes the duties that agents should follow when they act. Deontological theories include divine command theories, justice-based theories, and rights based theories.

2. Structurally, one person's right results in another person's, or other persons', correlative duty, a direct duty owed to the right holder.

3. Moral rights have been justified derivatively by indirect utilitarianism and theories of justice and directly by natural rights theories. Natural rights theories justify an entity holding a right through the entity's possession of inherently valuable natural features that need protection. Potential justifying features are autonomy, subjective interests, and objective interests. Autonomy applies only to competent humans, subjective interests may apply to many animals, and objective interests may apply to any entity that can flourish.

4. Kant's ethic sees only rational, autonomous human beings as morally considerable. It does not grant rights to infants, the comatose, or animals. From the utilitarian perspective, an overly stringent respect for rights may lead to terrible consequences, as in the Axe Murderer case.

5. Moral rights must be distinguished from legal rights. Negative rights impose a duty on others not to interfere, and are limited by the Harm Principle that says that rights cannot be exercised in a way that harms others. Positive rights impose a duty on others to assist the right holder.

6. Many environmental problems lead to accumulative harms, which are the additive consequence of many individually harmless acts. Rights cannot protect people from accumulative harms because no individuals have a duty to stop their harmless acts. Nor will the Harm Principle prevent

accumulative harms because it will not limit the freedom of individually harmless polluters.

ONLINE READING QUESTIONS

The book's website contains reading questions on this chapter. Working through these questions will help you understand, remember, and apply important concepts from the chapter. Some of the questions supply useful hints for the study questions.

STUDY QUESTIONS

Using the text and hints from the online reading questions, write out, type, dictate to your computer, or at least formulate in your head answers to the following questions.

1. Describe what is meant by the rights-based approach to morality.
2. Explain the relationship between a right and its correlative duty.
3. What is the difference between a natural right and a derivative right?
4. On what natural feature is Kantian natural rights based? Why might this be too restrictive?
5. Why does a case like the Truth-teller and the Axe Murderer count against the rights-based approach and potentially in favour of the utilitarian approach?
6. Why does the rights-based approach to ethics have difficulties protecting people against non-point source pollution?

QUESTIONS TO PONDER

Spend a few minutes thinking about the following questions, or, better yet, discuss them with fellow readers of this book.

1. Do you know of, or can you invent, a deontological ethical theory that is not divine command, rights-based, or justice-based? Would it be useful in environmental ethics?
2. How can we distinguish the subjective interests that are important enough to lead to rights from those that are not?
3. Can rights-based ethical theories avoid the utilitarian objection that they can lead to terrible consequences, as in the case of the Truth-teller and the Axe Murderer?
4. Libertarians criticize positive rights because it is unclear who owes the correlative duty to assist. On whom does the duty to enforce negative rights fall?
5. In accumulative harm cases, can you see a way to assign correlative duties to harmless polluters?

Chapter 8

JUSTICE

MANY ENVIRONMENTAL PROBLEMS INVOLVE A CONFLICT BETWEEN THE PRIVATE property rights of individuals or companies on the one hand, and considerations about the environment on the other. For example, the property rights of the owner of a factory that is emitting pollution affecting nearby houses will conflict with the property rights of the owners of these houses. A resolution of the conflict will involve a trade-off between the property rights of the factory owner and the property rights of the householders in the environment around the factory. Theories of distributive justice are theories of the fair distribution of property rights to resources, goods, and services. They have the potential to help us understand how to resolve conflicts like this.

Theories of justice, like theories of rights, are deontological. They tell us to follow principles of fairness in developing and implementing environmental policy. Theories of justice take us into the realm of political philosophy. Political philosophy applies ethics to the basic structure of a country's legal system. Distributive justice is concerned with the fair allocation of benefits and burdens across those with moral standing. Ethics has ordinarily been concerned with justice at the national level, with how a government should distribute benefits and burdens across the citizens of one country. However, we also need to decide on fair terms of international trade and on fair levels of development assistance. This leads to ethical concerns about international justice, which is concerned with the fair distribution of benefits and burdens between the citizens of different countries. As well, we need to decide on a fair distribution of the benefits of resource extraction and the burdens of environmental pollution between the present generation and future generations. This leads to consideration of intergenerational justice. We need to decide, too, on what constitutes fair treatment of animals, and this leads to consideration of interspecies justice.

Environmental problems often arise as the unintended consequences of producing goods and services within a market-based economic system. Some theories of distributive justice imply that governments should leave the free market to fix environmental problems as well as it can. Other theories of justice justify a strong role for governments in solving environmental problems, and put constraints on how governments may achieve these solutions. This chapter will survey the strengths and weaknesses of a range of important theories of justice.

Learning Objectives

1. To understand the notions of justice, fairness, equality, sameness, and difference.
2. To distinguish between compensatory, retributive, and distributive justice.
3. To understand the strengths and weaknesses of a libertarian theory of justice.
4. To understand the weaknesses of a utilitarian theory of distributive justice.
5. To acquire some understanding of John Rawls's theory of justice as fairness.

SAMENESS AND DIFFERENCE

At its most basic level, justice is about moral equality. Justice requires that we treat all ethically considerable entities as moral equals. Justice does not require that we treat all these entities in exactly the same way. What moral equality requires is that governments, organizations, and individuals do not treat people differently based on morally arbitrary features. Commonly accepted, though sometimes disputed, morally arbitrary features include:

1. Race (racism).
2. Sex (sexism).
3. Age (ageism).
4. Religious preference.
5. Sexual orientation.
6. Economic class.
7. Familial relationships to those in power.

Moral equality has another side. Treating people as equals also requires that we recognize morally relevant (non-arbitrary) differences between people. Examples of cases where it seems reasonable to treat people equally by treating them differently include:

1. Parents treat their own children differently from the children of others.
2. Disabled people are entitled to reserved, convenient parking.

3. Society punishes only those who deserve it.
4. Workers who put in more effort get greater rewards.
5. Restaurants reserve different washrooms for men and women.
6. Women are eligible for pregnancy leaves that men are not.

Distributive justice may require that the rich pay income tax at a higher rate than do the poor. Interspecies justice will not give to animals the political rights that liberal democracies give to humans (rights to vote, to form political parties, to freedom of expression) because animals are incapable of exercising such political rights. Justice is not as simple as treating every entity with moral standing in the same way.

Developed countries with a majority of citizens of European descent have had a tendency to pay more attention to fixing and preventing pollution problems in communities of people of European descent, than in communities of people of African descent. ENVIRONMENTAL RACISM occurs when environmental burdens fall unequally on people of different racial or ethnic descent. Race is a morally arbitrary feature of people from the point of view of moral equality. Governments have also often allowed environmental pollution to fall on poor people. Sometimes the reasoning is economic. An economist could argue that the Gross Domestic Product will suffer less if poor people are off work because of environmental illnesses than if rich people are. On the economic utilitarian view that utility is measured by willingness to pay, the best policy is the one that maximizes GDP. This economic utilitarian policy would lead to ENVIRONMENTAL CLASSISM, which occurs when environmental burdens fall unequally on poor people.

VARIETIES OF JUSTICE

When people think of the notion of justice, they most often think of criminal justice and the fines and jail time with which society punishes convicted criminals. This is corrective or RETRIBUTIVE JUSTICE and its function is to ensure that punishments are fair. It is concerned with questions such as whether society should fine or jail convicted polluters. Different ethical approaches have different views about what makes retributive justice fair. Utilitarian retributive justice will emphasize future consequences and will judge punishments according to how well they deter future pollution. Deontological retributive justice will assess punishments according to how they fit the crime. It will be concerned with whether the polluter gets the punishment she deserves for her polluting activity. Virtue ethic retributive justice will emphasize the educational role of punishment and be concerned with changing the character of the polluter to make her more thoughtful, careful, and environmentally aware.

Another type of justice is COMPENSATORY JUSTICE whose role is to ensure that people who harm others give their victims fair compensation for their injury. It would deal with the question of the amount of compensation that a polluting firm owes to those on whom the pollution falls. It would deal with whether industrialized countries that have used up the atmosphere's assimilative capacity for carbon dioxide owe compensation to developing countries that have emitted almost no greenhouse gasses.

The third type of justice is DISTRIBUTIVE JUSTICE, which is concerned with how to distribute benefits and burdens in a fair way in society. A theory of distributive justice does not actually take physical economic goods or services and pass them around. Rather it justifies a particular system of legal rights and responsibilities regarding these economic goods and services. These rights may include personal liberties like the right to freedom of movement, political rights like the right to vote, and property rights like the legal right to possess or sell an economic good or productive resource. These rights impose correlative duties on other people and thus generate responsibilities. One person's property right in her mobile phone places a legal responsibility on others not to use it without her permission. In this chapter, we will be particularly interested in theories regarding the just distribution of property rights. These theories will become particularly important when we discuss the economic approach to the environment in section three.

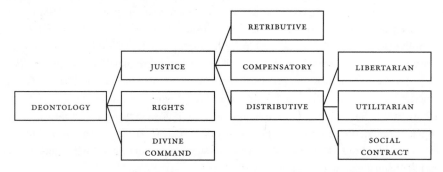

FIGURE 8.1: Approaches to distributive justice

There are two approaches to justifying the distribution of private property rights to people. One, a direct way, is to justify legal property rights as legal protections for pre-existing natural moral rights. LIBERTARIAN theories of justice justify a system of private property through the existence of natural moral rights to liberty and self-ownership. A second, indirect, way to justify a system of private property rights is to derive them from another type of ethical theory. We will look at the justifications offered by indirect utilitarian theory, and by the social contract theory of the American philosopher, John Rawls.

THE LIBERTARIAN THEORY OF JUSTICE

Libertarian political theory often attempts to justify a system of unrestricted private property rights by tracking property rights back to a morally relevant natural feature of particular human beings. The morally relevant feature is autonomy and the moral rights that protect autonomy are the negative rights of self-ownership. Self-ownership sees people as having the maximal liberty compatible with other people having the same, and includes the right to personal security, to freedom of movement, and so on. In particular, it includes the right to manage and sell a person's own labour. Being a self-owner is the opposite of being a slave. The autonomy-protecting rights of self-ownership are all negative rights. They impose duties on others not to interfere, but do not impose any duties to assist.

The most important libertarian argument for justifying a system of private property rights goes as follows:

1. All people have a natural right of self-ownership to their labour.
2. People who "mix" their labour with something un-owned come to own it, as long as they leave enough, and as good, for others.
3. Therefore, people have a natural right to their initially acquired property.
4. This property right includes the right to give, sell, or trade with others.
5. Therefore, people have a natural right to any property that they have acquired either by initial acquisition or by just transfer from others.

A libertarian system of property rights entails a minimally regulated, free enterprise economic system.

The second premise in this argument is the crucial one. It comes from the tremendously influential theory of the initial acquisition of property due to the seventeenth century English philosopher, John Locke (1632–1704). He formulated his theory in the following passage.

> Though the earth, and all inferior creatures, be common to all men, yet every man has a property in his own person: this no body has any right to but himself. The labour of his body, and the work of his hands, we may say, are properly his. Whatsoever then he removes out of the state that nature hath provided, and left it in, he hath mixed his labour with, and joined to it something that is his own, and thereby makes it his property. It being by him removed from the common state nature hath placed it in, it hath by this labour something annexed to it, that excludes the common right of other men: for this labour being the unquestionable property of the labourer, no man but he can have a right to what that is once joined to, at least where there is enough, and as good, left in common for others. (Locke 1689: Chapter 2, Section 27)

Locke's presentation of this argument suffers from several weaknesses. The first concerns his metaphor of mixing self-owned labour with un-owned nature to create a privately owned economic good. Mixing what an agent owns with un-owned nature need not result in private ownership of the mixture. For example, in the days before environmental regulations came into effect, when a factory emitted pollutants into a lake, the factory owners did not claim to own the lake on the grounds of mixing their effluent with the lake water. They were likely to take quite the opposite view, and try to claim that when the effluent mixed with the lake water, they no longer owned the effluent, and it was no longer their problem.

The second weakness concerns the requirement that enough, and as good, be left in common for others. Locke may have had in mind the acquisition of farmland that was going on in North America during his lifetime. Ignoring the property rights of Native Americans, colonists were busily clearing what they regarded as un-owned land and claiming to own it. Because, to them, North America was so vast, they could claim to be leaving enough, and as good, for other colonists. Of course, farmland in North America was limited, and the process of initial acquisition eventually ended. Individual acts of acquisition of farmland only appeared to leave enough, and as good, because colonists were ignoring the accumulative consequences of their actions. Individual acquisitions eventually added up to a situation where there was not enough, and as good, left in common. (Kernohan 1993: 59–65) A similar situation is going on today, as individual emitters of carbon dioxide appropriate the assimilative capacity of the atmosphere, while claiming that their individually insignificant appropriations leave enough, and as good, for future generations. Individual appropriators of non-renewable resources, like rare metals, can claim that they are leaving enough, and as good, for future generations, but the accumulative consequence of massive resource extraction will be to leave very little for the future.

A third weakness concerns the historical nature of these justifications. Unjust initial acquisitions that happened in the past infect contemporary systems of property rights. Since documentation of these injustices has been lost, we have no way of knowing which contemporary property rights are morally justified. Knowing what we do of the way the original colonists trampled on the moral rights of the native population of North America, we can reasonably conclude that contemporary land titles in all of North America are suspect. No country in the world is immune to this problem.

The libertarian response to these problems has been to shift focus from the mixing metaphor to the idea of adding value. The argument instead claims that, by her labour, the initial appropriator adds value to natural objects and thereby deserves to own these modified natural objects. The argument then makes the factual claim that, because of the productive efficiency of property-based economic systems, some of this value will accrue to those who missed the initial appropriation, leaving them better off than they would have been in a state of un-owned nature. Thus, the value added approach satisfies the requirement that enough, and as good, be left in common. For example, industrialized countries might argue that the benefits of their appropriation of the un-owned assimilative capacity of the Earth's atmosphere for carbon dioxide have trickled down to the least developed countries, thus leaving them enough, and as good.

The factual claims in the last paragraph are contentious. There is also still a theoretical problem with the version of libertarianism based on what individuals deserve. It depends on the assumption that people add value to nature in such a way that we can easily attribute the value added to the labour of particular individuals. As Adam Smith pointed out, the source of most value added is not individual labour. Instead, the source is specialization and the division of labour. For example, suppose there are two hunter-gatherers, each with a different set of skills. *He* is a good gatherer and a poor fisher. He can find 7 edible roots per hour, but only catch 1 fish. *She* is a good fisher and a poor gatherer. She can find only 1 root per hour, but she can catch 7 fish. We will assume that proper nutrition requires that they have equal amounts of roots and fish. Labouring individually for a standard eight-hour day, he can produce 7 roots in one hour and 7 fish in the other seven hours. She can produce 7 roots in seven hours and 7 fish in one hour. However, if they specialize in what they do best and divide their labour efficiently, then, in an eight-hour day, he can produce 56 roots and she can produce 56 fish.

	HE		SHE	
	Roots	Fish	Roots	Fish
Productivity per hour	7	1	1	7
Production from self-sufficiency in 8 hours	7	7	7	7
Production from specialization and division of labour	56	0	0	56
Equal distribution of product of cooperation	28	28	28	28

TABLE 8.1: Increased production from the division of labour

The value added by the division of labour, the extra roots and fish, is not brought about by any increased effort on the part of either party, but is produced by the way they organize their labour. Neither he nor she can claim to deserve the additional roots and fish. The fairest distribution is plausibly an equal distribution, not a distribution based on desert or labour expended. In a modern society, nearly all the goods and services are the product not of individual artisans, but of specialization and the division of labour on a huge scale. This makes it practically impossible to attribute value added to the labour of an individual, as required by libertarian theory.

Libertarian justice treats people as moral equals by giving people equal rights to their own labour and to property that they initially acquire from nature or exchange with one another. It does not lead, however, to a system of property rights in which everyone has equal shares. Libertarianism justifies an unrestricted capitalist economic system in which some people can acquire great wealth while others have very little.

THE INDIRECT UTILITARIAN THEORY OF JUSTICE

Libertarianism justifies a distribution of property rights directly by tracking down the historical connection between autonomous acts of property acquisition, through various voluntary transfers by gift or purchase, to contemporary property rights. Utilitarianism justifies a distribution of property rights indirectly, by claiming that a particular pattern of property rights is justified because it produces the greatest utility for everyone. Direct or act utilitarianism is of little help in deriving a theory of justice because direct utilitarianism insists that we assess each act by a calculation of its welfare consequences. Indirect utilitarianism, which uses maximizing preference satisfaction as a way of justifying an assignment of rights and responsibilities, can be used to justify a distribution of property rights in goods and services, particularly in that all-purpose good, monetary income. We can apply utilitarianism indirectly to justify a distribution of property rights in income. The best income distribution is the one that maximizes utility. Some utilitarians argue that the distribution that maximizes utility is also a just distribution.

The utilitarian theory of moral equality is that people are treated as equals when we give equal consideration to the interests of everyone. Each person's preference satisfaction counts in the same way in utilitarian calculations. When we aggregate preference satisfaction, we weight the value of each person's utility score by the same factor. For example, when we assess an option by aggregating the utilities of the affected persons, we count one times Alice's utility plus one times Bob's utility plus one times Carol's utility. We do not count one times Alice's utility plus three times Bob's utility plus one times Carol's utility on the grounds that Bob is male. Doing so would give unequal consideration to the interests of men and women, and that would be morally arbitrary.

Some utilitarians argue that this concept of moral equality will lead to an attractive account of distributive justice. They argue that the utilitarian standard of rightness will lead to an equal distribution of goods because of the economic Law of Diminishing Marginal Utility, which we will explain.

The TOTAL UTILITY of a group of economic goods or services is the sum of all the utility produced by the consumption of those goods or services. For example, the total utility produced by the consumption of two ice cream cones might be eight utiles. The MARGINAL UTILITY of an economic good or service is the additional utility gained through the consumption of one additional unit of that good or service. For example, the marginal utility of a third ice cream cone is the additional utility produced when someone who has already eaten two cones goes on to eat a third one. In Table 8.2, the marginal utility of a third ice cream cone is 2 utiles.

ICE CREAM CONES	0		1		2		3		4		5
Total utility	0		5		8		10		10		7
Marginal utility		+5		+3		+2		0		−3	

TABLE 8.2: The diminishing marginal utility of ice cream cones

For many goods, like ice cream cones, the additional pleasure or satisfaction that a consumer experiences diminishes as he or she consumes more of them. The marginal utility may even go negative when the consumer starts to feel ill. In Table 8.2, while the marginal utility of the first cone is 5 utiles, the marginal utility of the second cone is only 3 utiles. The total utility of two cones is the sum of the marginal utility of the first cone (5 utiles) plus the marginal utility of the second cone (3 utiles), which is 8 utiles. The law of diminishing marginal utility generalizes from ice cream cones to all economic goods and services. The LAW OF DIMINISHING MARGINAL UTILITY states that as the consumption of a given economic good increases, the marginal utility produced by the consumption of one additional unit of the good tends to decrease.

Utilitarian justice derives from indirect utilitarianism because it is concerned, not with maximizing preference satisfaction directly, but in justifying a system of distributing property rights to all-purpose economic goods. It is the way that the all-purpose economic goods are distributed that, indirectly, maximizes preference satisfaction. The major all-purpose economic good is monetary income because owners can use their income to satisfy whatever preferences they choose. The marginal utility of monetary income, like the marginal utility of ice cream cones, decreases. Very rich people will get less satisfaction from an additional sum of money than will very poor people. The law of diminishing marginal utility applies to monetary income just as it applies to the particular goods and services that people can use income to buy.

MONTHLY INCOME	$0		$1000		$2000		$3000		$4000
Total utility	0		50		80		100		100
Marginal utility		50		30		20		0	

TABLE 8.3: The diminishing marginal utility of income

Table 8.3 shows a very simple model of how this works. The utility of a monthly income for a subject is measured in utility units from 0 to 100, the scale used by the von Neumann and Morgenstern method of utility measurement described in Chapter 5. The first $1000 of monthly income makes a bigger difference to the person's total utility level (50 utiles) than does the second (30 utiles). In this model, the marginal utility of the fourth $1000 is zero.

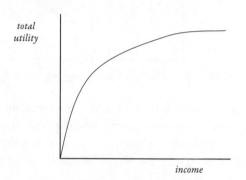

FIGURE 8.2: Diminishing marginal utility of income

Figure 8.1 sketches this information graphically. As income increases along the horizontal axis, the person's total utility rises less and less quickly. It rises less quickly because the additional utility produced by each unit of additional income diminishes with increased income.

Some utilitarians argue that the diminishing marginal utility of income leads to an equal distribution of income. For example, we will suppose that Otis and Paula both have the utility/income schedule of Table 8.3. Poor Otis has a monthly income of $1000 and a total utility of 50 utiles, whereas rich Paula has an income of $3000 and a total utility of 100 utiles. Table 8.3 shows that if we take $1000 of income from Paula, leaving her with $2000, and give it to Otis, giving him $2000 also, then we will raise Otis's total utility by 30 utiles while reducing Paula's by only 20 utiles. Because Paula has more income than Otis does, the marginal utility of $1000 is lower to her than it is to him. If we move from the unequal distribution to the egalitarian one, then we will get a net increase in utility of 10 utiles (+30 – 20). In general, poorer people get more satisfaction out of an extra dollar than do rich people. Therefore, we can maximize satisfaction by redistributing dollars from the rich to the poor. An indirect utilitarian can argue that, because it maximizes total utility, equal weighting of everyone's utilities, together with the diminishing marginal utility of income, leads to an equal distribution.

There are several problems with indirect utilitarian justice. The utilitarian argument for an equal distribution assumes that everyone gets the same incremental utility from each ice cream cone. This assumption is very questionable. Some people are more efficient at turning ice creams cones or monetary income into utility than are others. Philosophers affectionately call extremely efficient converters of goods into utility, "utility monsters."

Suppose that we have 4 ice cream cones to distribute between two people, Millie and Nathan. Each has the same utility function as given in Table 8.2. Because of diminishing marginal utility, we maximize aggregate utility when we give Millie and Nathan equal shares, as is shown in the next table.

MILLIE'S CONES	MILLIE'S UTILITY	NATHAN'S CONES	NATHAN'S UTILITY	TOTAL UTILITY
4	10	0	0	10
3	10	1	5	15
2	8	2	8	16
1	5	3	10	15
0	0	4	10	10

TABLE 8.4: Equal distribution of ice cream maximizes utility

When Millie and Nathan get 2 cones each, the total utility is at a maximum of 16 utiles. Some people are more efficient than are others in converting goods into utility (pleasure or satisfaction). Suppose Nathan is a utility monster who gets 5 times as much utility from each cone as Millie would get. In the following table, the utility Millie gets from her first cone is 5; the utility Nathan gets from his first cone is 5 times this, 25.

MILLIE'S CONES	MILLIE'S UTILITY	NATHAN'S CONES	NATHAN'S UTILITY	TOTAL UTILITY
4	10	0	$5 \times 0 = 0$	10
3	10	1	$5 \times 5 = 25$	35
2	8	2	$5 \times 8 = 40$	48
1	5	3	$5 \times 10 = 50$	55
0	0	4	$5 \times 10 = 50$	50

TABLE 8.5: Utility monster distorts equal distribution

Utility is maximized when Nathan gets 3 and Millie gets 1. In this case, utilitarianism still treats each unit of preference satisfaction equally, but, by distributing economic goods unequally, it does not treat Millie and Nathan equally as persons. Here is another example. Some wine-lovers get enormous satisfaction from an expensive bottle of wine, much more than the rest of us would. To maximize total utility, the rest of us should contribute money we would otherwise use to buy ourselves wine to buy them expensive bottles. We can maximize total utility by giving utility monsters more goods than are given to other, less efficient, convertors of ice cream or wine into utility. This seems unfair.

The basic utilitarian theory of moral equality is to give equal consideration to everyone's preferences, no matter what those preferences are. Utilitarian equality treats all preferences alike, even sadistic preferences, preferences that others have lesser liberties, and preferences that others receive less because of their race or gender. It seems unfair to count such preferences in making a distribution. Suppose Nathan has jealous preferences. Nathan gets −2 utiles for every cone that Millie gets as shown in Table 8.6.

MILLIE'S CONES	MILLIE'S UTILITY	NATHAN'S CONES	NATHAN'S UTILITY	TOTAL UTILITY
4	10	0	$0-2\times4=-8$	2
3	10	1	$5-2\times3=-1$	9
2	8	2	$8-2\times2=4$	12
1	5	3	$10-2=8$	13
0	0	4	10	10

TABLE 8.6: Unjust preferences distort equal distribution

Utility is maximized when Nathan gets 3 cones and Millie gets 1. Nathan gets more cones simply by preferring, unjustly, that Millie have less. Because indirect utilitarianism treats all preferences equally, it cannot rule out jealous or racist preferences. When we aggregate unjust preferences along with neutral ones, we get a distorted distribution of property rights.

A SOCIAL CONTRACT THEORY OF JUSTICE

We can maximize the size of the economic pie when incentives exist for people to take extra effort and risk. An INCENTIVE is an additional property right, to something such as more money, that motivates people to produce more. In order to create incentives, we will likely also have to permit unequal shares. However, the proper incentives given to well-off members of a society can actually benefit the poorest members of society. If the well-off members of a society have incentives to be more productive, then this can create a larger economic pie for the poorest members of the society to share. The poorest people in a society that has both incentives and an unequal distribution of income will receive more income than they would receive in a society that has an egalitarian distribution but no productivity incentives. Intuitively, an inegalitarian distribution where the poorest members of society do fairly well is fairer than an egalitarian distribution where the poorest members of society do less well.

In Table 8.7, the utilitarian distribution of money between three individuals Pat, Quincy, and Rita maximizes total income. Intuitively, though, the simple egalitarian distribution, which contains no incentives and is thus less productive, is fairer than the utilitarian distribution since it treats each person equally. Yet the prioritarian distribution that puts a priority on Pat, the poorest individual, seems fairer still. It allows for incentives to the best-off individual,

Rita, provided those incentives make the worst-off individual, Pat, better off than she, Pat, would be with simple equality. Perhaps moral equality involves, not making each individual the same, but making the worst-off individual as well off as possible.

	PAT	QUINCY	RITA	TOTAL
Utilitarian	$500	$1000	$3000	$4500
Simple egalitarian	$1000	$1000	$1000	$3000
Prioritarian	$1200	$1300	$1400	$3900

TABLE 8.7: The prioritarian distribution seems fairer than the equal distribution

Dealing fairly with incentives is an important issue for the work of American philosopher, John Rawls (1921–2002). In his 1971 book, *A Theory of Justice*, Rawls proposed a general conception of justice:

> All social primary goods—liberty and opportunity, income and wealth, and the bases of self-respect—are to be distributed equally unless an unequal distribution of any or all of these goods is to the advantage of the least favored. (p. 301)

He articulates this conception as two principles:

> First Principle
> Each person is to have an equal right to the most extensive total system of basic liberties compatible with a similar system of liberty for all.

> Second Principle
> Social and economic inequalities are to be arranged so that they are both:
>   (a) to the greatest benefit of the least advantaged, consistent with the just savings principle, and
>   (b) attached to offices and positions open to all under conditions of fair equality of opportunity. (p. 302)

The first principle is "lexically prior" to (trumps) the second principle. He calls the second principle, the "difference principle."

Rawls has a theory of the just distribution of rights: liberty rights (negative rights) and property rights. His theory treats all entities with moral standing (humans only for Rawls) as equals by treating them the same unless there is a good moral reason for treating them differently. Therefore, everyone is entitled to the same rights and liberties. He argues that race, gender, economic class, and (most controversially) genetically acquired natural abilities are all morally arbitrary reasons for distributing political or property rights. Therefore, his principle 2(a) permits economic inequalities only if they provide incentives to increase the size of the economic pie in a distributive system that maximally benefits the least advantaged (poorest) group in society. Rawls's theory of justice is liberal, and social democratic. It would lead to the sort of welfare-state capitalism that predominates in countries like Sweden and France.

Rawls justifies his theory of justice by means of a hypothetical social contract. This is very different from the actual contract that we imagine a state to enforce on ethical egoists in a contractarian theory. Rawls argues that a system of distributive justice is fair only if persons, who could completely discount all the morally arbitrary features of people like their race, sex, etc., would choose that system. To visualize how people could properly discount morally arbitrary features, he imagines people meeting to choose the principles of justice in a hypothetical "original position" behind a "veil of ignorance" such that

> ... no one knows his place in society, his class position or social status, nor does
> any one know his fortune in the distribution of natural assets and abilities, his
> intelligence, strength, and the like. (p. 12)

The system that parties to the original position choose behind the veil of ignorance becomes a social contract between them, and the social contract is a fair one because of the selective ignorance of the parties choosing it. The question remains, though, of why parties in the original position would choose Rawls's principles instead of choosing a maximizing, utilitarian theory.

The utilitarian argues that a *rational, maximizing person* behind the veil of ignorance would choose utilitarianism because this theory would maximize the total goods available. If he has an equal chance of being in any position in society, rich or poor, then he would maximize his expected utility in a utilitarian society. Rawls replies that a *reasonable person* would take the precaution of insuring herself against being enslaved or destitute. She would sacrifice some expected aggregate utility in return for living in a society that guaranteed basic liberties and that gave the greatest possible benefit to the least advantaged.

Rawls argues that parties in the original position would agree to a social contract that gives priority to the least advantaged because they would think as reasonable persons, not as rational persons. There is empirical evidence that people are often reasonable rather than rational. Buying insurance is a reasonable precaution for a person to take, but it is irrational in the sense that it does not maximize her economic self-interest. For example, suppose she owns a $100,000 house that has a 1% chance of burning down each year. Her expected cost for the year will be 1% of $100,000 = $1,000. If she buys insurance for the house, she will have to pay the insurance company a premium that will cover the risk of losing the house ($1,000) plus administrative costs and profit for the insurance company (say, $500), totalling $1500. Her expected cost for the year will be $1000 if she buys no insurance and $1500 if she does. She will maximize her expected benefit, through minimizing her expected costs, by not buying insurance. Yet, reasonable people take the precaution of buying insurance against large and irreversible losses, even though they would maximize their expected utility by not doing so.

Possibly precautionary reasoning only appears to be irrational because we are measuring costs in financial terms. As we have seen, income has declining marginal utility. Assuming that the householder is moderately well off, the utility loss of $1500 per year may be relatively small, whereas the utility loss of $100,000 from a burned-down house may be far greater than the monetary units indicate. The loss of her house would make her very poor, and decrease her utility drastically. Conversely, a very wealthy person, to whom $100,000 is a trivial amount, would likely self-insure.

Rawls argues that a reasonable person, who does not know her position in the society created by the social contract, will take the precaution of choosing a social structure that will protect her from large and irreversible misfortune. She will choose a society ordered with basic liberties and to the greatest benefit of the least advantaged in order to protect herself from the large and irreversible misfortunes of being enslaved or destitute in a less egalitarian, though more efficient, society ordered by a utilitarian decision procedure. This type of reasoning is important in discussions of the Precautionary Principle in environmental economics.

From the perspective of environmental ethics, one weakness of any social contract view is that justice applies only locally, between the parties to the contract, whereas many important environmental issues are global in scale. Rawls envisioned the citizens of a nation state like the US meeting behind the veil of ignorance to design a basic structure of distributive justice for the US. However, decisions about the economic structure of the US will have unintended consequences for the rest of the world. The level of fossil fuels used, the amount of greenhouse gasses emitted, and the use of food crops to produce biofuels will all affect the welfare of people in other countries. The interests of affected foreigners are not represented in negotiating a social contract for the US. Thus, it is difficult for a social contract theory of national justice to take into account issues of international, intergenerational, or interspecies justice.

SUMMARY

1. A theory of justice will treat people as moral equals. This is not the same as always treating people the same way. Treating people as equals requires treating people differently if there are morally relevant differences between them.
2. Three types of justice are retributive, compensatory, and distributive justice.
3. A theory of distributive justice is about the fair distribution of benefits and burdens among entities with moral standing. It concerns the distribution of rights and responsibilities, where the distribution of rights for human recipients includes the distribution of private property rights.
4. Libertarian theories of justice treat all humans equally by seeing them as all having the same natural rights. One natural right is the right to acquire private property in un-owned objects by being the first person to add value to the object. This natural right is limited by the requirement to leave enough, and as good for others. People may transfer property rights to others through gift or purchase, thus justifying a capitalist economic system.
5. Difficulties for libertarianism include these issues: People usually labour cooperatively to produce economic goods. Historically, people often acquired initial property rights in an unjust fashion. The accumulative consequences of initial acquisition usually involve not leaving enough

and as good for others. A libertarian system will produce a very unequal distribution of property rights.

6. Indirect utilitarian theories of justice treat people as equals by weighting each person's utilities by the same factor when adding them up. Some utilitarians argue that, since the marginal utility of income diminishes as income increases, maximizing total utility will involve redistributing income from rich to poor.

7. Because of their conception of equality, utilitarians try to satisfy all preferences regardless of their form or content. People can have very different income/utility schedules, creating the possibility of utility monsters. People can have unjust, racist, or sexist preferences that others have less. Including preferences such as these in utility aggregations will result in unjust distributions of utility.

8. Rawls's social contract theory of justice allows people to receive financial incentives to produce more, as long as this is to the benefit of the least advantaged. Rawls justifies his system of distributive justice on the basis that reasonable people, who were ignorant of what role they would personally play in society, would choose it.

9. In situations of risk and uncertainty, reasonable people will take precautions to avoid worst-case scenarios, whereas rational people will choose to take gambles that maximize their expected pay-offs.

ONLINE READING QUESTIONS

The book's website contains reading questions on this chapter. Working through these questions will help you understand, remember, and apply important concepts from the chapter. Some of the questions supply useful hints for the study questions.

STUDY QUESTIONS

Using the text and hints from the online reading questions, write out, type, dictate to your computer, or at least formulate in your head answers to the following questions.

1. Explain why justice does not always require that we treat people in the same way.
2. Why is environmental racism unjust?
3. Explain in words why, if people have identical marginal utility schedules, then maximizing utility should result in an equal distribution of goods.
4. Why is it a problem for utilitarian theories of justice that some people get more pleasure than others out of a given amount of economic goods?
5. How does Rawls's theory of justice allow for incentives?
6. Rawls supposes that a fair principle of justice is the one that would be chosen by people who did not know their own natural abilities and

social status. Why does he think such people would take the reasonable precaution of choosing a principle that distributed goods to the greatest benefit of the least advantaged?

7. What are the weaknesses of Locke's theory regarding the initial acquisition of private property rights in environmental resources?

QUESTIONS TO PONDER

Spend a few minutes thinking about the following questions, or, better yet, discuss them with fellow readers of this book.

1. Race and gender are morally arbitrary. So are affirmative action policies always unjust? How could you justify an affirmative action policy?
2. How would a libertarian reply to the objections made in the text to the Lockean theory of initial acquisition?
3. If monetary income has declining marginal utility, what does this mean for the use of willingness to pay as a measure of utility in environmental economics?
4. Are reasonable precautions always economically irrational, or, as suggested in the text, might the diminishing marginal utility of income make them a rational way to maximize expected utility? How might these thoughts apply to calculations of the expected costs and benefits of nuclear power stations that very occasionally melt down? Remember Chernobyl.
5. Human beings live cooperatively with food animals and companion animals. Speculate on a way that Rawls's apparatus (an original position, a veil of ignorance, and a social contract) could apply to the question of interspecies justice.

Part II

ENVIRONMENTAL ETHICS

Chapter 9

OBLIGATIONS
TO DISTANT PEOPLE

IN SEPTEMBER 2000, 147 HEADS OF STATE AGREED TO THE MILLENNIUM DEVELOPMENT Goals at the United Nations Millennium Assembly. The Millennium Development Goals were a promise by the rich, industrialized countries of the world to improve the welfare of people in developing countries. Rich countries promised to do the following by the year 2015:

1. Eradicate extreme poverty and hunger.
2. Achieve universal primary education.
3. Promote gender equality and empower women.
4. Reduce child mortality.
5. Improve maternal health.
6. Combat HIV/AIDS, malaria, and other diseases.
7. Ensure environmental sustainability.
8. Develop a global partnership for development.

Rich countries made some progress on keeping their promises until the financial crisis of 2008. Then, many rich countries froze overseas development assistance levels as they borrowed money to stimulate their own collapsing economies.

So far, we have been looking at ethical theories governing our obligations to ourselves, to nearby people, and to our fellow citizens. Yet people in distant countries also form part of the global environment, and we now need to address the question of their moral standing. Do we have moral obligations to people outside of our national borders? If so, then what is the extent of those moral obligations? Does a person living in Sydney have a different obligation to an unknown fellow Australian living across the country in Perth than he does to an unknown citizen of India living in Mumbai? Are the Millennium Development Goals morally required? Are present levels of foreign aid morally acceptable?

It is a commonplace to say that globalization is making our world more interdependent. Multi-national firms extract non-renewable natural resources, such as rare minerals and oil, from countries in Africa and the Middle East, and sell them to customers in Europe and North America. Firms and individuals emit pollution, particularly greenhouse gasses, in wealthy countries, and thereby increase levels of these emissions in poor countries on the other side of the planet. The global extent of many major environmental problems forces us to examine the moral consideration that we give to distant people.

Learning Objective

To understand ethical egoist, contractarian, utilitarian, rights-based, and distributive justice approaches to the extent of our moral obligations to distant people.

THE MORAL STANDING OF DISTANT PEOPLE

Saying that a human or non-human entity has moral standing means that we must consider it for its own sake when we are making an ethical judgment. Historically, ethical development has involved extending moral standing to larger and larger classes of humans. Modern environmental ethics considers the extension of moral standing to the non-human world, as pictured in Figure 9.1.

Entities possess moral standing for a reason, and that reason is generally some morally important feature of the entity. Each of the different types of ethical theory that we examined in the first eight chapters requires the entities to which it applies to have a different type of feature. Ethical egoism grants moral standing only to the self. Hedonistic utilitarianism requires entities with moral standing to have psychological experiences and sensations. A hedonistic utilitarian calculation can only count an entity as having moral standing if the entity can experience pains and pleasures, and so cannot count plants in its moral calculations. Preference-satisfaction utilitarianism requires entities to have wants and desires in order to have moral standing. Teleological consequentialism requires morally considerable entities to have natural purposes. Common good consequentialism permits only communities to have moral standing, not individuals. Rights-based theories require entities with moral standing to have one of autonomy, subjective interests, or objective interests, depending on the variant. Theories of justice require us to point to some morally relevant difference between entities that have moral standing and entities that do not.

Arguing that distant people have moral standing is thus straightforward. Nearby people have moral standing in all the ethical theories that we have considered, except ethical egoism

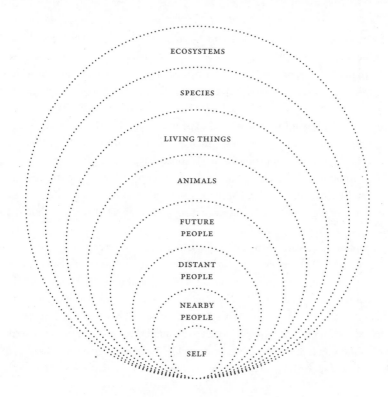

FIGURE 9.1: Expanding circles of ethical concern

and possibly the community-based version of objective consequentialism. Distant people have all the same natural features as nearby people. Whatever natural feature is sufficient for moral standing in these theories, distant people have it also. Therefore, distant people must also have moral standing.

The only difference between nearby people and distant people is their physical distance from us. Should physical distance be a morally relevant feature grounding differential moral concern? We can assess the moral relevance of physical distance by considering the converse situation. Suppose Sally lives near to her mother in Sydney, Australia. We, and she, all recognize that she can have moral obligations to her mother. Her mother then moves to London, England. Do Sally's moral obligations to her mother disappear when her mother moves to a distant country? If not, then this suggests that physical distance does not affect moral standing. Moral standing is not like a radio signal that becomes weaker at greater distances from the transmitter.

ETHICAL EGOISM AND DISTANT PEOPLE

To the ethical egoist, only the self has moral standing. Other nearby people, people not yet born, and the non-human environment have no moral standing. It follows immediately that distant people have no moral standing either. In the contractarian variant of ethical egoism, ethical egoists will welcome a coercively imposed system of private property rights and contract law that enables them to cooperate and avoid the war of all against all. Such a system will not extend, however, to people outside the circle of cooperation, and so will not extend to distant people.

In an influential 1974 paper, "Living on a Lifeboat," Garrett Hardin gave both utilitarian and ethical egoist reasons for rich nations to adopt a policy of not helping poor nations (Hardin 1974). Hardin offered his metaphor that rich nations are similar to well-stocked lifeboats containing a comfortable number of people to support his ethical egoist argument. Poor nations are similar to over-crowded lifeboats stocked without sufficient food or other resources. Hardin thinks that people in rich lifeboats have no obligation to share their food with people in poor lifeboats, or to admit people from poor lifeboats onto their rich ones. To do either, he claimed, would exhaust the food and resource of the rich lifeboats more quickly. By analogy, people in rich nations, acting in their own self-interest, should not give food aid to people in poor countries.

The metaphor of self-sufficient lifeboats was more apt in 1974 than it is in an era when global interactions are more evident. Rich and poor nations are not isolated and self-sufficient as the metaphor would indicate, but are thoroughly connected. Firms from rich countries mine the mineral and fossil fuel resources of poor countries, utilize the agricultural land of poor southern countries to grow tropical crops for rich northern consumers, employ inexpensive labour in poor country factories to manufacture goods for sale in rich countries, and emit pollutants that do not respect national boundaries. When rich lifeboats interact economically with poor lifeboats, the rhetorical force of the metaphor is much weaker.

UTILITARIANISM AND DISTANT PEOPLE

Distant people have the capacity for pain and pleasure just as nearby people do. Distant people have preferences that they want to satisfy, just as nearby people do. For utilitarians, the question about distant people is not one of moral standing. Instead, it is a question of the extent of our obligations to distant people. On one side of the question, Garrett Hardin, in his lifeboat article, offered a utilitarian argument against obligations of foreign aid to supplement his ethical egoist argument described above. On the other side of the question, Peter Singer, in a 1972 article, "Famine, Affluence, and Morality," written in response to a famine in what is now Bangladesh, offered a utilitarian argument for strong obligations of foreign aid. Both of these arguments accept the moral standing of distant people, but come to different conclusions based on different assumptions.

Hardin assumes that the human population of a country, like the population of organisms in any ecosystem, will exhibit exponential growth in the presence of an adequate food supply. The population will then experience a dieback once it surpasses the carrying capacity of the country or ecosystem. The CARRYING CAPACITY of a species in an ecosystem is the number of individual organisms it can support indefinitely given its fixed resources. A population experiences GEOMETRIC GROWTH when the change in the size of the population in each generation is proportional to the size of the population in the preceding generation. Geometric growth approximates exponential growth when the length of a generation becomes small. We can see how population growth is geometric if we imagine a simple model in which each generation of organisms produces two babies for each adult (four babies per female). The first generation will have 2 members, the second will have 4, the third will have 8, the fourth will have 16, and so on. As time goes forward, the rate of growth of the population will increase. Table 9.2 shows examples of linear and geometric growth for a series of numbers.

GENERATION	1	2	3	4	5	6
LINEAR GROWTH	2	4	6	8	10	12
GEOMETRIC GROWTH	2	4	8	16	32	64

FIGURE 9.1: Examples of linear and geometric growth of a series of numbers

A given ecosystem can feed only a certain number of any organisms in a sustainable way. The population of the ecosystem may over-shoot its carrying capacity for a time, but eventually there will be a dieback in the population to a new carrying capacity. Because of the environmental degradation caused by overpopulation, the new carrying capacity will likely be lower than the old one. The graph in Figure 9.2 pictures geometric population growth past carrying capacity followed by a dieback to below the original carrying capacity.

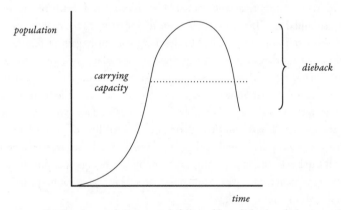

FIGURE 9.2: Geometric population growth followed by a dieback to below carrying capacity

Without aid, the population of a poor country will be in equilibrium at its carrying capacity. Hardin argued, however, that giving food aid each time there is a famine in a poor country will create a "ratchet effect" that will raise the population of a poor country well above its carrying capacity. Finally, a food emergency with which donated food aid cannot cope will cause catastrophic hardship to huge numbers of people. Because of the great dieback in population, the consequences created by the ratchet effect will be much worse than the consequences that would have happened if rich countries originally had given no food aid, and the population of the poor country had reached its natural equilibrium. Hardin concluded that to minimize the catastrophic consequences, rich countries should not give food aid to poor countries. This is a utilitarian argument against food aid and other assistance. Hardin extended this argument to future generations, arguing that huge outflows of food assistance and exponential population growth in poor countries will result in environmental ruin for future citizens of rich countries.

Peter Singer, on the other hand, argued in favour of food aid to famine-stricken poor regions like Bengal in 1971. Singer begins his argument with the utilitarian premise that

> ... if it is in our power to prevent something bad from happening, without thereby sacrificing anything of comparable moral importance, we ought, morally, to do it. (1972: 231)

We can see this to be a principle that maximizes good consequences by thinking as follows. If we sacrifice something of less moral importance to prevent a harm of greater moral importance, then we will increase the moral goodness of the world. If we go on doing this until the moral importance of what we sacrifice is equal to the moral importance of the harm that we prevent, then we will maximize moral goodness. If we continue and sacrifice something of greater moral importance to prevent something of lesser moral importance, then we will start to decrease the moral goodness of the world, which would be the wrong thing for a utilitarian to do.

Singer then assumes that the suffering and death caused by lack of food and other necessities is bad. It follows from these two premises that individuals in rich countries who can donate to famine relief without causing comparable suffering and death to themselves or their dependents should do so. They should continue to donate up to the point at which their marginal utility loss from donating is equal to the marginal utility gain to famine-stricken Bengalis. Singer points out that we may find equalizing marginal utility in order to maximize total utility too demanding, so that utilitarianism is asking us to do something that we are unable to do. For example, what Singer appears to advocate is that while there are starving children anywhere in the world, people are obligated to take food away from their own children (leaving just enough to keep them alive) in order to save the lives of the starving children. He suggests, however, that we are morally obliged to make the world better, even if we cannot make it the best it can be. If we can prevent great harm by sacrificing something with a small amount of moral significance, then we are obliged to do so. He argues for his principles with his well-known drowning-child analogy,

> ... if I am walking past a shallow pond and see a child drowning in it, I ought to wade in and pull the child out. This will mean getting my clothes muddy, but this is insignificant, while the death of the child would presumably be a very bad thing. (1972: 231)

Proximity or distance, he argues, is morally arbitrary. It is just as important that he help a Bengali child as a neighbour's child. No principle of equal consideration of interests will discriminate between people based on how far away they are. Nor does he think that lack of knowledge of the consequences of our actions, caused by our distance from the famine, should keep us from donating. Aid agencies, working in famine-stricken areas, compensate for our ignorance by directing aid to needy people.

He also uses the drowning child analogy to argue that it makes no difference to his (or our) obligations that there are millions of people who could also donate to famine relief, but do not do so. He asks the rhetorical question,

Should I consider that I am less obliged to pull the drowning child out of the pond if on looking around I see other people, no further away than I am, who have also noticed the child but are doing nothing? (1972: 233)

This question shows the absurdity of thinking that if others could help, but do not, then this somehow lessens our moral obligations.

Singer concludes that utilitarian reasoning applied to foreign aid and disaster relief will lead to a radical change in our ethical conceptual scheme. Our obligations are far more stringent than we think. Acts, like donating to disaster relief, that we have previously judged to be charitable, we can now see to be moral obligations. He implicitly disagrees with Hardin's objection that food aid will lead, through a ratchet effect, to great future suffering and death through catastrophic diebacks. He claims that our concern must be with relieving suffering now, and that this concern outweighs a concern with what might possibly happen in the future.

THE RIGHTS OF DISTANT PEOPLE

Distant people have the same capacities for autonomous choice that nearby people do. Distant people have the same important interests that nearby people need rights to protect. For rights-based theories, the question is not whether distant people have rights, but what rights they have with respect to us.

The rights of people in poor countries impose correlative duties on other people, including the citizens of rich countries. The responsibilities on the citizens of rich countries and their governments will depend, in part, on whether citizens of poor countries have positive or negative rights. Positive rights impose correlative duties of assistance on others; negative rights impose correlative duties of non-interference.

The existence of positive rights is controversial. For example, libertarian political philosophers deny that people have any positive duties of assistance toward others, only negative duties not to interfere with them or harm them in any way. Proponents of positive human rights do see the rights of distant people as imposing duties of assistance on all of us. For example, the twenty-fifth and twenty-sixth articles of the Universal Declaration of Human Rights, adopted and proclaimed by UN General Assembly resolution 217 A (III) of 10 December 1948, reads as follows:

Article 25
(1) Everyone has the right to a standard of living adequate for the health and
well-being of himself and of his family, including food, clothing, housing and
medical care and necessary social services, and the right to security in the event
of unemployment, sickness, disability, widowhood, old age or other lack of liveli-
hood in circumstances beyond his control.
(2) Motherhood and childhood are entitled to special care and assistance.
All children, whether born in or out of wedlock, shall enjoy the same
social protection.

Article 26

(1) Everyone has the right to education. Education shall be free, at least in the elementary and fundamental stages. Elementary education shall be compulsory. Technical and professional education shall be made generally available and higher education shall be equally accessible to all on the basis of merit.

If the governments of wealthy countries properly recognized the Universal Declaration of Human Rights, then they would pursue the Millennium Development Goals much more vigorously than they do at present.

The positive rights articulated in the Universal Declaration of Human Rights are not as demanding of the citizens of rich countries as are the obligations generated by Singer's utilitarian reasoning. The human rights of articles twenty-five and twenty-six are rights to a basic minimum level of welfare, a level that would not be that costly for rich countries to fund. The strong utilitarian principle would require that transfers of wealth continue until the marginal utility loss in rich countries equalled the marginal utility gain in poor countries. Maximizing total welfare in this way would be very costly for rich countries, and not something that their citizens would accept.

Negative rights impose a correlative duty on others not to interfere with our activities. Examples are private property rights, which block others from interfering with how we use what we own, and liberties, which are negative rights to do as we choose so long as we do not cause harm to others. Libertarians believe that people do not have positive rights, or rights to the aid or help of others. On the face of it, there are no duties to provide foreign aid in a libertarian political philosophy.

Thomas Pogge objects to this simple conclusion because it neglects the way that rich countries have violated the negative rights of citizens of poor countries in the past, and are continuing to violate them now (Pogge 2001). The simple libertarian conclusion assumes, as Garrett Hardin does, that rich and poor countries are isolated and self-sufficient. Libertarians, he argues, think as though distant people were like newly discovered inhabitants of the planet Venus. Even if the Venusians were very poor, and we could transport goods to them very cheaply, we would have no negative duties to help them. We might think we have positive duties to assist them, but libertarians do not believe in positive rights.

However, on Earth, the actual relationship of rich and poor countries has involved a history of violent conquest, colonization, and expropriation. For example, the Spanish conquest of Mexico in the sixteenth century killed a huge number of native Mexicans through warfare and disease, forcibly converted most native Mexicans to Christianity, and involved the theft of large amounts of gold and silver.

Such violations of the negative rights of distant people continue into the present. For example, Pogge notes that when the corrupt dictator of a poor country incurs a debt in his nation's name and then transfers the proceeds to his Swiss bank account, the citizens of the poor country must pay this debt. Negotiations between a dictator and a bank on Wall Street decided on the loan. Yet, international laws hold the citizens collectively liable for a loan on which they did not decide. International law, backed by the threat of sanctions, insists on repayment of such a debt, and violates the negative rights of citizens of poor countries.

The firms and citizens of rich countries are extracting non-renewable resources from the world, and using the assimilative capacities of the world's oceans and atmosphere, at an increasing rate. On a libertarian view of the initial acquisition of previously un-owned property, this is acceptable only if it leaves enough, and as good, for others, including distant people in poor countries. Of course, it is not leaving enough, and as good, for the poor and distant. Nevertheless, this would still not violate their rights, on the modified version of Locke's theory, if the poor and distant were benefiting from this resource extraction. On the contrary, Pogge argues, the number of people living in extreme poverty in countries around the world shows that the "enough, and as good" proviso is not being met, in violation of the negative rights of distant poor people.

The weakness of the simple libertarian account of our obligations to distant people is that it fails to take into account how people, firms, and governments near to us have violated, and are violating, the negative rights of distant people. For these rights violations, justice requires that the rich countries and their citizens pay compensation. Foreign aid is not charity; it is recompense.

TREATING DISTANT PEOPLE AS EQUALS

Treating people as equals requires that governments, organizations, and individuals do not treat them differently based on morally arbitrary features. Examples of morally arbitrary features include race, sex, age, sexual orientation, economic class, and family relationships to those in power. Is citizenship or country of birth a morally arbitrary feature of people?

Rawls thinks that any person who could completely discount all the morally arbitrary features of people, like their race, sex, and so on, would choose his social contract theory. To visualize this, he imagines people meeting to choose the principles of justice in a hypothetical original position behind a veil of ignorance where they were unaware of their own, morally irrelevant, personal characteristics like social status or level of natural abilities.

Should we apply this procedure to distant people? Should distant people be included in the hypothetical original position? Should people behind the veil of ignorance be aware of their citizenship? If Rawls's theory of justice did apply to distant people, then his difference principle, which permits inequalities only if they benefit the least advantaged, would entail that people in wealthy, developed countries have a justice-based reason for aiding people in developing countries.

Rawls himself thought that his theory of justice applied only to people who were part of the same system of social cooperation. Therefore, he thought that national borders, place of birth, and citizenship were not morally arbitrary. He thought, instead, that citizens of rich countries owed a duty of assistance to people in poor countries. This duty of assistance had a cut-off point, which was reached when the poor country was wealthy enough to institute a just society of its own. The world has changed since 1971 when Rawls was writing. Globalization has brought previously separate economies and self-sufficient nations together into a common system of cooperation. Philosophers like Thomas Pogge have disagreed with Rawls, claiming that treating people as equals requires accepting that citizenship is a morally arbitrary feature of persons, and claiming that the difference principle does require rich countries to redistribute resources to the least advantaged citizens of poor countries.

SUMMARY

1. Each type of ethical theory requires that entities with moral standing have certain features. Possession of these features is a necessary condition for the theory to apply to the entities.

2. To argue that an entity has moral standing, we must argue that it has a feature that is required by a type of ethical theory, that this ethical theory is a good one, and that the feature in question is sufficient for the entity to have moral standing in the theory.

3. Distant people share all the features of nearby people who do have moral standing. Physical distance is a morally arbitrary feature of people; people do not lose their moral standing when they relocate to greater distances.

4. The ethical question regarding distant people is not their moral standing. It is to determine the extent of our moral obligations to them.

5. Ethical egoism and contractarianism claim we have no moral obligations to distant people.

6. Garrett Hardin gave a utilitarian argument that giving food aid will eventually lead, through a ratchet effect, to great suffering in poor countries. This will happen because of a population dieback that he predicts will happen after geometric growth pushes population over carrying capacity.

7. Peter Singer gave a utilitarian argument in favour of food aid. He argued that rich people should, ideally, donate to famine victims so as to equalize marginal utility between rich and poor, and thus maximize total utility. Since "ought" implies "can," and if equalizing is too demanding, the rich still have an obligation to make the world better by donating what is of small significance to them.

8. If distant poor people have positive rights to food and other necessities, then these impose correlative duties of assistance on rich people in other countries.

9. If distant poor people have only negative rights, then libertarians can argue that rich countries have no duties to help them.

10. Against the simple libertarian position, Thomas Pogge argues that a history of colonial violence, unjust international law, and rich country appropriation of non-renewable natural resources are clear violations of the negative rights of distant poor people.

11. John Rawls thought that since we do not cooperate with distant people, then they are outside his social contract theory. Rich nations owe poor nations duties of assistance, but not the obligations of distributive justice

spelled out in his difference principle. Other philosophers have disagreed, arguing that citizenship is morally arbitrary, and that distributive justice should be global in extent.

ONLINE READING QUESTIONS

The book's website contains online reading on this chapter. Working through these questions will help you understand, remember, and apply important concepts from the chapter. Some of the questions supply useful hints for the study questions.

STUDY QUESTIONS

Using the text and hints from the online reading questions, write out, type, dictate to your computer, or at least formulate in your head answers to the following questions.

1. Describe Hardin's lifeboat ethics argument that rich countries have no obligations to poor and distant people.
2. What is the simple libertarian position on the obligations of the rich to poor and distant people?
3. Describe how human rights like those in the UN charter entail obligations of rich countries to poor and distant people.
4. Describe Hardin's ratchet effect argument that rich countries have no obligations to poor and distant people.
5. Describe Singer's drowning child example and explain, in a simple fashion, how he uses it to argue that we have obligations to poor and distant people.
6. Explain why international distributive justice apparently applies to economic relations between rich countries and poor countries.

QUESTIONS TO PONDER

Spend a few minutes thinking about the following questions, or, better yet, discuss them with fellow readers of this book.

1. The empirical theory of the benign demographic transition holds that as people become richer, and as children become more expensive to raise, have a better chance of surviving to be adults, and as people can count on pension funds when they retire and will not need the support of their children, people will voluntarily choose to have less children. What effect would the existence of a benign demographic transition have on Hardin's ratchet effect argument?
2. Do the benefits of industrialization in rich countries trickle down to distant poor people in a way that adequately compensates them for the rich countries using up non-renewable resources? Are the poorest people

in Africa better off now than they would have been if they had no history of interaction with Europeans? How is this relevant to the negative rights of Africans?

3. If Pogge is right about the violation of the negative rights of the poor and distant by the nearby and rich, what does this imply about the compensation that the rich owe to the poor and distant? Does this raise issues of retributive justice?

4. Is citizenship morally relevant to distributive justice, as the social contract theory of John Rawls would claim? Alternatively, is citizenship morally arbitrary, as the critics of Rawls claim? Should the difference principle therefore govern distributive justice between rich and poor countries?

5. Hardin thinks we have a utilitarian reason for avoiding population diebacks in the future. Singer thinks that the need to stop hunger, starvation, and malnutrition in the present outweighs worries about what might happen to future generations. Who is right and why?

Chapter 10

FUTURE
GENERATIONS

MANY ENVIRONMENTAL ISSUES ARE OF LITTLE CONSEQUENCE FOR PEOPLE LIVING now, but will become major problems for people who are alive in the future. For example, the emission of greenhouse gasses, such as carbon dioxide and methane, is causing only mild climate change today, showing up now as heat waves and the melting of polar ice. But one hundred years in the future, if the world continues with business as usual, its effects may include severe droughts, decreased food production, flooding of low-lying coastal areas in countries such as Bangladesh, and the forced migration of millions of people. The disposal of radioactive waste from nuclear reactors, the depletion of non-renewable resources such as fossil fuels, and the exhaustion of agricultural resources by soil erosion, are causing small problems now, but have the potential to be severe problems for people not yet born. None of us, however, will be alive in a hundred years, so why should we care about what happens to future people?

Many people are ethically committed to the idea of sustainable development, which the Brundtland Report of 1987 defined as "development that meets the needs of the present without compromising the ability of future generations to meet their own needs." Many farmers are committed to the idea of sustainable agriculture, agricultural processes that do not undermine our future capacity to successfully practice agriculture. We should have ethical reasons for these commitments, yet developing these is not as easy as it might seem. Extending moral standing to future generations creates some conceptual puzzles that environmental policy-makers should be aware of, and take into consideration in their analyses.

Learning Objectives

1. To understand what ethical egoist, contractarian, deontological, utilitarian, and justice-based approaches say about our obligations to future generations.
2. To understand some of the conceptual problems with the deontological approach regarding duties to posterity.
3. To understand some of the weaknesses of the utilitarian approach to obligations to future generations.
4. To understand the idea of discounting the interests of future generations and the effects of the choice of discount rate.
5. To understand some of the reasons people give for discounting the future, and the weaknesses of these reasons.

ETHICAL EGOISM AND FUTURE GENERATIONS

We will begin our survey of ethical theories and obligations to future generations with ethical egoism. Ethical egoism claims that the only entity with moral standing is oneself. So agents have no obligations to any people but themselves. Therefore, they have no obligations to future people.

Ethical egoism still has all the problems we have looked at before. For example, the ultimatum game shows that people are able to consider more than their own interests, and thus that the empirical theory, psychological egoism, on which ethical egoism is based, is false. The prisoner's dilemma game shows that consistent ethical egoists will have difficulty cooperating, and will thus be condemned to lives that are "nasty, brutish, and short." Ethical egoism is still an arbitrary approach because ethical egoists cannot point to any non-arbitrary feature of the self that other people do not share. Thus, it is difficult to accept the ethical egoist position in general, let alone in its conclusion that we have no obligations to future generations.

The contractarian approach allows ethical egoism to escape some of the difficulties of pure ethical egoism, but it, too, leads to the conclusion that we have no obligations to future generations. Agents need consider only other agents with whom they have entered into mutually advantageous, coercively enforced arrangements to avoid prisoner's dilemma type situations. Agents cannot make such contracts with future people because future people do not exist to contract with. Thus, agents have no obligation to future people. The typical contractarian lament is, "What has posterity done for me?" Again though, the contractarian approach is still susceptible to all the weaknesses of ethical egoism except its difficulty with cooperation. Contractarianism is still based on an implausible theory of human nature, psychological egoism. Contractarians are still susceptible to the paradox of egoism, which means some good things like true friendship are unavailable to them.

The deontological approach holds that what ethically matters is the principle that a moral agent follows when performing an action, and not the consequences of the action, or the character of the agent. In a natural rights version of deontology, duties are always correlative duties owed to the particular person who possesses natural rights. Natural rights are the rights of some particular person; they create correlative duties because of features that this particular person has. An existing person who actually has the capacity for autonomous choice has a natural right to liberty because of his or her actual possession of that feature. An existing person has a property right to an object because of a chain of actual historical transactions connecting him or her to an act of initial acquisition. This creates conceptual difficulties when we try to talk of correlative duties to people who are not yet born. A rights-based, deontological approach that requires direct correlative duties to particular people has difficulties accounting for the moral standing of unborn generations. The difficulties arise either because particular future people do not exist or because our policies will change the particular people who do exist in the future.

The first conceptual difficulty with applying the natural rights approach to future generations is the Temporal Location Argument. It goes like this:

1. Correlative duties are always direct duties to some particular person.
2. If a particular person does not exist, then we cannot have duties to him or her.
3. Future people do not exist.
4. Therefore, agents have no correlative duties to future people.

Another way of thinking of this conceptual problem goes as follows. Present people have no duties to imaginary people, such as Harry Potter, because imaginary people do not exist. However, future people do not exist either. Therefore, present people have no obligations to future generations of people. The problem arises because of the conceptual structure of rights. Rights alwasy require current duties to some particular person or entity, and future persons do not now exist and so cannot be the bearers of natural rights. This problem also arises for rights theorists who extend moral standing to entities other than people. Someone who believes in animal rights will have difficulty explaining why moral agents have duties to future animals.

The consequences of the Temporal Location Argument for the rights-based approach are very counter-intuitive. Before we were born, we did not exist. Before we were born, the previous generation had no obligations to our generation. Therefore, prior to our births, the previous generation had no obligation to conserve natural resources, or reduce pollution, for our generation. Similarly, we have no duty to future generations to mitigate greenhouse gas emissions, take care of our toxic waste, or preserve non-renewable resources. Unfortunately, the conceptual situation gets even worse.

A second way that correlative duties to a particular person cause conceptual difficulties for the rights-based approach is the Disappearing Beneficiaries Argument. The problem arises because of the extreme contingency of people. Who one is depends on one's genetic makeup, which, in turn, depends on which sperm fertilizes which egg at conception. If a person's parents had never met, or had met at a different time, or had not had sex at a particular time, or if another one of the millions of sperm produced by the father had won the race to fertilize the egg, then that person would not have been born. Other people would have been born instead. The coming into existence of any particular person is a very delicate matter that different circumstances could easily have changed.

If we accept the premise of the contingency of persons, then the Disappearing Beneficiaries Argument goes like this:

1. Correlative duties are always direct duties to a particular person.
2. The circumstances of one's conception determine who one is.
3. Different environmental policies will result in different people meeting and/or different times of conception.
4. Therefore, different environmental policies will result in different particular people being born in the future.
5. Therefore, policymakers have no correlative duties to any particular persons in the future to implement any particular environmental policies.

We would like ethics to give some guidance regarding the goals of environmental policy. For example, if we pursue policies that are more stringent on carbon dioxide emissions, then people may travel less. If people travel less, then they are likely to meet and mate with different people than they would have under a business-as-usual policy. Consequently, over a hundred years, climate change mitigation is likely to result in a completely different set of people being born than would have been born under a business-as-usual policy. The duty-based approach does not give much guidance here on what we should do. Do we owe the people born under climate change mitigation a duty to pursue climate change mitigation? Alternatively, do we owe the people born under business-as-usual a duty to pursue business as usual? If duties and rights are always duties to particular persons or the rights of particular persons, then duties and rights do not give ethical guidance to policymakers.

One way to argue for something like the moral standing of future generations within a rights-based approach would be to argue that present children have a natural right that present adults preserve the planet's environment and resources. Thus, present adults (generation A) owe a duty to present children (generation B) to preserve the planet for them. In another generation, these present children (B) will themselves be adults and will owe a duty to children in generation C to preserve the planet for generation C. In another generation, generation C will owe a preservation duty to a new generation D, and so on. Even though, at the present time generation A has no determinable duties to generation D, the whole structure of inter-generational duties will have the same results as though generation D did have moral standing for generation A.

THE UTILITARIAN APPROACH
TO FUTURE GENERATIONS

It appears that utilitarians can avoid the conceptual problems faced by the deontological approach. First, when a consequentialist agent is making a decision, the consequences are always in the future. Thus, utilitarians should have no problem with Temporal Location Argument. Second, utilitarians are not concerned with particular persons, but only with the satisfaction of preferences, the production of pleasure, or the avoidance of pain. It does not matter who has these preferences, pleasures, or pains. So it does not matter which set of people is the beneficiary of an environmental policy. Hence, utilitarianism has no problem with the Disappearing Beneficiaries Argument.

Accounting for obligations to future generations, however, raises a whole other set of problems for the utilitarian approach: ignorance of the future, population policy, whether to discount future lives, and how much to discount future preferences.

The first problem for the utilitarian approach regarding obligations to future generations is the Argument from Ignorance. It begins by observing that present people know very little about people who will be born far in the future, say, a hundred years from now. We are very uncertain about who will be born, what they will need, want, or be interested in, what technology they will possess, or even if any people at all will exist in the distant future. Yet we need to know what people are like in order to know what consequences our actions will have for them, and so what our obligations to them are. For example, if future people invent cheap fusion power, then we do not need to conserve fossil fuels for them. To the extent that present people do not have sufficient information about future people, present people have no obligations to them. Another form of ignorance is about the long-term effects of our actions. In some cases, we can predict them, but in many cases, especially regarding very long-term effects, we just do not know.

We can make a reasonably satisfactory reply to this argument that covers some of the uncertainties. We do know that future people will have certain basic interests. Whatever their lives are like, they will need sufficient food, clean, safe air and water, and a liveable climate. Thus, we have an obligation not to make the world such that they cannot satisfy those basic interests. We know, for example, that climate change is going to make their lives more difficult than otherwise, no matter what particular preferences may be in fashion in the far future. But the reply does not cover all cases. What we should do now to mitigate climate change will depend in part on how rich and technologically sophisticated future people will be. Some people argue that we owe posterity no obligation to mitigate climate change because future people will be so rich that they can easily absorb the costs of adaptation to the new climate.

A second problem with applying utilitarianism to future generations is the conclusions to which it appears to lead regarding population policy. There are two ways to understand the utilitarian injunction to cause the maximum amount of net utility. Average utilitarianism says that policies should bring about the highest possible amount of net utility per person. Total utilitarianism says that policies should bring about the highest possible amount of net utility without regard to how many persons the policy spreads that utility across. As long as the number of persons is the same in two policies that we are ethically assessing, then it does not matter which variety we use. In the near term, most environmental policies have no effect on the number of people affected by the policy. In the far future, this assumption breaks down. Environmental policies, which include population policies, will have an effect on the number of people alive in the far future. Environmental and population policy can change the size of future generations.

Total utilitarianism has what the philosopher Derek Parfit, who first pointed out the problem, called a "repugnant conclusion." If we can increase the total utility in the world by adding one more person, then we should do so. If the added person is even slightly happy, then the addition of that person will increase the total happiness. We should go on increasing the human population as long as each additional person is marginally happy. Total utilitarianism implies a population policy that keeps increasing the number of people in the world, even at the expense of environmental degradation, until the point at which the total world happiness begins to decline. This will result in an average level of happiness that is very low, even though it maximizes the total happiness. Most people will find this conclusion repugnant.

Unfortunately, average utilitarianism also has a difficulty once we consider applying it to the future and allow the possibility of changing the population size. Average utilitarianism enjoins us to adopt policies that result in the maximum amount of happiness per person. It follows that if anyone is born whose life will have less than the present average level of happiness, then that person will bring the average down. Thus, we should prevent from being born any person who is likely to be depressed or less happy than the average. This conclusion is also repugnant. It is likely possible, however, for the indirect version of average utilitarianism to avoid this difficulty. This version would argue that the implementation of such a population policy would cause so much anxiety among would-be parents that the utility costs of implementation would outweigh any effects of unhappy children on the average level of happiness.

A third problem for the utilitarian approach is that it appears to discount, or count for less, the lives of people born in the future. To see this problem, we need to consider the economic utilitarian argument for discounting the future. How much should a person be willing to pay now to get a $100 item that she wants very much, but which she will not receive until a year later? Would she pay $100 now? The answer is no, if she is reasoning rationally as an economic utilitarian would. An economic utilitarian will argue that she can get, say, a 7% return by investing her money in the stock market. If she will not get the item for a year then she should take $93 plus change now and invest it in the stock market. Then in a year's time, she should take the money, now $100, out of the stock market and buy the item. That way, it will have cost her only $93 plus change. To figure out the present value of a future cost, she should discount it by the relevant percentage rate. We call this percentage the DISCOUNT RATE. When economic utilitarians do cost-benefit analyses, the choice of discount rate is crucial to their policy recommendations. The discount rate that we should use in environmental economics is a huge ethical question, as will become clear in what follows.

We should also discount environmental costs that will fall on future generations when comparing them to costs in the present. The amount by which we should discount future costs can be quite large because of the power of compound interest. When someone is calculating the value of a $100 investment in the bank at 7% interest after 10 years, he should not just add $7 ten times to get $170. He should reason as follows: At the end of 1 year, he will have $107. In the second year, he will receive interest not on $100, but on $107. Thus at the end of the second year, he will receive $107, at 7% in interest, which is more than $7. His interest will compound. We could use a spreadsheet or financial calculator to calculate the future value (FV) of an investment whose present value is PV after t years at an interest rate of r. Instead, we will avail ourselves of a little trick that enables us to look at distant future values by estimating the doubling time of a present value at different interest rates.

To estimate the doubling time of a present value for a given interest (discount) rate we will use either the Rule of 70 or the Rule of 72. These rules are only approximations, so we will choose the version that makes the arithmetic easiest. To estimate doubling time use the

1. Rule of 70 for discount rates of 2%, 5%, 7%, 10%, 12%, 14%, which all divide nicely into 70 without remainder, or
2. Rule of 72 for discount rates of 3%, 4%, 6%, 8%, 9%, which all divide into 72 without remainder.

To apply one of the rules, we divide either 70 or 72 by the discount rate that we are considering. This gives the doubling time.

RULE OF 70	2%			5%		7%			10%	12%	14%
RULE OF 72		3%	4%		6%		8%	9%			
DOUBLING TIME	35	24	18	14	12	70/7=10	9	8	7	6	5 years

TABLE 10.1: Doubling (or halving) times at various discount rates

For example, using the Rule of 70, at a discount rate of 7%, the doubling time equals 70 divided by 7, which equals 10. At an interest rate of 7%, every 10 years the future value of an investment will double. Correspondingly, at a discount rate of 7%, every ten years the present value of a future cost will halve.

Now suppose that we want to know what happens in 50 years. In 50 years at 7%, a present value will double 5 times, that is, $2 \times 2 \times 2 \times 2 \times 2$, which is 32 times. Thus, at 7%, an investment of $1 will be worth $32 in 50 years. At a discount rate of 7%, after 50 years, we will need to use a discount factor of 32. Correspondingly, according to economic utilitarian reasoning, we should consider a cost of $32 incurred 50 years in the future to be the same as a cost of $1 in the present.

Discounting the future may seem a plausible way to proceed for investments and even costs in the short term, but it seems repugnant to apply this style of reasoning to human lives. Discounting the future seems wrong when applied to serious life and death concerns. If $1 today is worth $32 in 50 years, it seems to follow that one life today is worth 32 lives in the future. For example, if we are using economic utilitarian reasoning to evaluate a policy that saves 2 lives today but kills 32 people in the future, then we should save the 2 lives today at the expense of killing 32 people in 50 years. This is a controversial conclusion.

Utilitarian reasoning suggests that we should put a dollar value on the intensity of preferences and discount the intensity of future preferences according to some discount rate. A third problem for the utilitarian approach is determining what discount rate we should choose. The choice of discount rate has a large effect on what policy utilitarian reasoning will recommend.

Consider the following scenario drawn from a real environmental controversy. It models a debate between two economists, Nicholas Stern and William Nordhaus, about whether to take action now to prevent future climate change (Broome 2008). Both economists assume that climate change will cause one trillion dollars' worth of damage to the planet in 100 years. They agree that the cost, now, to prevent this damage is 50 billion dollars. The two economists, however, disagree about the appropriate discount rate: Stern says 1.4% while Nordhaus says 6%. We can use the rule of 70 (or 72) to show how the choice of discount rate affects the outcome of this cost-benefit analysis.

In Table 10.2, Stern chooses a discount rate of 1.4%. Using the rule of 70 for convenience, this gives an estimated doubling time of $70/1.4 = 50$ years. In 100 years, this will imply 2 doublings and a discount factor of $2 \times 2 = 4$. If the damage caused in 100 years is $1 trillion, then the present value of that future cost is 1/4 of $1 trillion, which is $250 billion. However, the present cost of climate change mitigation is only $50 billion, so Stern's policy advice is to reduce greenhouse gas emissions now.

Nordhaus, on the other hand, chooses a market discount rate of 6%. Using the rule of 72, this gives a doubling time of $72/6=12$ years. In 100 years, this will give $100/12=8.5$ doublings and a discount factor of 2 multiplied by itself 8.5 times, which is somewhat more than 256 ($2 \times 2 \times 2 \times 2 \times 2 \times 2 \times 2 \times 2 = 256$). If the damage caused in 100 years is $1 trillion, then the present value of that future cost is less than 1/256 of $1 trillion, which is less than $4 billion. However, the present cost of climate change mitigation is $50 billion, so Nordhaus's policy advice is not to reduce greenhouse gas emissions and instead leave climate change as a problem for future generations.

	STERN	NORDHAUS
Future value of damage in 100 years	$1 trillion	$1 trillion
Discount rate	1.4%	6%
Doubling (halving) time	$70/1.4 = 50$ years	$72/6 = 12$ years
Number of doublings (halvings)	$100/50 = 2$	$100/12 = 8.5$
Discount factor	$2 \times 2 = 4$	$2 \times 2 \times 2 \times 2 \times 2 \times 2 \times 2 \times 2 = 256+$
Present value of future damage	$250 billion	< $4 billion
Present cost of cleanup	$50 billion	$50 billion
Policy recommendation	Act now!	Delay!

TABLE 10.2: Effect of the choice of discount on policy recommendations

At least three ethical considerations affect our choice of a discount rate: pure time preferences, market discount rates, and the likelihood of a richer future.

In our own lives, we prefer to have something valuable now to having it in the future, or to pay a cost in the future rather than pay it now. This is partly due to impatience and procrastination (psychological) and partly due to knowing that there is a chance we will not be around in the future (risk). The technical term for this phenomenon is "pure time preference." The problem is that the choice of discount rate in a problem involving future generations involves comparisons between different lives, not a choice within a life. Pure time preference is relevant to choices within a life but not between different people's lives. If Tom is impatient and Vera is not, then it is not fair to impose Tom's implicit discount rate on Vera, or vice versa, without further justification.

Economists like to believe that economics is a science that does not make value judgments. Thus, they prefer to use a discount rate that they believe is revealed in the market. One such rate is the interest rate on investments that will induce people to postpone consumption now and invest their money for the future. People can usually get a 6% return on a not too risky investment in the financial market. Economists also argue that using the discount rate revealed in the market is democratic because it leaves ethical decisions to the public. There are several problems with this argument.

First, it is again illegitimate to argue from the principles that people do use to make decisions within their own lives (for example, their investment decisions regarding their own old age) to the principles that people should use to make decisions respecting the lives of different people in future generations.

Second, the market uses many different interest rates. There is the overnight bank rate determined by the central bank. There is the prime rate at which banks lend to their biggest customers. There are the mortgage rate, the rate of interest paid on savings accounts, the rate available on treasury bonds, the rate available on long-term government bonds, the rate available on corporate bonds, and the rate of return available in the stock market. They all differ from one another, and it is not at all clear which one we should use as the discount rate when dealing with future costs.

Third, it is not clear that the expression of preference for a certain interest rate by consumers of investment products is a very good guide to the beliefs about value that citizens hold. Democracy does not mean following consumer preferences, it means debate and deliberation in the political process.

Fourth, this argument seems to violate the is/ought gap. From the fact that it *is* the case that people use a 6% discount rate when dealing with future costs, it does not immediately follow that it *ought* to be the case that they use a 6% discount rate to make policy decisions that affect future generations.

Income, like every other good thing, has a declining marginal utility. As income increases, each additional increment provides a smaller and smaller amount of satisfaction. An additional $100 means more to a poor student than it does to a billionaire like Bill Gates of Microsoft. If, because of economic growth, people are richer in the future than they are now, then environmental policies will maximize utility if future people bear a proportionately larger share of the costs of cleaning up pollution. Policymakers can incorporate this consideration into policy recommendations by using a higher discount rate for future costs. One problem with this suggestion is that, with potential environmental catastrophes like climate change, it may be false that growth will continue and that the future will indeed be a lot richer than the present.

INTERGENERATIONAL JUSTICE

As we have seen, utilitarian policy prescriptions frequently raise distributive justice issues. The utilitarian tells us to maximize expected net benefits, but the theory by itself tells us little about how to distribute these benefits. We can see this problem in Nordhaus's policy advice above. He tells us that we will maximize net economic benefits if the costs of climate change are borne by future generations. This seems intuitively unfair because the people who are benefitting from burning fossil fuels and thus causing climate change are the present generation (us). Usually we think it is fair that the polluter pays, not the victim. His reasoning says that we polluters should escape any costs of cleanup just because of the time of our birth and the discount rate he has chosen. This conclusion neglects consideration of inter-generational justice.

Justice requires that environmental policy treat people as equals. This does not mean that it should treat everyone the same. Treating people as equals requires that organizations do not treat them differently based on morally arbitrary features. Examples of morally arbitrary features include race, sexual orientation, economic class, and perhaps country of birth. The question for inter-generational justice is whether *time of birth* is a morally arbitrary feature of people.

One way to think about this is to use the thought experiment suggested by John Rawls that we have looked at before. Rawls thinks his theory of distributive justice would be chosen by any person who could completely discount all the morally arbitrary features of people like their race, sex, etc. To visualize this, he imagines people meeting to choose the principles of justice in a hypothetical "original position" behind a "veil of ignorance." Should people in the original position behind the veil of ignorance be aware of their time of birth or generational membership? If they were aware of their generational membership, would they assign differential benefits and burdens based on this feature? If we answer No to these questions then we have a theory of intergenerational justice.

Intergenerational justice is concerned with the *distribution* of rights and duties. A moral right is not, in itself, fair or unfair. What is fair or unfair is who has it. What is fair or unfair is the distribution of rights. For example, the distribution of people in a geographic region is not the same as the people themselves. The distribution may be even or uneven, lumpy or smooth; the people themselves are neither even nor uneven and neither lumpy nor smooth. Consequently, distributive justice is not concerned with particular people. It treats all people, present and future, as equals.

The intergenerational justice approach apparently avoids the conceptual problems of the natural rights approach that we discussed earlier. Neither the indirect utilitarian approach nor the social contract approach distributes legal rights to particular people based on the actual possession of a natural feature by a particular person. Instead, they distribute rights and duties to whoever it happens to be who occupies certain roles in society. For example, some people occupy the role of police officers, and people in civilian roles have a correlative duty to obey them. The right of a police officer to be obeyed is not a natural right created by some special feature of that particular police person. The right of a police officer to be obeyed goes with the role the officer occupies, and the duty to obey the officer goes with the role the civilian occupies. Rights and responsibilities are assigned to these roles within a worked out theory of distributive justice. In a similar way, a theory of intergenerational distributive justice could assign duties and responsibilities regarding future generations to the roles that we occupy in the present.

SUMMARY

1. Though it may seem obvious that environmental ethics should assign moral standing to future people, there are some conceptual problems with this idea.
2. As we might expect, ethical egoism and contractarianism, with their concern only for maximizing self-interest, assign no moral standing to future people.
3. The natural rights approach, which concentrates on direct duties owed to particular people, has difficulty assigning moral standing to people who do not yet exist, and gives us no ethical guidance when we must choose between policies that will affect the identities of who will be born in the future.
4. Utilitarianism is oriented toward the production of future consequences, but it has trouble because of our ignorance of what these consequences will be in the far future.
5. Utilitarianism must apply in either its average or total form, but both of these lead to unattractive conclusions when applied to population policy.
6. Utilitarian reasoning, in its economic form, leads to the problem of how to weight the interests of future generations through the choice of discount rate.
7. A theory of inter-generational justice may allow us to distribute rights and responsibilities between generations without having to worry about duties to particular persons.

ONLINE READING QUESTIONS

The book's website contains reading questions on this chapter. Working through these questions will help you understand, remember, and apply important concepts from the chapter. Some of the questions supply useful hints for the study questions.

Using the text and hints from the online reading questions, write out, type, dictate to your computer, or at least formulate in your head answers to the following questions.

1. Explain why a contractarian ethics implies that people have no obligations to future generations.
2. Why does the argument from temporal location conclude that we have no correlative duties to future people?
3. Why does the disappearing beneficiaries argument conclude that we have no correlative duties to future people?
4. Why does the argument from ignorance conclude that we have no utilitarian obligations to future people?
5. What is the "repugnant conclusion" and how does it pose a problem for utilitarian obligations to future generations?
6. Explain why pure time preference might produce high discount rates in a cost-benefit analysis.
7. Explain why economists wish to use market interest rates as discount rates in a cost-benefit analysis.
8. Why is future growth an argument for using a relatively high discount rate in a cost-benefit analysis?
9. What is inter-generational justice?

QUESTIONS TO PONDER

Spend a few minutes thinking about the following questions, or, better yet, discuss them with fellow readers of this book.

1. Unborn people will actually exist at future times. They will then have natural features like a capacity for autonomous choice, and, in the future, they will have historically justified property rights. Will they not also have rights against us, rights that we are currently violating by failing in our duty to preserve the environment for them?
2. Why do you think that Stern and Nordhaus differ in their choice of a discount rate? Who is right?
3. Experiments in behavioural economics show that people discount the future in an inconsistent fashion over time. For example, if offered either $100 today or $110 a year from today, many people would choose $100 today. However, if offered either $100 ten years from today or $110 eleven years from today, many people would choose $110 in eleven years. The implicit choice of a discount rate by these subjects changes with time. They use a discount rate of more than 10% per year today, but see their future selves as using a discount rate of less than 10% per year. How is this dynamic

inconsistency relevant when an economic utilitarian tries to specify an empirically determined discount rate?

4. If robots could be police officers, would civilians still have a duty to obey them? Would robot police officers have any natural features grounding their rights to be obeyed?

5. Do you think that the following modification of the rights-approach could provide a way that the rights-approach could recognize the rights of future generations? An action is wrong when it has the *potential* to violate *somebody's* rights. There is not any particular person whose rights you violate when you park in front of a fire hydrant, but were there a fire, somebody's right to have that looked after efficiently by the fire department could be violated.

Chapter 11

ANIMAL WELFARE

IN THIS CHAPTER, WE BEGIN TO LOOK AT THE ETHICAL REASONING INVOLVED IN extending moral standing to beings that are not human. We have previously considered the moral standing of distant people and future generations, but have remained within an anthropocentric view of moral standing. Now we will look at issues involved in non-anthropocentric, zoocentric views of the moral status of animals.

The moral status of animals is relevant to global environmental policymaking. The effects of climate change on human beings provide one sort of ethical reason for mitigating it. Do its effects on animal habitat and animal welfare provide an additional ethical reason for policies that mitigate climate change?

The moral status of animals is relevant to policies regarding animal agriculture. Should we ban, or heavily regulate, factory farming, to increase the welfare of farm animals? Should we ban the keeping of veal calves in movement restricting crates, or the keeping of laying hens in over-crowded battery cages? Should we regulate slaughterhouses, putting animal welfare concerns ahead of lowering economic costs? What kinds of animals can we legitimately eat: cattle, fish, lobsters, or insects? Should we even eat animals at all? Should we become vegetarians, eating eggs and dairy, or vegans, eating only plant products?

The moral status of animals is relevant to policies regarding scientific experimentation on animals. Under what conditions is it morally permissible to use animals in medical research? Is it ever morally permissible to use animals in the safety testing of cosmetics?

The moral status of animals is relevant to policies regarding the hunting and trapping of wild animals. Is it morally permissible to hunt animals for food or for sport? Are the hunting practices of indigenous hunter-gatherers morally permissible? Can animal biologists legitimately cull animals to preserve fragile ecosystems, especially when humans have already eliminated the other top predators? Is it ethically permissible to hunt down and kill a grizzly bear that has started to attack humans?

The moral status of animals is relevant to policies regarding the human use of animals for purposes other than food. Is it ethically permissible to use horses to pull carts or oxen to pull ploughs? Is it ethically permissible to spay, neuter, or curtail the natural behaviours of dogs and cats when we keep them as companion animals in our homes? Is it permissible for city zoos and aquariums to keep wild animals in captivity for educational and recreational purposes?

This chapter and the next offer no definitive answers to the above questions, but they do show how to think about these issues from the perspective of ethical theory. We will examine the utilitarian animal welfare perspective in this chapter, and the deontological animal rights perspective in the next.

Learning Objectives

1. To understand some of the reasons for assigning moral standing to a type of entity.
2. To understand the difference between the animal welfare and animal rights approaches.
3. To understand the connection between utilitarianism and the animal welfare approach.
4. To understand the influential utilitarian argument of Peter Singer for equal consideration of the interests of animals.
5. To understand some of the weaknesses of the utilitarian approach to ethical obligations to animals.

THE MORAL STANDING OF ANIMALS

Different types of ethical theory require that the entities to which they apply have different sorts of features. For example, a hedonistic utilitarian calculation can only count an entity as having moral standing if the entity can experience pains and pleasures. Hedonistic utilitarianism cannot count trees and other plants in its moral calculations. Teleological consequentialism can consider plants and other living things in its moral deliberations provided they have some way of flourishing. The will theory of rights cannot apply to plants because they have no capacity for autonomous choice. Nor can the subjective interest theory of rights apply to plants because plants cannot receive any psychological benefit from the satisfaction of their interests. The objective interest theory of rights, however may apply to plants because we may be able to use their teleological properties to make a case that plants can receive non-psychological benefits. Table 11.1 summarizes the features required for moral standing by various ethical theories.

TYPE OF ETHICAL THEORY	FEATURE REQUIRED FOR MORAL STANDING
Ethical egoism	*Self*
Hedonistic utilitarianism	*Psychological experiences and sensations*
Preference-satisfaction utilitarianism	*Wants and desires*
Teleological consequentialism	*Natural purposes, mode of flourishing*
Common good consequentialism	*Organized community*
Will theory of rights	*Autonomy*
Subjective interests rights	*Capacity for psychological benefit*
Objective interests rights	*Capacity for non-psychological benefit*

TABLE 11.1: Features required by various ethical theories for possession of moral standing

The capacity for mental sensations is *required for* moral standing in hedonistic utilitarianism because the theory uses them in its calculations. The capacity for psychological sensations is a *necessary condition* for moral consideration by hedonistic utilitarianism. Entities can have moral standing in the theory only if they have this capacity. However, we can still ask whether this capacity for mental sensations is *enough for* moral standing. The question of moral standing for the theory is the question whether the capacity for psychological sensations is a *sufficient condition* for moral standing in hedonistic utilitarianism. If entities have this capacity, then do they have moral standing in the theory? Many complex animals appear to experience pain and pleasure. Is this a sufficient condition for the moral standing of these animals in hedonistic utilitarianism, or must they have some other feature? Do they, for example, also have to be members of the species, *Homo sapiens*?

If the capacity for pain and pleasure were enough to give moral standing to human beings, would it be enough to give it to animals? Let us suppose that the only difference between the capacity for pain and pleasure in animals and the capacity for pain and pleasure in humans is that the latter occurs in members of the species, *Homo sapiens*. Is that a morally relevant distinction? None of the ethical theories that we have looked at explicitly limits its required features to features of the species, *Homo sapiens*. This is not a required feature for the application of any ethical theory. Let us suppose that human beings were to encounter extraterrestrials that had all the morally relevant features of human beings, except that they are members of an alien species. They are just as clever, kind, civil, fair-minded, brave, and benevolent as humans are. They live according to similar moral principles, and they have a similar emotional makeup. It would be morally arbitrary to deny that these sophisticated aliens had moral standing just because they were not human. Species membership is not, in itself, grounds for denying moral standing.

Can we point to a morally relevant distinction between humans and animals? It is surprisingly difficult to point to a feature that is morally relevant, possessed by all human beings, and not possessed by at least some animals. This latter caveat is important. Species of animals differ in the features that they have. If we were to decide that some particular feature was important for moral standing, it would then follow that only those animals that possessed this feature would have moral standing. Other species of animals without the feature would not have moral standing. Let us suppose, for the sake of an example, that the morally relevant feature is the capacity to form family ties. Humans can do this, mammals can do this, most birds can do so as well, but fish and many reptiles cannot. Therefore, if the capacity for family ties is the determinant of moral standing, then humans and dogs would have it, while salmon would not. Even if we successfully argue that some animals possess a feature sufficient for moral standing, there is still a problem demarcating which animals have this feature and which do not.

In contemporary environmental ethics, there are two influential forms of argument regarding the moral standing of animals. One is the utilitarian approach of Peter Singer, which is concerned with Animal Welfare. The other is the deontological approach of Tom Regan, which is concerned with Animal Rights.

One difference is that the animal welfare approach permits a trade-off between the interests of humans and the interests of animals. This trade-off follows from the utilitarian decision procedure, which involves measuring and aggregating the interests of both humans and animals, before deciding which course of action maximizes the total net benefits of all species considered together. For example, the animal welfare approach would decide the vegetarianism issue by weighing the pleasures of human meat eating against the pains of animals reared for meat, and deciding which outweighs the other. The animal rights approach assigns direct, correlative duties to human moral agents not to harm animals, with no procedure for allowing a trade-off between the interests of animals and the interests of these human moral agents. The rights approach would not decide the vegetarianism issue by weighing the interests of meat-eating humans against those of farm animals, but argue instead that the rights of animals trump the interests of meat-eating humans. The animal rights approach would allow exceptions only in very few cases, for example, the right to kill an animal (or human being) in self-defence.

Another difference between the two approaches is that the utilitarian approach holds that the interests of entities have intrinsic value, whereas the rights-based approach holds that the entities themselves have intrinsic value. Tom Regan offers the analogy of a cup full of liquid. On the utilitarian approach, the liquid has intrinsic value, not the cup. If the liquid is fine wine, then it has more value than if it is a sugary soft drink. In this analogy, humans or animals, who are the containers of interests, have no intrinsic value, only the satisfaction of their interests does. On the rights-based approach, the cup containing the liquid has intrinsic value. In this analogy, it is the humans and animals who are morally important, not the satisfaction of their interests (Regan 1986: 19–20).

UTILITARIANISM AND ANIMAL WELFARE

The first utilitarian was the English philosopher and legal theorist, Jeremy Bentham (1748–1832). In a famous and often quoted passage, he wrote,

> The French have already discovered that the blackness of the skin is no reason
> why a human being should be abandoned without redress to the caprice of a tor-
> mentor. It may one day come to be recognized that the number of the legs, the
> villosity [hairiness] of the skin, or the termination of the *os sacrum* [tail bone],

are reasons equally insufficient for abandoning a sensitive being to the same fate. What else is it that should trace the insuperable line? Is it the faculty of reason, or perhaps the faculty of discourse? But a full-grown horse or dog is beyond comparison a more rational, as well as a more conversable animal, than an infant of a day, or a week, or even a month, old. But suppose they were otherwise, what would it avail? The question is not, Can they reason? nor, Can they talk? but, Can they suffer? (Bentham 1823: Chapter 17, Note 122)

This question, "Can they suffer?" is the foundation of the utilitarian approach to the moral standing of animals. Because complex animals can suffer, or experience pleasure, they are sentient. A being is SENTIENT if it is conscious or capable of feeling. Bentham thought we should consider the painful feelings of animals in ethical thinking. Sentient animals should have moral standing.

More recently, Peter Singer argues that utilitarianism must take into account animal welfare (Singer 1976). He begins from the basic moral principle that we should give equal consideration to the interests of all entities capable of having interests. Because complex animals are capable of feeling suffering and enjoyment, they have subjective interests. It is possible to psychologically benefit or harm them by satisfying, or thwarting, their interests. From the perspective of ethical thinking, he says, we should not regard interests as of any less weight just because of whose interests they are. We should not weight the interests of any being with moral standing by a lesser factor than those of any other when we are adding them up to do a calculation of utility. We should weight the interests of each being by a factor of one, and we should weight the interests of no being by either more or less than a factor of one. Equal consideration of interests is the utilitarian ideal of moral equality that we looked at in Chapter 8. It is not the same as factual equality. Singer is not saying, for example, that all human beings are equally strong, smart, attractive, or the same in any other feature. He is saying, instead, that these features are not important from a moral point of view. In our ethical decisions, we should not weight the interests of the strong any higher than we weight the interests of the weak. Strength, cleverness, and beauty are morally arbitrary; they are not morally relevant to treating people as equals.

Singer next argues that all entities with sentience have moral standing. Sentient beings can suffer, and suffering is a bad thing no matter in which type of being it occurs. Beings with moral standing are entitled to equal consideration of their interests. Suffering is not only bad, it is just as bad whether it occurs in one type of being or in another. To deny that the suffering of a being of a different species matters, or to say that it matters less than the suffering of human beings, is what Singer calls "speciesism." SPECIESISM is the denial of equal moral concern based on species membership. Singer called it so to bring out the analogy to racism and sexism. The history of ethical development is in part the story of how people have recognized the moral standing of more and more of their fellow beings. The Ancient Greeks thought people who did not speak Greek were barbarians, and thought it ethically permissible to enslave them. Until the nineteenth century, Europeans thought of Africans as potential slaves, and until the twentieth century Europeans failed to give full legal standing to women.

The next step in Singer's argument is the empirical claim that complex animals, like people, are sentient. This empirical premise is based on observations of animal behaviour and evidence of similarity between the nervous systems of complex animals and those of human beings. However, because some animals are sentient, it does not follow that all animals are sentient. Some animals, for example primates, cats, dogs, and farm animals, clearly are. Others, such as microscopic one-celled animals clearly are not. In the middle are difficult cases. Mussels, which passively graze on plankton, probably are not sentient, but clams, which are more responsive to their environment, possibly are, though their nervous systems are very simple, perhaps too simple for them to have the capacity to suffer. The sentience criterion for moral standing does not solve the demarcation problem, but it does move it from the border between human and non-human animals to the border between complex and simple animals. The border between sentience and its absence will also depend on whether we take the capacity of suffering or the capacity for pain as the criterion. Pain is a sensation, and sensation requires a central nervous system of some minimal complexity. Suffering is an emotion and emotion requires a more complex central nervous system that contains a particular structure, the limbic system.

At this stage, Singer can conclude that the interests of animals and people deserve equal consideration. By this, he does not mean to imply that the interests of animals and humans are the same. Humans have an interest in voting in elections, whereas pigs or dogs have no such interest. We do not thwart the interests of animals by making no provision for them to vote in elections. It is meaningless to worry about satisfying interests of animals for which they have no capacity.

It now follows that a moral agent should act to maximize the interests of both people and animals. The utilitarian principle states that moral agents should act so as to the cause maximum aggregated satisfaction of all interests. We give equal consideration to the interests of all sentient beings, human or non-human, by aggregating their interests through a procedure that weights all interest by the same factor. In order to maximize aggregated interests, we may sometimes have to trade off the welfare of animals and the interests of humans.

It does not follow that complex animals are moral agents. Moral agency requires more than sentience. It requires the capacity for understanding the interests of other beings, the capacity to understand moral principles, the capacity to reflect critically on various moral principles and to endorse some rather than others, and the capacity to choose, freely and autonomously, to obey a moral principle. A house cat is not doing anything morally wrong when it tortures a mouse because, though it has moral standing, it does not possess the capacity for moral agency. In Singer's interpretation of utilitarianism, moral standing is not the same as moral agency.

DIFFICULTIES WITH THE UTILITARIAN APPROACH

The utilitarian approach to animal welfare inherits many of the problems faced by utilitarianism itself. It faces new versions of the comparison and measurement problems. Utilitarian theory requires that sensations or preferences be aggregated, and thus presupposes that the intensities of sensations or preference satisfactions can be measured. The methods proposed by utilitarian economists for measuring the intensity of preferences obviously cannot apply to animals. Willingness to pay cannot be used as a measure of preference intensity in animals because the use of money is beyond the capacity of even chimpanzees or dolphins. No one would propose the capacity to use money as a criterion of moral standing. Nor does the von Neumann and Morgenstern method of using indifference to gambles to measure utility apply to animals, again because it is beyond their cognitive capacities. It is difficult to compare the effects of actions on animals and humans because of their different sizes and adaptations. The shove that a rider needs to move the rear end of her horse would be entirely inappropriate if applied to another human. It is more difficult to know what is in the interests of an animal than it is to know what is in the interests of another human being.

The problem of adaptive preferences arises also for the animal welfare position. If people are dissatisfied with their present circumstances, then we can improve net utility in two ways: either by changing their circumstances to something more satisfactory or by changing their preferences so that they are now satisfied with their present circumstances. The latter procedure may well work from a utilitarian perspective, but it can seem very unfair from a justice perspective. If poor and destitute humans have adapted their preferences to their reduced circumstances, we are not thereby relieved of any obligation to help them. Many animals are adaptable and easy to train. Farmers that rear chicks inside a barn find that, when they open a door to allow the chickens access to sunlight and pasture, the grown chickens refuse to go outside. Does this mean that the chickens have no interest in access to the outdoors? To deal with the problem of adaptive preferences, the animal welfare position could appeal to the notion of the natural interests of chickens, the interests that chickens would have in their natural state. The problem then is that humans have bred chickens to create certain behaviour traits genetically. The interests of tame chickens may differ drastically from the interests of their genetic ancestors.

Animal rights advocates argue that animal welfare theory does not go far enough in offering protection to animals. As we have seen, animal welfare theories, because of their utilitarian origins, permit a trade-off between the interests of animals and the interests of humans. In principle, the animal welfare position could permit the use of an animal in painful medical research programs if the benefits to human beings are sufficiently large. We should note, however, that the utilitarian position would permit the use of human beings in the same experiment. According to rights theorists, to use one being as a resource for others, or to treat a being as though he, she, or it has only instrumental value, fails to show that being proper respect.

The utilitarian animal welfare position does not offer the sort of total protection for animals that the animal rights position would require. Jeremy Bentham, in the passage preceding the above quotation, a passage that utilitarians remark on much less, claims that even though we have an obligation not to cause animals to suffer, we have no obligation not to kill and eat them.

> If the being eaten were all, there is very good reason why we should be suffered
> to eat such of them as we like to eat: we are the better for it, and they are never
> the worse. They have none of those long-protracted anticipations of future mis-
> ery which we have. The death they suffer in our hands commonly is, and always

may be, a speedier, and by that means a less painful one, than that which would await them in the inevitable course of nature. If the being killed were all, there is very good reason why we should be suffered to kill such as molest us: we should be the worse for their living, and they are never the worse for being dead. But is there any reason why we should be suffered to torment them? Not any that I can see. Are there any why we should *not* be suffered to torment them? Yes, several. (Bentham 1823: Chapter 17, Note 122)

In this passage, Bentham appears to allow that if we can kill an animal painlessly, or less painfully than how it would die in nature, then we may do so. Since suffering is what is intrinsically bad, it is suffering we must avoid causing, not loss of life. We have no obligation not to kill animals painlessly, says Bentham, because they do not have "... those long-protracted anticipations of future misery which we have." Again, from the animal rights perspective, the animal welfare position fails to adequately protect animals.

Tom Regan, whose argument for animal rights we will examine in the next chapter, attacks the animal welfare approach and its sentience criterion for moral standing. He argues that utilitarianism, the theory that requires the sentience criterion for moral standing, is an inadequate theory. Sentience is the criterion for moral standing only if utilitarianism is the correct ethical theory. If, for independent reasons, utilitarianism is not the correct ethical theory, then sentience is not the criterion for moral standing. Regan argues that utilitarianism is not the correct moral theory because utilitarianism fails to respect individual persons properly. The problem, he claims, comes from the way that utilitarianism aggregates interests, a problem that we have already observed in the Transplant Case. Interest-utilitarianism assigns a measure to the satisfaction or frustration of interests, adds the satisfactions, subtracts the frustrations, and totals the whole lot. In doing so, it pays no attention to the individual persons whose interests it aggregates. Suppose, he imagines, that he, Regan, has a rich, solitary, and miserly Aunt Bea who is going to leave him all her money in her will. If he were to murder his Aunt Bea painlessly, he would give most of her money to a children's hospital and cause a great improvement in the welfare of hundreds of children. According to the utilitarian approach, the increased welfare of hundreds of children outweighs the welfare loss due to the death of Aunt Bea. Therefore, according to utilitarianism, he should murder his Aunt Bea. This conclusion, he says, is incorrect because,

> ... the utilitarian's position leads to results that impartial people find morally
> callous. It is wrong to kill my Aunt Bea in the name of bringing about the best
> results for others. A good end does not justify an evil means. Any adequate
> moral theory will have to explain why this is so. Utilitarianism fails in this
> respect and so cannot be the theory we seek. (Regan 1986: 21)

The utilitarian aggregation procedure fails to show proper respect for Aunt Bea, a respect that a rights-based theory would better acknowledge. Utilitarianism is not the correct ethical theory when applied to human beings, nor is it the correct ethical theory when applied to animals. Thus, sentience, its criterion for moral standing, is not adequate either.

The animal welfare perspective's zoocentric view of moral standing also faces objections from more inclusive views of moral standing. A biocentric view extends moral standing to all living beings, not just humans and animals. It implies that we may need to trade off the interests of animals with the interests of plants. For example, we may have to cull elephants to protect their habitat from over-grazing, or we may need to shoot a porcupine to protect a majestic tree from the porcupine eating all its bark. An ecocentric view of moral standing extends moral standing to ecosystems. It implies that we may need to subordinate the interests of individual animals to the health of the ecosystem. For example, we may need to shoot white-tailed deer in order to save the forest ecosystem to which they belong, or introduce a disease to rabbits in order to save native Australian ecosystems. Singer's animal welfare theory grants equal consideration only to the interests of individual people and animals. However, the moral standing of ecosystems and the species that make them up, raise holistic concerns. Do the last remaining members of a nearly extinct species have any special moral status? Is it permissible to shoot goats on a west coast island to protect a rare species of plants? In later chapters, we will look at the reasons offered for biocentric and ecocentric views of moral standing.

SUMMARY

1. Different types of ethical theory require that entities have different features in order for the theory to apply to them.
2. Species membership is not an explicitly relevant feature in any ethical theory.
3. That some animals possess a natural feature sufficient for moral standing does not imply that other animals without that feature also have moral standing.
4. The animal welfare approach to moral standing is consequentialist and utilitarian. The animal rights approach is deontological and rights-based.
5. Peter Singer bases his utilitarian, animal welfare view on equal consideration of the interests of animals and humans. Any animal that can suffer is sentient and has subjective interests. Singer argues that we should give the interests of animals the same weight as the corresponding interests of humans in the utilitarian aggregation process.
6. Like any utilitarian theory, Singer's view faces the problem of how we should compare and measure the intensity of interest satisfaction, and the problem of why we should not just adapt preferences to circumstances. These problems are even more difficult across different species than they are within a single species.
7. Tom Regan argues that the animal welfare, sentience approach to moral standing is inadequate because the ethical theory grounding it, utilitarianism, is inadequate. Utilitarianism is inadequate because its decision procedure involves aggregating the interests of beings, and thus fails to respect the value of individual beings properly.
8. Biocentric views of moral standing ask why only animals, and not all living things, should be thought morally considerable. Ecocentric views ask why

the interests of animals should always outweigh concerns with the health of ecosystems and the preservation of endangered species.

The book's website contains reading questions on this chapter. Working through these questions will help you understand, remember, and apply important concepts from the chapter. Some of the questions supply useful hints for the study questions.

STUDY QUESTIONS

Using the text and hints from the online reading questions, write out, type, dictate to your computer, or at least formulate in your head answers to the following questions.

1. Explain some of the differences between the animal welfare and animal rights approaches.
2. What does "equal consideration of interests" mean to a utilitarian animal welfare supporter?
3. What is sentience and why is it important to utilitarians?
4. Describe some of the measurement and comparison problems for the animal welfare approach.
5. Explain why the animal welfare approach would face problems if species have moral standing.

QUESTIONS TO PONDER

Spend a few minutes thinking about the following questions, or, better yet, discuss them with fellow readers of this book.

1. Suppose scientists were to design genetically modified pigs, chickens, and cattle that could not feel pain or suffer. Should an animal welfare supporter accept eating them? Should the animal welfare approach advocate that scientists design them?
2. We can design thought-experiments, like Robert Nozick's experience machine (see the chapter on Utilitarianism), to show that sensations, feelings, and experiences are not what have ultimate intrinsic value. Singer's view appears to assume that feelings of suffering are intrinsically bad. Does Nozick's thought experiment refute Singer's view?
3. Though John Stuart Mill vigorously defended Jeremy Bentham's application of utilitarian principles to animals, he tried to avoid objections to Bentham's simple hedonistic version of utilitarianism by claiming that "It is better to be a human being dissatisfied than a pig satisfied; better to be Socrates dissatisfied than a fool satisfied" (1863: Chapter 2). Pleasures have

different qualities, and push-pin is not as good as poetry (see the chapter on Utilitarianism). The implication is that the satisfaction of the interests of a human being is morally more important than the satisfaction of the interests of a pig, and the satisfaction of the interests of an insightful philosopher are more important than the satisfaction of the interests of a fool. Does Mill abandon equal consideration of interests?

4. Should we count the interest of a predator in hunting, or a house cat in playing with its prey, in a utilitarian aggregation? Does equal consideration of interests require that we treat the same interests in human beings as having the same weight as do these interests in predatory animals? If a house cat has an interest that in a human we would call, sadistic, should we recognize that interest in the cat morally?

5. A man is in a lifeboat with his pet dog and another human. The lifeboat will only hold two, and the man has the only gun. He loves the dog, but the human is a stranger. He counts all interests equally. Because of his love for the dog, saving the dog and ordering the other human out of the boat maximizes utility. Is this the right action?

Chapter 12

ANIMAL RIGHTS

THE ANIMAL WELFARE POSITION IS UTILITARIAN IN ITS JUSTIFICATION. ACCORDING to Peter Singer, utilitarianism should give equal consideration to the interests of both animals and humans. Interest-utilitarianism works by aggregating a measure of satisfied interests for each alternative policy, and then implementing the policy that will maximize total satisfaction. Because it is aggregative, utilitarianism permits us to trade off human interests against those of animals, and equally to trade off the interests of animals against those of humans. Humans and animals are resources for one another. In principle, animals can be compassionately farmed and painlessly killed, if human interests in meat-eating outweigh any discomfort for the animals. Human interests in medical research can outweigh the interests of humanely kept and properly anaesthetized laboratory animals. Human interests in hunting can outweigh the interests of cleanly shot game animals. Animal welfare objections to these practices cannot be made in principle; they must be made in practice, by pointing out the difficulty of painless killing, or how rare are clean kills by hunters.

The animal welfare case against animal agriculture, animal experimentation, and animal hunting can be very strong, but it is not a definitive, principled case. These arguments are not strong enough for proponents of animal rights. Tom Regan, who has given the most influential defence of the rights of animals, argues for the total abolition of scientific experimentation on animals, the total dissolution of commercial animal agriculture, and the total elimination of animal hunting and trapping (Regan 1986: 13). What is wrong with human treatment of animals is not that humans cause animals to suffer or die, but that humans use animals as resources and thus fail to respect their rights. According to the animal rights approach, we have strong principled reasons against ever making a trade-off between the interests of animals and the interests of humans.

In this chapter, we will set Regan's argument in its historical context, spell it out in more detail, and look at some of its weaknesses. We will also look at what a theory of interspecies justice might say about sameness and difference in how we assign rights to animals and humans.

Learning Objectives

1. To understand the position of Immanuel Kant on animal rights.
2. To understand Tom Regan's influential argument for animal rights.
3. To understand some of the weaknesses of the animal rights position.
4. To understand the notion of interspecies justice.

SOME HISTORICAL VIEWS ON DUTIES TO ANIMALS

Throughout the history of philosophy, philosophers have disagreed on the moral standing of animals. Aristotle (384 BCE–322 BCE), the intellectual parent of virtue ethics, thought that humans and animals differed in degree but not in kind. However, he thought that the lesser abilities of animals made them morally inferior to humans. Aristotle was no friend to equality of respect or consideration; he also thought that women and slaves were of less moral importance than adult male citizens. René Descartes (1596–1650), the intellectual parent of modern philosophy, thought there was a difference of kind between humans and animals. Descartes claimed that the mind and the material world were two different substances. In order to explain human behaviour, we need to postulate that humans have minds, whereas we can explain the behaviour of animals by assuming merely that they are complex machines or automata. David Hume (1711–76), whose view on the fact/value distinction we have studied, disagreed. He argued that we can explain the behaviour of animals and humans in the same way, so animals and humans are not distinct in kind.

Immanuel Kant (1724–1804), whose work in philosophical theory tried to reconcile the rationalism of Descartes and the empiricism of Hume, located the difference between animals and humans in the human capacities for self-consciousness and autonomous choice. These capacities enable human beings to reflect on moral principles and act as moral agents. Kant thought that humans could not owe duties directly to animals. In notes that his students took of his lectures on ethics, he claimed, "But so far as animals are concerned, we have no direct duties. Animals are not self-conscious and are there merely as a means to an end. That end is man.... Our duties towards animals are merely indirect duties toward humanity" (1976: 122). Because we do not have direct duties to animals, Kant's view is that animals cannot have rights. If an animal could have a moral right, then that right would impose a correlative duty on some or all human moral agents. These correlative duties would have to be direct duties, duties owed to the animal. Indirect duties, duties regarding the animal, but owed to some human being are not the correlative duties that create rights. For example, a dog has a right that a human not kick it only if the human owes a duty to the dog not to kick it. If the human merely has a duty to the dog's owner not to hurt her pet, then the dog itself has no moral right that the human not kick it.

Just because animals do not have natural rights like humans do, it does not follow that humans have no obligations regarding animals. Kant thought that cruelty to animals was a vice, and that kindness to animals was a virtue. He had virtue-theoretic reasons for treating animals well.

> If then any acts of animals are analogous to human acts and spring from the same principles, we have duties towards the animals because thus we cultivate the corresponding duties towards human beings. If a man shoots his dog because the animal is no longer capable of service, he does not fail in his duty to the dog, for the dog cannot judge, but his act is inhuman and damages in himself that humanity which it is his duty to show towards mankind. If he is not to stifle his human feelings, he must practise kindness towards animals, for he who is cruel to animals becomes hard also in his dealings with men. (1976: 122)

The virtue of kindness to animals is, for Kant, a derivative virtue. It does not directly contribute to the flourishing of the human being who possesses it. Instead, it is a derivative virtue. Its importance stems from aiding its possessor to fulfill his duties to other human beings better. It is an anthropocentric virtue, derived ultimately from the rights of other human beings. It does not truly recognize the moral standing of the animals it protects.

A Kantian theory of rights is a theory of natural rights. The assignment of rights in the theory does not derive from some other, non-rights-based theory like indirect utilitarianism or a social contract theory of distributive justice. A Kantian theory does not assign people rights because making people feel more secure maximizes utility indirectly. Instead, on a Kantian theory, rights belong to people because of particular natural features inherent in them, their capacity for autonomy and for moral agency. Moral agency includes the capacity for free and rational moral action, the capacity to take moral responsibility for an action, and the capacity to fulfil duties to others. Humans have rights because they possess these natural features.

Because of its emphasis on autonomous choice, the Kantian theory of natural rights fits best with the will theory of the nature of rights. The will theory emphasizes that a rightholder has the power to decide whether or not to hold other people to the duties that they owe to her. For example, in the case of a contractual right, a person can decide whether to compel the man who she has hired to mow her lawn to finish the bit down by the edge. Rights require choices like this only if the capacity for making autonomous choices is something that is morally important.

On this view, only fully functioning, adult human beings have moral standing, and can have moral rights. The major weakness of the Kantian theory of rights is that it is too restrictive. It fails to extend moral standing, and moral rights, to beings who do not have the natural feature on the basis of which the theory justifies rights, but whom we would normally think to possess moral standing. Human infants, human beings with severe cognitive deficits, and human beings in an irreversible coma are morally considerable beings. Yet they lack the capacity for autonomy that they need to be moral agents and to be ascribed moral standing in the Kantian framework. They are MORAL PATIENTS, not moral agents, individuals who do not have the capacity to act morally or immorally, but who can still be acted on morally or not. The will theory is not the only theory of the nature of natural rights. Perhaps the interest theory can fare better. This is Tom Regan's claim.

REGAN'S RIGHTS-BASED ARGUMENT

Regan's defence of animal rights bases the moral standing of animals on their possession of a natural feature different from that of autonomy. The natural feature is that of being an "experiencing subject of a life," a feature that is not confined to well-functioning adult humans, and a feature that means its possessors will have subjective interests. Some of these subjective interests will be important enough to generate rights. Any such interests that are important enough to generate moral rights in humans will generate equal moral rights in animals. For example, animals that are experiencing subjects of a life have a subjective interest in continuing to live. Humans have this important interest, and it gives them a natural right to life. Thus, animals equally have this same right to life.

Regan has both a negative and a positive argument for his position. His negative argument consists in showing that other contrary views do not withstand rational scrutiny. He thinks that Descartes's no mind, no sentience, no moral status view fails because we have no more evidence that other humans have sentient minds than we do that animals have sentient minds, and we do ascribe moral standing to humans.

He argues that contractarian ethics, which rules out moral standing for animals because they cannot be party to contracts, is an inadequate moral theory for human beings as well as animals. Contractarian ethics allows many human beings to fall outside the contract. For example, we could understand the former apartheid government of South Africa as a contract between South Africans of European descent that excluded South Africans of African descent. Contractarian ethics has no way of saying that this apartheid contract was unfair, since according to contractarian thinking, only the white South Africans who are party to the contract had moral standing.

He also argues that the virtue ethics approach is inadequate because it cannot say whom the virtue of kindness or the vice of cruelty should take as their objects. We can imagine a kind racist who is kind only to members of his own race. The kind racist still has the virtue of kindness, but we would judge that his kindness does not go far enough. We need further reasons for saying that his kindness should not stop at racial boundaries. Similarly, we also need further reasons for saying the kindness should not stop at species boundaries.

He argues that the utilitarian approach, which relies on sentience as its criterion for moral standing, is inadequate for reasons that we looked at in the last chapter. The attraction of utilitarianism is that it treats all interests with equal consideration, but the weakness is that its decision procedure aggregates all interests together in a way that does not properly respect individual persons. To use Regan's example, utilitarian reasoning would permit him to painlessly euthanize his rich Aunt Bea, if he could make better use of the money to help hundreds of sick children. This conclusion is morally callous and indicates a problem with utilitarian theory. Utilitarianism allows individuals to be treated merely as resources for others.

He disagrees with the Kantian approach that requires the capacity for moral agency in order for a being to have moral standing. The problem, as we have seen before, is that the Kantian criterion of moral agency fails to extend moral standing to human infants and small children, to human beings with severe cognitive deficits, and to comatose human beings. Because these are all beings that should have moral standing, the moral agency criterion is defective. Figure 12.1 classifies various positions on the moral standing of animals, and locates Regan's views on animal rights as a version of the interest theory of the nature of moral rights.

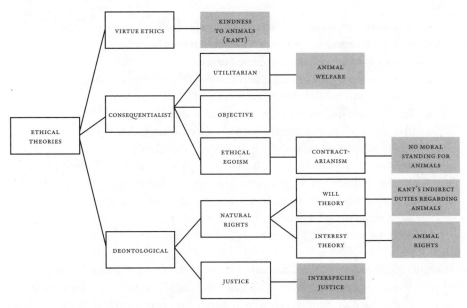

FIGURE 12.1: A taxonomy of ethical positions on the moral standing of animals

The search for a criterion of moral standing is the search for some natural feature that is common to all beings that, in our considered judgment, have moral standing. Regan argues that what is similar between beings with moral standing is not that they have sentience or the capacity for autonomy, but that they are experiencing subjects of a life. He writes:

> And the really crucial, the basic similarity is simply this: we are each of us the experiencing subject of a life, a conscious creature having an individual welfare that has importance to us, whatever our usefulness to others. We want and prefer things, believe and feel things, recall and expect things. And all these dimensions of our life, including our pleasure and pain, our enjoyment and suffering, our satisfaction and frustration, our continued existence or our untimely death— all make a difference to the quality of our life as lived, as experienced, by us as individuals. As the same is true of those animals that concern us (the ones that

are eaten and trapped, for example), they too must be viewed as the experiencing subjects of a life, with inherent value of their own. (Regan 1986: 22)

Beings who are experiencing subjects of a life have an inherent value. Their inherent value means we cannot treat them purely instrumentally. We must not treat them as resources for ourselves or others. We must not treat animals as utilitarianism treats Aunt Bea in Regan's thought experiment.

Regan's positive argument for the rights of animals depends on the basic moral principle that all entities with inherent value are to be shown equal respect. If we recast Regan's' positive argument in terms of the interest theory of the nature of rights, it goes like this:

1. All entities that are experiencing subjects of a life have subjective interests.
2. Animals, like humans, are experiencing subjects of a life.
3. Animals, like humans, have subjective interests.
4. All entities that are experiencing subjects of a life have inherent value.
5. All entities that have inherent value have equal inherent value.
6. Therefore, animals have inherent value equal to that of humans.
7. All entities with both inherent value and subjective interests have a crucial interest in not being treated merely as resources for others.
8. Therefore, animals have a crucial interest in not being treated as resources for others that is morally equal to that interest in human beings.
9. The crucial interest of inherently valuable entities in not being treated as resources for others implies that they have moral rights.
10. Therefore, animals and humans have equal moral rights.

Regan's argument depends on the notion of inherent value. Something has instrumental value if, and only if, it brings about, directly or indirectly, something of intrinsic value. Something that has only instrumental value is merely a resource for others. Something has intrinsic value if, and only if, it is valuable for its own sake, and not for what it brings about. Something can have intrinsic value because of some natural feature that it possesses, or it can have intrinsic value because of some special relationship that it has to other things. The former type of intrinsic value is inherent because it is grounded in a feature that inheres in the entity. The latter type of intrinsic value is not inherent in the entity itself but instead is grounded in the entity's relationship to other entities. For example, a rare but useless plant may have intrinsic value because of its uniqueness. The rareness of a particular plant is not an inherent feature of the plant, but instead depends on the almost universal absence of other plants of that species. So a rare plant may have no instrumental value because it is useless, it may have intrinsic value because of its uniqueness, and it may have no inherent value because its uniqueness is not an inherent feature of the plant.

Regan argues that being an experiencing subject of a life is a sufficient condition for having inherent value. If something is an experiencing subject of a life, then it has inherent value. He allows that other beings besides experiencing subjects of a life may also have inherent value, but claims that all he needs to establish animal rights is the inherent value of experiencing subjects of a life. As we have seen, he argues that being an experiencing subject of a life is a sufficient condition for having inherent value by pointing out that it is a common feature among all those human beings that, in our considered judgment, have inherent value. In the same way, he argues that having inherent value is not a hierarchical concept. All human beings whom we consider to have inherent value have it to the same degree. Inherent value does not vary with intelligence, health, strength, or any other variable. Thus, all beings that have inherent value have it equally. Finally Regan argues that since inherent value is distinct from instrumental value, we must not treat beings with inherent value merely as resources for others. We must not treat beings with inherent value as Aunt Bea was treated in his anti-utilitarian thought experiment. Beings with inherent value have interests that must be protected by equal moral rights. Since complex animals are experiencing subjects of a life, they have equal moral rights to human beings.

The consequences of Regan's abstract and complex argument are that we should implement policies that permit no commercial animal farming, that forbid meat eating, that forbid trapping and hunting, and that do not use animals in scientific research. As far as his argument is concerned, however, our environmental policies do not need to show moral concern for plants, nature, species, or ecosystems, since he has not shown us to have any direct duties to them.

PROBLEMS WITH THE ANIMAL RIGHTS POSITION

Philosophers developed each of the major ethical approaches in response to problems that they perceived in competing approaches. Thus, we can look for weaknesses in the animal rights position by considering it from within virtue ethics, consequentialist, justice-based, and holistic ethical theories. For example, to the virtue ethicist, any form of rights theory will appear too absolute, too rigid, too lacking in flexibility, too lacking in the application of judgment and wisdom, to be the best approach for human moral agents to take toward animals.

Consequentialists will point out that moral agents will face situations where they cannot avoid weighing the aggregate consequences of their actions. For example, the world's farmers cannot plough their fields to grow vegetarian food for people without inflicting suffering and death on the small animals that live in these fields. As moral agents, we must weigh the rights of mice and toads against the interests of humans in having enough to eat. Even vegans are complicit in some animal rights violations. The animal rights position cannot avoid making trade-offs.

Regan's suggested test for moral standing, being an experiencing subject of life, does not give a precise demarcation between beings with and without moral standing. Instead, it moves the demarcation boundary from a line between humans and other species of animals to a line between those animals that have and those animals that do not have a particular set of capacities. From his description of an experiencing subject of a life, we can see that this set includes all of the following: a capacity for consciousness, a capacity for preferring, a capacity for believing, a capacity for recalling, a capacity for expecting, a capacity for enjoyment, a capacity for frustration, and a capacity to be concerned about continued existence. Complex animals will pass this test, and simple ones will not. Regan does not think the lack of a clear boundary matters, so long as farm animals, wild animals, and experimental animals clearly pass the test for moral standing. He leaves open the possibility that the real criterion may be weaker and thus give moral standing to a wider class of entities.

From the perspective of other theories of moral standing, the animal rights approach, like the animal welfare approach, is individualistic. It cannot easily recognize holistic moral considerations. Regan's animal rights theory gives rights only to individuals. Yet, we are familiar with considering the interests of entities that are not reducible to their component individuals, entities such as business corporations, municipal and condominium corporations, provinces and nations, which all have legal standing in the courts and perhaps also moral standing in ethics. If holistic entities have moral standing then their interests may come into conflict with the rights of animals. Is it ethically permissible for us to cull animals to protect endangered species of plants? May we cull large herbivores that are destroying ecosystems through overgrazing?

Philosophers and legal theorists have identified three theories of the nature of rights. Either rights derive from theories of justice or other ethical theories, or they are natural rights grounded in inherent, innate features of their possessors. Natural rights arise either in recognition of the capacity for autonomous choice (the will theory), or in recognition of the crucial interests of the right-holder (the interest theory). Regan's theory of animal rights clearly falls into the latter category. The notion of an interest is somewhat abstract. The legal theorist, Joel Feinberg, who also introduced the distinction between individual and accumulative harms, described interests in the following way. We can have a duty regarding the Taj Mahal, a duty not to injure it or a duty to maintain it, but we do not owe that duty to the Taj Mahal itself because the Taj Mahal is a thing with no interests and no good of its own:

> A mere thing, however valuable to others, has no good of its own. The explanation of that fact, I suspect, is that mere things have no conative life; neither conscious wishes, desires, and hopes; nor urges and impulses; nor unconscious drives, aims, goals; nor latent tendencies, directions of growth, and natural fulfillments. Interests must be compounded somehow out of conations; hence mere things have no interests. *A fortiori*, they have no interests to be protected by legal or moral rules. (Feinberg 1976: 195)

Feinberg probably intended to describe only subjective interests since a conation is a psychological process. However, his list of examples includes "latent tendencies, directions of growth, and natural fulfillments," which are non-psychological capacities that we could understand to permit objective interests, the sort of capacities in which a teleological theory of ethics is interested. In the next chapter, we will look further into the idea that other beings besides humans and animals have objective interests or a good of their own. We will note here, though, that if there are objective interests, and if they can ground rights, then, from a biocentric view of moral standing, Regan's extension of rights to animals has not gone far enough.

Singer argues for equal consideration of the interests of animals and humans. Regan argues for equal rights for animals and humans. Both arguments implicitly assume theories of interspecies justice. Justice requires that we treat all beings with moral standing as moral equals. This does not require, however, that we always treat them in the same way. Instead, it requires that we treat them the same, unless there is a morally relevant reason for treating them differently. Conversely, we must not treat moral beings differently for morally arbitrary reasons. Some morally relevant reasons for treating beings differently stem from their different interests.

Simple forms of utilitarianism treat interests as differing only in the degree of psychological fulfilment produced by their satisfaction. Utilitarianism must then consider the immoral interests of sadists in torturing animals, and the unjust preferences of racists, in its calculations. From the justice perspective, and in the considered judgment of most of us, this seems wrong; sadistic and unjust preferences should not be counted at all. There are morally relevant reasons for treating some categories of interests differently. We still treat people as moral equals even though we do not treat their sadistic and racist interests in the same way as their other interests.

The interest theory of rights, too, distinguishes different categories of interests. Some interests are important enough to engender rights and some are not. For example, wild animals have interests both in avoiding suffering and in obtaining mates. The first interest grounds a right that humans not cause wild animals to suffer. The second interest does not ground a right that humans provide wild animals with mates, even if that were possible. Interest theories of rights must distinguish important interests requiring rights from everyday interests that do not, otherwise every whim will become an entitlement. Important interests are those interests that must be respected in order to show respect for the being itself. Rights protect interests, such as an interest in avoiding suffering or physical injury, that are of crucial concern to the being. Everyday interests, such as a wish for pizza at lunch, do not have the same sort of moral relevance.

Whether or not an entity has a particular interest will depend on the nature of the entity. For example, unlike humans, animals do not have a crucial interest in freedom of speech or in having freedom of assembly for political purposes. Peter Singer writes:

> Many feminists hold that women have the right to an abortion on request. It does not follow that since these same people are campaigning for equality between men and women they must support the right of men to have abortions too. Since a man cannot have an abortion, it is meaningless to talk of his right to have one. Since a pig can't vote, it is meaningless to talk of its right to vote. There is no reason why either Women's Liberation or Animal Liberation should get involved in such nonsense. The extension of the basic principle of equality from one group to another does not imply that we must treat both groups in exactly the same way, or grant exactly the same rights to both groups. Whether we should do so will depend on the nature of the members of the two groups. The

basic principle of equality, I shall argue, is equality of consideration; and equal consideration for different beings may lead to different treatment and different rights. (Singer 1976: 150)

A right to vote requires the capacity to have a subjective interest in voting. Being prevented from voting must have the potential to harm the right-bearer in some way. The capacity for an interest in voting requires the capacity to understand political issues. From the justice perspective, that of treating beings as moral equals, the presence or absence of a capacity to understand political issues is a morally relevant reason for treating beings differently when we assign the right to vote. In justice-based theories, we can disregard immoral and unjust interests, treat crucial interests as trumping everyday interests, and consider only those interests of a being for which the being has the underlying natural capacity.

Some animals, though they are aware, conscious, and sentient, are not self-conscious or self-aware. Self-consciousness requires that animals have a sense of personal identity over time and a sense of their own future. Animals without these capacities do not have a crucial interest in continued life. Painlessly euthanizing them would not be a harm to them, any more than denying a pig the right to vote would harm the pig. Controversially, this would imply that animals without this capacity do not have a right to continued life. Some cognitively sophisticated animals are plausibly self-aware, while others are obviously too simple to be so. Drawing the boundary is a profoundly difficult question. One suggested test for the presence of self-awareness in animals is the mirror test. The experimenter marks the animal, puts the animal in front of a mirror, and observes whether the animal can recognize itself as the marked animal in the mirror. Apes, dolphins, and elephants seem to pass the test, whereas cats and dogs do not. This suggests the question, which we will not pursue further, of whether interspecies justice should assign a right to continued life to chimpanzees, but not to cats.

Table 12.1 lists some morally relevant capacities and the crucial interests that they create in various types of animals and types of human beings. A being cannot have a right unless it has the corresponding crucial interest.

CAPACITY	CRUCIAL INTERESTS (RIGHTS)	WHO HAS CAPACITY	WHO DOES NOT
Sentience	Absence of suffering	Humans, complex animals	Simple animals
Self-consciousness	Continued life	Most humans, primates, dolphins	Fetuses, comatose, most animals
Autonomous choice	Liberty, private property	Most humans	Infants, comatose, all animals
Moral agency	Hearing truth, education	Most humans	Infants, comatose, all animals
Self-governing social cooperation	Democratic expression, vote, assembly	Most adult humans	Children, comatose, all animals

TABLE 12.1: Natural capacities, the crucial interests that they generate, who has these capacities, and who does not

Thinking about the ethical treatment of animals from the perspective of interspecies justice does not solve all the ethical questions we have raised, but it does suggest some useful distinctions. Moral equality and the equal consideration of different categories of interests would rule out harm to animals in research on cosmetics since an animal's crucial interest in avoiding suffering would always trump a human's everyday interest in using cosmetics, no matter how many humans were involved. Similarly, animal suffering in factory farms would trump the substitutable, everyday interest of humans in eating meat. Controversially, if animals are not moral agents, then it is permissible to deceive them. Also controversially, if farm animals do not have a crucial interest in continued life, then eating benignly reared, humanely slaughtered animals would be permissible.

Singer's equal consideration of interests, Regan's equal rights for animals, and the concern of interspecies justice with moral equality, all presuppose that those beings with moral standing have it to the same degree. They have the same moral significance. It is possible to think of alternative positions where entities that have intrinsic value, and thus some sort of moral standing, have less moral significance than do humans. For example, whereas we might injure an inaccessible wilderness area of no economic value to protect a human being's life, we would not injure it to protect a human being's property rights. Such judgments of moral significance do not fit easily into egalitarian approaches such as the animal rights approach and we will examine them more fully in later chapters.

SUMMARY

1. The animal rights approach prevents a utilitarian trade-off between the interests of animals and the interests of humans.
2. Kant's will theory of natural rights does not justify rights for animals because they lack the capacity for autonomous choice required by the will theory. Instead, Kant thinks people should avoid the vice of cruelty to animals, not for the sake of the animals, but because avoiding the vice of cruelty helps people fulfil their duties to other human beings.
3. Tom Regan argues that the Kantian approach to animals is wrong because it cannot account for the moral standing of infant, comatose, and severely cognitively impaired human beings. He argues that the utilitarian approach is the wrong one because it will permit individuals to be sacrificed or otherwise used in order to maximize the aggregate good.
4. Regan argues that animals have equal rights with human beings. Because animals, like humans, are experiencing subjects of a life, they have the same inherent value as humans have. The capacity to experience their lives gives them a crucial subjective interest in not being treated as resources for humans, and thus rights equal to those of humans.
5. Virtue ethicists will see the animal rights position as too rigid. Consequentialists will argue that it cannot account for conflicts between rights.

6. Biocentric egalitarians will argue that the animal rights position does not go far enough because it does not recognize the important objective interests of plants and other living things.

7. Ecological holists will argue that it does not properly resolve conflicts between the interests of animals and the preservation of species and ecosystems.

8. Interspecies justice recognizes that different types of interest may legitimately be treated differently, but treats equivalent animal and human interests equally. It rules out consideration of sadistic and racist interests, gives crucial interests, though not everyday interests, the protection of rights, and recognizes that different beings have different capacities and thus need different rights.

ONLINE READING QUESTIONS

The book's website contains reading questions on this chapter. Working through these questions will help you understand, remember, and apply important concepts from the chapter. Some of the questions supply useful hints for the study questions.

STUDY QUESTIONS

Using the text and hints from the online reading questions, write out, type, dictate to your computer, or at least formulate in your head answers to the following questions.

1. If humans have only indirect duties to animals, then this means that animals do not have rights. Explain.
2. What is Kant's criterion for moral standing and what are its weaknesses?
3. Explain how the rights approach and the utilitarian welfare approach differ in the way that they treat beings as equals.
4. What is Regan's criterion of moral standing and why does it give rights to animals?
5. Explain the potential conflict between the animal rights approach to moral standing and a holistic approach that gives moral standing to ecosystems.
6. Compare the animal welfare and animal rights approaches to medical experimentation on animals.

Spend a few minutes thinking about the following questions, or, better yet, discuss them with fellow readers of this book.

1. What is the relationship between inherent intrinsic value and rights? Does everything that has inherent intrinsic value have moral standing? Does everything that has moral standing have rights?

2. Is the animal rights approach practical? What would happen to the environment if all farm animals were immediately released from captivity? If they were not released, and not sold to be eaten, who should pay for their food?

3. Suppose a pseudo-vegetarian were to argue that eating hamburgers is ethically permissible because hamburgers are made up of tiny bits of meat from hundreds of beef cattle, and the tiny bit of meat from each animal that he eats would have no effect on whether or not any individual animal was killed for meat. What do you make of this argument?

4. Cats have a right to torture mice. Animals and humans have equal rights. Therefore, humans have a right to torture mice. What is wrong with this argument?

5. Rights are limited by the harm principle. For example, someone's right of movement is limited by the duty not to move in a way that harms others. Animals cannot understand the harm principle, so can they have rights?

6. Pigs can pass the mirror test for self-awareness, whereas human infants cannot. Does this mean that painlessly euthanizing a pig violates the pig's rights to continued life, whereas painlessly euthanizing a human infant does not violate the infant's right to continued life?

Chapter 13

BIOCENTRIC ETHICS

IN PREVIOUS CHAPTERS, WE TOOK REGULAR ETHICAL THEORIES AND EXTENDED them so that they apply to more and more aspects of the environment. We started by accepting that our own selves have moral standing. Then we observed that no morally relevant distinction exists between ourselves and other people around us. Next, we extended our moral concern by noticing that people in distant countries and in future generations are similar in all morally relevant ways to the people around us. We therefore have good reason to be morally concerned about them as well. Finally, we looked at arguments that complex animals are similar to human beings in morally relevant ways and that animals too can have moral standing.

In the next few chapters, we will look at philosophical views that are less about extending applied ethics and more about constructing new environmental philosophies. Underpinning a new environmental philosophy is a new conceptual framework for understanding the world. A good analogy is that a conceptual framework is like a lens through which we see the world. If we change the shape or colour of the lens, then we will see the world differently. In order to appreciate and come to adopt a new environmental philosophy, people must make a basic change in the way they see the world and take on a new system of core beliefs about human nature and the natural world. A change in conceptual framework is like a scientific revolution. During the Renaissance, Europeans made a huge shift in their understanding of the cosmos. They abandoned the Ptolemaic conceptual framework that placed the Earth at the centre of the universe with the Sun, Moon, planets, and stars all rotating round it, and adopted the Copernican conceptual framework which put the Sun at the centre of the universe. With this revolution in astronomy went a revolution in their thinking about the importance of human beings. Ousted from the centre of the universe by science, Renaissance Europeans were better prepared to lose their privileged position in the Medieval Great Chain of Being, a hierarchical conceptual framework that placed God at the top, and human beings just below the angels but well above animals and the environment.

Scientific revolutions happen gradually. One scientific paradigm slowly replaces another as argument and evidence accumulate and change the balance of intellectual power between the worldviews. The worldviews that we will examine, reverence for life, biocentric egalitarianism, ecofeminism, and deep ecology, do not offer knockdown arguments for their positions. Instead, they urge the adoption of new conceptual frameworks for understanding the environment and the place of human beings in it.

Learning Objectives

1. To understand the reverence for life theory of Albert Schweitzer.
2. To understand the biocentric egalitarianism of Paul Taylor.
3. To understand some of the problems faced by biocentric egalitarianism.

ALBERT SCHWEITZER'S REVERENCE FOR LIFE

A biocentric ethic is an ethical theory in which all living things have moral standing. An early version of a biocentric ethic in Western philosophy occurs in the work of the German physician, organist, theologian, missionary, and philosopher, Albert Schweitzer (1875–1965). Schweitzer reacted against what he perceived as the overly abstract conceptual framework of modern philosophy. He rather harshly condemned this framework as it has descended from René Descartes. He urged, instead, that philosophy adopt a different, life-centred conceptual framework.

> With Descartes, philosophy starts from the dogma: "I think, therefore I exist." With this paltry, arbitrarily chosen beginning, it is landed irretrievably on the road to the abstract. It never finds the right approach to ethics, and remains entangled in a dead world- and life-view. True philosophy must start from the most immediate and comprehensive fact of consciousness, which says: "I am life which wills to live, in the midst of life which wills to live." This is not an ingenious dogmatic formula. Day by day, hour by hour, I try and move in it. At every moment of reflection it stands fresh before me. There bursts from it again and again, as from roots that can never dry up, a living world- and life-view which can deal with all the facts of Being. A mysticism of ethical union with Being grows out of it. (1923: 213–14)

Adopting this life-centred conceptual framework, he thought, will lead a person to also adopting a fundamental emotional attitude of awe and wonder toward living things that he called "reverence for life."

> Ethics consist, therefore, in my experiencing the compulsion to show to all will-to-live the same reverence as I do to my own. There we have given us that basic principle of the moral which is a necessity of thought. It is good to maintain and encourage life; it is bad to destroy life or obstruct it. (1923: 214)

So a change in a person's intellectual worldview leads to a change in her fundamental attitude toward living things, and that leads to adoption of a fundamental moral principle: A person is good when she preserves living things and evil when she harms them.

Reverence for life does not articulate a defined set of rules or principles, as a deontological ethic would. Nor does it advocate weighing the consequences of an act or policy, as a consequentialist ethic would. Rather it embodies a fundamental attitude toward the world that underpins a stable disposition to act in certain life-affirming ways toward the environment. The attitude of reverence for life grounds a certain set of character traits. Perhaps the best way to interpret Schweitzer's biocentric ethic is as a virtue ethic, where life-affirming virtues in humans are part of what makes for the flourishing of life on Earth.

Is it ethically permissible for a person to defend himself against an attacking predator? Is it ethically permissible for a person to harvest plants in order to eat? Schweitzer sees all such questions as moral dilemmas. They have no answers. Human beings must harm other living beings in order to live; they cannot live without doing wrong. They have no way to avoid committing crimes against life, or to avoid the feelings of guilt that go with such killing. This is the ethical tragedy of human existence. Nevertheless, human beings can avoid unnecessary harms to life. Schweitzer writes:

> The countryman who has mowed down a thousand blossoms in his meadow as fodder for his cows should take care on the way home he does not, in wanton pastime, switch off the head of a single flower growing on the edge of the road, for in so doing he injures life without being forced to do so by necessity. (1923)

A person who reveres nature will try to live as lightly in the world as she can. She will eat low on the food chain, she will avoid disturbing nature, and she will brush aside a bothersome insect rather than squash it.

Schweitzer's biocentric ethic illustrates the way a person comes to see the world through a different conceptual lens. She begins to see herself as just one living being amid other living beings all with the same will to live. This leads to a new attitude toward living beings and a new morality. Rather than looking for the weaknesses in Schweitzer's views, we will instead look at a more recent, and more philosophically sophisticated, argument for a biocentric ethic.

Paul Taylor has given an influential argument that moral agents must give the same respect to all living things that they give to human beings. He calls his position of biocentric egalitarianism, "respect for nature." His view is egalitarian because not only do all living beings have moral standing, they also have equal moral standing. He argues as follows:

1. Some entities have an objective good of their own.
2. An entity has an objective good of its own if, and only if, it is a teleological centre of life.
3. All living things are teleological centres of life.
4. Therefore, each living thing has an objective good of its own.
5. We have good reason to adopt the biocentric outlook on nature according to which the objective good of any living thing is of no more inherent worth than that of any other.
6. All living things, including humans, have equal inherent worth.
7. Rational agents should give to all living things the same respect that they do to human beings.

The crucial step in this argument is the fifth one, where he argues that we have good reason to change our conceptual framework from an anthropocentric outlook on nature to a biocentric outlook on nature. The biocentric outlook on nature is roughly the outlook of the science of biology, an outlook in which the species *Homo sapiens* is just one species among many. Its members have no special biological features that would ground their having a moral worth that is superior to that of other living beings. All seven steps of the argument require further explanation.

1. Some entities obviously have a good of their own, for example, a child, whereas some entities obviously do not. For example, no one would claim that a pile of sand, or the Taj Mahal, had a good of its own. Preventative maintenance might be good for the Taj Mahal, but it is only good because we humans who value the Taj Mahal want it preserved. We do not maintain the Taj Mahal for its own sake (Feinberg 1976: 195). An entity's SUBJECTIVE GOOD is what it wants for itself, or what it believes to be good for itself. No one would think that a tree had a subjective good because a tree does not have the psychological capacity to want something for itself. There is, however, another sense in which an entity can have a good. An entity's OBJECTIVE GOOD is what is really good for the entity, not what the entity actually wants. For example, what a child actually wants, its subjective good, is often not what is really good for the child, its objective good. A child's parents can often determine what is good for a child better than the child herself can. It is in the sense of having an objective good that a tree can have a good of its own. Thus, some entities have an objective good of their own.

2. Even in this more expansive sense, many things do not have an objective good. Neither a pile of sand, nor the Taj Mahal has a good in either the subjective or objective sense. The difference between a pile of sand and a tree is that we can make sense of a tree as having conditions that are objectively good for the tree. When we examine the life cycle of a tree and look

at the environmental conditions in which it will grow, reproduce, remain healthy, and even flourish, then we can see that certain conditions will benefit the tree and other conditions will harm the tree. A pile of sand is not the sort of thing that can be healthy or flourish. Beings that we can benefit or harm in ways that enhance or diminish their ability to flourish, Taylor calls TELEOLOGICAL CENTRES OF LIFE. A tree is not complex enough to have a subjective good but it can have an objective good because it is a teleological centre of life. An entity has an objective good of its own if, and only if, it is a teleological centre of life.

3. All living things have goals or ends like growth, development, sustenance, and propagation. They exhibit goal-directed activities, which enable their self-preservation and well-being. All living things are teleological centres of life.

4. As a matter of logic, it follows from the forgoing premises that each living thing has an objective good.

5. Taylor does not think that it follows as a matter of deductive logic that, just because a being has an objective good, it therefore has inherent moral worth. Instead, he argues that we have good reasons to replace our anthropocentric outlook on nature with a biocentric outlook on nature. Just as we are justified in replacing the geocentric (Earth-centred) conceptual framework of Ptolemy with the heliocentric (Sun-centred) conceptual framework of Copernicus in our understanding of the solar system, so too we are justified in replacing the anthropocentric outlook on nature that has done so much harm to the environment with the biocentric outlook of modern biology. The biocentric outlook on nature is the conceptual framework of the biologist. For Taylor it contains four crucial features:

(1) Humans are members of the Earth's ecosystem, the same as any other living things.
(2) This ecosystem is a complicated, interconnected web of living things.
(3) All living things pursue their objective goods in their own way.
(4) Human beings are not superior in inherent worth to other living things.

As a consequence of adopting this coherent, unified and rational "picture" or "map" of the world, we will come to see that, all living things have the same inherent worth as human beings (Taylor 1981: 205). If humans have no inherent worth, then neither do other living things. However, if humans do have inherent worth, then so do other living things, and equally so. We have good reason to adopt the biocentric outlook on nature according to which the objective good of any living thing is of no more inherent worth than that of any other.

6. BIOCENTRIC EGALITARIANISM is the view that all living things have equal inherent worth and we must treat them as moral equals in ethical reasoning. Biocentric egalitarianism follows from the crucial fourth feature of the biocentric outlook on nature, the denial of human superiority. It is true that human beings have certain capacities that other living things do not. Taylor mentions rational thought, aesthetic creativity, autonomy and self-determination. These capacities are central to human lives and human society. However, they are important only within an anthropocentric outlook on nature; they are important only from the point of view of human beings. It begs the question to infer that these capacities

are the only capacities that are important from a moral point of view. In the anthropocentric outlook on nature, human beings are superior according to human standards only. Other living beings have capacities that indicate their superiority from the point of view of their species. For example, capacities for rationality, creativity, and autonomy are of little use to a cheetah that relies on its amazing capacity for short bursts of speed to catch its food (1981: 212). The features of human beings that justify their moral superiority in the anthropocentric outlook on nature are revealed as morally arbitrary in the biocentric outlook on nature. All living things have equal inherent worth.

7. Taylor concludes that human beings must adopt an ultimate moral attitude of respect for nature in which moral agents give to all living things the same respect that they give to human beings. An ultimate moral attitude is not a developed ethical theory. Ethicists need to do more work to turn a moral attitude into specific ethical judgments applying to particular cases. His picture of a biocentric ethic is one in which ethical judgments must be faithful to the ultimate moral attitude of respect for nature, which in turn is grounded in adopting the conceptual framework of the biocentric outlook on nature.

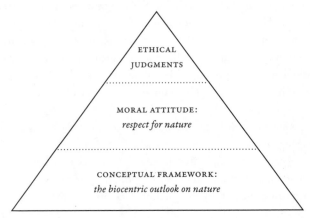

FIGURE 13.1: Ethical judgments resting on the biocentric conceptual framework

The attitude of respect for nature is a disposition to have certain moral emotions, to feel indignation at the senseless destruction of trees, to feel guilt at participating in the killing of living things, to admire activists who oppose the clubbing of baby animals, or to be ashamed at one's own lack of effort on behalf of the non-human world. These emotions are not just feelings or sensations; they have considerable cognitive content. They depend on beliefs about the world, and they will change if these underlying beliefs change. This is the premise of the most common form of psychotherapy, Cognitive-Behavioural Therapy. Here the therapist treats someone's depression, for example, by getting the person to articulate his automatic devaluations of himself, and to see that they are unjustified. By changing his cognitive outlook on himself, the therapist can get him to change his emotional attitude toward himself. Similarly, by changing their conceptual framework from anthropocentric to biocentric, people will change their attitude toward nature to one of respect. Rational agents should give to all living things the same respect that they do to human beings.

One question is how to classify Taylor's biocentric egalitarianism in a taxonomy of ethical theories. Is Taylor's view a rights-based, justice-based, consequentialist, or virtue ethic? Is it holistic or individualistic? Taylor is clear that he does not believe that non-human living beings have moral rights (1981: 218). He does think, however, that one way human societies could express their respect for nature would be to assign legal rights to non-human living beings. He has established that non-human living beings have objective interests, so what we need to do is to set up a system of human legal guardians who can use the courts and legal system to protect the objective interests of living beings. Taylor sees his work as establishing "both standards of character and rules of conduct" for human treatment of nature (1981: 197). Beyond this, it is difficult to classify the ethical theory that he develops. It uses rules of conduct that impose obligations of duty, principles of interspecies justice that apply when these rules of conduct conflict, and green virtues that support people in following these rules and principles. His four rules of conduct for moral agents are (1986: 172):

1. Nonmaleficence: Do not harm any organism with a good of its own.
2. Noninterference: Do not restrict or meddle with individual organisms or their ecosystems.
3. Fidelity: Do not trick or deceive other organisms.
4. Restitutive Justice: Breaking the other rules requires compensating the affected organisms.

Nonetheless, his position is definitely individualistic rather than holistic.

> The good of a population or community of such individuals consists in the population maintaining itself from generation to generation as a coherent system of genetically and ecologically related organisms whose average good is at an optimum for the given environment. (Here *average good* means that the degree of realization of the good of *individual organisms* in the population of community is, on average, greater than would be the case under any other ecologically functioning order of interrelations among those species populations in the given ecosystem.) (1981: 199)

Taylor is concerned primarily with increasing the average good of individual organisms, and only derivatively with promoting the good of whole biological communities insofar as that aids individual organisms.

Second, we might want to ask if it is good biology to say that plants are "teleological centres of life." Taylor is constructing a life-centred ethic, not a thing-centred ethic; he needs to distinguish between living beings that have an objective good, and mere things, like a pile of sand, that do not. He needs a teleological conceptual framework to make this distinction, and he claims to find this in biological science. As biological science develops, however, it makes less and less use of teleological metaphors like flourishing, goal-directedness, and healthiness, and gives more and more detailed explanations of the biochemical mechanisms that explain biological systems. It is possible that the concept of a teleological centre of life will eventually drop out of the conceptual framework of biologists and that the biocentric outlook on nature may become reductionist and mechanistic. In the biocentric outlook of the future, the notions of harming and benefiting living things that underlie the notion of the objective good of living things may become purely metaphorical.

Third, we may wonder whether Taylor has committed the naturalistic fallacy by deriving an ethical "ought" from a scientific "is." Taylor acknowledges the possibility of committing the naturalistic fallacy when he notes that we do not logically contradict ourselves if we assert that a being with an objective good lacks inherent worth. However, he avoids it by recommending the adoption of a certain scientifically based belief system, the biocentric outlook on nature, rather than trying to give a deduction of an ethical proposition from a factual one. In the first chapter, we noted that there are two senses of the word "ought." There is the "ought" of ethics that tells us how we ought to act, and there is the "ought" of normative rationality that tells us what we ought to believe, given our evidence or assumptions. From the evidence of sunlight streaming through the window, we ought to conclude that it is a fine day outside, and we ought not to conclude that it is raining. One way to interpret Taylor's argument is as claiming that we rationally ought to adopt the biocentric outlook on nature because the balance of biological evidence is in its favour. His claim is agreement-seeking in that it appeals to biological evidence and is action-guiding in the sense of guiding our acts of inference. A similar quest for agreement went on when the heliocentric outlook on the solar system replaced the geocentric outlook. Eventually it became a rational inference to adopt the Copernican, heliocentric outlook. Taylor crosses the is/ought gap, not by mistake, but by arguing that we ought rationally to accept the biocentric outlook, and that this outlook rationally grounds a set of emotional dispositions that can be summarized as an attitude of respect for nature.

Fourth, we may ask how Taylor is to resolve conflicts between the objective goods of different life-forms like humans and plants. Here he develops a theory of interspecies justice. He resolves these conflicts by observing first that beings with an objective good also have objective interests, and second that these interests are of different moral importance (1986: 256–313). Living beings have basic interests in securing the conditions for their continued existence, and non-basic interests in securing conditions that enable them to flourish in better rather than worse ways. Human beings, who are moral agents, though not other living beings who are not moral agents, have two types of non-basic interests, those that are in accord with the attitude of respect for nature and those that are not. Human interests that do not respect nature are interests like killing elephants for their ivory, fishing for sport or collecting rare wildflowers (1986: 274). Human interests that do not respect nature have zero weight when they conflict with other interests. Human interests that do respect nature further subdivide into those that are important to developing human civilization and to the basic life plans of individual human beings, and those that are more trivial. One of Taylor's examples of an important nonbasic interest is the building of a library or art museum that will destroy natural habitat (1986: 276).

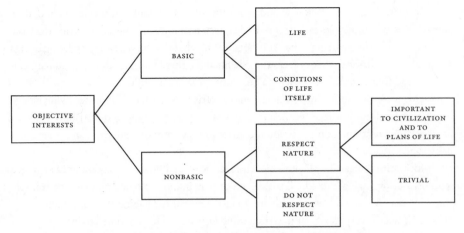

FIGURE 13.2: Taylor's taxonomy of the objective interests of moral agents

According to Taylor's principle of self-defence, a human being may protect her basic interest in life itself by destroying another living being that is attacking her. She has just as much inherent worth as the attacking lion, and thus has no obligation to sacrifice herself for the lion. Self-defence does not violate biocentric egalitarianism. According to Taylor's principle of proportionality, nonbasic human interests that do not respect nature do not count in the adjudication of a conflict. Thus, she may not hunt lions for sport. Taylor's principle of distributive justice covers situations in which the basic interests of human beings come into conflict with the basic interests of other living beings. For example, in environments like that of subsistence hunters in the far north, where humans must eat meat to live, they may kill seals to eat. Humans do not have less inherent worth than seals, and are not obliged to sacrifice their own lives to protect the lives of seals. In environments where a healthy diet of plants may be grown, human beings should be vegetarians. This is not because animals have more inherent worth than plants, but because animals live higher up the food chain, and so farming animals will kill more plants than will harvesting plants for food directly (1986: 293–96). Otherwise, humans must make every effort to share the planet fairly with other species by, for example, setting aside permanent habitat for other living beings.

According to his principle of minimum wrong, important non-basic human interests that respect nature may override the basic interests of other living beings as long as humans minimize the wrongs that they thereby commit. Taylor is not a rights theorist. He does not conceive of the basic interests as always trumping nonbasic interests, as crucially important interests always trump everyday interests in a rights-based theory. Thus, human beings may build an art gallery even though doing so will destroy some natural habitat, as long as they minimize such destruction. Human beings create environmental pollution as a by-product of maintaining their civilization, and may continue to do so, again as long as they minimize the wrongs done to other living beings. It is here that Taylor's theory faces a dilemma. On the one hand, if he does not allow respectful, important, nonbasic human interests to override the basic interests of other living things, then he will have created an ethic that is too stringent for humans to be able to follow. Since "ought" implies "can," it follows that an ethical theory that is too strict for humans to follow would be no ethical theory at all. On the other hand, if he allows respectful and important yet nonbasic interests of human beings to override the basic interests of other living beings, then it is not clear in what way he is treating all living beings as moral equals. Taylor's theory faces the dilemma of either being an ethic that humans can endorse and follow, or not truly being a biocentric egalitarian ethic.

Finally, according to Taylor's principle of restitutive justice, harms to other living beings, brought about by application of the principles of minimum wrong and distributive justice, deserve compensation. Compensation may also take the form of wilderness and permanent habitat preservation.

A fifth question regarding Taylor's biocentric ethic is what he should say about cases where we must sacrifice living individuals to preserve and maintain ecological wholes. For example, should human beings cull large herbivores to save their natural habitat from destructive over-grazing? Taylor is very clear that moral standing is possessed by individual living beings and not by ecological wholes (1986: 118). It is a fallacy to argue that because the individual organisms that make up an ecosystem have moral standing, the ecosystem itself has moral standing. The FALLACY OF COMPOSITION says that it is incorrect to argue from the premise that a part has a certain property to the conclusion that the whole has that property. For example, the following argument is obviously fallacious:

1. Trees are made up of cells as parts.
2. Cells are invisible.
3. Therefore, trees are invisible.

Similarly, in ethics, it does not follow that if the individual parts have moral standing, then the whole has moral standing. The FALLACY OF DECOMPOSITION (or fallacy of division) says that it is incorrect to argue from the premise that a whole has a certain property to the conclusion that any of its parts have that property. For example, the following argument is obviously fallacious:

1. The tree in the courtyard weighs more than a ton.
2. The tree is made of cells.
3. Therefore, the cells of the tree weigh more than a ton.

In ethics, it does not follow that if the whole has moral standing, then the individual parts have moral standing. Even if all individual living things have moral standing, it does not follow that species or ecosystems have moral standing, and vice versa.

Many biological and ecological entities are not individuals. A SPECIES is a category defining a group of individual organisms that are capable of interbreeding. It is different from the POPULATION of a species, which is a group (not a category) of individual organisms belonging to the same species living in a specified area or habitat. A species is an abstract entity, whereas a population is an unstructured collection of individuals. BIODIVERSITY (or biological diversity) is the number or variety of species of organisms in a particular area. An

ECOSYSTEM is a biological community, together with its physical environment, functioning as a whole.

There is a saying that the whole is greater than the sum of its parts. In philosophy, we could mean three very different things by this saying (Des Jardins 1997: 165–67). One is METAPHYSICAL HOLISM, which is the claim that a whole has an existence that is just as real as that of its parts. The parts could exist, but if they are not organized in a certain way, then the whole will not exist. If the parts are organized in the right way, then a new, holistic entity comes into existence. For example, one early interpretation of an ecosystem was as a superorganism, just as real as the individual organisms of which compose it. It is also possible to think of a human being as a highly differentiated and organized community of trillions of human cells and trillions of microorganisms. Another form of holism is METHODOLOGICAL HOLISM, which is the philosophical view that we cannot have a complete understanding of a system just by knowing everything about its parts. The science of ecology again is an example; we cannot reduce knowledge of the intricate interrelationships of the ecosystem to knowledge about its component species. A third form of holism is ETHICAL HOLISM, which is the view that wholes have moral standing either as well as, or instead of, their constituent parts. For example, ethical holism might consider the good of a biotic community over and above the good of its members. We will look more closely at ethical holism in the next chapter.

SUMMARY

1. Theories about obligations to future generations, animal welfare, or animal rights all involve extending applied ethics into new areas while accepting the standard conceptual framework for interpreting the world.

2. New environmental philosophies like biocentric egalitarianism or ecofeminism involve changing our underlying conceptual framework, the metaphorical lens through which we understand the world.

3. Albert Schweitzer urges adoption of a new attitude toward the world, reverence for life, based on adoption of a new life-centred worldview. Reverence for life is a disposition to have emotions of awe, wonder, and reverence toward all living beings.

4. Paul Taylor urges adoption of a fundamental moral attitude of respect for life, based on adoption of a new conceptual framework for understanding humans and their relationship to nature, the biocentric outlook on life.

5. In the biocentric outlook on life, humans have no more inherent worth than do other living beings. Living beings are teleological centres of life, each with an objective good of its own, and morally equal in their inherent worth to human beings. Biocentric egalitarianism is the view that all living beings are equal from the moral point of view.

6. We should adopt the biocentric outlook, the outlook of the biological sciences, because it is rational to do so, not because it is morally required to do so. One question for Taylor's argument is whether teleological explanations are as important in biology as he thinks they are. Adopting the

new cognitive framework of the biocentric outlook will lead us to adopt a new emotional framework of respect for life, upon which we can base a new environmental ethic.

7. Another question for Taylor's position is how it will handle conflicts between the objective interests of human beings and other living beings. Human beings have equal moral worth to other living beings and thus do not have to sacrifice their basic interests (interests in the conditions of life itself) for other beings. Nonbasic human interests that do not respect nature, like killing for sport, carry no weight in conflicts with the interests of other living beings. Taylor thinks that important human nonbasic interests that do respect nature may override the basic interests of other living beings provided that humans do minimum wrong, treat other living beings fairly, and compensate them in some way for their injury. Humans should be vegetarians, not because animals have more inherent worth than plants, but because animals eat plants, and eating animals will involve doing more wrong overall than will eating the plants themselves.

8. Biocentric egalitarianism is an individualistic environmental ethic, not a holistic one. It assigns moral standing only to individual organisms and does not assign moral standing to the ecological system of which they are a part.

ONLINE READING QUESTIONS

The book's website contains reading questions on this chapter. Working through these questions will help you understand, remember, and apply important concepts from the chapter. Some of the questions supply useful hints for the study questions.

STUDY QUESTIONS

Using the text and hints from the online reading questions, write out, type, dictate to your computer, or at least formulate in your head answers to the following questions.

1. Why is Albert Schweitzer's theory of Reverence for Life a virtue ethic?
2. Explain the distinction between an organism having a subjective and an objective good.
3. How does Taylor avoid Hume's Guillotine?
4. How does Taylor's biocentric egalitarianism resolve conflicts between humans and non-human living things?

QUESTIONS TO PONDER

Spend a few minutes thinking about the following questions, or, better yet, discuss them with fellow readers of this book.

1. Complex machines, like cruise missiles, exhibit goal-directed behaviour, and we can give teleological explanations of what they do. Would a sophisticated future robot be a teleological centre of life?

2. Where is the demarcation between living beings and natural objects? Are bacteria, viruses, or prions teleological centres of life?

3. If a biocentric egalitarian's only choice was to eat either a pig or a quarter acre of soybeans weighing about the same, which should he eat, and why?

4. If a biocentric egalitarian's only choice was to eat either a pig or a human being of the same weight, which should she choose, and why?

5. When Taylor says important nonbasic human interests that respect nature can override the basic interests of nonhuman living beings, does he really give up his biocentric egalitarianism or does he still respect the equal inherent worth of all living beings?

6. Is it a consequence of Taylor's position that it is ethically permissible to kill seals respectfully, and with minimum pain and wastage, to make fur coats?

Chapter 14

ECOCENTRIC
ETHICS

SYMPATHETIC PHILOSOPHERS DEVELOPED THE ETHICS OF ANIMAL WELFARE AND animal rights because they thought standard anthropocentric ethics did not adequately protect the well-being and lives of animals. Similarly, environmentally minded philosophers have developed biocentric ethics because they did not think that zoocentric ethics adequately protected the environment. Ecocentric ethics, the view that ecosystems have moral standing, goes even further. In this view, we should protect ecosystems or biotic communities because they have an inherent worth that is over and above their usefulness to the lives of plants, animals, and human beings.

An ecocentric ethic would make sense to someone who adopts a holistic conceptual framework, an ecocentric outlook on nature. However, an ecocentric outlook on nature is different from a biocentric outlook only if, in some important way, ecology is different from biology. If we can fully explain the behaviour of an ecosystem through knowledge of its physical environment and the biological character of its component species, then the ecocentric outlook is not truly a new conceptual framework for understanding the world. Local ecosystems, or the whole planetary ecosystem, must be more than the sum of their parts in order to support the idea of basing an ethic on their moral standing.

We can take any of several possible positions on the role of ecosystems in environmental ethics. The default position is that ecosystems have only instrumental value to the entities that live in them. They provide ecosystem services to humans, and provide food to animals and plants. A second position is that ecosystems do have intrinsic value, but have less moral significance than do individual entities. A third position is that of ecocentric egalitarianism, the view that ecosystems have moral standing and an inherent worth equal to that of individual entities. Finally, we might hold the position that ecosystems are the only entities with moral standing. Individual living beings are merely of instrumental value, ethically important only for the role they play in maintaining the stability and health of ecosystems. The latter is the interpretation often given to Aldo Leopold's influential Land Ethic: "A thing is right when it tends to preserve the integrity, stability, and beauty of the biotic community. It is wrong when it tends otherwise" (1949: 262). This interpretation appears to sacrifice the interests of humans and other living beings to preserve the ecosystems in which they live.

Learning Objectives

1. To understand the notion of a holistic theory.
2. To understand the Land Ethic of Aldo Leopold.
3. To understand some of the weaknesses of holistic theories in environmental ethics.

CRITERIA FOR MORAL STANDING

So far we have looked at four different theories regarding what natural feature something should possess in order to be morally considerable, and we are about to look at a fifth. Immanuel Kant thought that moral agency was necessary and sufficient for moral standing. Moral agency includes the capacity for free and rational moral action, the capacity for taking moral responsibility, and the ability to have duties to others. Strictly speaking, Kant's criterion implies that only competent, adult human beings have moral standing; children, the cognitively challenged, and the comatose are left out.

Peter Singer takes sentience, the ability to feel pleasure and pain, to be the criterion for moral standing. The criterion of sentience implies that human beings and, roughly, all animals more complex than an oyster are morally considerable. Singer takes the moral standing of humans and somewhat complex animals to imply that we should give their interests equal consideration, or weight them equally in utilitarian calculations regarding the best policies to implement.

Tom Regan takes something more than sentience to be the criterion for moral standing. All beings that are experiencing subjects of a life are morally considerable. Being an experiencing subject of a life includes having beliefs and desires, memory, a sense of the future, emotions, preferences, and goal-directedness. The being's welfare must matter to it. Regan's criterion includes all human beings and all mammals over one year of age (1983: 78). Regan argues that all experiencing subjects of a life have equal inherent worth, and thus are entitled to equal respect for their moral rights.

Paul Taylor argues that even though only humans and animals can have subjective interests, other living beings can have objective interests and are thus morally considerable. To have objective interests, a being must be capable of being benefited or harmed. Thus to have moral standing, a being needs to be a teleological centre of life; it must be goal directed. Taylor argues for biocentric egalitarianism, the view that all living things, including humans and animals, have equal moral worth. Table 14.1 summarizes these four positions, together with Aldo Leopold's ecocentric Land Ethic.

AUTHOR	THEORY	CRITERION	APPLICATION
Kant	Human rights	Moral agency	Competent *homo sapiens*
Singer	Animal welfare	Sentience	Somewhat complex animals
Regan	Animal rights	Experiencing subject-of-a-life	Quite complex animals
Taylor	Biocentric	Teleological centre of life	Living things
Leopold	Ecocentric	Biotic community	Ecosystems

TABLE 14.1: Summary of criteria for moral standing

Aldo Leopold takes biotic communities to be morally considerable because they have integrity, stability, and beauty. Biotic communities are holistic entities, composed of individual animals and plants of different species in a complicated relationship to the land on which they live. The land ethic sees ecosystems as having moral standing, but potentially denies moral standing to individual plants, animals, and even humans.

ECOLOGY AND INTRINSIC VALUE

The ecocentric outlook forms a new, holistic conceptual framework only if methodological holism is true. Does ecology reduce to biology? Can we give a complete account of an ecosystem in terms of the interactions of its biological components and their physical environment? Do we think that, in principle, we can construct computer simulations of complex ecosystems that model our observations of them? To some extent, the answer depends on how we interpret ecosystems.

One, older interpretation of an ecosystem is as a complex super-organism. The different species of plants and animals in the system relate to the whole ecosystem as organs, like the heart and liver, relate to the body of an animal. Ecosystems, like organisms, develop to maturity. For example, in north-eastern North America, a forest fire will lead first to ferns, then leafy bushes, then deciduous trees like birch, then small conifers like spruce and fir, and finally to a pine or hemlock forest. Ecosystems develop toward stable natural equilibrium or climax community.

A second interpretation uses the metaphor of ecosystems as biotic communities organized into a food web. Species occupy ecological niches in a food chain. Energy from the sun is taken into the community from photosynthesis by plants that are the primary producers. These are consumed by members of herbivorous species, which are in turn consumed by members of carnivorous species. Bacteria and fungi in the soil decompose waste material and dead consumers, and return nutrients to the plants. This is a simple food chain, but actual ecosystems are much more complex, and a better metaphor is that of a food web. Individual members are characterized by the food function they perform in the ecosystem.

The community as a whole is reasonably stable over time, even though individual plants and animals are continually dying and being replaced.

A third interpretation of ecosystems stresses the flow of energy in the system. An ecosystem includes both biological and non-biological elements, and ecologists also study the cycling of nutrients like carbon, nitrogen, and phosphorous through the system.

The first interpretation of an ecosystem fits nicely with the teleological approach to intrinsic value described in Chapter 6. The ecosystem, as super-organism, has a natural purpose or goal that is to preserve and maintain itself as a stable, homeostatic system. The teleological approach then sees the stability of the ecosystem as having intrinsic value. The stability of the ecosystem is more than just instrumentally valuable to humans, animals, or plants. It is valuable in and of itself because it is a goal of the ecosystem. The problem with this approach is that teleological explanations, and talk of ecosystems as super-organisms, is becoming out of date in modern scientific thinking.

The second interpretation of an ecosystem fits nicely with the common good approach to intrinsic value. The stability of an ecosystem is intrinsically valuable because it contributes to the betterment of the biotic community. A biotic community is an organized collection of individual plants and animals, and maintaining the health, integrity, and stability of the community's organizational structure is intrinsically valuable. The stability of the biotic community is intrinsically valuable, rather than just something of instrumental value to the community's members, only if the community is more than the sum of its parts. Currently we marvel at the complexity of ecosystems and are unable to comprehend how such stable interrelationships are maintained. However, future scientists may create comprehensive computer models of ecosystems that will support the view that we can understand ecosystems through knowledge of the behaviours of their individual components.

Dispositional or informed preference theories may also assign intrinsic value to ecosystems. If an imaginary person who was fully informed and reasoning rationally about ecosystems would prefer that they were preserved, then ecosystems would have intrinsic value. Arguably this sort of value is not instrumental. No actual human beings are fully informed and perfectly rational. Instead, informed preference theories of value make a claim about what possible, but not actual, human beings would be disposed to prefer. Ecosystems would have this type of value even if they were completely unknown or useless to actual human beings. A possible objection to the dispositional theory of value is that, since it appeals to the informed preferences of possible human beings, it is fundamentally anthropocentric. However, this objection would also apply to non-anthropocentric theories. Schweitzer grounds his ethical theory in an attitude of reverence, and both Regan and Taylor ground their ethical fundamental attitudes of respect. Reverence and respect are also attitudes that only beings with the emotional makeup of human beings can adopt.

These three ways of valuing ecosystems—teleological, common good, and dispositional— are of particular use within an objective consequentialist ethical theory. Such an ethical theory would examine the intrinsic values of different policy outcomes, somehow weigh their moral significance, make any necessary trade-offs, and recommend the policy which maximized intrinsic value.

We have earlier looked at some holistic criticisms of individualistic ethical theories, particularly of animal welfare and animal rights. The holistic outlook raises questions regarding conflicts between individual organisms and species. For example, do the last remaining members of a species have any special moral status? May we shoot goats living on an island in order to protect a rare species of plants found only on that island? The holistic outlook also raises questions regarding conflicts between individual organisms and ecosystems. For example, in the absence of any other top predator, may we cull deer in order to save a forest ecosystem?

Kant, Singer, Regan, and Taylor all gave equal consideration or respect only to the interests of individual people, animals, and living things. We are familiar, however, with considering the interests of entities that are not reducible to their component individuals. Business corporations have the standing of legal persons under law, and have many, though not all, the legal rights and responsibilities of human persons. Business corporations are characterized by a high degree of organizational structure that enables them to exist as stable entities in a market economy. Their legal rights protect their stable existence both externally, from other firms in the economy, and internally, from their employees and shareholders. Condominium corporations, universities, municipalities, provinces, states, and nations too have legal rights and duties, and exist as stable, complex, highly organized entities.

In 1949, Aldo Leopold proposed that ecosystems should also have moral standing. He wrote that "A thing is right when it tends to preserve the integrity, stability, and beauty of the biotic community. It is wrong when it tends otherwise" (1949: 262). Leopold's definition of his land ethic has been very influential in the development of non-anthropocentric ethical theories. Human beings live in human communities and need ethics to enable them to cooperate both for mutual advantage and for the sake of preserving the community. "The land ethic simply enlarges the boundaries of the community to include soils, waters, plants, and animals, or collectively: the land" (1949: 239).

A preliminary question that we may ask is whether the land ethic commits the naturalistic fallacy. The naturalistic fallacy is the fallacy of arguing from statements of fact to judgments of value without adequate reasons or additional ethical premises. Does the land ethic fail to observe the fact/value distinction between descriptive statements about scientific facts and normative judgments about ethical issues? A way for Leopold to cross the is/ought gap would be to embrace one of the objective theories of intrinsic value that we canvassed earlier. For example, suppose we assume that all ecosystems tend toward a stable state. Then, the ethical premise that fulfilling the natural purpose of goal-directed entities is intrinsically valuable, together with the empirical premise that ecosystems do have the goal of stability would, without fallacy, yield the conclusion that the stability of ecosystems has intrinsic value. Similarly, the ethical premise that preserving communities is intrinsically good, together with the idea that ecosystems are biotic communities, yields the conclusion that preserving ecosystems is intrinsically valuable.

Another way that Leopold could avoid the fallacy would be to argue, like Taylor, that it is rational for people to adopt an ecocentric outlook on nature, and that this will lead to an attitude grounding the land ethic. Leopold writes "[n]o important change in ethics was ever accomplished without an internal change in our intellectual emphasis, loyalties, affections and convictions" (1949: 246). It is possible that we could expand these remarks, following Taylor, to rationally justify our adoption of a new intellectual framework, new emotional attitudes, and thus new ethical convictions.

Another important question to ask is how to interpret the land ethic as an account of the moral standing of ecosystems. Two interesting interpretations are:

1. Ecosystems are the only entities with moral standing.
2. Ecosystems have moral standing, and other individual entities have equal moral standing.

There are other possibilities, but we will look at only these two. It is difficult to interpret Leopold's view here. On the one hand, he describes how moral standing has been extended as human societies developed. The beautifully written opening paragraphs of his essay, "The Land Ethic," tell how the ancient Greek hero, Odysseus, thought about his wife, Penelope, in an ethical way but not about the slave girls of his household, twelve of whom he hanged for suspected misbehaviour. Since that time, "ethical criteria have been extended to many fields of conduct" (1949: 237). Usually when a criterion or principle extends to new cases, it still applies to the cases where it applied before the extension. On this interpretation, humans and other living beings would keep their moral standing within the land ethic.

On the other hand, Leopold's formulation of the land ethic can easily be taken to imply that the land is the only entity with moral standing. The first part of his definition says that an action is right when it tends to preserve the stability of ecosystems. So preserving the stability of ecosystems is sufficient for an action to be right. The first part of his definition does not say that this is the only way for an action to be right. The first part of the definition leaves it an open question whether other actions may also be right because, for example, they respect the rights of animals.

The second part of his definition has two possible readings. One reading takes it to mean that an action is wrong when it is not the case that it tends to preserve the stability of ecosystems. This reading means that the only way for an action to be right is for it to preserve the stability of ecosystems. The first part of Leopold's definition says that preserving the stability of an ecosystem is enough for an action to be right, and the second part of his definition, on the present reading, says that preserving the stability of an ecosystem is required for an action to be right. The conclusion is that only ecosystems can have moral standing, because preserving their stability is the only way to perform a right action. This conclusion seems much too strong. Surely, there are other ways to perform a right action, for example, by making everyone happy, or by promoting the interests of all living things.

Another reading of the second part of Leopold's definition, "It is wrong when it tends otherwise," takes it to mean that an action is wrong when it tends to not preserve (that is, to have an adverse effect on) the stability of ecosystems. The difference between the two readings comes out in what the second part of the definition says about neutral actions. Neutral actions have no effect on the stability of ecosystems. Since neutral actions do not tend to preserve the stability of ecosystems, they are wrong under the first reading. Since neutral actions have no adverse effect on the stability of ecosystems, they are not wrong under the second reading.

The second reading allows that the land ethic does not cover neutral actions. It does not cover actions that tend neither to preserve nor to affect ecosystems adversely. It allows that ecologically neutral actions may be right or wrong under different moral standards from the land ethic, that other entities besides ecosystems may have moral standing, and that we need a theory of environmental justice to decide conflicts between the interests of ecosystems and living things generally. This reading is the more natural reading of the second part of the land ethic: "A thing is wrong when it tends otherwise." An action is wrong when it tends to affect the stability of an ecosystem adversely.

Nevertheless, the view that only ecosystems have moral standing has been influential in environmental ethics. Reading the land ethic to say that only ecosystems have moral standing leads to a purely holistic ethic, which is in conflict with individualistic ethics like those of Singer, Regan, and Taylor. A purely holistic ethic gives only instrumental value to the individuals that make up ecosystems. Individual living things, humans included, are only of value insofar as they tend to preserve the stability of the ecosystem. If they tend otherwise, then we should stop or destroy them. This train of thought can lead to a holistic ecocentric ethic that is non-anthropocentric, and also anti-anthropocentric or misanthropic. It puts the health and stability of ecosystems not only ahead of the basic interests of animals and plants, but also ahead of the basic interests of human beings. Such an ethic would be very demanding on human beings, and, since "ought" implies "can," would need to be developed carefully to make it a possible ethical system for humans to follow. Maybe we could avoid doing what this ethic says is wrong: switching on a light, heating our houses—indeed building houses in the first place. We might survive in dark cold caves, but an ethic that advocates this is ridiculously demanding.

THE MORAL STANDING OF ECOSYSTEMS

Earlier we pictured the extension of moral standing in various theories of environmental ethics as a series of concentric circles, with ecosystems represented as an outer circle that encompasses all the others. However, if we accept an ecocentric ethic in which the moral significance of ecosystems is superior to that of individual living things, then the picture will look more like that it Figure 14.1. In this picture, the moral standing of ecosystems partially eclipses, rather than encompasses, that of individual living beings.

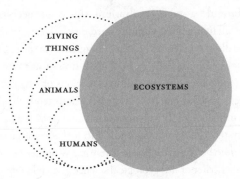

FIGURE 14.1: Moral significance of ecosystems as superior to that of other living things

In political philosophy, one huge problem with ethical theories based on the common good is that the good of the community too easily overrides the interests and rights of individual people. The fascism of Hitler and Mussolini was distinguished by a thoroughgoing priority of communal values over individual rights. Tom Regan writes:

> The implications of this [Leopold's] view include the clear prospect that the individual may be sacrificed for the greater biotic good, in the name of 'the integrity, stability and beauty of the biotic community.' It is difficult to see how the notion of the rights of the individual could find a home within a view that ... might be fairly dubbed "environmental fascism." (1983: 361–62)

Animals and human beings are only members of biotic communities. It could be, writes Regan, that some rare wildflower is of more importance to the stability of the biotic community than are its animal or human members. On this view, we would be doing no wrong if we destroyed the humans to protect the wildflowers. Regan cannot abide this conclusion because it violates the rights of individuals. How should we interpret the land ethic to avoid the charge of ecofascism? Is the land ethic (1) the only source of right and wrong, (2) the most important source of right and wrong, or (3) merely one source of right and wrong among many?

Even if we interpret the land ethic in the weakest sense, we should still ask how we are to understand conflicts between ecosystems and individual plants, animals and humans. When we tried to adjudicate conflicts within zoocentric and biocentric theories, we appealed to the notion of interests. We looked at equal consideration of interests in utilitarianism, the distinctions between immoral, everyday, and crucial subjective interests that are at work in rights- and justice-based theories, and the basic and nonbasic interests at work in Taylor's biocentric egalitarianism. So it seems that in order to take account of the moral standing of ecosystems, we need to investigate whether ecosystems can have objective interests.

In Taylor's account of the objective interests of plants, he pointed out that plants could be benefited or harmed because they have goals that can be facilitated or thwarted. They are goal-directed, teleological centres of life. Harley Cahen has argued that it is much harder to make out a case that ecosystems are goal directed (Cahen 1988). Ecosystems have the apparent goal of striving to achieve and maintain a stable equilibrium state. However, though an ecosystem may tend toward a stable equilibrium, this is not necessarily a real goal of the system. For example, all living beings tend toward death. Death is a stable state for any living being, but it is hardly the real goal of any living being (1988: 209). Death is instead a by-product of the biology of living beings. Real goals do not just describe the direction toward which a system tends; they also provide explanations of why the system tends that way. Behaviour is directed toward a goal both if the behaviour tends to bring about the goal, and if the behaviour occurs *because* it brings about that goal (1988: 205).

Whether or not ecosystems have moral standing in a theory of environmental justice depends on whether or not they have objective interests. Whether or not they have objective interests depends on whether or not ecological science gives teleological explanations of their behaviour. Whether or not science gives teleological explanations of their behaviour depends on whether the behaviour of ecosystems occurs because it "tends to preserve the integrity, stability, and beauty of the biotic community," or whether the stable equilibrium of the ecosystem is just a by-product of the activity of individual living beings acting in their environment. For example, in an earlier chapter we looked at Adam Smith's claim that an "invisible hand" would produce the maximum aggregate income for the members of an economic system, even though each member of the economic system acted only for his or her own self-interest. Of course the invisible hand is a metaphor. Under perfect conditions, the economic system behaves only *as if* it tends to maximize aggregate income. Maximizing aggregate income is not a real goal of the economic system; it is a by-product of the self-seeking behaviour of participants. Modern economic science explains why an economic system in perfect competition will maximize overall economic welfare in terms of economic models of the behaviour of self-interested rational agents without appeal to an invisible hand. Whether or not ecosystems can have objective interests depends on whether or not modern ecological science requires non-metaphorical teleological explanations to explain their stability and resilience.

THE GAIA HYPOTHESIS

Our Sun, like any star of its magnitude, is slowly getting hotter. In a billion years or so, it will have become so hot that it will have burned off all the Earth's atmosphere and evaporated all of its water. By that point, Earth will have become uninhabitable for life as we know it, just as Mars is now. Even though the Sun has become significantly hotter in the last half billion years, the temperature of the Earth, with some exceptions, has remained remarkably constant in a range that is hospitable to life. Struck by this and other facts pointing to the stability of the Earth's biosphere, the atmospheric scientist, James Lovelock, suggested the GAIA HYPOTHESIS that Earth itself is a self-regulating system that has stability as its goal. Provocatively, he called this system, Gaia, after the ancient Greek goddess of the Earth, thus suggesting that the system is some sort of complex super-organism. Over time, the biosphere adapts to the Earth's physical environment because Darwinian evolution modifies its species membership. At the same time, though, the Earth's biosphere modifies the Earth's physical environment, for example, by absorbing carbon dioxide from the atmosphere and trapping it underground in the form of coal and oil. These feedback mechanisms tend to maintain the Earth's temperature at a level that preserves the stability of the Earth's community of living beings.

The question of the Gaian system's moral standing depends on the same sort of considerations on which the moral standing of ecosystems depends. Does the Gaian system have intrinsic value? Is it the only entity with moral standing, or is it just one of many entities with moral standing? Can we meaningfully say that the Gaian system has objective interests? Are teleological explanations of the Gaian system true teleological explanations, or are they just useful metaphors? Is the apparent teleology of the Gaian system merely a by-product of the workings of Darwinian evolution at an individual level coupled to the scientifically unsurprising effects of living things on their physical environment?

SUMMARY

1. Different environmental ethics each have a different criterion for moral standing. For Kant, it is moral agency. For Singer's animal welfare theory, it is sentience. For Regan's animal rights theory, it is being an experiencing subject of a life. For Taylor's biocentric ethic, it is being a teleological centre of life. For Aldo Leopold's land ethic, it is being a biotic community or ecosystem.

2. If ecosystems are goal-directed super-organisms, then they could have intrinsic value in the teleological approach. If ecosystems are biotic communities, then they could have intrinsic value in the common good approach. They could also have intrinsic value according to the dispositional, or informed preference, account.

3. According to Leopold's land ethic, "A thing is right when it tends to preserve the integrity, stability, and beauty of the biotic community. It is wrong when it tends otherwise" (1949: 262).

4. The land ethic has been taken to mean either that only ecosystems are morally considerable, or that ecosystems are morally considerable and other individual entities are too.

5. The strong interpretation can lead to ecofascism.

6. The weak interpretation has difficulty accounting for conflicts of interests between ecosystems and living beings. To have objective interests, a system must be goal-directed. So the question is whether ecosystems simply tend to a stable equilibrium, or whether they behave as they do *because* their behaviour tends to maintain that stable equilibrium.

7. The Gaia hypothesis takes the planet Earth to be a coupled system in which species in the biosphere evolve to fit their environment while, at the same time, changing that environment so that it tends to preserve conditions hospitable to life. The methodological question is whether the Gaia hypothesis is a genuine teleological explanation or just a useful metaphor.

ONLINE READING QUESTIONS

The book's website contains reading questions on this chapter. Working through these questions will help you understand, remember, and apply important concepts from the chapter. Some of the questions supply useful hints for the study questions.

Using the text and hints from the online reading questions, write out, type, dictate to your computer, or at least formulate in your head answers to the following questions.

1. Explain three different interpretations of the view that ecosystems have moral standing.
2. Describe an example of a holistic criticism of an individualistic theory of moral standing.
3. Why can the Land Ethic be accused of ecofascism?
4. Suppose members of a species have moral standing. Why does it not immediately follow that the species itself has moral standing?

QUESTIONS TO PONDER

Spend a few minutes thinking about the following questions, or, better yet, discuss them with fellow readers of this book.

1. Do you think that an ecosystem is either a super-organism or a biotic community?
2. Do you think a dispositional, informed preference account of intrinsic value is necessarily anthropocentric?
3. Does Leopold commit the naturalistic fallacy in formulating his land ethic?
4. Are ecosystems the only entities with moral standing? Or, do ecosystems and living beings all have equal moral standing? Or, do ecosystems just have intrinsic value? Or do they merely have instrumental value? To whom?
5. Do we need to give teleological explanations of ecosystem behaviour? Does ecosystem behaviour not only tend to preserve stability but also occur because it tends to preserve stability? Can we fully account for ecosystem behaviour through complicated computer models?

Chapter 15

ECOFEMINISM

JUSTICE REQUIRES AN END TO RELATIONSHIPS OF UNEQUAL AND UNFAIR POWER, where one party dominates the other and uses the subordinate party to serve his own ends. Does this apply to relations between humans and the natural world? Human beings have power over nature. They dominate animals, plants, and the land and use the environment to serve their own purposes. Abuse of this power causes most of the Earth's environmental problems.

Power takes different forms. Coercive power is the ability to dominate through force or the threat of force. Between one person and another, it is the power of the gun and the jail cell. Between humans and nature, it is the power of the bulldozer and the slaughterhouse. Economic power is the ability to dominate through economic incentive or economic threat. It allows one person to hire another to operate the bulldozer or to work in the slaughterhouse. Ideological power is the ability to dominate through internalized beliefs and attitudes. Ideological power works both ways. It leads subordinates to see their unquestioned submission as natural, and it leads the dominant to understand their dominance as ordinary and normal. The machinery operator bulldozing the rainforest does not think to question his orders, and the farmer who hired him thinks it is progress to clear-cut trees and grow soybeans. Human domination of nature is taken for granted by everyone.

Ideological power depends on the existence of a widely held, mutually supporting, and resilient set of core beliefs about the world and about human nature, together with the attitudes that these beliefs sustain. In other words, ideological power depends on a shared worldview or conceptual framework. Ecofeminists point out that shared conceptual frameworks are often oppressive; they implicitly contain an unquestioned logic of domination. Further, there are interesting connections between the patriarchal conceptual framework that makes the domination of women by men seem natural and the anthropocentric conceptual framework that makes the domination of nature by humans seem normal and ordinary. Both types of domination must be understood together.

To some feminists, all the ethical theories that we have looked at so far are part of a patriarchal conceptual framework. Looking at ethical problems through the lens of moral rights, principles of justice, and calculations of utility is a masculine approach. Women, with their experience of looking after children, old folks, and dependent others, have a different approach, an ethic of care. An ethic of care emphasizes special relationships between people and the emotions that validate them. An environmental ethic of care emphasizes the attachments people make to animals and the land.

Learning Objectives

1. To understand the notion of having and changing a conceptual framework.
2. To understand how a conceptual framework can facilitate injustice.
3. To understand the idea of an oppressive conceptual framework in ecofeminism.
4. To understand the feminist ethics of care.

CONCEPTUAL FRAMEWORKS

A factual conceptual framework is a widely held, mutually supporting, and resilient set of core beliefs about the world and about human nature. Conceptual frameworks are resilient because they are able to maintain their structure while making only small changes in response to contrary evidence. We have met a factual conceptual framework before in Paul Taylor's biocentric outlook on nature. The biocentric outlook is the conceptual framework of the biologist:

1. Human beings are members of the Earth's ecosystem, the same as all other living beings.
2. This ecosystem is a complicated, interconnected web.
3. All living things flourish in their own way.
4. Human beings are not inherently superior in strength, speed, size, etc. to other living things.

If we change our conceptual framework to the biocentric outlook, then we will also move, he argues, to the ethical position of biocentric egalitarianism.

A paradigm of a change in conceptual frameworks was the move from the geocentric (Earth-centred) outlook of Ptolemy to the heliocentric (Sun-centred) outlook of Copernicus and Galileo during the European Renaissance. That the Sun, Moon, planets, and stars went round the Earth in perfect circles was an almost universally held and fundamental belief of Medieval European science. It was also a very resilient set of beliefs. It had external support because it fitted in with the account of the heavens in the Christian Bible, and there was not, at the time, a clear distinction between science and religion. It had internal support because of its ability to absorb all contrary empirical observations through the device of epicycles. In the geocentric framework, the planets were supposed to go around the Earth from east to west. Nevertheless, sometimes they appear to move from west to east. Astronomers can easily explain the retrograde motion of the planets in the modern, heliocentric framework. The Earth moves more quickly around the Sun, and on a smaller orbit, than does an outer planet like Jupiter. When the Earth is on the opposite side of the Sun from Jupiter and moving faster, Jupiter will appear to move in one direction against the fixed stars. When the Earth is on the same side of the Sun as Jupiter and moving faster, Jupiter will appear to move in the opposite direction against the fixed stars. The medieval, geocentric outlook can explain this only in terms of the planets moving in small circles, epicycles, around their proper position on their great orbits around the Earth. Using the device of epicycles, the geocentric framework gave an accurate account of all astronomical observations made until the Renaissance.

Factual conceptual frameworks are resilient in part because scientific theories are difficult to falsify. In an over-simplified account of scientific method, scientists work by formulating hypotheses and then performing crucial experiments, which either confirm or falsify them. In a more accurate account of scientific method, scientists do formulate hypotheses, but they can test these hypotheses only in conjunction with many assumptions about other theories and about how their apparatus works. For example, a hypothesis in theoretical physics can only be tested by assuming a great deal of other physics to be true and assuming a great deal of technology works as planned. An observation contrary to the hypothesis may either disconfirm the hypothesis or indicate a problem in other parts of the theory or in the experimental apparatus. From the logical point of view, it is not possible to tell whether an observation falsifies the proposed hypothesis or an auxiliary assumption. It is always logically possible to maintain the original hypothesis by changing the auxiliary assumptions instead. In a similar way, just one counter-argument or one crucial experiment cannot falsify and overthrow a conceptual framework. The move from wide acceptance of one conceptual framework to wide acceptance of another involves an accumulation of ill-explained evidence, an accumulation of dissatisfaction with the clumsy explanations offered by the earlier framework, and even the passing of an older generation of scientists. The heliocentric conceptual framework is not just a modification of the geocentric one; it is a completely new worldview, a new conceptual lens for viewing the universe. The transition from the geocentric to the heliocentric framework is the Copernican Revolution. It affected the way that Renaissance Europeans thought of their relationship to the natural world.

Up to this point, we have been working with factual or scientific conceptual frameworks, and have considered them as separate from the attitudes and ethical values that they support. For example, we interpreted Taylor as arguing that norms of rationality should move us to adopt the biocentric outlook, and that adopting this biological conceptual framework would then lead us to adopt an attitude of respect for nature and the ethical values that come with that attitude. However, we can also think of conceptual frameworks more generally. We can think of them as including the attitudes and ethical values that naturally go with the factual conceptual framework. Karen Warren defines a conceptual framework as "... a set of basic beliefs, values, attitudes and assumptions which shape and reflect how one views oneself and one's world. It is a socially constructed lens through which we perceive ourselves and others. It is affected by such factors as gender, race, class, age, affectional orientation, nationality, and religious background" (Warren 1990: 127). A CONCEPTUAL FRAMEWORK is a mutually supporting, seldom questioned, and resilient set of fundamental assumptions about the world, about human nature, and about ethical values that affects how people think and act in the world.

It is easier to see and analyze the conceptual frameworks of others than it is to see and analyze one's own. The astronomy and cosmology of Medieval Europeans was not distinct from their religion. The cosmology that supplemented the Ptolemaic, geocentric conceptual framework in astronomy was the creation story in the Book of Genesis. In the beginning, God created heaven and the Earth, then light and darkness, then water and dry land, then plants, then the Sun and stars, and then animals. Finally, God created human beings:

> 26. And God said, Let us make man in our image, after our likeness: and let them have dominion over the fish of the sea, and over the fowl of the air, and over the cattle, and over all the earth, and over every creeping thing that creepeth upon the earth.
> 27. So God created man in his own image, in the image of God created he him; male and female created he them.
> 28. And God blessed them, and God said unto them, Be fruitful, and multiply, and replenish the earth, and subdue it: and have dominion over the fish of the sea, and over the fowl of the air, and over every living thing that moveth upon the earth.
> 29. And God said, Behold, I have given you every herb bearing seed, which is upon the face of all the earth, and every tree, in the which is the fruit of a tree yielding seed; to you it shall be for meat [i.e., food]. (King James Version: Genesis, Chapter 1)

Genesis contains a cosmology in which God creates the heavens and Earth, and a view of human nature in which humans are created in the image of God. The bible has a divine command ethical theory in which God ordered that human beings "have dominion over" or dominate all other living things and use them for human purposes. This conceptual framework, consisting of a cosmology, a geocentric astronomy, a theory of human nature as like that of God, and a divine command theory of ethics, justified a thoroughly anthropocentric environmental ethic in which nature had only instrumental value. We can see how such a conceptual framework would make human domination of nature seem natural and normal, and how it would lead people to take for granted their exploitation of the environment. In an influential 1967 essay, "The Historical Roots of Our Ecological Crisis," Lynn White, Jr.

argued that this ancient and medieval conceptual framework is still influential in sustaining exploitative western attitudes toward the environment (White 1967).

KAREN WARREN ON OPPRESSIVE CONCEPTUAL FRAMEWORKS

Karen Warren argued that there are important historical, metaphorical, and theoretical connections between the domination of women by men and the domination of the environment by human beings. Oppressive conceptual frameworks enable both types of domination. Warren writes that an oppressive conceptual framework "is one that explains, justifies, and maintains relationships of domination and subordination. When an oppressive conceptual framework is patriarchal, it explains, justifies, and maintains the subordination of women by men" (1990: 127–28). An OPPRESSIVE CONCEPTUAL FRAMEWORK is a conceptual framework that makes relationships of domination and subordination seem normal, natural, and unquestionable. A conceptual framework like that described in the Book of Genesis was oppressive since it explained, justified, and maintained relationships of domination and subordination between human beings and their environment. Warren identified three important features of oppressive conceptual frameworks:

1. Value hierarchical thinking,
2. Value dualisms, and
3. A logic of domination.

VALUE HIERARCHICAL THINKING is "'updown' thinking which places higher value, status, or prestige on what is 'up' rather than on what is 'down'" (1990: 128). An example of updown thinking is the picture of international relations which is subverted by a south-up map.

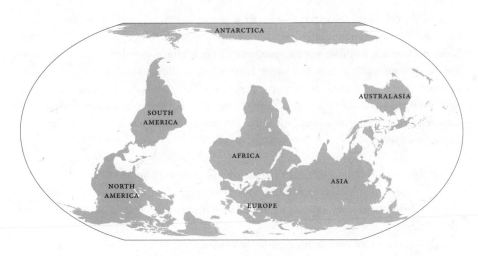

FIGURE 15.1: South-up map of the world

The map in Figure 15.1 seems odd to many people because what is most normal is to see the rich, powerful, industrialized countries of the north represented as above, and thus more important than, the poorer, developing countries of the south. Of course, there is no such direction as "up" in space. Any reason for representing the North Pole of the spinning Earth as up, and the South Pole as down, is arbitrary. A south-up map is just as accurate as a north-up map, yet it has the interesting capacity to subvert our usual thinking about the relative importance of rich and poor countries.

VALUE DUALISMS are "disjunctive pairs [that is, of the form x *or* y] in which the disjuncts are seen as oppositional (rather than complementary) and exclusive (rather than as inclusive), and which place higher value (status, prestige) on one disjunct rather than the other ..." (1990: 128). Some examples are reason/emotion where higher value is placed on reason, mind/body where higher value is place on the mind, and male/female where higher value is placed on the male.

UP	DOWN
Reason	Emotion
Mind	Body
Male	Female
Human	Natural
Mental	Physical
Rationality	Irrationality
Culture	Nature

TABLE 15.1: Value dualisms

Thirdly, a LOGIC OF DOMINATION is a structure of argumentation that justifies relationships of domination and subordination. "A logic of domination is not just a logical structure. It also involves a substantive value system, since it needs ethical premises to permit or sanction the 'just' subordination of that which is subordinate. The justification typically is given on grounds of some alleged characteristic (e.g. rationality) which the dominant (e.g. men) have and the subordinate (e.g. women) lack" (1990: 128). For example, Warren claims that a patriarchal conceptual framework implicitly sanctions an argument with the following structure (1990: 130):

1. Men have the characteristic of rationality and women do not.
2. Whoever is rational is morally superior to whoever is not.
3. Whoever is morally superior is justified in dominating whoever is morally inferior.
4. Therefore, men are morally superior to women.
5. Therefore, men are justified in dominating women.

The first premise of the logic of domination is the [false] empirical belief about human nature that men are rational and women are not. It presupposes the dualism of rational/emotional. The second premise, which is an ethical premise, is updown, value hierarchical thinking. Rationality is up, its absence is down, and whoever is rational is morally superior to whoever is not. The third premise, which is also an ethical premise, comes from the substantive value system of the logic of domination. The three premises may seem normal within a patriarchal conceptual framework, but that does not make them true. The two conclusions follow logically from the premises, and would be supported by true premises, but the premises are not true.

Similarly, an anthropocentric conceptual framework implicitly sanctions an argument with the following structure (1990: 129):

1. Human beings have minds and other living beings do not.
2. Whoever has a mind is morally superior to whatever does not.
3. Whoever is morally superior is justified in dominating whatever is morally inferior.
4. Therefore, human beings are morally superior to other living beings.
5. Therefore, human beings are justified in dominating other living beings.

This logic of domination presupposes a dualism of mind and body, a value hierarchy of mental over physical, and the ethical assumption that the morally superior are entitled to dominate the morally inferior. The argument embodies fundamental beliefs about human and non-human nature, involves seldom-questioned value assumptions, and is embedded in an oppressive conceptual structure.

Again, it is easier to see the oppressive structure of the conceptual frameworks of others than it is to see the oppressive structure of our own. For example, the oppressive conceptual structure of Ancient Greece is apparent in the following quotation from Aristotle's *Politics*.

> And it is clear that the rule of the soul over the body, and of the mind and the rational element over the passionate, is natural and expedient; whereas the equality of the two or the rule of the inferior is always hurtful. The same holds good of animals in relation to men; for tame animals have a better nature than wild, and all tame animals are better off when they are ruled by man; for then they are preserved. Again, the male is by nature superior, and the female inferior; and the one rules, and the other is ruled; this principle, of necessity, extends to all mankind. Where then there is such a difference as that between soul and body, or between men and animals (as in the case of those whose business is to use their body, and who can do nothing better), the lower sort are by nature slaves, and it is better for them as for all inferiors that they should be under the rule of a master. (Aristotle 350 BCE: Book I, Part V)

In the shared conceptual framework of Aristotle's Greece, slavery was natural and ordinary, the rule of men over women was taken for granted, and the domestication of animals for human purposes was thought justified. The value hierarchical dualisms of soul over body and of rational over passionate or emotional were core beliefs of the framework.

Karen Warren's ecological feminism is committed to rejecting both the domination of women by men and the domination of nature by human beings. It sees a conceptual connection between these two systems of domination in that both are enabled by oppressive conceptual structures with a structurally similar logic of domination. We can see a historical connection between the two systems of domination in the thinking of Aristotle. We can also see a metaphorical connection between the two systems of oppression in the feminization of Mother Nature and in the Greek goddess, Gaia.

Warren's ecofeminism poses a challenge to environmental ethics interpreted as the extension of moral standing from humans to animals, plants, and possibly ecosystems. The wholesale rejection of oppressive conceptual frameworks involves the rejection of value dualisms, value hierarchies, and logics of domination. Yet the notion of moral standing has the properties of a value dualism and a value hierarchy. It divides the world into those who satisfy a criterion for being morally considerable and those who do not, and ethically privileges the former. It makes it ethically permissible for human beings to dominate non-human entities that have no moral standing. If we draw the boundary between animals and plants using sentience, for example, to create a hierarchical value dualism, then ethics will permit humans to use plants as they see fit. If we draw the boundary to include all life, then ethics will permit humans to use water, rocks, and minerals for their own purposes. Ecofeminism challenges the conceptual framework of environmental ethics as we have discussed it by pointing out that it, too, is oppressive.

THE ETHICS OF CARE

If the conceptual framework of environmental ethics is oppressive, then we must make a choice. On the one hand, we can take this conclusion as a *reductio ad absurdum* of Warren's critique of the logic of domination. On this view, the concept of an oppressive conceptual framework is so broad that even environmental ethics becomes oppressive, and that seems absurd. On the other hand, we can take the conclusion as indicating the need for a rethinking of conventional ethics within a framework that is not oppressive, such as a feminist ethic of care.

Contemporary feminist ethics has taken two divergent paths. One view is that of LIBERAL FEMINISM, which denies there are morally relevant differences between men and women that prevent women having moral standing equal to that of men. We should give the interests of women the same consideration as the interests of men. From the point of view of equality, gender is usually morally irrelevant, and justice should be mostly gender neutral. The exceptions are where justice must consider conditions like motherhood that are specific to women. Unequal respect for women is sexist. The other broad view is RADICAL FEMINISM, which affirms that there are morally relevant biological differences between men and women, and argues that these create, not different rights, but an alternative feminist perspective in ethics. For example, childbearing and motherhood give women a special perspective on ethics. Instead of starting ethics from the standpoint of abstract principles of justice and calculations of utility, radical feminist ethics would begin from the standpoint of private family life with its special relationships between mothers and other family members, the strong emotional attachments that family members form, and the ways in which they care for one another.

In an ethic of care, the paradigmatic relationship between mother and child is a relationship of unequal power. Mother and child do not meet as two businesspeople trying to negotiate a mutually advantageous contract, with each party looking out for itself. Infants are powerless and children almost so. Nevertheless, mothers and children are not in a relationship of domination and subordination. Good mothers do not use their children for their own purposes; instead, they nurture and train their children to help them develop into adults. A care-based ethical framework is not oppressive; it contains no logic of domination. An ethic of care is an ethic based in the special relationships that people have to one another, like that of mother and child, and in the emotions that make such attachments possible. Within a care-based ethical framework, the devices of conventional ethics, such as principles of justice, calculations of utility, and rights to non-interference, are neither useful nor productive. A feminist ethic of care emphasizes the importance of social context over the application of abstract principles, the importance of cooperation over conflict and competition, the importance of relationships over individualism, the importance of caring for others over the claiming of rights, and the importance of wise judgment over the calculation of costs and benefits.

CONVENTIONAL ETHICS	FEMINIST ETHICS OF CARE
Abstract principles	Context
Competition and conflict	Cooperation
Atomistic individuals	Relationships
Rights and duties	Caring
Calculation of consequences	Wisdom

TABLE 15.2: Feminist and conventional ethics

It is easy to see how an ethic of care can encompass some aspects of the environment. People form emotional attachments to their companion animals and to the parts of the land that are their homes. They care for their pets, they care for their homes and gardens, and they care for their families and their communities. What is more difficult to see is how to extend an ethic of care to distant others. An ethic of care is founded on special relationships with specific others. Caring generally for unknown others in distant countries, or for unrelated people born a century in the future, or for exotic tropical ecosystems, requires a different type of emotional attitude. While the justice-based approach can say the national boundaries and time of birth are morally arbitrary features of persons, a care-based approach must struggle to go beyond special attachments to specific persons. It is easier for ethical theories based on universal moral consideration to look after the interests of distant and future people, unknown animals, and unvisited wilderness areas than it is for ethical theories based on special relationships to particular people, pets, and homes. Against this objection, however, a defender of the ethic of care can point to the lack of success of universalizing moral theory in actually protecting distant others. Perhaps abstract principles of justice are unable to guide the actions of real people, whose motivations are more concrete and specific. If abstract moral theory cannot, in practice, perform the function of protecting the interests of distant others, then the best that ethics can do is to try to create concrete relationships between nearby people and faraway people, animals, plants, and places. For example, the non-governmental organization, Plan International (Foster Parent Plan), raises aid for international development projects through a system of child sponsorship. Though Plan International actually spends aid money on community development, this system allows donors to correspond with a particular sponsored child in the community and form a relationship with him or her.

A second problem for an ethic of care to solve is defining just how much care we should give. A caretaker must care both for others and for herself. How much care is appropriate for others and for self? A mother may sacrifice her life for her infant child, but as children grow older, she must establish some psychological boundaries between herself and her growing child, for both the child's sake and for her own. The appropriate level of care in mother/child relationship may be determined as a matter of psychological health, but the appropriate level of care between a person and her adult friends and family requires an analysis. The justice-based approach offers a ready solution; a person is entitled to a fair share, just as others are. The justice-based approach models a system of caring relationships as a system of reciprocity. Caretakers are entitled to feel hard done by if their needs are not also met. The role of justice within families and friendships, however, is controversial.

One way of conceptualizing this problem without resorting to principles of justice is to interpret an ethic of care as analogous to a virtue ethic. A virtue is often a mean between two vices. For example, courage is metaphorically the mean between cowardice and foolhardiness.

Cowardice/Courage/Foolhardiness

It requires practical wisdom to determine when courage becomes foolish recklessness on one side, and when courage becomes weak fearfulness on the other. Analogously, care is the mean between selfishness and self-sacrifice.

Selfishness/Care/Self-sacrifice

It requires practical wisdom, not a theory of justice, to determine the boundaries between care and selfishness and between care and self-sacrifice. On this interpretation, an ethic of care advises development of the practical wisdom and the caring relationships of a good mother, and application of her wise caring attitudes to non-human nature.

In a virtue ethic, a person develops virtues because being a virtuous person is what constitutes a flourishing and objectively happy life. Virtues are character traits that an individual person possesses. They are part of the person, who is a unitary, individual self with the mental properties of being courageous, benevolent, honest, and so on. A virtue ethic is individualistic and atomistic; the virtues are properties of the self within the skin. In an ethic of care, a person develops caring relationships with others. Caring relationships are not character traits of an individual self, but are properties of a network of interactions between persons and others. In an ethic of care, the self is not a psychological atom, but is a node in a network of relationships. Whether or not the self is flourishing is the same question as whether or not the network of special relationships that constitutes the self is flourishing. The network of special relationships that constitutes the relational self is a flourishing one if the relationships are healthy, caring, and loving. To take a flourishing relational self as being what a meaningful and happy life is all about, a person must move from the conceptual framework of the atomistic self to the conceptual framework of the relational self. In the next chapter, we will look at another framework that also asks us to rethink who we are, and to rethink the nature of the self.

SUMMARY

1. Power can be coercive, economic, or ideological. Ideological power can involve a shared conceptual framework that makes domination and subordination seem natural and normal.
2. A conceptual framework is an enduring, shared set of interrelated fundamental assumptions about the non-human world, human nature, and ethical values that forms an intellectual lens through which people understand and act in the world.
3. A conceptual framework can be oppressive in that it justifies unquestioned relationships of domination and subordination.
4. Karen Warren identifies three aspects of an oppressive conceptual framework: value dualism, hierarchical moral thinking, and a logic of domination. She contends that feminism and environmentalism have a conceptual connection because patriarchal and anthropocentric conceptual frameworks have structurally similar logics of domination.
5. Liberal feminists accept the framework of standard ethics, but demand that it give women equal respect and consideration. Radical feminists reject the framework of standard ethics and propose alternatives based in women's distinctive forms of moral reasoning.
6. A feminist ethic of care begins ethics from women's moral experience of special relationships with others and their accompanying emotional attachments. The ethic of care must solve problems regarding the ethical treatment of distant others and the proper distinction between care and self-sacrifice. It sees the human self not as an isolated, atomistic individual but as constituted by a network of caring social relationships.

ONLINE READING QUESTIONS

The book's website contains reading questions on this chapter. Working through these questions will help you understand, remember, and apply important concepts from the chapter. Some of the questions supply useful hints for the study questions.

Using the text and hints from the online reading questions, write out, type, dictate to your computer, or at least formulate in your head answers to the following questions.

1. Describe how someone might see the origins of human damage to the environment in the conceptual framework of the Judeo-Christian religious tradition.
2. Describe how Warren thinks a patriarchal conceptual framework connects to human damage to the environment.
3. Explain the difference between liberal and radical feminism.
4. Describe how radical feminism suggests an ethic of care and how an ethic of care might prevent human damage to the environment.

QUESTIONS TO PONDER

Spend a few minutes thinking about the following questions, or, better yet, discuss them with fellow readers of this book.

1. Are ethical judgments relative to conceptual frameworks? Does the existence of alternative cultural frameworks imply cultural relativism in ethics?
2. What is the difference between care and benevolence? Is the feminist ethic of care already implicit in a virtue ethic that emphasizes the virtue of benevolence?
3. Is the conceptual framework of environmental ethics, with its emphasis on discovering the correct criterion for moral standing, actually an oppressive conceptual framework?
4. Do you think that an ethic of care founded in special relationships between specific people can be extended to show ethical consideration for unknown distant and future people?

Chapter 16

DEEP ECOLOGY

DEEP ECOLOGY IS AN ENVIRONMENTAL MOVEMENT AND ENVIRONMENTAL PHILOSOPHY founded by the Norwegian philosopher, Arne Naess. Deep ecology is "deep" because it entails fundamental changes in the way that human beings understand themselves. If human beings change their self-understanding, then they will also radically change their relationship to the environment. This deep change in human self-understanding is not an incremental change whose justification develops from the self-conception that human beings currently have. To adopt a deep ecological conception of themselves, people will need to make a revolutionary change from their present worldview to the deep ecology world view. Deep ecology requires that people adopt a new conceptual framework, one that contains a very different view of human nature.

Deep ecology has a holistic view of the human self. The feminist ethic of care gives up an atomistic view of the individual human self in favour of a relational view in which the self is constituted by its relationships with others. Deep ecology gives up the atomistic self in favour of a wide self that identifies itself with its non-human environment. This identification between self and nature creates a deep connection between the two. Because the human self and its non-human environment are one whole, their relationship will become more harmonious.

To move from what most people believe about themselves to the deep ecological outlook, people will need to change their conceptual framework in a radical way. We have looked at several examples of changing conceptual frameworks: Paul Taylor's biocentric outlook on nature, the Old Testament's theological outlook that justifies human mastery of nature, the scientific revolution that took us from a geocentric to a heliocentric view of the universe, and Karen Warren's rejection of the conceptual framework of the logic of domination. In this chapter, we will examine Arne Naess's metaphysical holism and the deep ecological world-view. We cannot produce an argument for deep ecology from standard ethical premises. We can look, however, at its historical roots, its cultural parallels, and its strengths and weaknesses to assess whether it is rational to adopt deep ecology as an environmental philosophy.

Learning Objectives

1. To understand the holistic conception of the self.
2. To see how changing the conceptual framework of a person's self-understanding to a wide holistic view can make a person see the entire natural environment as part of him or herself.
3. To interpret deep ecology in the context of broad ethical egoism and virtue ethics.
4. To understand some of the criticisms of deep ecology.

THE WIDE HOLISTIC SELF

The French philosopher, René Descartes (1596–1650) was influential in promoting our modern conception of who we are. For Descartes, the essence of himself was an immaterial thinking substance, his mind. It included all the doubts, fears, hopes, beliefs, and other mental states that made him who he was. The mind, as a unitary substance with mental properties, was distinct from the material substance that made up his body and rest of the external world. The material substance had physical properties such as mass and size, whereas the mental substance had psychological properties like thought and emotion. Descartes described an individualistic view of the self in which the self was a unit of mental substance that is distinct from the material world with which it interacts. The Cartesian self is atomistic in two senses: internally, it is a unified substance, and externally it is separate from other selves and from its environment.

The English philosopher, David Hume (1711–76), proposed a more holistic account of the internal self. While still holding that the mind was distinct from the external world, he argued that there was no unified thing among the mind's ideas and impressions that was the self as a unified substance. Among all the ideas and impressions in his mind, he could find no clear impression of the mind itself. Thus, instead of seeing the mind as a unitary substance, he saw it as more like a community of thoughts, a whole consisting of organized parts.

> As to causation; we may observe, that the true idea of the human mind, is to consider it as a system of different perceptions or different existences, which are linked together by the relation of cause and effect, and mutually produce,

destroy, influence, and modify each other. Our impressions give rise to their correspondent ideas; [and] these ideas in their turn produce other impressions. One thought chases another, and draws after it a third, by which it is expelled in its turn. In this respect, I cannot compare the soul more properly to any thing than to a republic or commonwealth, in which the several members are united by the reciprocal ties of government and subordination, and give rise to other persons, who propagate the same republic in the incessant changes of its parts. And as the same individual republic may not only change its members, but also its laws and constitutions; in like manner the same person may vary his character and disposition, as well as his impressions and ideas, without losing his identity. (Hume 1740: Book 1, Part IV, Section VI)

Hume's holistic view of the self sees the self as being like an ecosystem where individual plants and animals may live or die, but the ecosystem, as a whole, remains the same. The same ecosystem persists despite changes in its individual members. Hume's view of the self is holistic regarding the internal contents of the mind, but he sees these internal mental contents as separate and distinct from the external environment of the self.

The American philosopher and psychologist, William James (1842–1910) identified a sense of the self, which he called the "Empirical Self," that extended the holistic self to include all those external or non-mental things that are emotionally important to a person.

The Empirical Self of each of us is all that he is tempted to call by the name of me. But it is clear that between what a man calls me and what he simply calls mine the line is difficult to draw. We feel and act about certain things that are ours very much as we feel and act about ourselves. Our fame, our children, the work of our hands, may be as dear to us as our bodies are, and arouse the same feelings and the same acts of reprisal if attacked.... The body is the innermost part of the material Self in each of us; and certain parts of the body seem more intimately ours than the rest. The clothes come next.... Next, our immediate family is a part of ourselves. Our father and mother, our wife and babes, are bone of our bone and flesh of our flesh. When they die, a part of our very selves is gone. If they do anything wrong, it is our shame. If they are insulted, our anger flashes forth as readily as if we stood in their place. Our home comes next. Its scenes are part of our life; its aspects awaken the tenderest feelings of affection; and we do not easily forgive the stranger who, in visiting it, finds fault with its arrangements or treats it with contempt. (James 1890: Chapter 10)

If someone ridiculed one of our mental capacities, such as our feelings for nature, then we would feel ashamed and be angered. If someone took from us one of our mental capacities, such as our ability to solve problems or our capacity for pleasure, then we would feel angry at the loss. Through such emotions, we identify with our mental capacities. These same emotional attitudes, of pride, shame, and indignation, however, extend beyond our inner mental world to include parts of our outer world too. Because we have the same sort of emotional attitudes to components of our outer world as we do to components of our inner world, these parts become aspects of our self in a wider sense.

Hindu theology contains a very wide notion of the self. The wise person can achieve oneness with the universe through spiritual practices that reveal this oneness. In the *Bhagavad Gita* it is written:

> One perfectly realized and perfected in the science of uniting the individual consciousness with the Ultimate Consciousness, identifying with this consciousness everywhere and in everything perceives the realized self situated in all living entities and all living entities in the realized self. (Chapter 6, Verse 29)

In the Hindu spiritual tradition, after long meditative practice, a person can fundamentally change her view of her own self. She will give up the view of herself as a separate entity isolated from her world and come to see that there are no boundaries between her mind and her environment. Moving from the Cartesian conceptual framework of isolated, atomistic selves to the wide holistic conceptual framework of selves identified with their environments is not easy. It is not just a matter of understanding one clever argument or hearing one pertinent counterexample. It requires persistence, determination, and rigorous, disciplined practice.

ARNE NAESS'S WIDE HOLISTIC VIEW OF THE SELF

Drawing on the insights of William James and the *Bhagavad Gita*, the Norwegian philosopher, Arne Naess (1912–2009) claims that the self is not an individual "atom" consisting in the unity of a person's own internal mental states, but instead is a whole that includes all those external things to which a person has deep psychological attachments. This holistic self has an independent existence that is just as real as that of its parts. Once people come to see their environment as part of themselves, they will protect and maintain it. People will do this, not because the environment is instrumentally valuable in satisfying human interests, but because the environment is intrinsically valuable in the same way that people themselves are.

Naess thinks that psychological identification with nature is the source of deep ecological attitudes toward the environment. The original use of the concept of psychological identification is in psychoanalysis. Freud thought of primary identification as the original emotional attachment between mother and child in which the child makes no distinction between itself and its mother. More generally, IDENTIFICATION occurs when a person has emotional attitudes toward the qualities of other persons or objects that are the same as those that the person has toward those qualities in herself. For example, when parents take pride in the accomplishments of their children, they identify with their children. William James describes the process of identification, though he did not call it that, in the following passage:

> *In its widest possible sense*, however, *a man's Self is the sum total of all that he* CAN *call his*, not only his body and his psychic powers, but his clothes and his house,

his wife and children, his ancestors and friends, his reputation and works, his lands and horses, and yacht and bank-account. All these things give him the same emotions. If they wax and prosper, he feels triumphant; if they dwindle and die away, he feels cast down,—not necessarily in the same degree for each thing, but in much the same way for all. (James 1890: Chapter 10)

Naess described identification in terms of interests: "Identification is a spontaneous, non-rational, but not irrational, process through which *the interest or interests of another being are reacted to as our own interest or interests*" (1985: 261). For example, all children have an interest in having enough food. When parents react to their child's interest in having food as though it were their own interest, they have identified with their child.

Naess defines a person's Self as all those entities and situations with which the person identifies. He indicates this notion of a comprehensive Self by capitalizing it and indicates the Cartesian notion of a narrow self by not capitalizing it. Maturity, for Naess, is the widening and deepening of our identification with other living things, as well as species, ecosystems, and landscapes (1985: 263–64).

> Identification is not limited to beings which can reciprocate: any animal, plant, mountains, ocean may induce such processes.... Through identification, higher-level unit[y] is experienced: from identifying with "one's nearest," higher unities are created through circles of friends, local communities, tribes, compatriots, races, humanity, life, and, ultimately, as articulated by religious and philosophi-cal leaders, unity with the supreme whole, the "world" in a broader and deeper sense than the usual. (1984: 263)

Deep ecology requires that we seek a wide identification with both the human and non-human world. This is the requirement of SELF-REALIZATION, with a capital "S," and it leads to the view that all living things have a right to live and flourish.

By breaking down the distinction between the comprehensive Self and the non-human world, deep ecological identification brings to the non-human world the same moral stand-ing that the narrow self has. Ethical egoism claims that only the self is ethically consider-able, and that only the satisfaction of narrow self-interest is of intrinsic value. Deep ecology widens the Self to include individual living things, species, ecosystems, and landscapes. Thus, we can think of deep ecology as a form of ethical egoism with a very wide understanding of Self-interest.

> Against the beliefs in fundamental ego-alter conflict, the psychology and phi-losophy of the (comprehensive) Self insist that the gradual maturing of a person *inevitably* widens and deepens the self through the process of identification. There is no need for altruism towards those with whom we identify. The pursuit of self-realization conceived as actualization and development of the Self takes care of what altruism is supposed to accomplish. Thus, the distinction egoism-altruism is transcended. (1985: 263–64)

Wide Self-interest includes the interests of all living things, species, ecosystems, and land-scapes. Therefore, satisfying the interests of all living things, species, ecosystems, and land-scapes has intrinsic value.

The analogy between deep ecology and a wide form of ethical egoism is useful in capturing the action-guiding aspect of an environmental ethic. Narrow ethical egoism explains why people are generally motivated to do what they believe they should do; doing so is in their narrow self-interest. Wide ethical egoism can give a similar explanation of why people who adopt the conceptual framework of deep ecology will become motivated to promote the interests of the environment; doing so is in their wide Self-interest. As they identify with their environment, they will develop interests in protecting and maintaining it. Nevertheless, the analogy between deep ecology and ethical egoism breaks down at two crucial points.

First, when a standard ethical egoist pursues his narrow self-interest, he feels under no obligation to think critically about the interests he pursues. He just accepts his interests as he finds them, and has no need to wonder if they are good or bad. In the theory of ethical egoism, the satisfaction of his wants and preferences just is what is intrinsically valuable. This contrasts, for example, with a virtue ethic. A virtue ethic will be very concerned that a person should flourish by developing good interests, the interests of a person with a virtuous character, and avoiding interests that lead to vice. The regular notion of self-realization involves the develop-ment of excellence or virtue in the capacities and character of a person. In the deep ecological worldview, a person develops Self-realization by identifying with other people, animals, living beings, species, ecosystems, and landscapes. She does this by reacting to their interests, subjec-tive or objective, as if to her own interests. However, not every entity in the environment is one with which a deep ecologist would want to identify. Her environment contains coal-fired electrical generators, huge super-highways, and millions of cars. If, as Naess claims, we can identify with oceans, mountains, and landscapes, then we can potentially identify with coal-fired electrical generating plants. Deep ecological identification requires some way of deciding with which aspects of her environment a person should identify.

Deep ecologists cannot avoid making value judgments about which non-human interests they should react to as to their own and which they should see as external to themselves. This ethical decision procedure could be rule-governed, in which case it would send us back to considerations of moral standing, moral rights, utility, and justice, or it could be a matter of wisdom, not rules, as in a virtue ethic. Either deep ecology relies on the theories of the intrin-sic value of nature and the moral standing of the non-human world that we have examined in previous chapters, theories such as those of Singer, Regan, and Taylor, or deep ecology is offering an alternative analogous to a virtue ethic.

The virtue ethic strategy is possibly more congenial to the notion of deep ecological Self-realization. In striving for regular self-realization, a person must decide which of his habits, attitudes, interests, and character traits are valuable and so are ones he should cultivate, and which are worthless and so are ones he should eliminate. Such decisions require practical wisdom. In striving for Self-realization, a deep ecologist must decide with which aspects of her environment she should identify and which non-human interests she should take on as her own. The spontaneous, but not irrational, process of identification also requires practical wisdom to get it right.

The second point at which the analogy between deep ecology and wide, holistic ethical egoism breaks down is dealing with conflicts between interests. Narrow, individualistic ethical egoism assumes that the agent is rational. A rational, self-interested agent will have a set of interests that are consistent and coherent. The interests of a rational agent will not conflict with one another. On the contrary, the deep ecologist who identifies her interests with those of the non-human world around her will need to adjudicate between conflicting interests. As Naess writes, "A high level of identification does not eliminate conflicts of interest: Our vital interests, if we are not plants, imply killing at least some other living things" (1985: 262). Deep ecologists identify with the interests of plants, yet the interests of people in food, clothing, shelter, and communication also conflict with the interests of plants. Deep ecologists identify with the interests of animals, yet the interests of people in self-defence conflict with the interests of dangerous animals.

Naess suggests that the deep ecologist handle the problem of conflicting comprehensive interests, not with practical wisdom, but with two rules:

(1) More vital interests have priority over less vital interests.
(2) The interests of entities that are nearer to us in space, time, culture, and species have priority over the interest of entities that are more remote. (1985: 266)

Even though interests are bound to conflict, he thinks that we can often reduce the conflict by imagining alternatives and compromises. For example, the vital interests of communities of human hunter-gatherers in food and clothing may conflict with the preservation of endangered species. Though the principle of nearness means that we should favour the interests of the humans over the interests of members of the endangered species, we may still avoid the conflict by providing alternative food and clothing from the wealth of rich industrial societies. The vital interests of a poisonous snake may include living in an area where children play, thus threatening the vital interests of the children. The principle of nearness justifies removing the snake instead of the children. However, an alternative would be to consider the vital interests of the snake when choosing where to create a playground for children (1985: 267). Naess's rules, which he admits are vague and ambiguous, go some way to resolving conflicts of interest. Nevertheless, it is important to exhibit practical wisdom in seeking to avoid or defuse such conflicts.

The ecological consciousness involved in wide, holistic identification with the non-human environment does not totally solve all ethical problems. It provides an account of how humans can become motivated to do something to preserve their environment by adopting it as part of themselves. Yet it must still answer both the question of what does or does not have intrinsic value and the question of how to resolve the inevitable ethical conflicts that arise.

THE DEEP ECOLOGY PLATFORM

Arne Naess and George Sessions articulated the basic practical principles of deep ecology in a way that they hoped would make the principles understandable and acceptable to people thinking about environmental problems from various different philosophical perspectives. These principles are not as controversial as one might expect:

(1) "The well-being and flourishing of human and nonhuman life on Earth have value in themselves (synonyms: inherent worth; intrinsic value; inherent value). These values are independent of the usefulness of the nonhuman world for human purposes" (Devall 2007: 70). This principle is inconsistent with both narrow ethical egoism and subjective consequentialism. Utilitarian ethical theories attribute intrinsic value only to pleasurable sensations and satisfied human preferences. The deep ecological view is, however, consistent with objective accounts of intrinsic value.

(2) "Richness and diversity of life forms contribute to the realization of these values and are also values in themselves" (Devall 2007: 70). This principle incorporates a holistic theory of intrinsic value. Richness and diversity are properties of wholes, not of individuals. For example, we cannot say that a single person exhibits diversity, but we can say that a room full of people does. Nevertheless, the second principle does not imply that only holistic entities have intrinsic value. It says that richness and diversity *also* have intrinsic value, leaving it open that individual entities can have intrinsic value too.

(3) "Humans have no right to reduce this richness and diversity except to satisfy vital needs" (Devall 2007: 70). Reducing the richness and diversity of life, which humans often do by destroying non-human individuals, is wrong unless it is necessary to satisfy vital human interests. This principle embodies a notion of environmental justice. We must always consider the interests of non-human entities, but vital human interests can outweigh them. Trivial or substitutable human interests cannot.

(4) "The flourishing of human life and cultures is compatible with a substantial decrease of the human population. The flourishing of nonhuman life requires such a decrease" (Devall 2007: 70). Though the flourishing of human culture requires a moderately large human population, it does not require that the population be as large as it is. The principle goes on to say that the flourishing of non-human life requires a decrease in the population of human beings. This is not especially controversial (theological beliefs about human population excepted) if it just means that we should bring human population growth under control, and shrink the human population in the long run. It is a different story, of course, if we interpret the principle to mean that we should kill human beings in order to allow non-human nature to flourish. The latter interpretation is inconsistent with the third principle that puts a priority on human vital interests.

(5) "Present human interference with the nonhuman world is excessive, and the situation is rapidly worsening" (Devall 2007: 70). Most environmentally aware people would accept this value judgment.

(6) "Policies must therefore be changed. The changes in policies affect basic economic, technological structures. The resulting state of affairs will be deeply different from the present" (Devall 2007: 70). Because of the intrinsic value of non-human nature in all its richness and diversity, economic policies must change. Business-as-usual as an economic policy is no longer viable. "Shallow" environmentalists who, unlike deep ecologists, think that we should conserve nature because of its instrumental value to human beings, will still agree that

economic policy must change, though they may hope that the results of new environmental policies will be lifestyles that are not greatly different from present ones.

(7) "The ideological change is mainly that of appreciating *life quality* (dwelling in situations of inherent value) rather than adhering to an increasing higher standard of living. There will be a profound awareness of the difference between big and great" (Devall 2007: 70). This claim locates the philosophy underlying a change in economic policy as one of abandoning the goal of growth in the standard of living in favour of the goal of increasing quality of life. Behind business-as-usual economic policies are ethical assumptions about the value of increasing economic output, such as growth in the Gross National Product. The next section of this book will look in detail at the ethical assumptions of the market-based economic system.

(8) "Those who subscribe to the foregoing points have an obligation directly or indirectly to participate in the attempt to implement the necessary changes" (Devall 2007: 70). These are ethical principles and, as such, should guide how people act. People who agree with the beliefs embodied in these principles should understand that they have an obligation to act on them to help preserve the non-human environment.

WEAKNESSES OF DEEP ECOLOGY

Some criticisms of deep ecology centre on the misanthropy of some of its supporters. For example, in an article criticizing deep ecology, Murray Bookchin quotes David Foreman of the environmental advocacy group, Earth First! as saying the following in an interview:

> When I tell people how the worst thing we could do in Ethiopia is to give aid—the best thing would be to just let nature seek its own balance, to let the people there just starve—they think this is monstrous.... Likewise, letting the USA be an overflow valve for problems in Latin America is not solving a thing. It's just putting more pressure on the resources we have in the USA. (Bookchin 1987)

It is not fair to use a quotation from an activist who happens to hold deep ecological views as representative of the theoretical view of the movement. We could read principle (4) of the deep ecology platform as obliging us to let people starve in order to achieve the decrease in human population required for the flourishing of non-human life. That reading, however, is not consistent with the priority that principle (3) puts on the vital interests of humans. Nor is that reading consistent with Naess's view, discussed above, that we should adjudicate conflicts of interest by giving priority to the interests of those nearest to us in species.

The name, "deep ecology," immediately associates this philosophical position with an ecocentric ethic. This may lead people to interpret an ecocentric ethic as entailing the view that only holistic entities, like ecosystems, species, landscapes, and wilderness, have moral standing. Then deep ecology may seem open to the charge of ecofascism because it will put the flourishing of ecosystems ahead of the interests of individual plants, animals, and human beings. This chain of thought, however, is not consistent with principle (2) of the deep ecology platform, which states that holistic qualities like richness and diversity of species *also* have intrinsic value along with individual living beings. As well, the use by principle (1) of the notion of intrinsic value, and its synonyms, instead of the notion of moral standing, suggests that the platform is open to making the sort of trade-offs that we see in an objective consequentialist ethical theory or in a theory of environmental justice. On this interpretation, we do not privilege the interests of holistic entities, as in the interpretation that begets the charge of ecofascism. Instead, we weigh them in the decision procedure along with the interests of individual living beings.

Many deep ecologists have been interested in wilderness preservation. Wilderness preservation in relatively sparsely populated countries like the US is an easier goal than it is in heavily populated countries like India. In India and other developing countries, wilderness preservation may be detrimental to the interests of the agricultural poor. Creating a tiger preserve in India, for example, will displace many small farmers, and expose their livestock to danger from the tigers (Guha 1989). While some deep ecologists may emphasize wilderness preservation in their activism, the deep ecology of Arne Naess is open to the possibility of conflicts of interests and in finding principled ways of resolving such conflicts.

Ecological consciousness and Self-realization conflict with a common-sense view of the self. Since the worldview of deep ecology is so different from the worldview of common sense, detractors may accuse it of fuzzy thinking. The requirement of deep ecology to seek wide identification and Self-realization may also seem to be too demanding to be an ethical requirement. The spiritual disciplines required to achieve oneness with the world in Eastern traditions take many years of practice. The scale of the change in conceptual framework that is required to attain ecological consciousness is vastly larger than the change to a biocentric outlook on nature, for example, that is required for Taylor's biocentric egalitarianism.

This completes our review of ethics and environmental philosophies. It has not, by any means, surveyed all the environmental philosophies that people have ever proposed. Nor, has it done full justice to all the nuances of the positions that we have surveyed. Nevertheless, it organizes various positions regarding normative ethics and moral standing so that we can use them to examine environmental policy.

SUMMARY

1. Our common-sense view of the self is similar to that of Descartes. A mental substance or soul is distinct from the body and other material substance, yet somehow interacts with the body. Because the soul is distinct from the material body, it is possible to imagine it existing after the death of the body.

2. William James proposed a different view of the self, in which the self is constituted by all those persons and things to which a person forms strong emotional attachments. This wide, holistic view of the self is also a theme of Hindu philosophy.

3. Arne Naess proposed that, like James, we think of our self as everything with which we identify. He proposed that we have an ethical obligation to seek Self-realization and expand our range of identifications from narrow

self-interest to wide Self-interest so as to see the environment as part of ourselves.

4. Adopting this new ecological consciousness will involve a large change in the conceptual framework in which we understand ourselves.
5. We still need reasons why we should identify with wilderness areas but not with nuclear power stations or devastating earthquakes. As well, we need a way of adjudicating conflicts of interest among the entities with which we identify. Naess proposed that we give priority to vital interests over non-vital ones, and to the interests of those that are nearer to us in space, time, and species over the interests of those who are more distant.
6. We can interpret the deep ecology platform in more and less radical ways. The radical interpretations are open to criticisms of ecological fascism and misanthropy, but have less textual support that do other, less radical interpretations.

ONLINE READING QUESTIONS

The book's website contains reading questions on this chapter. Working through these questions will help you understand, remember, and apply important concepts from the chapter. Some of the questions supply useful hints for the study questions.

STUDY QUESTIONS

Using the text and hints from the online reading questions, write out, type, dictate to your computer, or at least formulate in your head answers to the following questions.

1. Describe Arne Naess's conception of wide identification with the non-human environment.
2. Explain the analogy between deep ecology and a form of ethical egoism with a very broad and holistic conception of the self.
3. Explain how Arne Naess would resolve conflicts between the interests of a poisonous snake and the interests of children playing in its habitat.

QUESTIONS TO PONDER

Spend a few minutes thinking about the following questions, or, better yet, discuss them with fellow readers of this book.

1. Is the conception of a widely identified Self in deep ecology a piece of fuzzy thinking?
2. Naess says this about his conceptions of vital interests and nearness: "The more vital interest has priority over the less vital. The nearer has priority over the more remote—in space, time, culture, species. Nearness derives its

priority from our special responsibilities, obligations and insights" (1985: 266). What would Naess's view be regarding international development assistance, and would you agree with it? What about future generations?

3. Naess writes about nearness: "The importance of nearness is, to a large degree, dependent upon vital interests of communities rather than individuals. The obligations within a family keep the family together, the obligations with a nation keep it from disintegration" (1985: 267). In the same vein, do obligations between the parts of the deep ecological Self keep the Self together? If the deep ecologist achieves identification with the universe, then what happens to nearness as a rule of priority? Does this quotation suggest that Naess primarily has a holistic or an individualistic view of moral standing?

Part III

ETHICS, ECONOMICS, AND THE ENVIRONMENT

Chapter 17

ETHICS
AND ECONOMICS

IT IS IMPOSSIBLE TO THINK ABOUT ENVIRONMENTAL POLICY WITHOUT ALSO thinking about economic issues. Economic markets have become a dominant force in modern life. Markets govern production and consumption decisions, govern resource extraction and pollution emission, and generally govern human interaction with the environment. Once upon a time, people asked their priests to predict the future and give advice in times of crisis. In the contemporary world, we ask economists the same questions, and expect that their answers, at least regarding market behaviour, will be more accurate than those of the ancient priests.

Economists distinguish carefully between positive and normative economics. POSITIVE ECONOMICS is economic analysis that offers scientific, cause-and-effect explanations of market behaviour that observational data can, in principle, confirm or refute. NORMATIVE ECONOMICS is economic analysis that embodies ethical judgments about the right or best policy options. In formulating environmental policy, it is very difficult to keep positive and normative economic judgments apart. If someone thinks that the free-market system is ethically justified, and thinks that positive economics says that the market will behave in such-and-such a way, then, rationally he should, think that such-and-such market behaviour is ethically justified. It is essential, then, for environmental ethics to examine the ethical assumptions that justify market-based approaches to the environment. Introductory economics textbooks often begin by promising to help the reader view the world through the lens, or conceptual framework, of economic theory. An introductory environmental ethics textbook, then, should promise to help the reader view economic approaches to the environment through the lens of ethical theory.

Economists well know that the ability of markets to maximize preference satisfaction breaks down under certain conditions. The conditions under which markets do not maximize preference satisfaction, economists call MARKET FAILURES. Most important environmental problems correlate with forms of market failure. For example, producers seldom intend to create pollution for its own sake; pollution is commonly a by-product of the production of something useful. Pollution falls not just on the producer, but also on everyone around the production site. The market system does not properly take into account the effects of pollution on costs to other living beings and will thus fail to maximize preference satisfaction. Climate change is a gigantic example of market failure. Fixing market failures requires collective action such as government intervention in the market.

We can distinguish three responses to the market failures generated by environmental problems, each with its own ethical justifications, and each with its own ethical weaknesses. MARKET FUNDAMENTALISM is the view that, whatever the environmental effect of an economic market based on existing individual property rights, those effects are ethically permissible. Individuals may sue under tort laws to fix any perceived environmental harms. Governments have, in principle, no role in fixing environmental problems. FREE-MARKET ENVIRONMENTALISM is the view that the bad environmental effects of market behaviour are not ethically permissible, but that the best solution to environmental problems is to privatize the environment properly. If people have well defined private property rights to the whole environment, then they will be able to work out solutions to all their environmental problems efficiently. Governments have, in practice, no role in fixing environmental problems. ENVIRONMENTAL ECONOMICS is an approach that recognizes market failures regarding the environment and studies how we can take collective action to fix environmental problems in a cost-effective manner. Governments have, in this approach, a large role in fixing environmental problems. Fixes could involve governments issuing regulations, granting subsidies, creating systems of marketable emission permits, or imposing emission taxes.

Regarding climate change, a hard-headed market fundamentalist might hold that whatever people choose to do with their private property, including emitting carbon dioxide, is ethically permissible. If other people do not like it, then they can individually sue the emitters without involving the government. A free-market environmentalist might try to fix climate change by privatizing the atmosphere. Each person would own a portion of the absorptive capacity of the atmosphere based on how much he was currently using, and others should sue if he used any of their absorptive capacity, again without involving the government. An environmental economist might suggest that an emission tax, levied by the government according to how much carbon dioxide a person produced, would give emitters an incentive to cut back emissions to sustainable levels. Studying the ethical assumptions of proposals like these will be the task of this section of the book.

Learning Objectives

1. To understand contractarian and libertarian justifications for markets.
2. To understand the economic utilitarian justification for markets.
3. To understand the role of markets in distributive justice.
4. To understand market fundamentalism, free-market environmentalism, and environmental economics as approaches to environmental problems.

ETHICAL JUSTIFICATIONS FOR MARKETS

Markets are organized collections of sellers and buyers, some of them producing goods and services, some of them consuming goods and services, and some of them just transferring goods from one person to another. Markets organize our lives. Our morning coffee, our rent or mortgage, our internet connections, our clothes, our jobs, all of these we connect to through market transactions. Though there is no central agency which plans how goods and services will be distributed, myriads of individual market transactions coordinate, for example, the distribution of food to a large city with little shortage or surplus.

Under certain circumstances, simple markets can arise spontaneously. If two Stone-Age hunters of equal strength and ferocity meet in the woods, they may possibly arrange an exchange of a rabbit for a pheasant without any stealing or fighting. Complex modern economies, however, require detailed rules to govern sophisticated market transactions. These rules, in turn, are backed by vast amounts of commercial law and precedent, all ultimately enforced by the legal system of the state. Modern systems of commercial law do not arise spontaneously; they have developed over the years as governments and courts bring order to new types of market transactions. So accustomed are we to the rules of a market economy that we tend to forget that the rules are there. We internalize the rules. We do not expect, when we pick up milk at the grocery store, that we can leave without paying. Money itself, as a claim on the goods and services of others, becomes so normal that we never pause to think of its basis in the continued confidence of everyone that such claims will be recognized. With a sophisticated market economy goes a whole conceptual framework for thinking about the world that seems so natural that we forget that it is a historical and cultural creation. Only when confronted with cultures that produce and distribute goods in different ways, do we notice that the market worldview is not universal.

Modern market economies are organized through sets of legal rules that are ultimately enforced by the state. Such a system of legal rights will include:

1. Property law that defines, defends, and permits the transfer of property rights in goods.
2. Tort law that prevents the harmful use of property.
3. Contract law that enforces the contracts that people create with one another.

For a market economy to work efficiently, people need to know who owns what and how. The state must define ownership of land and resources. The state must make clear the different types of property rights. A person's private property rights in her toothbrush are different from her property rights in the company in which she owns 50 shares. The state must defend rights in property through the criminal law, the court system, the police, and ultimately the armed forces. The state must clarify the conditions under which we can give property to others or exchange it with them. When one person harms the property of another, or uses his property to harm another person, the state must create a set of tort laws that permit the victim to sue the alleged perpetrator for compensation, and a court system to settle such claims. If a factory smokestack makes a downwind house uninhabitable, the householder needs a way to sue for compensation. Exchanging goods and services is no longer as simple as laying down a dead rabbit and picking up a dead pheasant. People need contracts to govern promises in the present regarding performance in the future. A builder needs legal assurance that the landowner will pay for the house she is starting to build when she completes the work in six months' time. The landowner wants similar assurance that the house will be as promised. Both parties need lawyers and judges who can enforce such contracts.

Legal rights are not the same thing as moral rights. Nevertheless, a system of legal rights must be ethically right, or at least ethically permissible. If we think a law is ethically wrong, then we are not bound, morally, to accept it. Different ethical theories will make different judgments regarding the best legal system to govern the market. We will study four such ethical theories. Each justifies a different approach to the interaction of a market economy and the environment. First, from the ethical egoist approach, we can see the state-enforced rules of the market as a way for ethical or psychological egoists to avoid the dilemmas of cooperation. Second, from the libertarian approach, we can see the legal rules of the market as embodying natural rights to acquire and exchange goods and services. Third, from within an indirect utilitarian approach, we can see the rules of the market place as a way for psychological egoists, each acting in their own best interest, to produce the maximum possible amount of goods and services. Fourth, from within the social contract approach to justice, we can see

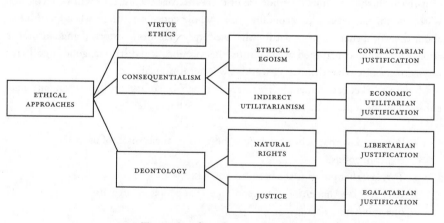

FIGURE 17.1: Taxonomy of justifications for a market economy

the market as a means to maximize the goods and services available to the least advantaged members of a society. Figure 17.1 classifies these different justifications for a market economy in terms of the ethical approaches from which they arise.

1. CONTRACTARIAN JUSTIFICATION

Consider a society of ethical egoists each maximizing his or her own narrow self-interest. They will face prisoner's dilemma situations regarding all of the following:

1. Keeping contracts with each other.
2. Stealing each other's property.
3. Injuring each other's property.

Each of them will steal, cheat, and harm whenever it would maximize his or her self-interest. Thus, they will end up in sub-optimal equilibriums. They will find it rational to establish a state with the power to punish cheaters who steal or break contracts. In other words, they will find it rational to set up a free-market system enforced by state coercion.

We can see how this works if we imagine two Stone Age hunters who must decide whether to trade their catches or fight over them. Suppose that Frank has caught a rabbit, but that he would rather have a pheasant. He would get twice as much utility from a pheasant, but would get the most utility from having both. Conversely, Bert has caught a pheasant but he prefers to have a rabbit. He would get 1 unit of satisfaction from a pheasant, 2 from a rabbit, or 3 from having both. Frank and Bert meet in the woods and must decide whether to trade with one another or to fight and steal the other's catch. The best outcome for each is a successful theft, but if the other fights back, then they will each leave with what they caught. If the payoff matrix for units of satisfaction is as in Table 17.1, then we can see that it is a prisoner's dilemma situation. If Frank thinks that Bert expects to trade, then his best strategy, as an egoist, is a surprise attack to steal Bert's pheasant, gaining him 3 utiles instead of 2. If Frank thinks that Bert plans to attack him, then his best strategy is to fight back because 1 utile is better than 0. By similar reasoning, Bert has a dominant strategy, which is also to fight. Therefore, the two hunters will end up in the lower right cell. This is worse for both of them than the top left square which they can only access if they both trade.

		FRANK	
		Trade	Fight
BERT	Trade	2 2	✓ 3 0
	Fight	0 3 ✓	✓ 1 1 ✓

TABLE 17.1: Unregulated choices between trading and fighting

The game in Table 17.1 is a prisoner's dilemma. It suggests that people who cannot keep agreements will be condemned to Hobbes's war of all against all, leading lives that are "nasty, brutish, and short."

Suppose now that Frank and Bert live in a tribe whose matriarch enforces property rights, facilitates exchange, and makes perpetrators of harms compensate their victims. In effect, the matriarch imposes a free-market economy. In particular, she will penalize any hunter who fights and steals with a penalty of 2 units of satisfaction. The new situation is shown in Table 17.2 where any payoff that involves fighting is penalized by 2.

		FRANK	
		Trade	*Fight*
BERT	*Trade*	√ 2 2 √	3 − 2 = 1 0 √
	Fight	0 3 − 2 = 1	1 − 2 = −1 1 − 2 = −1

TABLE 17.2: Regulated exchange

We can now see that Frank will trade no matter what Bert does because 2 > 1 (= 3 − 2) and 0 > −1 (= 1 − 2). Similarly, Bert will also have a dominant strategy of trading, and the two hunters will find equilibrium in the top left cell with 2 units of satisfaction each. This is an improvement over the prisoner's dilemma outcome in the lower right cell.

The contractarian justification of markets will appeal to those who think that people are innately selfish and that selfishness is a virtue. Though it solves a dilemma of cooperation for ethical egoists, it has business-as-usual implications for environmental policy. It justifies a market-fundamentalist approach to environmental problems. It limits the hunter's ethical concern to present members of the matriarch's tribe. They are not required to show concern for the environment of another tribe that is not party to the contract. Nor are they required to show ethical concern either for future generations, or for any non-human beings. Only if they cause environmental harm to other members of their own tribe will they have to pay compensation.

2. NATURAL RIGHTS JUSTIFICATION

The Libertarian theory of justice also justifies a market economy. The theory, as we have seen, starts from the premise that each person has a natural right of self-ownership. This right is based in people's actual possession of the capacity for autonomous choice over their own actions. Self-ownership includes maximal liberty, rights to personal security, freedom of movement, and so on, and the right to manage and sell the person's own labour. In the state of nature, anyone who mixes his or her labour with an un-owned thing comes to own that thing, so long as he or she leaves "enough, and as good," for others. People thus have a natural right to their initially acquired property. This property right includes the right to contract, that is, to give away, to sell, or to trade their property with others. Therefore, a person has a natural right to any property that he or she has acquired either by initial acquisition or by exchange with others.

We can see that the libertarian justification of the market economy is somewhat stronger in its implications for preventing environmental harms than is the contractarian justification. People have a natural right that the activities of others not harm them, a right based in their possession of a natural feature, the capacity for autonomous choice. Possession of a natural right is thus independent of whether or not someone is party to a contract enforced by the state. For example, a member of another tribe would have a natural right not to be harmed by members of the matriarch's tribe, even though he or she was not protected by any implicit contract. Citizens of Kenya have rights that the polluting activities of a firm in the US not harm them, even though citizens of Kenya are not citizens of the US.

This justification of markets, however, has difficulty justifying ethical concern for future generations. On a natural rights-based account of ethical obligations, we owe a duty to a person not to harm him or her because they possess a natural right. As we have seen before, the conceptual difficulty with obligations to future generations is that future people do not exist in the present. Thus, they do not possess the natural features that are the basis for their claims to our moral duties. Furthermore, the policies that we implement now will affect who is born in the future, making it impossible to decide just whose natural rights we are supposed to respect in our policymaking.

Another difficulty for the natural rights justification of markets is that many of the environmental harms done by the polluting by-products of economic activity are accumulative harms and not individual harms. A duty on everyone else not to interfere with a person's private property protects that person's property. Additionally, the Harm Principle limits a person's property rights; a person cannot use his or her property in ways that cause harm to others.

When we can clearly trace environmental harms to the activities of an individual, then a system of rights will work to protect people from harm. A person who uses her property to produce widgets is free to do this provided she does not cause harm to other people, and other people have a duty to her not to interfere with her use of her property. If her widget production causes pollution that harms the property of her neighbours, then she must cease. The Harm Principle puts limits on her freedom to use her property. Natural rights can protect people from individual environmental harms. The situation is different when there is no identifiable point source for the environmental harm, or when pollutants from many different sources accumulate in the environment. For example, the carbon dioxide emissions from millions of cars accumulate in the atmosphere and contribute to climate change. Though climate change may cause the flooding of low-lying river deltas and force millions of people from their homes, none of the people forced from their homes could successfully sue any of the car drivers for violating their property rights. The contribution to the flooding that any particular driver makes is vanishingly small. Scientific knowledge of the causal chains connecting drivers, carbon dioxide, warming, flooding, and refugees is incomplete.

Similarly, we cannot justify interfering with the freedom of people to drive on the basis of the Harm Principle because we cannot accurately point to any particular harm that they are causing. A rights-based justification of the market system has great difficulty preventing many of the biggest environmental problems.

3.INDIRECT UTILITARIAN JUSTIFICATION

The most influential ethical justification of the market economy is the indirect utilitarian justification. It argues that the free-market system, a system within which all pursue their own self-interest will produce the maximum aggregate preference satisfaction for everyone. This is an indirect utilitarian justification because it asks everyone to use an ethical egoist instead of a utilitarian decision procedure. Direct utilitarianism holds that we should use the principle of maximizing aggregate preference satisfaction as a decision procedure to govern each action. Indirect utilitarianism holds that we should not apply the maximizing principle to each action, but should instead use it as a justification, or standard of rightness, for a set of ethical rules setting out legal rights and obligations for everyone.

Adam Smith in *The Wealth of Nations* of 1776 first observed that in a market economy the butcher, the brewer, and the baker are all motivated by self-interest and not benevolence. Yet they are led, as if by an invisible hand, to maximize the total well-being of society. This happens despite the fact that maximizing aggregate preference satisfaction is not what they intend to do. Economists have shown that a free market system can maximize total economic welfare. If people, each buying and selling according to his or her own self-interest, cause maximum aggregate preference satisfaction, then this is a good indirect utilitarian reason for having the economy run by markets.

Maximization happens, however, only under certain conditions. First, the price someone is willing to pay for a good or service must measure the preference satisfaction that they expect from it. Second, the market must be in perfect competition, with many buyers and sellers who can easily enter and exit the market place. The market must not be a monopoly or oligopoly with only one or just a few sellers. People must have adequate information to make buying and selling decisions. Third, there must be no market failures. Particularly there must be no external costs or benefits and no open-access or public goods. External costs are costs that are by-products of market transactions and that fall on people who are not part of the transaction. Environmental pollution is generally an external cost. Open-access and public goods are, roughly, goods from which we cannot easily exclude people, and which we cannot easily turn into private property. Clean air and other desirable environmental states of affairs are public goods. We will return to external costs and public goods in detail because of their importance to environmental problems.

A simplified example will illustrate how, under ideal conditions, the self-interested behaviour of producers and consumers within a market will maximize aggregate welfare. First, we will show how our example has a production and consumption point that maximizes the net benefits to the participants. Second, we will look at how the self-interested behaviour of the participants will lead them to this same point. That self-interested behaviour leads to maximum net benefit will be an indirect utilitarian justification for regulated egoism within this miniature market.

In order to understand ethical issues regarding the economic approach to the environment, we cannot avoid looking at some economic reasoning. We began our study of where utilitarian ethical reasoning shades into economic reasoning in our discussion of utilitarian justice. There we distinguished the total utility caused by consuming a stock of goods and the marginal utility caused by consuming one more increment of the good in question. We also studied the diminishing marginal utility of income; as people get wealthier, the marginal utility that they get from each extra $100 gets smaller. Here we will talk about the total and marginal benefits caused by the consumption of an item.

NUMBER OF ITEMS	0		1		2		3		4		5		6
TOTAL BENEFIT (TB)	0		5		9		12		14		15		15
MARGINAL BENEFIT (MB)		5		4		3		2		1		0	

TABLE 17.3: Total benefit and marginal benefit

In the abstract example in Table 17.3, we can see that as someone consumes more and more of the item, for example cans of beer or chocolate bars, the total benefit she receives rises, but at a diminishing rate. This is an example of the economic Law of Diminishing Marginal Utility. It reflects a basic assumption about human nature. The marginal benefit of consuming each additional item will tend to diminish. The total benefit grows, but at a diminishing rate. Figure 17.2 shows a graph of the total benefit for different numbers of items consumed.

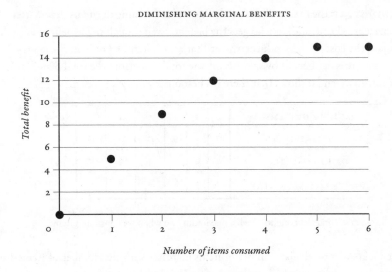

FIGURE 17.2: Chart of total benefit against number of items consumed showing diminishing marginal benefit

The items that we consume do not just appear by magic. They must be produced by someone, and production will have a cost or disutility. The total cost will increase as the number of items produced rises. The second big assumption of economic reasoning is that the marginal cost of producing each additional item will tend to increase in the short term. This is the LAW OF INCREASING MARGINAL COST. It follows from the rationality of human behaviour. A rational person will produce items in the cheapest and easiest way possible. She will use her cheapest alternative to produce the first item, then her use her next cheapest alternative to produce the second item, and so on. A common example is that a person will choose the low-hanging fruit on a tree first. Fruit higher in the tree is more difficult and costly to pick. We can see a simple, abstract example of this in Table 17.4.

NUMBER OF ITEMS	0		1		2		3		4		5		6
TOTAL COST (TC)	0		0		1		3		6		10		15
MARGINAL COST (MC)		0		1		2		3		4		5	

TABLE 17.4: Increasing marginal costs

The total cost increases more and more quickly as the number of items produced increases. The cost of producing one more item (its marginal cost) rises with the number of items produced. The first item is free; its cost is zero. The second costs one unit, the third two, and so on. (We should note that the Law of Increasing Marginal Cost only holds in the short run, where factory size and technology stay the same. In the long run, technology will change, firms will achieve economies of scale, and large-scale mass production will usually lower the cost per item.)

To a utilitarian, it is the net benefit of producing and consuming the items that matters. It does not matter to the utilitarian who gets the benefit. Even though the benefit goes to the consumer and the cost to the producer, the utilitarian is interested only in the aggregated benefit. We find this net benefit by subtracting the total costs from the total benefits. This is done in Table 17.5, and it shows that there is a best output, which is 3 items.

NUMBER OF ITEMS	0	1	2	3	4	5	6
TOTAL BENEFIT (TB)	0	5	9	12	14	15	15
TOTAL COST (TC)	0	0	1	3	6	10	15
NET BENEFITS (TB – TC)	0	5	8	9	8	5	0

Table 17.5: Total net benefits reach a maximum of 9 when we consume 3 items

The total benefits of a particular number of items increases with the number of items, but after 3 items, the costs grow faster than the benefits. The net benefit is a maximum or 9 when 3 items are produced and consumed.

Another way to show that net total benefit is at a maximum when 3 items are produced and consumed is to think in terms of net marginal benefit. For each number of items, we have to ask whether producing and consuming one more item will increase the total net benefit. Will the total net benefit increase if the producer and consumer move from 2 items to 3? From Table 17.6, we can see that the marginal benefit of this increase is 3 and its marginal cost is 2. The increase in items will contribute a net marginal benefit (MB – MC) of +1. Thus, an increase in items from 2 to 3 will also increase the total net benefit. As long as the marginal benefit of one more item exceeds the marginal cost of one more item, an increase in the number of items will increase the total net benefit. What will happen if the producer and consumer move from 3 items to 4? This will contribute a net marginal benefit of −1, a negative number, and will thus decrease the total net benefit. If the marginal cost is higher than the marginal benefit then one more item will decrease the total net benefit. As before, the quantity of items that maximizes total net benefits is 3.

INCREMENT	MB	MC	MB-MC
0 to 1	5	0	5
1 to 2	4	1	3
2 to 3	3	2	1
3 to 4	2	3	−1
4 to 5	1	5	−4

TABLE 17.6: Net marginal benefit (MB − MC) of an increase in production and consumption

Figure 17.3 charts the marginal benefits and marginal costs of an increase of one item. As long as the dark grey column (MB) is higher than the light grey column (MC), total net benefit will increase through the production and consumption of one more item. Total net benefit will be at a maximum at 3 items.

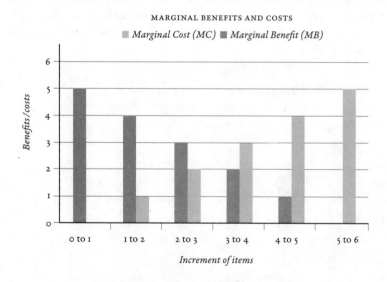

FIGURE 17.3: Chart of falling marginal benefit (MB) and rising marginal cost (MC)

Therefore, according to utilitarian ethical theory, this miniature economy ought to produce and consume 3 items. The production and consumption of 3 items will maximize the total net benefits for the two parties.

Now let us look at the same example in a different way. We want to see if producers and consumers, acting only in their own self-interest, will also maximize total net benefits by producing and consuming 3 items. If self-interested agents, acting with respect for property rights and contracts of exchange, will also arrive at maximum net benefits, then the example will illustrate an indirect utilitarian justification of this miniature market economy. To see how this works, we have to assume that the self-interested agents in our example put a price on their marginal benefits and marginal costs. They measure their marginal benefits according to their maximum WILLINGNESS TO PAY (WTP) for each additional item consumed, and they measure their marginal cost according to their marginal WILLINGNESS TO ACCEPT (WTA), the smallest amount that they would require for each additional item produced. As we have mentioned previously, and as we will discuss in detail again, this will prove to be a very controversial assumption. (One criticism is that Willingness To Pay does not just indicate marginal benefit, but also Ability To Pay. A rich person is willing, because able, to pay more than a poor person for an additional item from which the rich person derives the same benefit as does the poor person. Therefore, WTP, as a measure of preference satisfaction, does not work when comparing people of different income levels.)

Ignoring these criticisms for the moment, if we measure marginal benefits and costs in dollars, Figure 17.3 will look like Figure 17.4. Whenever the price of an additional item is above its marginal cost, a self-interested producer will be willing to produce one more item. If the price of an item is $4.50, and the marginal cost to the producer of producing 5 items instead of 4 items is $4.00, then it will be in the self-interest of the producer to produce 5 items. A price of $4.50, however, is higher than the marginal benefit for the consumer of increasing her consumption from 1 item to 2. Therefore, it will not be in her self-interest to consume more than 1 item at that price. The price will have to fall in order for both producer and consumer to be satisfied.

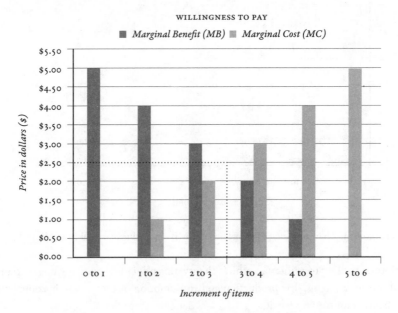

FIGURE 17.4: Willingness To Pay (WTP) versus increments of items

At a price between $2.00 and $3.00, both the producer and consumer can satisfy their self-interest. At $2.50, for example, the price will provide the producer with an incentive to increase his production from 2 items to 3 because $2.50 is more than the $2.00 that he would be willing to accept to cover his marginal cost of producing the 3rd item. However, he will not be willing to produce a 4th item because the marginal cost of $3.00 is higher than the price of $2.50. Likewise, the consumer will buy a 3rd item because her marginal benefit of $3.00 is higher than the price, but she will not buy a 4th item because her marginal benefit of $2.00 is lower than the price of $2.50. Bargaining in their own self-interest, the producer and consumer will arrive at a production and consumption level of 3 items. As we have seen, the production and consumption of 3 items also maximizes total net benefits.

In this simple example, the producer and seller are led, as if by an invisible hand, to maximize total net benefits. This provides an indirect utilitarian justification for the self-interested behaviour of market participants. We can extend this type of argument to a market with many participants. When there are many participants, MB and MC will become smooth lines as graphed in Figure 17.5. The MB line shows the quantity of items demanded by thousands of consumers at any given price, whereas the MC line shows the quantity of items the producers will supply at any given price.

EQUILIBRIUM PRICE AND QUANTITY

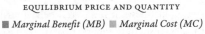

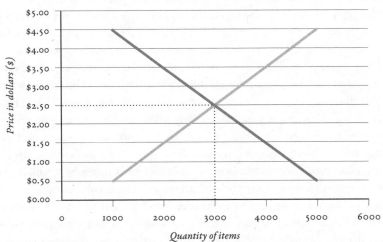

FIGURE 17.5: A market with many participants, showing price and quantity of items

If the price is above $2.50, producers will want to supply more items than the consumers are willing to pay for. If the price is below $2.50, consumers are willing to pay for more items than the producers can supply without losing money. Self-interested behaviour will result in an equilibrium quantity of 3000. Below 3000 items, marginal benefit per additional item is greater than marginal cost, and individual market participants will increase their total net benefit by producing and consuming more items. Above 3000 items, the marginal cost of an additional item is greater than its marginal benefit, and participants will increase their total net benefit by producing and consuming fewer items. Total net benefit is at a maximum when participants produce and consume 3000. Again, self-interested behaviour by individual market participants results in an equilibrium that has maximum aggregate net benefit for everyone.

Philosophers will say that in equilibrium the perfectly competitive market maximizes net utility. Economists will say that, at the equilibrium price and quantity of items reached through the self-interested behaviour of buyers and sellers, the perfectly competitive market is Pareto efficient. A market equilibrium is PARETO EFFICIENT if no change can be made in the quantity produced that will make someone better off without also making someone worse off. Let us suppose that the quantity produced is below 3000, say 2500. Then at a price of $2.50, someone can produce an additional item for $2.00 and someone else will be willing to pay $3.00 for it. Hence, the production and consumption of one more item will make two people better off without making anyone worse off. Any quantity below 3000 will not be Pareto efficient. Any quantity above 3000 will not be Pareto efficient because the marginal cost of producing it will exceed the benefit to anyone of consuming it. The only Pareto efficient point is the market equilibrium, the point that maximizes total net benefits. The advantage of the concept of Pareto efficiency over that of maximizing total net utility is that the economist needs only suppose that people can say that they prefer one outcome to another without needing to suppose that people can say by how much they prefer that outcome to the other.

Indirect utilitarian reasoning justifies self-interested behaviour in a market. If we focus only on the constrained ethical egoism of the market participants, we will arrive at a market-fundamentalist approach to the environment. The duty of an individual in the market is to maximize his own self-interest; the market will take care of the rest. Market failures, like the pollution that falls on distant people or the unsustainable use of resources whose consequences fall on future generations, are not the concern of market participants. If we focus on the underlying utilitarian reasoning that justifies self-interested market behaviour, we will start to consider the interests of distant and future people outside the market. This will lead us to see that the bad side effects of a market economy, pollution and unsustainable resource use, are failures of the market system that we must fix. There are two alternative strategies for fixing these failures: Free-market environmentalists believe that we can fix the market's failures by extending market rules to all aspects of the environment, that is, by privatizing the environment. Environmental economists believe that we need to take collective action to correct the problems caused by individual, self-interested behaviour, and advocate government intervention to mitigate market failures. We will examine free-market environmentalism from an ethical perspective in the next chapter, and the ethical assumptions of environmental economics in succeeding chapters.

4. JUSTICE-BASED JUSTIFICATION

Unfortunately, the markets justified by contractarian, libertarian, and indirect utilitarian reasoning have no tendency to produce just distributions of consumer items. The market economy may end up concentrating wealth and income in the bank accounts of only a few very rich people. None of these justifications has anything to say about the fairness or unfairness of an unequal distribution of income.

A simple egalitarian theory of justice would take the distribution of consumable items out of the hands of the market, and put distribution into the hands of central planners. One problem with this strategy is that it would remove the incentives the market system gives to participants acting mostly out of self-interest to produce these consumable items. A centrally planned economy is not as efficient at producing goods and services as is a free-market economy. In a centrally planned, egalitarian economy, the economic "pie" would be smaller than in a market society, and there would be fewer goods and services to distribute. A better strategy would be to use the market to produce a maximal amount of goods and services and then redistribute entitlements through the tax system. This is the strategy behind the difference principle of John Rawls. As we have seen, Rawls's difference principle says we should distribute income equally unless an unequal distribution makes the least advantaged members of society better off. A less than equal distribution may make the least advantaged better off than they would be in a simple egalitarian society if it provides incentives for the more advantaged to work harder, and if some of the additional income trickles down to the least advantaged. Thus, a complex egalitarian theory of distributive justice like that of Rawls may also provide a justification for a market economy, though one with a large role for the state in redistributing income.

SUMMARY

1. Most people now live in market economies. The emission of pollution and the unsustainable use of natural resources are a by-product of economic activity governed by market forces.

2. Market fundamentalists believe that we are justified in ignoring the by-products of economic activity that fall on others outside the market. Free-market environmentalists believe that we will avoid the harmful by-products of market activity if we extend property rights to cover the whole environment. Environmental economists believe that fixing such market failures will take changes in government policy.

3. Markets of any complexity do not arise spontaneously, but require state enforcement and intervention. This state action requires an ethical justification.

4. The coercive enforcement of contracts and private property rights and the prevention of harms to others by the state will allow a society of self-interested ethical or psychological egoists to avoid dilemmas of cooperation like the prisoner's dilemma. This provides a contractarian justification of a market economy, but justifies no concern for people or beings outside the contract.

5. Libertarians think that people have natural rights to property, including the right to transfer or exchange it, and thus think that the legal rules of the market are morally required. The rights-based approach has difficulty protecting people from, and preventing people from creating, accumulative environmental harms.

6. A perfectly competitive market between self-interested participants will maximize aggregate net benefits for all participants. This provides an indirect utilitarian justification for a market economy. Market participants do not have to behave as utilitarians; they can be purely self-interested. They just have to follow the rules of the market in order to maximize aggregate net benefits. In principle, an indirect utilitarian framework will also allow us to take into account environmental harms falling on those outside a particular market.

7. A perfectly competitive market may result in maximum aggregate net benefits as measured in financial terms, but there is no guarantee that it will distribute these benefits fairly. Modern theories of distributive justice take advantage of the efficiency of the market, but then redistribute the net benefits according to principles of justice.

ONLINE READING QUESTIONS

The book's website contains reading questions on this chapter. Working through these questions will help you understand, remember, and apply important concepts from the chapter. Some of the questions supply useful hints for the study questions.

STUDY QUESTIONS

Using the text and hints from the online reading questions, write out, type, dictate to your computer, or at least formulate in your head answers to the following questions.

1. Briefly explain the contractarian justification of a market-based approach to the environment.
2. Briefly explain the natural rights justification of a market-based approach to the environment.
3. Briefly explain the indirect utilitarian justification of a market-based approach to the environment.
4. Briefly explain the Rawlsian justice-based justification of a market-based approach to the environment.

QUESTIONS TO PONDER

Spend a few minutes thinking about the following questions, or, better yet, discuss them with fellow readers of this book.

1. Speculate about combining an indirect utilitarian justification of the legal rules for a two-person economy with a two-person game theory justification for the same rules.

2. All four justifications for a market economy are thoroughly anthropocentric. Can you see any way of modifying one or more of them to include an ethical concern for the non-human environment?
3. Which justification does the best job of showing ethical concern for distant people? Can you see any way of modifying one or more of them to include an ethical concern for distant people?
4. Which justification does the best job of showing ethical concern for future generations? Can you see any way of modifying one or more of them to include an ethical concern for future generations?

Chapter 18

FREE-MARKET
ENVIRONMENTALISM

FROM THE POINT OF VIEW OF THE NON-HUMAN WORLD, A MARKET ECONOMY IS A very efficient device for extracting resources from the environment, adding to human welfare, and discharging pollution back into the environment, which, to some extent, gets recycled into resources.

It is impossible for human beings to live without consuming some natural resources as food, clothing, and shelter, and without emitting some pollution as respired carbon dioxide and sewage. The question is one of scale and sustainability. It helps that some resources naturally replenish themselves, and that some of the products of the economy can be recycled or reused. Problems arise, however, when people exhaust natural resources and when their polluting emissions exceed the assimilative capacity of the environment. In some cases, the activity of an individual or small group may cause these problems. Yet the most serious of these problems—climate change, soil degradation, declining water supplies, stagnant levels of food production, and the end of oil—are not the work of evil individuals, but are an unintended by-product of economic activity. In the contemporary world, markets govern most of this economic activity. Thus, it is essential to think about the relations between market economies and the environment from an ethical point of view.

One view of the matter, free-market environmentalism, holds that the environmental problems apparently caused by the market economy actually arise because the market is not extensive enough. Overuse of resources, for example, arises because people have open access

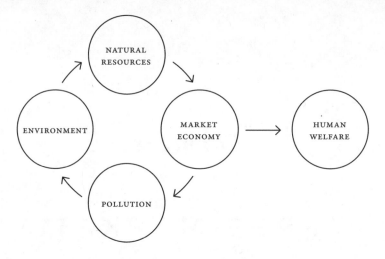

FIGURE 18.1: The market economy and the environment

to un-owned resources and thus have an incentive to overuse them. The paradigm example of this is the tragedy of the commons, where a commonly owned pasture is exhausted because sheep farmers do not have well-defined property rights to portions of the pasture. We can efficiently fix pollution problems, according to an argument of Ronald Coase, if property rights to pollute and not be polluted are clearly defined and enforced. It does not matter, according to his argument, whether the polluter owns the right to emit pollutants or if the victim owns the right not to be polluted. As long as one right or the other is adequately enforced and can be bought or sold, and as long as the two parties can bargain cost-effectively, then they can reach an optimal agreement without government intervention. In this chapter, we shall critically examine the ethical assumptions of free-market environmentalism and see if we should use only market mechanisms to solve environmental problems.

Learning Objectives

1. To understand the tragedy of the commons as a collective action problem, as the source of many environmental problems, and as a potential justification for free-market environmentalism.
2. To understand how market transactions can give rise to environmental problems in the form of externalities.
3. To understand the Coase theorem as a free-market response to the problem of external pollution costs and to understand its weaknesses.
4. To understand the notion of a socially optimum amount of pollution and its basis in preference-satisfaction utilitarianism.

THE TRAGEDY OF THE COMMONS

Before the nineteenth century, English villages had a common grazing area where all residents could graze their sheep. The commons was often over-grazed and the sheep on it did very poorly. The commons had a carrying capacity—the maximum number of grazing sheep allowing the grass to grow back. When the commons had reached its carrying capacity, each farmer had an incentive to graze an additional sheep. The benefits of the additional sheep all came to him, but the costs, in reduced weight gain per season, were spread over all the farmers. Thus, each farmer always had an incentive to add one more sheep to the commons. The common pasture then deteriorated and the sheep did not thrive. Garrett Hardin, who first formulated this argument and named this sort of problem, the "tragedy of the commons," concluded that the solution is to replace common property with a system of private property in order to protect the environment (Hardin 1968). If people can sell it as a resource in the future, then they will have an incentive to maintain its value. Hardin's argument supports the market-based environmentalist position.

In the terminology of economics, a COMMON RESOURCE is a resource whose consumption by one individual diminishes its availability for others, yet is a resource from which it is difficult to exclude other individuals. A shared pasture is a common resource with a carrying capacity. The carrying capacity of a resource is the rate of use of a resource that it can tolerate without deteriorating.

We can think of the tragedy of the commons as a dilemma of cooperation similar to the prisoner's dilemma. Because it is a multi-party prisoner's dilemma, we cannot fully represent it in a small payoff matrix. We can gain a sense of the reasoning involved, however, if we look at the situation from the point of view of an arbitrary farmer, Farmer Fred. Suppose that 10 farmers each graze 10 sheep on a community pasture that they own in common and that has a carrying capacity of 100 sheep. As long as the total number of sheep on the pasture is 100 or below, the farmers will make a profit of $30 per sheep, or $300 for 10 sheep grazed. If the number of sheep on the pasture exceeds the carrying capacity of 100, then the profits will fall for every farmer by $1 per sheep for each extra sheep grazed. Table 18.1 shows a partial payoff matrix for arbitrary Farmer Fred. If all the other farmers continue to graze 10 sheep each and Farmer Fred decides to pasture an 11th sheep, then profits per sheep will go down to $29, but Farmer Fred will now have 11 of them and so will make $290 + $29 = $319 instead of $300 by choosing to graze an 11th sheep on the common pasture. If all the 9 other farmers each graze 11 sheep and if Farmer Fred grazes 10 sheep, then he will make 10 × $21 = $210 because the carrying capacity is exceeded by 9 sheep. If all the 9 other farmers each graze 11 sheep and if Farmer Fred grazes 11 sheep, then he will make 11 × $20 = $220 because now the carrying capacity is exceeded by 10 sheep.

		FARMER FRED	
		11 Sheep	*10 Sheep*
OTHER FARMERS	*11 Sheep*	✓ $220	$210
	10 Sheep	✓ $319	$300

TABLE 18.1: Payoff matrix for arbitrary farmer in the tragedy of the commons

Whatever the other 9 farmers do, Farmer Fred will be better off by grazing 11 sheep. Farmer Fred has a dominant strategy. Farmer Fred, as a rational agent maximizing his self-interest, will graze 11 sheep instead of 10. Since Farmer Fred's situation is the same as that as all the rest of the farmers, all farmers have a dominant strategy which is to add one sheep. No matter what the other farmers do, each farmer will graze an extra sheep. Thus, each farmer has an incentive to keep adding sheep until the commons is spoiled.

Another way to approach this situation is through thinking of the internal and external costs of Farmer Fred's decision. When all farmers are grazing 10 sheep and Farmer Fred decides to graze an 11th sheep, there is an internal or private cost to Farmer Fred. Because Farmer Fred's decision causes the carrying capacity of the pasture to be exceeded, he will now make only $29 instead of $30 per sheep, which is a loss to him of $10 on the 10 sheep that he is already pasturing. He gains $29, however, because of his profit on the 11th sheep, for a net benefit of $19. At the same time, he imposes a cost on the other 9 farmers. They will each lose $1 of profit from each of their 10 sheep because collectively they exceed the carrying capacity, all because of the decision of Farmer Fred. The other farmers will now each make 10 × $29 = $290 instead of $300. The cost to the other 9 farmers is an external cost from the point of view of Farmer Fred. He does not have to bear the cost of his decision himself. Instead, he inflicts it on the other farmers. The total external cost that he inflicts on the other 9 farmers is 9 × $10 = $90. The external cost of $90 to the other 9 farmers caused by Farmer Fred's decision to exceed the carrying capacity is greater than the private net benefit of $19 gained by Farmer Fred from his 11th sheep.

From an economic utilitarian point of view, Farmer Fred's action is wrong because it reduces total net economic benefits. From the point of view of distributive and compensatory justice, it is unfair that Farmer Fred inflicts these uncompensated costs on the other 9 farmers. From the ethical egoist point of view, the tragedy of the commons is a dilemma of cooperation, since ultimately all 10 farmers will be worse off. From a libertarian point of view, Farmer Fred's action is not permissible because he has not left enough, and as good, for the other 9 farmers. From the point of view of virtue and vice, Farmer Fred is being selfish and greedy.

The TRAGEDY OF THE COMMONS is a particular type of external cost situation in which the external costs of an individual participant's actions are spread over all the participants in the situation. This gives each participant a positive net internal benefit and an incentive for doing the action, yet the result of similar actions by all participants is a worse situation for all.

More generally, external costs can also fall on distant people who are not participating in the commons, on generations of people not yet born, and on living beings and ecosystems who lack the capacity to participate in any decisions about the use of the commons. Many environmental problems seem to have the structure of a tragedy of the commons: the costs of overgrazing in Darfur at the southern border of the Sahara fall on the pastoralists, though at the same time creating conflicts with settled agriculturalists. Overfishing of the Grand Banks off the coast of Newfoundland led to a collapse of the cod fishery and the end of a way of life for fishing people. The problems of roads congested with cars are problems mainly for the drivers themselves. Pollution of the Great Lakes and overuse of the Colorado River are problems mainly for those doing the polluting and overusing. Whaling in international waters has caused a huge decline in whale populations. This is an economic problem mostly for whalers, but it is also a loss for all those who admire whales. Other environmental problems are created partly by open access to resources, but create external costs not only for participants, but also for other living beings on the planet: Rainforest destruction in Brazil and carbon dioxide emissions into the atmosphere cause climate change for everyone. The accumulative climatic harms created by fossil fuel consumers in North America will fall on people living on the Ganges delta in Bangladesh who do not themselves consume much fossil fuel.

Free-market environmentalists often cite the tragedy of the commons as a reason for market-based environmentalism. The tragedy of the commons example suggests that states can sometimes protect the environment by turning common resources into private resources. This sounds plausible in the previous example where 10 farmers each had 10 sheep on a pasture with a carrying capacity of 100 sheep. The natural suggestion is that the government could divide the common pasture into 10 equal plots, and allow the farmers to fence their now private pastures so that only their own sheep can graze there. The shares are equal, so this sounds fair. All farmers would now have the incentive to preserve the grass by grazing only 10 sheep on their individual pieces of pasture. The shares of land do not have to be equal to have the same positive effect. If we suppose that historically, one farmer grazed 20 sheep, two grazed 15 sheep each, three grazed 10, and four grazed 5, then a fair solution is not so obvious. Should the farmers receive land in accord with their historic use of it? Should they get an equal share of the land even though they have historically used different amounts of it? Should farmers in the next valley also get shares? Should the farmers have to buy their shares of the land from the government? Privatizing an open resource may well prevent its overutilization, but it also raises many questions of justice.

The free-market environmentalist solution of privatizing open access resources can prevent the tragedy of the commons for certain environmental situations. For example, issuing lobster fishing licenses and assigning FM radio frequencies have worked well in the past. However, the solution does not easily extend to international situations where jurisdiction is unclear. Consider the case of whaling in international waters or the conflicts between animal herders and crop farmers in the Sahel. On the international scene, there is no world state to enforce implementation coercively. Nevertheless, international agreement is sometimes possible, though the agreements do not usually involve the assignment of property rights. For example, the Montreal Protocol to prevent depletion of the ozone layer by chlorofluorocarbons (CFCs) and other substances has worked well. The free-market environmentalist solution does not work well where property rights are not enforceable. For example, the assimilative capacity of the Earth's atmosphere for greenhouse gases is an open-access resource that is not easy to divide among the people of the world in any sort of fair and enforceable way.

The tragedy of the commons scenario is a particularly vivid representation of what can go wrong with common or open-access resources. Yet it is a weak argument for the necessity of private property rights because there can be other forms of governance for the commons (Rowe 2008). For example, when people own cooperative or condominium apartments, their buildings typically have a common element such as the hallways, gardens, and exercise facilities that are not the private property of any one apartment-owner. The common element is typically not an un-owned, common resource ripe for overexploitation. Instead, there are condominium corporation rules against, for example, leaving garbage in the hallways.

Dividing a common pasture up into privately owned fields is not the only way to prevent tragedy. Common resources are often managed resources; human beings have invented many ways of administering the commons besides privatizing it. As well, they have created communities that instil virtues of sharing and moderation in the use of resources. This communitarian solution helps people internalize the rules that allow successful management of the commons.

NEGATIVE EXTERNALITIES

There is still another problem with activities concerning private property. Sometimes private activities affect others who are not party to a free-market transaction. For example, suppose Bob's neighbours in the next apartment hire a band for a weekend party. The activity is on their private property, and the market transaction is between them and the band. However, as a by-product of this activity, Bob, who is external to the transaction, will hear a lot of music (or noise pollution). If Bob likes the music, then this is an external benefit (positive externality) for him. If Bob does not like the music, then this is an external cost (negative externality) for him.

An EXTERNAL COST or negative externality is a cost arising from the economic activity of an agent that is born by others because the cost is not incorporated into the market price of the product. An EXTERNAL BENEFIT or positive externality is a benefit arising from the economic activity of an agent for which the agent is not compensated because the cost is not incorporated into the market price of the product. People engage in economic activity without intending to cause pollution, but it is nonetheless a side effect of their activity, and they do not always have to pay for the costs they inflict. Economists think of externalities as examples of market failure. However, the Coase Theorem suggests that, under certain circumstances, the market will actually be able to handle externalities and maximize total net social benefits.

The net social benefit of a polluting agent's activity includes both the private benefits and costs for the agent and the external costs to everyone else.

- + Internal benefit to agent of polluting activity
- − Internal cost to agent of polluting activity
- − External cost to everyone else of polluting activity
- = Net social benefit for everyone of activity

THE COASE THEOREM

Ronald Coase argued that if private property rights are clearly defined and agents can negotiate, with no transaction costs, the buying and selling of rights to do activities that cause external costs, then bargaining can always find solutions that maximize preference satisfaction through minimizing total social costs. Counter-intuitively, the parties will be able to achieve a socially efficient outcome regardless of how the property rights are initially assigned (Coase 1960).

This result is called the COASE THEOREM, and it lends support to the idea that, if transferable private property rights are clearly defined for everything, then the market can, by itself, maximize aggregate net social benefits in the presence of external costs like pollution. We can construct a simple example to illustrate Coase's argument. Suppose that the Acme Co. builds a widget factory upwind of Bob's house, and emits noxious pollution that makes Bob's house a less desirable place to live. If Acme operates with no pollution control it will have a net internal benefit of $1200 instead of the $1000 it would get if it used pollution controls. Bob, however, will have a $1000 net benefit from his house if Acme uses pollution controls, but only a $400 net benefit if Acme does not. Table 18.2 summarizes the payoffs.

Suppose, first, that there are no property rights governing pollution emissions. Acme will use no pollution control and total social benefits will be $1600 as shown in the right hand column. Total social benefits will not be maximized because using pollution control will produce a higher aggregate net benefit of $2000. Acme, however, considers only its internal costs, and it is cheaper for Acme, though not for Acme and Bob together, for Acme to provide no pollution control.

	POLLUTION CONTROL	NO POLLUTION CONTROL
ACME'S NET BENEFIT	$1000	$1200
BOB'S NET BENEFIT	$1000	$400
TOTAL NET SOCIAL BENEFIT	$2000	$1600

TABLE 18.2: Acme and Bob with no defined property rights

Now suppose that Bob has the right not to suffer pollution. Bob uses his right to force Acme to install pollution control equipment. Acme suffers a $200 loss, whereas Bob has a $600 gain. This situation optimizes total social benefit at $2000. The pollution control column of Table 18.3 shows the situation of Bob and Acme as it is now. This is not surprising. If Bob has a legal right not to suffer from pollution, then he can force Acme to internalize the cost of pollution control.

	POLLUTION CONTROL	NO POLLUTION CONTROL
ACME'S NET BENEFIT	$1000	$1200
BOB'S NET BENEFIT	$1000	$400
TOTAL NET SOCIAL BENEFIT	$2000	$1600

TABLE 18.3: Bob has property right not to suffer from pollution

What is more surprising is that if Acme has the saleable right to pollute and Acme and Bob bargain as two rational, self-interested agents, then they will still arrive at the optimum social benefit. For Bob can offer Acme a payment of $400 to install and use pollution control. Acme will accept because, after the deal, Acme has the $1000 benefit under the pollution control scenario plus the $400 payment from Bob. This is better for Acme than the $1200 it makes with no pollution control. Bob is also better off because he receives the $1000 benefit of pollution control minus the $400 he pays Acme, which is still a higher level of benefit than the $400 benefit he would have received without pollution control. Both Acme and Bob are better off, though Bob is not as well off as when he owned the right not to suffer from pollution. Net social benefits are $2000, which is optimum. The payment from Bob to Acme is a "side payment." A SIDE PAYMENT is a payment made from one party to the other to induce them to internalize an external cost.

	POLLUTION CONTROL	NO POLLUTION CONTROL	AFTER DEAL
ACME'S NET BENEFIT	$1000	$1200	$1000 + $400 = $1400
BOB'S NET BENEFIT	$1000	$400	$1000 – $400 = $600
TOTAL NET SOCIAL BENEFIT	$2000	$1600	$2000

TABLE 18.4: Acme has right to emit pollution, but Bob's side payment results in optimal social benefits

From the economic utilitarian point of view, that of reducing the external costs of pollution, it does not matter whether Acme or Bob is assigned the property rights. They can still bargain to an optimum scenario. Any side payment between $201 and $599 would result in both parties being better off. It is crucial to this result that there be well defined property rights, and that these property rights can be bought and sold. In the very first scenario, there were no property rights. Acme just emitted pollutants, but had no right to do so that it could sell to Bob. Defined, transferable property rights make reaching the optimum outcome possible.

From the deontological, justice-based point of view, it seems unfair that Bob would have to pay to reduce Acme's pollution of his house. Suppose, however, that Acme's widget factory was there first, and then Bob came along and built his house. Then it might seem fair for Acme to have the right to emit pollution, and Bob should have to pay to have Acme reduce its emissions. Coase pointed out that property rights determine who can impose external costs on whom. If Acme has the right to emit pollutants, then Acme can freely impose a $600 loss of benefit on Bob. Similarly, though, if Bob has the right not to suffer from pollution, then Bob can similarly impose a $200 loss of benefit on Acme.

The assumptions of the Coase theorem are that parties have perfect information and that parties can negotiate with little or no transaction costs. TRANSACTION COSTS are the costs of reaching and enforcing an agreement between negotiating parties. They include the costs of researching information about the situation, negotiating the agreement, and legally enforcing the agreement. The basic weakness of the Coase approach is that many important environmental problems do not satisfy these assumptions. The assumptions are satisfied only in very simple cases, when there are few parties affected and when they can communicate easily. The transaction costs of negotiations become expensive when there are many recipients of pollution, many polluters, non-point source pollution, or accumulative pollutants. When the cause of pollution is difficult to prove, when parties cannot trust one another, when parties have little information about other parties' incentives, when those polluted have little information about the polluters' emissions, or when there are legal fees involved, Coase's approach breaks down. Applying Coase's approach requires that we identify a direct connection between the rights of one party and the rights of another. Many environmental problems are cases of accumulative harms, and as we have seen, a rights-based approach does not work properly in the presence of accumulative harms. As well, Coase's approach maximizes efficiency with no regard for rights or fairness. From the point of view of economic utilitarian efficiency is does not matter who has the legally transferable property rights. From the point of view of distributive justice, it matters very much. The initial distribution of transferable legal property rights determines who will have to compensate whom for the harms of pollution or the opportunity costs of cheaper production.

THE SOCIALLY OPTIMAL LEVEL OF POLLUTION

There is a common moral intuition that the only ethically defensible level of pollution is zero. Pollution is wrong, and those who are emitting it ought to stop. We have a moral duty and ethical obligation never to pollute the planet. On reflection, we see that this cannot be quite right. It is impossible to live without creating some undesirable emissions, and any ethical theory that demanded zero pollution would be too demanding for us to follow. The free-market environmentalist approach embodied in the Coase theorem would recommend pollution when the benefits of production outweigh the costs of pollution. Suppose that the net benefits for Acme and Bob are as in Table 18.5, and that initially Bob owns the right not to suffer from pollution. Aggregate net benefits are highest if Acme can produce widgets without pollution controls.

	POLLUTION CONTROL	NO POLLUTION CONTROL	AFTER DEAL
ACME'S NET BENEFIT	$1000	$1900	$1900 − $700 = $1200
BOB'S NET BENEFIT	$1000	$400	$400 + $700 = $1100
TOTAL NET SOCIAL BENEFIT	$2000	$2300	$2300

TABLE 18.5: Bob owns right not to be polluted and social optimum is no pollution controls

Following Coase's approach, Acme can offer a side payment of $700 to Bob to allow Acme to produce widgets without pollution control. Acme will still be better off with $1900 − $700 = $1200 worth of benefits rather than producing with pollution controls for $1000. Bob will accept because he will now be better off with $400 + $700 = $1100 in net benefits instead of $1000. Having Acme produce with no pollution control is financially better for both parties. The socially optimal level of pollution is not zero.

More precisely, to the economic utilitarian, the SOCIALLY OPTIMAL LEVEL OF POLLUTION is the point at which the human beings in a market place value the next consumer good more highly than they do the reduction in pollution that could be bought with the same money. The socially optimal level of pollution is not equal to zero pollution, but is determined by both the costs caused by pollution and the benefits brought about by the production which led to the pollution. Economic utilitarians measure costs and benefits by the willingness of people both to pay for being free of pollution and to pay for the goods produced by the polluting activity.

A clear example of the economic determination of the socially optimal level of pollution is an auction. Suppose that cattle farmers want their cattle to have access to Bumpers Brook. Local anglers want to keep the river free of pollution. The economic utilitarian approach is to have an auction to see how much anglers and farmers are willing to pay to reduce pollution. Let X be the maximum pollution Bumpers Brook will tolerate. Divide X into 100 shares, and auction the shares among the anglers and farmers. Suppose the anglers buy 42 shares, and decide not to pollute their quota in order to protect the brook. The farmers buy 58 shares, and allow their cattle to pollute this quota. In this case, the optimal level of pollution is .58X.

A utilitarian justification of the determination of the optimal level of pollution by a free-market auction starts with the premise that utilitarianism says to cause maximum aggregate utility. The preference-satisfaction utilitarianism assumption is that satisfying preferences maximizes utility, and that we create more utility by satisfying more intense preferences. The economic utilitarian assumption is that people reveal the intensity of their preferences by how much they are willing to pay for whatever will satisfy them. Hence, we maximize utility by distributing things to whoever will pay the most for them. In a free-market auction, whoever pays the most for something gets it. Therefore, utilitarianism implies that the result of a free-market auction will appropriately determine the optimal level of pollution.

In a more general situation than that of a simple auction, we can use marginal costs and benefits to determine the optimal level of pollution. The marginal cost (MC) of decreasing pollution equals how many dollars it would cost to decrease pollution by one increment. The marginal benefit (MB) of decreasing pollution equals how many dollars, for example, we would save in health care costs by decreasing pollution by one increment. As we move from maximally dirty to 100% clean, we ask at each point whether the added benefit of a policy of increasing cleanliness by one increment outweighs the cost of doing so. If it does, then total benefit will be increased by the clean-up. If it does not, then total benefit will be decreased by the clean-up. Therefore, maximal net utility (net total benefits minus net total costs) is at the point where MC = MB. This point is the socially optimum level of pollution, OL.

Figure 18.2 shows a graph of the marginal benefits of a cleaner environment and the marginal costs of cleaning the environment up, as measured by willingness to pay, against the level of cleanliness going from 0% clean (or maximally dirty) to 100% cleaned up (or no pollution at all). MC is the marginal cost of decreasing pollution by one increment, MB is the marginal benefit of decreasing pollution by one increment, and OL is the optimal level of pollution. The graph assumes that the added cost of an increment of cleanliness rises as the water (or whatever) gets cleaner, and that the added benefit of an increment of cleanliness falls as the water gets cleaner. This is because of the laws of diminishing marginal utility and of increasing marginal cost. We can see the intuitive validity of these assumptions if we reflect on cleaning up a house. We get the maximum impact for the least cost with a simple tidying up. Dusting gives us less impact and takes longer. We get less impact again, though at the cost of more time, by sweeping the floors, then a still smaller additional impact by washing them, and yet less impact by scrubbing them.

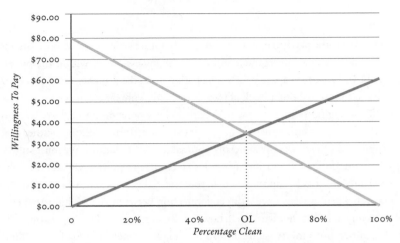

SOCIALLY OPTIMAL LEVEL OF POLLUTION

■ *Marginal Benefit (MB)* ■ *Marginal Cost (MC)*

FIGURE 18.2: Marginal costs (MC) and marginal benefits (MB)
versus level of cleanliness showing socially optimal level of pollution (OL)

Environmental economics represents these notions differently in order to facilitate economic reasoning. Environmental economists use the notion of a Marginal Damages curve
(MD) to represent the benefits forgone by failing to clean up pollution, and the notion of
a Marginal Abatement Cost curve (MAC) to represent the incremental costs of preventing
pollution or of cleaning it up. The horizontal axis of their graph has level of emissions on
an increasing scale. The marginal abatement cost (MAC) is zero when there is no pollution
control. Thus, the MAC line slopes downward from the left and crosses the horizontal axis at
the level of emissions when no one makes any effort to prevent pollution. Marginal damage
increases with emissions, so the MD line slopes upward from the left.

WEAKNESSES OF FREE-MARKET
ENVIRONMENTALISM APPROACH

One problem with free-market environmentalism is that its theory of moral standing is narrowly anthropocentric: Only humans participating in the free market have moral standing.
Arguing in support of a market-based approach to environmental problems, William Baxter
famously wrote the following regarding the idea of eliminating the use of the pesticide DDT
to protect penguins from damage.

> My criteria are oriented to people, not penguins. Damage to penguins, or sugar
> pines, or geological marvels is, without more, simply irrelevant. One must go
> further, by my criteria, and say: Penguins are important because people enjoy
> seeing them walk about on rocks; and furthermore, the well-being of people
> would be less impaired by halting use of DDT than by giving up penguins. In

short, my observations about environmental problems will be people-oriented, as are my criteria. I have no interest in preserving penguins for their own sake. (Baxter 1974: 5)

Distant people outside the particular market in question, future generations whose costs and preferences are unknown and unrepresented by any willingness to pay within the present market, animals who lack the capacity for participating in markets, plants, and ecosystems are all outside the conceptual framework of free-market environmentalism.

From the deontological point of view, free-market environmentalism neglects issues of duties, rights, and harms. Perhaps people have a duty to create zero pollution, rather than a utilitarian obligation to create only a socially optimal level of pollution. We must still ask why people have this duty. One possible answer is that emitting pollution violates the rights of others to personal security by injuring them in some way. This works fine in a case like that of Acme and Bob where we can trace a direct connection between Acme's industrial emissions and Bob's injury. It does not work well, however, for cases of accumulative harm. If the pollution that caused Bob's injury is due instead to smog from the tailpipes of the millions of cars in a huge city, then we can no longer trace a direct connection to the activity of any particular driver. Each driver can reasonably argue that her driving is not causing enough smog to injure Bob, and so she is not violating his rights. Further, she can argue that since she is not harming Bob, the Harm Principle gives the government no justification for interfering with her right to drive her car. A rights-based argument for zero pollution has difficulty with non-point source pollution and pollution that accumulates over time. On the other hand, someone might think that we have a duty to cause zero pollution because pollution creates costs for other people. This, however, is a utilitarian argument, and, as such must consider both the costs and the benefits of the polluting activity to all parties including the polluter and its customers. Considering the benefits as well as the costs of pollution will lead us back to a socially optimal level of pollution.

From within the teleological form of objective consequentialism, someone could argue that humans should strive for zero pollution for the sake of the health of the planet, in order to maintain the balance of nature that will never benefit anyone, or to preserve the beauty of a pristine wilderness that nobody will ever enjoy. This objection to the socially optimal level of pollution would require us to defend a notion of natural flourishing that could serve as a goal for the environment as a whole, which might be difficult to do. We could also phrase an objective consequentialist argument of striving for zero pollution in terms of protecting the Earth's biotic community, or the biotic and abiotic system that is Lovelock's Gaia.

The dispositional, informed preference, approach to intrinsic value immediately suggests that we think critically about how preferences provide a basis for the notion of the socially optimal level of pollution. This approach reminds us that what people actually want will often differ from what they would want if fully informed, and that the latter is what is valuable for them. The preferences in the calculation of a socially optimal level of pollution are the actual, often uninformed, preferences of market participants. Many of these preferences may depend on a false understanding of the human/environment interaction. It is entirely possible that, if market participants had full information about the world, then they would see the costs of pollution as much higher than they do now. Consequently, the optimal level of pollution generated by hypothetical, fully informed, market participants would be lower than the socially optimal level generated by actual, imperfectly informed, market participants.

From within the virtue ethics approach, someone could criticize the market determination of a socially optimal level of pollution by saying that she does not want to be the sort of person who thoughtlessly harms the environment that way. She does not want to be a member of a community that does not strive for the least amount of pollution possible. The market-based approach, she might argue, includes the vices of thoughtless selfishness and extractive, short-sighted greed that constitute a non-flourishing human life.

Finally, the economic utilitarian theory of instrumental value based on measuring the intensity of preferences by the willingness of people to pay to have them satisfied is, as mentioned frequently, a suspect theory of value. If willingness to pay is not an accurate or valid measure of value, then the socially optimal level of pollution, which we have defined in terms of it, is not accurate or valid either.

SUMMARY

1. A fundamental theorem of welfare economics holds that under conditions of perfect competition the free market will maximize participants' welfare. Free-market environmentalism holds that we can correct market failures by expanding the domain of transferable property rights and thus perfecting the market.

2. One source of market imperfection is open-access resources. Where private ownership is not well-defined, self-interested behaviour by each individual will lead to the spoiling of the resource. In the tragedy of the commons, each farmer has an incentive to graze additional sheep beyond the carrying capacity of the common pasture because she gets a net benefit from each extra sheep and is able to externalize most of the costs of the extra sheep onto the other farmers.

3. Privatizing the commons is one way to prevent tragedy, but it may not be a fair and just way. Nor is privatization the only way to govern the commons.

4. A polluting individual does not pay all the environmental costs that the individual causes. The costs caused by an individual's actions, but passed on to others, are external costs. External costs may fall on other market participants, on distant people, on future generations, and on animals, plants, and ecosystems.

5. Ronald Coase argued that if there are well-defined, saleable property rights in environmental situations, then parties can always negotiate solutions to external cost situations that maximize net social benefits, provided transaction costs are negligible. If property rights are not saleable, then the parties cannot do this. The parties can achieve a socially efficient outcome regardless of whether one party initially owns the right to emit pollutants or another initially owns the right not to suffer from pollution.

6. The Coase approach does not work well when many parties must negotiate, when pollution is not point source, when pollution accumulates, when pollution crosses international boundaries, or when future generations are involved.

7. Because economic utilitarians take into account both the costs of pollution and the benefits of the productive activity that caused it, they do not believe that the best level of pollution is zero. The socially optimal level of pollution is the level where the marginal cost caused by an increment of pollution equals the marginal benefit of the additional goods produced by the activity that caused the increment of pollution.

8. Other ethical approaches hold that the morally right level of pollution should be as close to zero as we can reasonably achieve. The concept of a socially optimal level of pollution is narrowly anthropocentric. It ethically neglects distant people, future people, and the non-human world. It permits violations of the right not to be harmed by other people's pollution, endangers the healthy flourishing of the planet. It encourages selfish, greedy behaviour, and will result in higher levels of pollution than fully informed citizens would negotiate.

ONLINE READING QUESTIONS

The book's website contains reading questions on this chapter. Working through these questions will help you understand, remember, and apply important concepts from the chapter. Some of the questions supply useful hints for the study questions.

STUDY QUESTIONS

Using the text and hints from the online reading questions, write out, type, dictate to your computer, or at least formulate in your head answers to the following questions.

1. Explain the tragedy of the commons.
2. Why is pollution often an external cost?
3. Why is the Coase theorem often not useful in formulating environmental policy?
4. Why do economic utilitarians believe in a non-zero socially optimal level of pollution?
5. What ethical reasons do people give for zero pollution?

Spend a few minutes thinking about the following questions, or, better yet, discuss them with fellow readers of this book.

1. In *People or Penguins*, William Baxter argues we must accept the free-market approach to the environment and its appeal to human self-interest because no other approach "corresponds to reality" (Baxter 1974: 5). Do you agree? Why or why not?

2. Baxter claims that the economic approach will not lead to destruction of the non-human environment because human beings depend on that environment (1974: 5). Do you agree? Why or why not?

3. Baxter also claims that what is good for people is also good for penguins, so economic markets will protect the environment (1974: 5–6). Do you agree? Why or why not?

4. "But many of the more extreme assertions that one hears from some conservationists amount to tacit assertions that they are specially appointed representatives of sugar pines, and hence that their preferences should be weighted more heavily than the preferences of other humans who do not enjoy equal rapport with 'nature.' The simplistic assertion that agricultural use of DDT must stop at once because it is harmful to penguins is of this type" (Baxter 1974: 6–7). What are Baxter's ethical assumptions? Do you agree? Why or why not?

5. "[I]f polar bears or pine trees or penguins, like men, are to be regarded as ends rather than means, if they are to count in our calculus of social organization, someone must tell me how much each one counts, and someone must tell me how these life-forms are to be permitted to express their preferences, for I do not know either answer. If the [answer] is that certain people are to hold their proxies, then I want to know how those proxy-holders are to be selected: self-appointment does not seem workable to me" (Baxter 1974: 7). What are Baxter's ethical assumptions? Do you agree? Why or why not?

6. "Questions of *ought* are unique to the human mind and world—they are meaningless as applied to a nonhuman situation. I reject the proposition that we *ought* to respect the 'balance of nature' or to 'preserve the environment' unless the reason for doing so, express or implied, is the benefit of man" (Baxter 1974: 7). What are Baxter's ethical assumptions? Do you agree? Why or why not?

Chapter 19

EXTERNAL COSTS AND PUBLIC GOODS

THE BRANCH OF ETHICS THAT EXAMINES ETHICAL JUSTIFICATIONS FOR ECONOMIC systems is political philosophy. Political philosophy tries to discover what ethical principles should govern the role of state governments. These principles will involve treating people as moral equals, but, as we have seen, there are different ways to do this. The utilitarian approach gives equal consideration to the interests of everyone. The rights-based approach gives equal respect to every person. The distributive justice approach gives fair shares to everyone. Environmental ethics reminds government policymakers that the non-human world should also have moral consideration.

As we have seen, the contractarian and libertarian approaches morally justify only a minimal role for the government. The contractarian approach sees state enforcement of contracts and private property as a covenant between ethical egoists. The libertarian approach sees the state as unfortunate but unavoidable, required to protect natural rights to private property and liberty. Both approaches justify only the most minimal possible type of government, often called a "night-watchman" state, which has little role in protecting the environment.

The utilitarian approach allows a contingent role for the government in protecting the environment. The indirect utilitarian view is that markets in perfect competition provide maximum total preference satisfaction, but that we may need the state to fix market failures. Individually self-interested behaviour, constrained only by the rules of the market, does not yield maximum aggregate net benefit where there are external costs, like those caused by accumulative pollution, and where there is a need to provide public goods, like clean air. The justice-based approach sees an essential role for the state in ensuring that net benefits are fairly distributed. The state should distribute the costs of preventing pollution and the costs of providing public goods in a way that treats everyone as morally equal.

This chapter will look, in more detail, at environmental pollution and resource depletion as external costs of economic activity, and at the provision of a healthy environment as a public good. Markets fail to provide efficient solutions to external environmental costs and fail to provide optimum amounts of environmental public goods. Thus, we need to examine ethically the role of government environmental policy in providing environmental public goods.

Learning Objectives

1. To understand more about the ethical implications of external environmental costs.
2. To understand the notion of an environmental public good.
3. To understand some of the ethical issues regarding environmental public goods.
4. To understand that environmental economics has a measurement problem for external costs and public goods because they are outside the market.

ENVIRONMENTAL NEGATIVE EXTERNALITIES

Economic activities involving private property often create environmental problems. Sometimes private activities affect others who are not party to market transactions because the market price of the product does not incorporate the cost to others. People engage in economic activity without intending to cause pollution, but it is nonetheless a side-effect of their activity, and they do not always have to pay for the costs they inflict. These are the negative externalities, or external costs, of economic activity.

In a tragedy of the commons situation, a farmer chooses to exceed the carrying capacity of the commons and graze an extra sheep. This farmer's action causes external costs, in the form of lost income, that fall on all the farmers who use the common pasture. The competitive overgrazing that follows hurts all the farmers, and, if the common pasture is irreversibly injured, it will hurt the farmer's descendants too. These are anthropocentric external costs. If we consider the situation from the point of view of the nonhuman environment, we can see that there are also zoocentric external costs in the form of the sheep that are now hungry, biocentric external costs to the overgrazed grass, and ecocentric external costs in the destruction of the grassland ecosystem. We must note, however, that a market-based representation of the situation will necessarily neglect external costs incurred by any entities other than the original farmers. Only the original farmers can have a willingness to pay which the market can measure; their descendants, their sheep, and the grassland cannot.

Privatizing the commons is one possible way to solve the problems created by common resources. A common resource is a resource from which it is difficult to exclude other individuals, yet is a resource whose consumption by one individual diminishes its availability for others. However, privatization has problems. How are we to assign initial shares in the common resource fairly? For example, the assimilative capacity of the atmosphere for greenhouse gasses is currently a common resource. To prevent climate change, how are we to assign initial shares in its use among large, carbon-intensive, industrial firms? In assigning private property rights to an open access resource, we are actually restricting liberty. Before privatization of an open-access resource, all people have a negative right to use the resource as they see fit. After privatization, those common rights are restricted. If we do assign tradable private property rights in common resources, then the Coase theorem shows that market participants will be able to negotiate a socially optimal level of pollution, but only if transaction costs are very low. Unfortunately, for many of the worst environmental problems facing the Earth, transaction costs are not low. Because so many environmental problems involve non-point source and accumulative pollution, it is extremely difficult to trace direct causal chains connecting human activities and the accumulative harms that they bring about. Without knowledge of such direct causal chains, determination of legal liability will be difficult, and negotiations will be expensive, if not impossible in practice.

If a market economy cannot internalize the costs of environmental damage through a procedure like that of Coase, then the actual marketplace will not take into account the costs of environmental damage. If, for example, the production of widgets causes pollution, then the market for widgets will produce more widgets, and at a lower price, than an economic utilitarian would judge to be optimal. The producers and consumers of widgets, thinking only of their own self-interest, make their buying and selling decisions based on their private or internal marginal costs (MC) and marginal benefits (MB). The pollution costs created by the production of widgets get spread over all of society, and the individual producers and consumers of widgets do not pay them. The costs of pollution are external costs (XC) from the point of view of the producers and consumers. Producers and consumers do not take into account external costs in their buying and selling decisions. Consequently, the market will not maximize the aggregate net benefits to all the society.

To see how this works, we will first consider an example where there are no external costs. Table 19.1 shows the internal or private marginal benefits of consuming one more widget (MB) and the internal or private marginal costs of producing one more widget (MC). From the point of view of an economic utilitarian, the point is to maximize net costs and benefits. It does not matter to the economic utilitarian that the benefits go to the consumer and the producer pays the costs. The economic utilitarian is concerned only with the aggregate net benefits. The net private or internal benefits, for all producers and consumers, are MB – MC.

INCREMENT OF WIDGETS	0 to 1	1 to 2	2 to 3	3 to 4	4 to 5	5 to 6	6 to 7	7 to 8
MB ($)	9	8	7	6	5	4	3	2
MC ($)	1	2	3	4	5	6	7	8
MB-MC ($)	8	6	4	2	0	−2	−4	−6

TABLE 19.1: Internal marginal costs and benefits for the production and consumption of widgets

External Costs and Public Goods

Suppose this miniature economy is producing 3 widgets. Will the aggregate net benefits increase if the economy produces another widget? The fourth widget will produce an incremental benefit of $6 and cost $4, for a positive net benefit of $2. Thus, to maximize total net economic benefits, the economy should produce a fourth widget. Should the economy produce a fifth widget? According to the table, increasing widget production from 4 to 5 will produce $0 net marginal benefits. Producing a fifth widget will not increase total net benefits. Therefore, when there are no external costs because there is no pollution from widget making, then total net benefit is maximized when MB = MC which is the production of 4 widgets.

Now we will change the example to include external costs. Suppose that widget production produces pollution that causes costly damages to everyone else in the market society. Table 19.2, shows this as an additional social cost of $2 for each widget produced. In Table 19.2, MC is the internal marginal private cost of producing one more widget and XC is the external marginal social cost of the pollution. MC + XC is the total marginal social cost and MB – (MC + XC) is the net marginal social benefit.

INCREMENT OF WIDGETS	0 to 1	1 to 2	2 to 3	3 to 4	4 to 5	5 to 6	6 to 7	7 to 8
MB ($)	9	8	7	6	5	4	3	2
MC ($)	1	2	3	4	5	6	7	8
MB-MC ($)	8	6	4	2	0	−2	−4	−6
XC ($)	2	2	2	2	2	2	2	2
MB- (MC+XC) ($)	6	4	2	0	−2	−4	−6	−8

TABLE 19.2: External costs to all of society

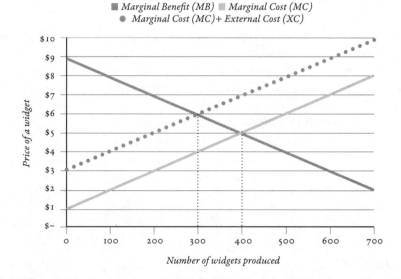

FIGURE 19.1: Optimal levels of widget production with and without external costs

We can see in Table 19.2 that when the external costs of the pollution caused by widget production ($2 per widget) are included, total net social benefits reach maximum when 3 widgets are produced. The production of a 4th widget will add $0 to the total benefits.

If we now change the example again, and think about the production of hundreds of widgets, then we can show what is going on here in a graph (Figure 19.1). Because they consider only internal marginal costs, widget producers and consumers, acting rationally in pursuit of their self-interest, will reach an equilibrium of 400 widgets at a price of $5. If there were no external costs, then this quantity and price would maximize aggregate net social benefits. When there are external costs, however, the equilibrium fails to maximize aggregate net social benefits. Economic utilitarian thinking must include all costs, including the external pollution cost of $2 per widget that falls on all members of the market society, not just the producers and consumers of widgets. When we consider the full social cost of widget production, as shown by the MC + XC line, we see that aggregate net social benefits is at a maximum with 300 widgets at a price of $6. In the presence of the external costs of environmental damage, the self-interested behaviour of producers and consumers (equilibrium = 400 widgets @ $5) fails to maximize aggregate net social benefits (maximum = 300 widgets @ $6).

Failure to take into account the full social costs of the pollution created by widget production will, from an economic utilitarian point of view, result in:

1. The production of too many widgets (400 instead of 300), and
2. The production of widgets at too low a price ($5 instead of $6).

The economic utilitarian considers all costs and benefits. The total net social benefit must include:

1. The benefits to individuals of the goods produced,
2. The internal costs to individuals of the goods produced, and
3. The external costs, spread over the whole market society, of the goods produced.

Therefore, economic utilitarian reasoning points to the need for government intervention to regulate polluters. Alternatively, the government can make polluters internalize the external social costs that they create by placing an emissions charge or pollution tax on their production of pollutants.

One of the problems with the utilitarian approach to ethics is its measurement problem. Economic utilitarians use willingness to pay as a measure of preference intensity. However, the market does not assign a monetary value to external costs like the costs of pollution. In order to apply economic utilitarian reasoning to external costs we must assign them a monetary value. This creates a problem. How do we assign monetary values to external costs that are not the subject of market transactions? For example, how do we assign a dollar value to the costs to human health of sulphur dioxide emissions from a coal-burning power plant? The answer is Cost-Benefit Analysis, also known as Benefit-Cost Analysis, which is the subject of the next chapter.

ENVIRONMENTAL PUBLIC GOODS

An economic good is something that is the input or output of economic activity. This is the sense of "good" that we use when we talk of the goods and services produced by an economy. It is a positive concept and not a normative one. An ethical good, on the other hand, is something that an ethical theory evaluates as ethically good. We will be concerned here with public goods as public economic goods. It is often the case that public economic goods are also ethically good, and people sometimes conflate economics and ethics and talk of "public bads."

A PUBLIC GOOD is as an economic good that is non-rival and non-excludable. The latter two terms require definition. A NON-RIVAL GOOD is an economic good whose consumption by one individual does not diminish its availability to others. For example, when one person enjoys a fireworks display, that person's consumption of the fireworks display does not diminish its availability to others who can also enjoy it. By contrast, a RIVAL GOOD is an economic good whose consumption by one individual does diminish its availability for others. For example, when one person consumes an ice cream cone, that ice cream cone is not available for others to consume. A NON-EXCLUDABLE GOOD (an open-access good) is an economic good from which it is difficult to exclude other individuals who do not pay for the good. A fireworks show is also an example of a non-excludable good, as is the common pasture of the farmers in the tragedy of the commons. By contrast, an EXCLUDABLE GOOD is an economic good from which it is possible to exclude other individuals who do not pay for the good. Any form of private property is an example of an excludable good.

Using these concepts, we can classify economic goods in a way that is useful when applied to the environment. Table 19.3 summarizes this classification.

	RIVAL	NON-RIVAL
Excludable	Private good	Collective good
Non-excludable	Commons good	Public Good

TABLE 19.3: Classification of economic goods

PRIVATE GOODS are excludable and rival. They are economic goods from which it is possible to exclude others, and are such that their consumption by one person will prevent their consumption by others. Examples include food items, an enclosed pasture, or a personal computer. Private goods are goods that are suited for buying and selling in an economic market.

COLLECTIVE GOODS are excludable and non-rival. They are excludable economic goods whose use by one person does not diminish their availability to others. For example, national parks and museums approximate collective goods. People can be excluded from them, but up to their carrying capacity, their use by one person does not prevent others from using them also. Cable television and internet services are also excludable but approximately non-rival. Because collective goods are excludable, they are bought and sold in markets.

COMMONS GOODS are non-excludable and rival. They are open-access goods whose use by one person diminishes their value for others. Examples include a common pasture or an ocean fishery that have reached their carrying capacity.

PUBLIC GOODS are non-excludable and non-rival. They are open-access goods whose use by one person does not diminish their availability to others. Examples include national defence, police protection, and the judiciary. These are accessible to all citizens and not diminished by use. Many environmental goods are public goods. Examples include breathable air, clean water, reduced greenhouse gas build-up, the ozone layer, beautiful scenery, wilderness areas, and the absence of, or reductions in, noxious pollutants. Because public goods are non-excludable, people cannot buy or sell them in a market. These abstract types of economic goods apply only approximately in the real world. Public goods are usually only approximately non-excludable. For example, governments can exclude non-citizens from the benefits of national defence. They are also only approximately non-rival. For example, the court system is sometimes over-loaded, and the use of the atmosphere for absorbing carbon dioxide started to cause problems when human beings exceeded its assimilative capacity.

Environmental problems, like climate change, tend to be external costs in an economic market. Solutions to environmental problems, like reducing atmospheric carbon, tend to be public goods. If human beings do succeed in reducing carbon emissions, then it will not be possible to exclude anyone from those benefits, and the benefits to one person do not diminish the benefits to anyone else. The ethical question posed by environmental solutions as public goods is who should pay for them?

Environmental public goods usually cost money to provide. Because environmental public goods are non-excludable, the markets will not supply them. Since it is difficult or impossible to prevent non-contributors from enjoying them, each person has an incentive not to contribute to the provision of public goods. Such FREE-RIDERS enjoy the benefits of a public good without bearing the burdens of providing it. The free-rider problem produces two ethical difficulties:

From an economic utilitarian perspective, every person has an incentive to free-ride and let others pay for the public good. Thus, few, if any, people will contribute to providing the public good. Because no one pays, the result will be a less than socially optimal amount of the environmental good. For example, most of us are free-riders with respect to reducing greenhouse gas emissions.

From a justice-based perspective, free-riding is an injustice because it is an unfair distribution of benefits and burdens. Free-riders receive a benefit without contributing to the provision of the public good. Those who do not free-ride often pay more than their share of the costs of the good.

Some people argue for solving the public goods problem by turning public goods into private goods, like the enclosure of the commons. For example, its owner will protect a lake that becomes private property. Because public goods are non-rival, however, extending their consumption to more people always gives a benefit without incurring any additional cost. (A non-rival good is an economic good whose consumption by one does not diminish its availability to others.) Privatizing a public good does diminish its availability to those excluded, and prevents them from receiving its benefits. From the utilitarian point of view, extending the consumption of public goods to everyone will maximize net benefits. Private property solutions to the free-rider problem, like privatizing a lake in order to protect it from pollution, reduce aggregate utility, and hence are wrong according to the utilitarian approach.

As well, enclosing or privatizing public goods removes the rights of access previously held by everyone. For example, if we preserve the lake by privatizing it, then people who were previously at liberty to use the lake will now be excluded, which will interfere with their rights. Creating private property rights always infringes on the rights of those who do not become the new owners. Privatization of public goods raises issues of gaining consent from those whose rights we infringe and how we should compensate them.

Because of the free-rider problem and because of the difficulties with private property (enclosure) solutions, we generally need government to provide adequate levels of public goods. Governments will finance the provision of public goods through taxation. Social insurance, education, national defence, and a healthy environment are generally the responsibility of government. The need for government intervention implies that we need a theory of justice to govern the fair allocation of the benefits and burdens of producing public goods. The costs of preventing pollution and the costs of providing clean-up should be distributed in a way that treats everyone as moral equals.

We can see some of the justice issues that arise in paying for public goods if we extend the example of Mike and Nancy, the rational agents from the chapter on ethical egoism whose self-interested strategies led to a prisoner's dilemma situation and to the pollution of the lake on which they were building their cottages. Suppose that they now face the problem of cleaning up this pollution. Neither can exclude the other from enjoyment of a clean lake, and the enjoyment of a clean lake by one person does not prevent the other person from also enjoying it. From the perspective of this little two-person society, a cleaned up lake is an environmental public good. Both Mike and Nancy would be better off (receive positive net individual benefits) if the lake were cleaned up. Nevertheless, both would like to free-ride on the efforts of the other to clean up the lake, so nothing will get done unless they bring in the local government. The government will then face the problems of fairly distributing the benefits and burdens of the clean-up.

In what follows, we will investigate the fairness of different forms of taxation to pay for this environmental public good: a poll tax, a proportional income tax, and a progressive income tax. Suppose the cost of the clean-up is $800. The benefits of the cleanup will be measured by Mike's and Nancy's willingness to pay for a clean lake. Suppose that Mike and Nancy want a clean lake with equal intensity, but that they differ in their abilities to pay. Mike makes $400 per week whereas Nancy makes $800. Each is willing to give up a week's salary to have the lake cleaned up. It is reasonable to assume that Mike's willingness to pay for a clean lake is $400 and Nancy's is $800. Someone's willingness to pay for an economic good is the maximum amount of money that he or she is willing to give up to get the good. However, money is not what is important to the person; it is what the money will buy. What is important is the other economic goods that he or she must forego in order to get this particular good. To get money, Mike and Nancy must forego leisure time by working. So it is reasonable to say that if they both want a clean lake with the same intensity as they want a week's holiday, then both value a clean lake the same as they value a week's pay. So rich Nancy's WTP for a clean lake is $800 whereas poor Mike's WTP for the clean lake is $400.

Notice that this would probably not be how they would answer if a government official asked them how much they would be willing to pay for a clean lake. Both would have an incentive to understate their willingness to pay because they would know that the government official will use this information to calculate their share of the clean-up costs.

A just government policy will treat people as equals. The intuitive way to treat people as equals in funding the clean-up of the lake is to require that Mike and Nancy each pay the same amount of money. This is called either a "poll tax" or a "head tax." A POLL TAX requires the same payment from each person regardless of their income and is a REGRESSIVE TAX in the sense that a person who has a lower income will pay a higher proportion of their income as tax. Table 19.4 shows the results of a poll tax for Mike and Nancy.

	WTP	COST	POLL TAX	TAX/WEEK	NET BENEFIT
Mike	$400		$400	100%	0
Nancy	$800		$400	50%	$400
Total	$1200	$800	$800		$400

TABLE 19.4: Proportion of weekly income paid and net benefit received for a poll tax

If Mike and Nancy each pay $400, then they can jointly pay the cost of cleaning up the lake. This will cost Mike 100% of his weekly salary of $400, whereas it will cost Nancy only 50% of her weekly salary of $800. Mike's net benefit is the benefit he receives from the clean lake, measured as his WTP of $400, minus the poll tax that he must pay of $400, which is $0. On the other hand, Nancy's net benefit is her WTP of $800, less her tax cost of $400, which equals $400. If Mike and Nancy each pay the same amount for the public good of a clean lake, then poor Mike will pay a larger proportion of his income and receive a smaller net benefit than will rich Nancy. From the point of view of treating people as equals, an equal poll tax is not as attractive a way of paying for public goods as it first seems.

Another intuitively fair option for paying the costs of public environmental goods is a PROPORTIONAL TAX, where all people pay an equal percentage of their income. In this case, if Mike and Nancy each pay 67% of their weekly income, then this will raise the $800 needed to fund the clean-up. Table 19.5 shows this situation.

	WTP	COST	PROPORTIONAL TAX	TAX/WEEK	NET BENEFIT
Mike	$400		$267	67%	$133
Nancy	$800		$533	67%	$267
Total	$1200	$800	$800		$400

TABLE 19.5: Proportion of weekly income paid and net benefit received for a proportional tax

This tax is no longer a regressive tax as both Mike and Nancy pay the same percentage of their weekly income. Nonetheless, they each receive a different net benefit from the clean-up of the lake. Because rich Nancy, who is able to pay more, has a higher WTP ($800) than does poor Mike, her net benefit of $800 less her proportional share of the tax ($533) is $267. Mike, on the other hand, receives a net benefit that is his WTP of $400 less his tax cost of $267, which is only $133. From the point of view of treating people as equals, a proportional tax, one that requires an equal percentage of income from everyone, is better than a poll tax. However, it is still not a fair way of paying for public goods.

If we require that everyone contribute to the cost of providing an environmental public good in such a way that they each receive the same net benefit, then the result will be a PRO-GRESSIVE TAX in which those with more income pay a higher percentage of their income as tax than do those with less income. For Mike and Nancy, the total net benefit of the clean-up of the lake is $400. In Table 19.6, we distribute this net benefit equally between Mike and Nancy giving them $200 each.

	WTP	COST	PROGRESSIVE TAX	TAX/WEEK	NET BENEFIT
Mike	$400	.	$200	50%	$200
Nancy	$800		$600	75%	$200
Total	$1200	$800	$800		$400

TABLE 19.6: Equal net benefit requires a progressive tax

Working backwards, we see that to get a net benefit of $200, Mike will pay $200 in tax, whereas Nancy will pay $600 in tax. Poor Mike's $200 tax is 50% of his weekly income while rich Nancy's $600 tax is 75% of her weekly income. On the assumption that a person's willingness to pay for an environmental public good is higher, if his or her income is higher, then equalizing the individual net benefits of providing a public good will require a progressive tax system.

In passing, it is worth noting that these considerations also apply to public goods like national defence and a legal and police system able to safeguard marketable private property rights. In order for the minimal, night-watchman, state required by contractarian and libertarian justifications of the market to function, the state must provide national defence, police, and a judiciary as a public good for all its citizens. If it is reasonable to assume that wealthier citizens are willing and able to pay more for the protections afforded to private property than are poorer citizens, then to equalize the net benefits of even a minimal state, the minimal state should fund itself through a system of progressive taxation.

To know how much of a public good to provide, the government needs a way of measuring its benefits and costs. However, the government faces the same measurement problem for environmental public goods that it did for external costs. Because environmental public goods are non-rival and non-excludable, they do not get a value in the market. Market values apply only to economic goods if people who do not pay for them also do not get to enjoy them. By definition, there is no market for public goods and no market valuation of them. Hence, again, economic utilitarian policymakers must turn to the techniques of Cost-Benefit Analysis.

SUMMARY

1. Market-based economic activity often results in unintended side-effects of environmental pollution and resource depletion.

2. Producers and consumers do not usually pay the costs of these environmental problems. Environmental problems are external costs from their point of view. These external costs fall not only on other market participants, but also on distant people, on future generations, on non-human living beings, and on ecosystems.

3. Economic utilitarian thinking can take account of external costs only as they fall on other members of a market society, on humans whose willingness to pay measures the intensity of their preferences.

4. Individual market actors take into account only their own internal costs, while ignoring the external costs to the rest of society of the pollution generated by their activities. Their self-interested economic activity will then result in a market equilibrium in that it does not maximize aggregate net benefits for all members of the market society. They will produce too much of the polluting goods at too low a price, and they will produce more than the socially optimal level of pollution. Adam Smith's invisible hand fails to work when there are external environmental costs.

5. Government action can make private individuals internalize the external social costs of their activities through mechanisms like a pollution tax.

6. Solutions to environmental problems are often public goods. We cannot exclude a person from the benefits of the solved problem, and one person receiving the benefits does not reduce them for anyone else.

7. Because environmental public goods are non-excludable, people have an incentive to free-ride by letting others pay the costs of providing them. Environmental public goods are non-rival, so excluding free-riders reduces aggregate net social benefits. Free-riding is, however, unfair.

8. Creating a private market in public goods is difficult, results in the restriction of previously held liberties, and is economically inefficient because it excludes people from non-rival public goods.

9. Environmental public goods are best provided by governments, not private markets, and financed through taxation.

10. If willingness to pay for environmental public goods increases with ability to pay, then a progressive income tax to pay for them will equalize net benefits for each citizen.

ONLINE READING QUESTIONS

The book's website contains reading questions on this chapter. Working through these questions will help you understand, remember, and apply important concepts from the chapter. Some of the questions supply useful hints for the study questions.

Using the text and hints from the online reading questions, write out, type, dictate to your computer, or at least formulate in your head answers to the following questions.

1. Explain why pollution and other environmental harms are often negative externalities.
2. Why would less pollution be produced if industries took into account full social costs instead of just their individual costs?
3. Why is a reduced level of greenhouse gasses in the atmosphere a public good in the economic sense?
4. Explain why the free-rider problem results in less than the socially optimum level of environmental public goods.
5. Explain the ethical weakness of privatization (turning public goods into private property) as a solution to the provision of a socially optimum level of environmental public goods from both the utilitarian and the rights-based approaches.

QUESTIONS TO PONDER

Spend a few minutes thinking about the following questions, or, better yet, discuss them with fellow readers of this book.

1. Are individuals morally wrong when they ignore the external costs of their activities, such as pollution falling on others?
2. Should individuals acting in a market society be forced by the government to internalize the external costs of their activities for the benefit of others? Would doing so violate their rights? Why or why not?
3. Should individuals acting in a market society be forced by the government to help pay for environmental public goods, even if they do not themselves want the environment cleaned up? Why or why not?
4. Think critically about the argument in the text that a progressive income tax is the fairest way to pay for environmental public goods. Would a poll tax, a proportional tax, or no tax at all be more just?

Chapter 20

COST-
BENEFIT
ANALYSIS

ECONOMICS IS A SCIENCE. AS SUCH, IT MAKES FACTUAL STATEMENTS ABOUT HOW A
market economy *does* behave and not normative statements about how a market economy
ought to behave. Yet policymakers use the theories, the data, and the predictions of environmental economics in their policy decisions. Policy decisions guide the actions of governments
and other organizations, telling them what they ought to do. Moving from the factual statements of environmental economics to the normative, value judgments of policy recommendations and decisions requires assuming an ethical theory. Some ethical premise is required
to go from "is" to "ought" without committing the naturalistic fallacy.

The natural ethical theory for the economics approach to environmental policy is a form of
utilitarianism. Utilitarian ethical theory tells policymakers to implement those policies that
will cause the maximum aggregate net benefits for everyone with moral standing, where the
measurement of net benefits is in terms of the intensity of preferences satisfied. Economic
utilitarianism specifies how to measure the intensity of preferences. ECONOMIC UTILITARI-
ANISM is an ethical theory that tells policymakers to implement those policies that cause
maximum aggregate net benefits, where policymakers are to measure net benefits according to people's willingness to pay for economic goods and services. Economic utilitarianism is often the implicit ethical assumption turning economic results into environmental
policy recommendations.

If economic utilitarianism were the best ethical theory, it would have certain attractions. When economic markets are working perfectly, people will maximize aggregate net economic benefits by behaving selfishly. It would be easy to be good; the market would maximize benefits without people having to show any benevolence or concern for others. We have seen, however, that economic utilitarianism has many weaknesses as an ethical theory. It fails to consider the interests of any being who is not a participant in the particular market under discussion. Its production of maximum net social benefits may result in unjust distributions of net benefits to individuals. Its use of willingness to pay as a measure of the strength of preferences has difficulties that we will review in this chapter.

Pollution and resource depletion, the environmental side-effects of purely self-interested market behaviour, create market failures. Environmental problems are external social costs that individual market participants do not consider, and solutions to environmental problems are public goods that a free market will not provide. For environmental economics to take into account external costs and public goods, it must find some way of measuring people's willingness to pay for them. Market prices do not measure the WTP for external costs and public goods, so environmental economists must employ some other technique. This technique is cost-benefit analysis (CBA).

Learning Objectives

1. To understand why CBAs are needed in environmental economics.
2. To understand the weaknesses of WTP as a guide to environmental policy.
3. To understand the justice issues raised by using CBAs.
4. To understand how and why CBAs discount the future and the ethical problems that arise.

MEASURING COSTS AND BENEFITS

Environmental problems often originate in external costs, and their solutions often involve providing public goods. Government policymakers will be interested in measuring the costs and benefits associated with public goods and external costs. Unfortunately, they cannot measure the external costs of environmental damage and the value of environmental public goods by prices in a market economy. The market does not assign a price to external costs because producers and consumers do not consider them in their pricing decisions. The market does not assign a price to public goods because, since there is no way of excluding people from them, they are essentially free to all. Hence, environmental policymakers need another method for assigning monetary values to external costs and public goods.

A COST-BENEFIT ANALYSIS (CBA) is a technique whereby environmental economics measures the costs and benefits of different environmental policies according to people's willingness to pay for them. Environmental economists calculate the total net benefits of alternative policies, and use the results as a factual input to a policy decision, or as a way of making a policy decision. They measure costs by how much individuals are willing to accept as compensation for the negative consequences of the environmental policy. They measure benefits by the willingness of individuals to pay for the consequences of the environmental policy. Policymakers will consider *all* costs and benefits associated with a project. For example, the external costs associated with a new coal-fired power plant will include air pollution and CO_2 emission, and its internal benefits will include the preferences satisfied by the power produced.

Environmental economists use several methods of measuring costs and benefits. Sometimes they will compute the costs or benefits of a policy using existing market values. For example, if pollution causes a decrease in agricultural production, then they will calculate the cost of this directly from known market values for the products.

Sometimes environmental economists cannot compute the costs and benefits of a policy from existing prices. One method that they can use here is the CONTINGENT VALUATION METHOD. They use a carefully designed survey to ask people directly how much they would be willing to pay for some benefit, or how much compensation they would expect for a cost. For example, pollution causes increased health risks. A contingent valuation study will then ask people how much they would pay for various levels of reduced health risks.

Another indirect method is to look at similar goods that are different only in respect of their non-market cost, and use statistical methods to value the non-market cost. For example, an environmental economist might find two similar houses, one in a polluted area, the other not. The difference in price of the two houses will indicate the cost of pollution to homeowners.

To complete the CBA for the effects of different policies, the analyst adds up the costs and benefits for each policy under consideration for everyone involved. If the analyst accepts economic utilitarian ethical assumptions, then she will recommend the policy with the highest net benefit. For example, Table 20.1 shows the costs and benefits of two policies, business-as-usual (BAU) and Plan B, as they apply to two individuals, Ron and Sally.

	BAU	PLAN B
Ron's benefits	$500	$400
Ron's costs	−$400	−$200
Sally's benefits	$300	$600
Sally's costs	−$100	−$300
Total net benefits	$300	$500

TABLE 20.1: Adding up the costs and benefits of two policies

The net benefits of implementing Plan B are $500 and this is higher than the $300 net benefits of BAU. If we wish to maximize net benefits, then this cost-benefit analysis will recommend that we adopt Plan B rather than the BAU policy.

Notice that CBA presupposes rule utilitarianism as a justifying ethical theory. Policies are sets of rules and regulations. Policy makers are trying to choose the policy that, in conjunction with the free market economy, will provide the maximum net benefits, as measured by willingness to pay.

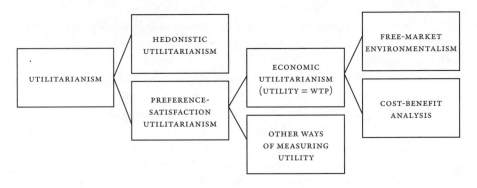

FIGURE 20.1: Cost-Benefit Analysis as a form of economic utilitarianism

WILLINGNESS TO PAY

When policymakers use cost-benefit analysis to make a policy decision or recommendation, they make utilitarian ethical assumptions. Utilitarian ethical theory has weaknesses
that we have examined earlier. Because it deals only with pains, pleasures, and the satisfaction of preferences, it is limited in the range of entities whose moral standing it can take
into account. Because it aggregates net benefits, it has trouble respecting individual rights,
like those of Tom Regan's Aunt Bea in the chapter on Animal Welfare or the victims of
the transplant surgeon in the chapter on Utilitarianism. Because it is concerned only with
maximizing aggregate net benefits, it ignores the question of fairly distributing benefits. In
addition, because it aggregates costs and benefits, it must do interpersonal comparisons, and
measure the intensities of the satisfaction of different people's preferences.

All of these difficulties carry over into economic utilitarianism. Economic utilitarianism
has additional problems, however, concerning its use of willingness to pay as an interpersonal measure of intensity of preference. Just as we had to distinguish marginal and total
benefits, we must distinguish between marginal willingness to pay and total willingness to
pay. Marginal willingness to pay is the maximum amount of money that someone would
be willing to exchange for one more increment of an economic good. Because of the law of
diminishing returns, marginal willingness to pay tends to diminish as someone consumes
more and more of the good. For example, someone might be willing to pay $3 for his first
cone of ice cream, $2 for his second, $1 for his third, and nothing at all for a fourth. His total
willingness to pay for three ice cream cones is $3 + $2 + $1 = $6. It is total net willingness to
pay that the economic utilitarian is concerned to maximize. Maximum total net willingness
to pay, however, is generally found by finding the point at which his marginal willingness to
pay equals his marginal cost of purchasing the good. This equilibrium will also determine
the price of the good in a market.

It is important to notice that someone's total willingness to pay is not simply the price
multiplied by the number of goods bought. For example, if the market determines a price of
$1.50 for ice cream cones, then he will buy two cones, but not a third. His total willingness
to pay is not 2 cones @ $1.50 = $3. This $3 is the total cost to him of the two cones. His gross

total willingness to pay is one cone @ $3 + a second cone @ $2 = $5. His net total willingness to pay for two cones of ice cream, what economists call his consumer surplus, is the difference between his gross total willingness to pay of $5 and his total cost of $3, which is $2.

Distinguishing between marginal and total willingness to pay helps resolve a paradox initially posed by Adam Smith. We are willing to pay very little for water that is absolutely essential to life, and willing to pay much more for diamonds, which are pretty, but relatively useless. Thus, it seems that we have our values wrong. Water is very available and we use a great deal of it, so our marginal willingness to pay for water is small. Our total willingness to pay for the enormous amount of water that we consume, however, is very large. Diamonds are rare, so our marginal willingness to pay for them is very high. Because we buy so few diamonds, our total willingness to pay for them is less than our total willingness to pay for water.

In a similar way, we measure costs as marginal willingness to accept. Someone's marginal willingness to accept is the minimum amount of money that he would be willing to take in exchange for producing and selling an economic good. The price that a person is willing to pay for a certain good and the price that the same person would be willing to accept for the same good are not always the same. For example, ability to pay affects willingness to pay more than it does willingness to accept. The price that someone would be willing to pay in return for receiving another year of life is limited by his ability to pay, but the price that someone would be willing to accept in return for not having that extra year of life is not limited by his ability to pay, and will usually be much higher.

One notorious weakness of WTP as a measure of the intensity of preferences is that it does not make proper comparisons between people of different wealth. Because she is *able* to pay more for a given good than a pauper is, a billionaire is *willing* to pay a lot more than a pauper is willing to pay for the same good. This holds true, even though the pauper wants the good just as much as the billionaire does. People are inclined to say that a dollar is a dollar, but doing so will give an unfair weight to the preferences of the rich over those of the poor.

A second notorious weakness of willingness to pay is that there are goods to which it is not appropriate to assign a dollar value. How should we value a pristine wilderness area? An environmental economist might do so by surveying people regarding how much they would be willing to pay to travel to the wilderness area in order to see it. An environmentalist will see this as a poor indicator of the instrumental value of the wilderness area, and no indicator at all of its intrinsic value. An economist might value someone's life as the present value of the yearly incomes that the person could expect to receive over the rest of his or her working life. From the perspective of a rights theorist, this economic valuation is too permissive regarding trading off one life against another. From the justice perspective, this economic valuation unfairly assigns higher values to the lives of rich people than to the lives of the poor. A rights theorist will argue that someone's personal liberty is not the sort of thing that can be valued by asking the person how much she would be willing to accept in return for selling herself into slavery. From the perspective of virtue ethics, the virtues of integrity and honesty are not the sort of thing on which we can put a price.

Willingness to pay purports to measure only the intensity of preferences. It does not make any distinctions between types of preferences. It does not distinguish a preference for an environmental public good from a sadistic preference for violent pornography or a jealous preference that some group of people receive less than their fair share. There are people who are willing to pay for these things.

Willingness to pay, as opposed to the market price, is difficult to measure. People usually know what they are willing to pay for one more increment of a good at their current consumption level. If we ask someone, however, what he would be willing to pay for a smaller consumption level of the same good, then he may well not know the answer. Someone may know what he is willing to pay for an additional bottle of water without knowing what he would be willing to pay for that same bottle when stranded in the desert. Additionally, people have an incentive to overstate how much they would be willing to pay for environmental public goods when they think that their answer will contribute to a government decision to provide a good without affecting how much they personally will have to pay. Conversely, people will have an incentive to understate their willingness to pay for the same environmental public goods when they think that their answer will determine how much they themselves will be required to pay.

Willingness to pay is a dispositional concept. A contingent valuation asks, for example, not what people actually pay for an existing good, but what they would be willing to pay for a good that they may or may not receive in the future. From the perspective of the dispositional theory of value, what is important is not what people actually pay, or what people would pay in their present state of knowledge, but what people would pay if they had full information about the good in question. Since people are not generally fully informed, finding out what they would pay in their present state of ignorance is a misleading guide to value.

A cost-benefit analysis will often use a mixture of net benefits calculated from market prices and net benefits discovered through a contingent valuation survey of people's willingness to pay. Since market price only equals willingness to pay for the last increment of a good, mixing prices paid with people's answers about their willingness to pay under nonmarket circumstances will be problematic.

Monetary values are not absolute. A $20 bill, in itself, is only a piece of paper; what are important are the economic goods for which we can exchange it. What people can buy with a $20 bill depends on the market in which they are. In a bar in the US, $20 might buy five bottles of beer, whereas in a bar in Mexico that $20, in Mexican Pesos, might buy 10 bottles of beer. If the only economic good that we were concerned with is beer, then we could say that $20 in the US is the same measure of preference intensity as is $10 in Mexico. Unfortunately, not all goods will exchange at the same rate. A music CD that costs $20 in the US might cost $15 in Mexico. This does not preserve the 2 to 1 exchange rate. If prices for goods vary in an irregular pattern between markets, then monetary units will not really be comparable or commensurable between markets. One implication is that cost-benefit analyses involving distant people in different markets can only be approximate at best. Another implication is that we should look with suspicion on cost-benefit analyses that extend into the future, when new production technologies and new consumption patterns will effectively create new markets.

If we accept CBA as a way of deciding on environmental policies, then this will imply that environmental burdens should fall unequally on poor people. In an infamous memo written in 1991, Lawrence Summers, then chief economist at the World Bank, wrote the following:

> Just between you and me, shouldn't the World Bank be encouraging *more* migration of the dirty industries to the LDCs [Least Developed Countries]? I can think of three reasons:
>
> (1) The measurement of the costs of health-impairing pollution depends on the foregone earnings from increased morbidity and mortality. From this point of view a given amount of health-impairing pollution should be done in the country with the lowest cost, which will be the country with the lowest wages. I think the economic logic behind dumping a load of toxic waste in the lowest-wage country is impeccable and we should face up to that. (Quoted in *The Economist* 1992: 82)

In the conceptual framework within which Summers is operating, the health costs of pollution are measured in terms of lost income. Poor people lose less income when they are sick than do rich people. Thus, a policy under which pollution falls on the poor will have higher net benefits than will a policy under which pollution falls on the rich. (The questions at the end of the chapter describe the other two reasons to which Summers refers.) Regarding this memo, Summers wrote, "... its intent was not to make policy recommendations, but only to clarify what had been a rather vague internal discussion" (Summers 1992: 4). Still, the memo nicely illustrates some of the fairness problems inherent in CBAs where ability to pay affects willingness to pay.

CBAs raise issues of distributive justice because CBAs look only at the total net benefits and not at how those benefits are distributed. Consider two policies, BAU and Plan B, and their net benefits for Ron and Sally.

	BAU	PLAN B
Ron's net benefits	$100	$50
Sally's net benefits	$200	$400
Total net benefits	$300	$450

TABLE 20.2: The distributional effects of two policies

According to a CBA, utilitarian policymakers should choose Plan B. Yet, all the benefits of policy Plan B accrue to Sally, who gains $200 under Plan B, while the burdens fall on Ron, who loses $50 under Plan B. Sally is a winner under Plan B and Ron is a loser. This seems unjust. Many policy choices have consequences that produce winners and losers. CBA does not itself deal with compensation of losers by winners.

Because, under Plan B, the total net benefits are larger, the *potential* exists for the winner to compensate the loser while still gaining from Plan B. By giving $50 to Ron, Sally can restore him to his net benefit under BAU and still have an increased net benefit under Plan B. Table 20.3 show this.

	BAU	PLAN B	PLAN B AFTER COMPENSATION
Ron's net benefits	$100	$50	$100
Sally's net benefits	$200	$400	$350
Total net benefits	$300	$450	$450

Table 20.3: Plan B distribution after compensation is paid

In most cases, because CBA recommends picking the policy with maximum net benefits, there exists the *potential* for the winners to compensate the losers. However, there is no economic reason for this compensation *actually* to take place.

From the point of view of compensatory justice, any CBA should include a plan for the winners to compensate the losers fairly. Policymakers should also implement this fairness plan if they implement the policy recommended by the CBA. In this case, Sally restores Ron to his original net benefits under BAU, but Sally still receives all the benefits of Plan B for herself. From the point of view of distributive justice, this is still unjust. Why should Sally receive all the additional benefits produced by the implementation of Plan B? Would it not be fairer to distribute the additional net benefits produced by the implementation of plan B in a way that treated Ron and Sally as moral equals?

Unfortunately, we can also describe situations where it does not make sense to talk of winners paying compensation to losers. Suppose that a CBA must take into account loss of life. Consider five persons affected by two policies as shown in Table 20.4.

	A	B
M		−1
N	−1	
O		
P		−1
Q		
TOTAL LOSS OF LIFE	−1	−2

TABLE 20.4: A CBA involving lives lost

A utilitarian policy maker would recommend policy A because only one life is lost, N's. M and P are clearly the winners under policy A because their lives are saved. However, because the loser N is dead under policy A, there is *no potential* for the winners, M and P, to compensate N for N's loss of life. This is unjust and violates N's right to life.

Another situation where compensation cannot take place will happen when the winners are too poor to compensate the losers fully. For example, suppose the policy choice is between business-as-usual and building a sewage treatment plant in a wealthy neighbourhood. People in both rich and poor neighbourhoods will benefit from the public good of having a sewage treatment plant. The costs, however, will fall more heavily on the wealthy neighbourhood. The sewage treatment plant will depress property values in the wealthy neighbourhood. The people in the poor neighbourhood, because they are poor in private income, will be unable to pay enough money to the people in the wealthy neighbourhood to compensate the wealthy for this depression in their property values. A purely maximizing cost-benefit analysis could recommend building the sewage treatment plant, even though it would be impossible for the poor people to fully compensate the wealthy.

FUTURE COSTS AND BENEFITS

When an individual does a CBA that applies only to herself, she should discount all future costs and benefits to their present values before comparing them. Similarly, environmental economists will discount all future costs and benefits to the present before they aggregate them. As we saw in the example in the chapter on Future Generations, where discounting was applied to the cost of mitigating or not mitigating climate change, the choice of discount rate can make a huge difference regarding which policy a cost-benefit analysis will recommend. In that example, Stern's choice of a low discount rate for future costs resulted in a recommendation for action now, whereas Nordhaus's use of a higher discount rate resulted in a recommendation for action only in the future. This example does not generalize to the conclusion that low discount rates are always more environmentally friendly. In a case where producing an environmental public benefit in the present will have large costs in the future, a higher discount rate for those future costs will favour action now.

In the examples that follow, we will use a simple rule of thumb that we have used before, the rule of 70, for calculating the present values of future costs and benefits. The rule of 70 says that the doubling time = 70 / discount rate. Suppose that the discount rate equals the interest rate on alternative use of funds of 7%. Then, the time for an investment to double is 70 / 7 = 10 years, approximately. Equivalently, the number of years for the value of a future cost to halve is 70 / 7 = 10 years. Thus, the present value (PV) of a future cost of $1000 in 10 years is now $500. The PV of a cost of $1000 to be incurred in 50 years at a discount rate of 7% can be calculated easily as follows:

1. Doubling time = 70 / 7 = 10 years.
2. In 50 years, present money will have doubled 5 times.
3. $2 \times 2 \times 2 \times 2 \times 2 = 32$.
4. So present value (PV) $\times 32 = \$1000$.
5. PV of $1000 in 50 years @ 7% = $1000 / 32 = $31.25.

We will use this present value of future costs in examining the justice issues that arise when environmental economists extend cost-benefit analyses into the future.

First, let us examine what happens when a single individual applies such a cost-benefit analysis within her own life. Suppose that she faces an environmental problem with two policy choices:

Policy A = clean it up now and pay the cost now.
Policy B = clean it up in 50 years and pay the cost in 50 years.

Only one individual is affected, and the discount rate is 7%. If she performs the cleanup now it will cost her $35, but if she performs the cleanup in 50 years, then it will cost her $1000. Table 20.5 shows her cost-benefit analysis.

	A (pay cost now)	B (pay cost in 50 years)
Net cost of cleanup	$35	$1000
PV of net cost of cleanup	$35	$31.25
CBA	x	✓

TABLE 20.5: CBA showing policy A of cleanup now and policy B of cleanup in 50 years for a single individual

For simplicity in what follows, we will assume that the benefits of both policies are the same, and that we only need to worry about their costs. Since the net costs of policy B are lower than those of policy A, a CBA would recommend implementing policy B. Under policy B, the individual's future self will pay the costs in 50 years. No justice problem exists in this example since the winner is identical to the loser. The individual can decide for herself whether she wishes to incur the cost of cleanup now or incur it in 50 years' time. Justice problems only arise when we apply a decision procedure that works well enough within a single life as a decision procedure for groups of individuals.

Second, let us examine what happens when a group of individuals is involved in a policy decision over a short period of 10 years in which no one is born, and in which no one dies.

	A (pay cost now)	B (pay cost in 10 years)
Net cost of cleanup	$550	$1000
PV of net cost of cleanup	$550	$500
CBA	x	✓

TABLE 20.6: CBA showing policy A of cleanup now and policy B of cleanup in 10 years for a group whose individual members stay the same

Since the net costs of policy B are lower than are those of policy A while the benefits are the same, a CBA would recommend implementing policy B. Under policy B, the group members will pay the costs in 10 years. Possible compensatory justice problems exist, since there may be winners and losers among the many individuals. However, since the economic pie is larger by $50 under B, and since the individuals are the same under policies A and B, the potential exists for the winners to compensate the losers.

Third, let us examine a policy choice where many different individuals are affected over a very long time period of 50 years, such that people die or are born, and the population affected in the future is different from the population in the present. In this example, the present value of the cost of fixing an environmental problem in the future ($31,250) is lower than the cost of fixing it in the present ($35,000).

	A *(pay cost now)*	B *(pay cost in 50 years)*
Net cost of cleanup	$35,000	$1,000,000
PV of net cost of cleanup	$35,000	$31,250
CBA	x	✓

TABLE 20.7: CBA showing policy A of fixing an environmental problem now and policy B of fixing it in 50 years for a group whose individual members change

Since the net costs of policy B are lower than are those of policy A, a CBA would recommend implementing policy B. Under policy B, the members of the group in 50 years' time will pay the cost of the cleanup. The present-day members of the group are the winners in this scenario, and the future members of the group are the losers. Most of the present-day winners may have died in 50 years and most of the future losers may not yet be born. Still, there is a way for the present day winners to compensate the future losers. The present winners should invest the sum of $31,250 so that it will grow, through compound interest, into the $1 million required to pay the cost of cleanup in 50 years' time. For example, our generation may decide not to pay the costs of mitigating climate change because it is less expensive for future generations to adapt to a changed climate. Instead, we may leave the adaptation costs for future generations to pay. To be fair, then, our generation should invest the present value of those future costs in a way that will compensate future generations for adapting to the damage that we have caused.

Fourth, let us examine a similar scenario where the present value of the cost of fixing a future environmental problem ($31,250) is higher than the cost of fixing it in the present ($30,000).

	A *(pay cost now)*	B *(pay cost in 50 years)*
Net cost of cleanup	$30,000	$1,000,000
PV of net cost of cleanup	$30,000	$31,250
CBA	✓	x

TABLE 20.8: CBA showing policy A of fixing a future environmental problem now and policy B of fixing it in 50 years for a group whose individual members change

Since the net costs of policy A are lower than those of policy B, a CBA would recommend implementing policy A. Under policy A, the present members of the group will pay the cost of fixing the future environmental problem. The future members of the group are the winners in this scenario, and the present-day members of the group are the losers. Here there is no mechanism for the future winners to compensate the present losers. Future winners cannot transmit any compensation backwards through time to present losers. For periods greater than the human life span, it will be impossible for future winners to compensate present losers.

Finally, we should observe again that costs and benefits in the far future might not be commensurable with costs and benefits in the present as measured using the willingness-to-pay method. The use of monetary figures to measure willingness to pay can be misleading. What is important is not monetary amounts, but what economic goods and services those monetary amounts will purchase. What goods and services a certain number of dollars will purchase will depend on the particular market in which the transaction is taking place. 50 years from now, the range of goods and services that are available in the market and their relative prices will be considerably different from now. It is not just a matter of uniform inflation; the prices of different goods will not all change at the same rate. New goods will be available that are not available now, and others that are available now will disappear. What one dollar means now will not be the same as what one dollar means in 50 years' time. Consequently, we should be very mistrustful of the meaning of a cost-benefit analysis that extends into the far future.

THE COMPENSATION TEST

Mainstream economists tend to avoid measuring the intensity of preferences according to willingness to pay. They are suspicious both of making interpersonal comparisons of preferences and of aggregating the welfare of different people. Instead of maximizing net benefits, they prefer to talk of a Pareto-optimal equilibrium, where no transaction can make anyone better off without making someone else worse off. There is a corresponding notion of a Pareto improvement. A change in the distribution of goods is a PARETO IMPROVEMENT if it makes at least one person better off without making any other person worse off.

The notion of Pareto efficiency fails to say anything about the justice of the initial distribution of goods. As Amartya Sen writes, "A state can be Pareto optimal with some people in extreme misery and others rolling in luxury, so long as the miserable cannot be made better off without cutting into the luxury of the rich" (Sen 1987: 32). Many would take it to be an improvement from the point of view of justice to take from the rich and give to the miserable; however doing so would not be a Pareto improvement.

Environmental economists, however, cannot make do with just the notion of a Pareto improvement. There are many situations, like that illustrated in Table 20.2, where an aggregate improvement, according to a cost-benefit analysis, makes someone like Ron worse off. Plan B is not a Pareto improvement because it makes Ron worse off. Yet it is an improvement from the perspective of a cost-benefit analysis because it maximizes total net benefits. To utilize their cost-benefit analyses, environmental economists require some notion of efficiency other than Pareto efficiency. Environmental economists might appeal to a different notion of efficiency, Kaldor-Hicks efficiency.

One situation is a Kaldor-Hicks improvement over another, even if some people in the old situation lose out, so long as, in the new situation, it is possible for those who become better off to compensate those who become worse off without themselves becoming worse off than they were in the old situation. For example, in Table 20.2 Plan B gives Sally $400 instead of the $200 that she gets under BAU, whereas Plan B gives Ron only $50 instead of the $100 that he gets under BAU. Plan B is not a Pareto improvement over BAU, despite Plan B maximizing net benefits, because it makes Ron less well off than does BAU. However, Plan B is a Kaldor-Hicks improvement because Sally could give Ron $50, thereby restoring him to his position under BAU, yet still having $350 and being better off herself than under BAU (see Table 20.3). The COMPENSATION TEST, or the notion of a Kaldor-Hicks improvement, requires merely the possibility of the winners paying compensation to the losers, and does not require that the winners actually pay the compensation. If the losers are also the least advantaged, then the mere possibility of compensation will not impress supporters of egalitarian justice. As Sen writes,

> Another—arguably more basic—difficulty [with the compensation test] relates to the question as to why the mere possibility of compensating the losers should be adequate to establish a social improvement even if the compensation is not, in fact, to be paid. The losers could include the worse off and the most miserable in the society, and that is little consolation to be told that it is possible to compensate them fully, but ('good God!') no actual plan to do so. If, on the other hand, the losers are in fact compensated, then the overall outcome—after compensation—is a Pareto improvement, and then there is no need for the compensation test as a supplement to the Pareto principle. So the compensation criteria are either unconvincing or redundant. (Sen 1987: 33, Note 4)

A new situation where the winners could possibly compensate the losers is not a Pareto improvement over the old situation, though it is a compensation test improvement. A new situation where the winners could and actually do compensate the losers is a Pareto improvement.

The notion of a compensation test improvement is not of universal application in cost-benefit analyses. We have already seen situations in which it is not possible for the winners to compensate the losers. When a policy choice involves the loss of life, it is not possible for those who keep their lives to compensate those who lose their lives. It may be impossible for the poor to compensate the rich for their losses under a policy that initially places most of the costs on the rich. It is not possible for unborn generations to compensate the present generation for paying costs in the present whose benefits will go to future generations. In these cases, the policy that maximizes net benefits according to a cost-benefit analysis will not be a compensation test improvement over the comparison policy.

People seldom create environmental problems on purpose. More commonly, they are the unintended by-product of beneficial economic activities. The costs created by environmental problems, unfortunately, are not usually borne by the people who decide what to produce and consume. Pollution and resource depletion create external costs that an economic market does not properly represent. Solutions to environmental problems are usually public goods. The law cannot exclude people from the benefits of the solution. Consequently, a free-market that supplies only private, excludable economic goods will not properly provide environmental public goods. One technique for dealing with external environmental costs and environmental public goods is cost-benefit analysis.

Policymakers can use a cost-benefit analysis of policy options in two ways. First, policymakers can use a cost-benefit analysis as a method of making decisions about public policy. If policymakers use it in this way, then they are making a strong ethical assumption. They are assuming the ethical theory that we have called economic utilitarianism, which is a form of preference satisfaction utilitarianism where we measure the intensity of people's preferences by their willingness to pay. Second, policymakers can use a cost-benefit analysis as information in a process of public deliberation. In the second use, the cost-benefit analysis merely provides information to a government committee or to a process of public and democratic discussion of policy options. In the second case, other ethical theories besides economic utilitarianism will become relevant. Public deliberation can consider the importance of respecting rights, compensating losers, distributing net benefits fairly, and the moral standing of distant people, future people, and other living beings who do not participate in the economic market.

SUMMARY

1. A cost-benefit analysis (CBA) measures the costs and benefits of different environmental policies according to people's willingness to pay for them, and calculates the total net benefits of each policy. It then uses the result either as a factual input to a policy decision, or as a way of making a policy decision.

2. If we use a CBA to make a policy decision then we implicitly assume the ethical theory of economic utilitarianism.

3. Willingness to pay (WTP) measures the intensity of people's preferences according to how much they are willing to pay to have their preferences satisfied in an economic market. WTP has many weaknesses as a measure of preference intensity. It cannot distinguish the effects of different abilities to pay. It has difficulties with goods that people see as priceless. It considers only the intensity of a preference without considering whether the preference is moral or fair. It considers poorly informed preferences at face value. It can measure strength of preference only within a particular market, and breaks down when applied in distant and future markets.

4. The results of a CBA can conflict with distributive justice. A policy that maximizes net benefits may create winners and losers. Because the

economic pie is larger, the winners can essentially compensate the losers. Compensatory justice requires that winners actually compensate losers. Distributive justice additionally requires that we distribute the total net benefits of the maximizing policy to all concerned in a fair manner.

5. Environmental economists often extend CBAs into the future using a discount rate to compare the present values of future costs and benefits. Choices made in the present regarding whether to pay the cost of environmental public goods now or in the future can raise problems of intergenerational compensatory justice.

6. Using willingness to pay in CBAs that extend into the far future involves problems of commensurability between present and future markets.

7. Mainstream economics tries to avoid using willingness to pay as a cardinal measure of utility. Instead, it uses the notion of a Pareto improvement and a Kaldor-Hicks compensation test. The compensation test requires the potential ability to compensate, but not the actual payment of compensation. There are cases where the WTP methods of environmental economics work, but the compensation test does not.

ONLINE READING QUESTIONS

The book's website contains reading questions on this chapter. Working through these questions will help you understand, remember, and apply important concepts from the chapter. Some of the questions supply useful hints for the study questions.

STUDY QUESTIONS

Using the text and hints from the online reading questions, write out, type, dictate to your computer, or at least formulate in your head answers to the following questions.

1. Explain why utilitarian economists use cost-benefit analysis in policy recommendations regarding negative pollution externalities and the provision of environmental public goods.

2. What are the ethical assumptions behind economic utilitarianism?

3. What difficulties does cost-benefit analysis encounter in measuring costs and benefits in terms of willingness to pay?

4. Why does cost-benefit analysis often lead to problems with compensatory justice?

5. Why does cost-benefit analysis work best when deciding policy on the basis of future consequences for a single individual, second best when deciding policy on the basis of near future consequences for an unchanging group of individuals, and least well for deciding policy on the bases of far future consequences for groups of individuals whose composition changes?

Spend a few minutes thinking about the following questions, or, better yet, discuss them with fellow readers of this book.

1. The second reason that Summers gives for locating polluting industries in poor countries is this. "(2) The costs of pollution are likely to be non-linear as the initial increments of pollution probably have very low cost. I've always thought that under-populated countries in Africa are vastly *under*-polluted; their air quality is probably vastly inefficiently low [sic] compared to Los Angeles or Mexico City ..." (quoted in *The Economist* 1992: 82). What principle of environmental economics is Summers implicitly appealing to here? Do you agree with his argument? Why or why not?

2. The third reason that Summers gives for locating polluting industries in poorer countries is this one. "(3) The demand for a clean environment for aesthetic and health reasons is likely to have very high income-elasticity. The concern over an agent that causes a one-in-a-million change in the odds of prostate cancer is obviously going to be much higher in a country where people survive to get prostate cancer than in a country where under–5 mortality is 200 per thousand ..." (quoted in *The Economist* 1992: 82). Do you agree with his argument? Why or why not?

3. The Summers memo concludes as follows. "The problem with the arguments against all of these proposals for more pollution in LDCs (intrinsic rights to certain goods, moral reasons, social concerns, lack of adequate markets, etc.) could be turned around and used more or less effectively against every Bank proposal for liberalisation" (quoted in *The Economist* 1992: 82). What does "liberalisation" mean in this context? Did Summers see environmental ethics as a threat to World Bank programs? Why?

Chapter 21

PRECAUTIONARY PRINCIPLES

DISASTERS WITH NUCLEAR POWER STATIONS SUCH AS CHERNOBYL IN THE UKRAINE and Fukushima in Japan, ruptured oil tankers such as the Exxon Valdez, explosions on oil rigs such as the one on the Deepwater Horizon, and looming disasters such as climate change, species extinctions, the release of genetically modified organisms, and the safety of medicines and food, all suggest that special precautions should be taken in decision-making regarding potential catastrophes. Is cost-benefit reasoning appropriate regarding such situations?

Environmental problems are by-products of economic activities that create costs that decision makers in the marketplace do not consider. Solutions to environmental problems are mostly public goods whose value the market cannot measure. To help make decisions regarding environmental problems and solutions, environmental economists use the method of cost-benefit analysis. Cost-benefit analysis either is a decision-making procedure itself, or is a useful input to a wider decision-making process. Policymakers apply it not only to the costs and benefits of environmental policies, but also to their future costs and benefits through the method of discounting future costs and benefits to present values. They also apply it when they do not know the actual outcome of a policy is precisely, but when they can assign probabilities to its different potential outcomes. In this case, the analysis will calculate the expected values of outcomes, which is a technique that we have seen before.

Using expected values in cost-benefit analyses works only when policymakers have enough prior information to determine the probabilities of outcomes. Many environmental problems, however, involve scenarios with which scientists have little experience because the scenarios happen very infrequently. On the one hand, medical scientists have enough experience with radiation sickness to be able to give accurate probabilities of sickness occurring for various doses of radiation. On the other hand, scientists, luckily, have much less experience with catastrophic problems at nuclear power reactors, so they cannot accurately estimate the probability that a nuclear reactor will fail and emit harmful radiation. When probabilities are unknown, expected value calculations are not accurate.

Cost-benefit analyses measure costs and benefits according to willingness to pay. Ability to pay heavily influences willingness to pay. Some environmental problems are so catastrophic that they severely reduce the incomes of the people they affect. After the catastrophe, people's ability to pay may be very different than before the catastrophe, and what they are willing to pay after the catastrophe may no longer be commensurate with what they were willing to pay before the catastrophe. Cost-benefit analyses are done using pre-catastrophe willingness to pay, and therefore will not accurately measure the costs to people after the catastrophe.

When environmental problems occur with unknown probability or result in large income drops for victims, it is best to apply a precautionary approach, instead of using a cost-benefit analysis to make decisions. We shall look at how to formulate a precautionary principle and how it may apply to uncertain and potentially catastrophic scenarios.

Learning Objectives

1. To understand the precautionary principle in its various versions.
2. To understand risk, uncertainty, and expected value.
3. To see how precautionary reasoning may preclude cost-benefit reasoning.
4. To understand why precautionary reasoning might be reasonable but not rational.

RISK AND EXPECTED VALUE

In some situations, policymakers do not know for sure what the outcomes of policies will be, but can only know the probabilities of consequences. When policymakers do a cost-benefit analysis in situations where they know only probabilities, how do they handle risk? The answer is that they calculate the expected values of net benefits.

For example, suppose that policymakers believe that policy A has a 30% chance of producing net benefits of $4,000 and a 70% chance of producing net benefits of $12,000, whereas policy B has a 40% chance of producing net benefits of $3,000 and an 60% chance of producing net benefits of $15,000. How will they proceed?

The expected net benefits of policy A = .3 × $4,000 + .7 × $12,000 = $1,200 + $8,400 = $9,600.

The expected net benefits of policy B = .4 × $3,000 + .6 × $15,000 = $1,200 + $9,000 = $10,200.

POLICY A			POLICY B		
Net benefits	Probability	Expected value	Net benefits	Probability	Expected value
$4,000	0.3	$1,200	$3,000	0.4	$1,200
$12,000	0.7	$8,400	$15,000	0.6	$9,000
		$9,600			$10,200

TABLE 21.1: CBA using expected values with known probabilities (risk)

Economic utilitarian policymakers would recommend choosing the policy that maximizes net benefits, which is B.

Calculations of expected net benefits only work when policymakers know the probabilities of outcomes. Suppose that policymakers do not know the probability with which policy B leads to a net benefit of $3,000 and the probability with which policy B leads to the net benefit of $15,000. Now policymakers cannot calculate the net expected value.

POLICY A			POLICY B		
Net benefits	Probability	Expected value	Net benefits	Probability	Expected value
$4,000	0.3	$1,200	$3,000	?	?
$12,000	0.7	$8,400	$15,000	?	?
		$9,600			?

TABLE 21.2: CBA using expected values when probablilies are unknown (uncertainty)

RISK is a condition where we cannot definitely predict the outcome, but where we *can* measure the probabilities of different possible outcomes. UNCERTAINTY is a condition where we cannot definitely predict the outcome and where we *cannot* measure the probabilities of different outcomes. We cannot do cost-benefit analyses using expected values accurately under conditions of uncertainty.

Other situations where a cost-benefit analysis may not be appropriate are ones involving catastrophic costs. Suppose that policymakers have a choice of a very risky policy C that has a 99% probability of leading to positive consequences, but has a 1% probability of leading to very serious costs that will impoverish the people who are affected. The expected value of the outcome of policy C is $296,000. Suppose that policymakers are comparing this with policy D that imposes no risk of very serious negative consequences, and that has an expected value of $296,000 as well.

POLICY C			POLICY D		
Net benefits	Probability	Expected value	Net benefits	Probability	Expected value
$400,000	0.99	$396,000	$500,000	0.32	$160,000
−$10,000,000	0.01	−$100,000	$200,000	0.68	$136,000
		$296,000			$296,000

TABLE 21.3: CBA with a risk of very serious negative consequences (Field 2002: 122)

Since the expected values of the outcomes of both policy C and policy D are the same, we must find a way to decide between the two policies. A policymaker who is RISK NEUTRAL would make a decision entirely based on the expected values of the outcomes. A policy-maker who is RISK AVERSE would make a decision in a way that avoids seriously negative consequences, even if they have a low probability of happening. Pure economic utilitarian policymakers will tend to be risk neutral, and will be willing to flip a coin in order to decide between the two policies. Ordinary citizens will tend to be risk averse, and will avoid policy C because of its catastrophic consequences. Most ordinary citizens would avoid policy C even if its expected payoff were higher than that of policy D. Risk neutrality may be rational, but risk aversion may be reasonable when harms are very serious. For example, it might be reasonable to take precautions to avoid serious climate change, even if a cost-benefit analysis were to suggest that business as usual would probably have higher net benefits.

PRECAUTIONARY PRINCIPLES

In dealing with situations involving the uncertain possibility of serious negative consequences, many policymakers recommend adopting a precautionary approach. Many English-language aphorisms recommend this. For example, people often say, "An ounce of prevention is worth a pound of cure," or, "Better safe than sorry."

The precautionary approach has been codified in many versions of a precautionary prin-ciple. The best known of these is the one adopted as principle 15 of the Rio Declaration at the United Nations Conference on Environment and Development in 1992.

> In order to protect the environment, the precautionary approach shall be widely applied by States according to their capabilities. Where there are threats of seri-ous or irreversible damage, lack of full scientific certainty shall not be used as a reason for postponing cost-effective measures to prevent environmental degrada-tion. (UNCED 1992: #15)

We can see how this principle contains the prescriptive use of the auxiliary verb "shall" to indicate that the principle is an ethical judgment. This version of a precautionary principle focuses on what to do in cases of uncertainty. It tells policymakers that, when there are poten-tially serious or irreversible negative consequences, they should not let scientific uncertainty prevent them from considering those serious negative consequences in decisions. In such cases, it recommends a policy of cost-effective measures to prevent damage to the environment.

The Wingspread Conference on the Precautionary Principle recommended a stronger ver-sion of a precautionary principle in 1998.

> When an activity raises threats of harm to human health or the environment, pre-cautionary measures should be taken even if some cause and effect relationships are not established scientifically. In this context the proponent of the activity, rather than the public, should bear the burden of proof. The process of applying the Precautionary Principle must be open, informed and democratic and must include potentially affected parties. It must also involve an examination of the full range of alternatives, including no action. (Wingspread Conference 1998)

We can see how this principle uses the verb "should" to indicate that it is making an ethical judgment. The Wingspread version of the precautionary principle is stronger than the Rio version in the sense that it sets the barrier for applying the principle at a lower level, and so will apply more frequently. It appears to suggest that any level of harm, not just serious or irreversible harm, is enough to trigger the precautionary principle. By shifting the burden of proof proponents of a new activity, it neglects the dangers of the *status quo*. For example, the alternative to building a nuclear power station, which has an uncertain probability of causing a catastrophe, may be to keep a coal-fired electric generator, which carries a risk of contributing to both respiratory disease and climate change.

Another version of the precautionary principle is that adopted by the Commission of the European Communities in 2000.

> Although the precautionary principle is not explicitly mentioned in the Treaty except in the environmental field, its scope is far wider and covers those specific circumstances where scientific evidence is insufficient, inconclusive or uncertain and there are indications through preliminary objective scientific evaluation that there are reasonable grounds for concern that the potentially dangerous effects on the environment, human, animal or plant health may be inconsistent with the chosen level of protection. (Commission 2000: 9–10)

This precautionary principle applies where consequences are uncertain, but where science gives reasonable grounds for concern. It also requires that there be potentially dangerous effects. Thus the European Communities precautionary principle is weaker than the Wingspread version because it sets the barrier for applying the principle at a higher level. When the precautionary principle applies, it says that policymakers should refer to the level of environmental protection chosen by the European Communities, presumably by a process of democratic political deliberation, in order to see how to proceed.

In its most general formulation regarding activities that may affect the environment, a precautionary principle has a three-part structure. First, it will specify what degree of damage the consequences of the activity must have in order to trigger a precautionary response. Second, it will specify the degree of certainty with which we should know the connection of activity to consequence before the activity would trigger a precautionary policy response. Third, it will specify the nature of the precautionary response that we must take (Manson 2002: 265–67). Table 21.4 summarizes the structure of some potential precautionary principles.

We can construct many different versions of a precautionary principle in this framework. For example, the table includes imaginary principles that are overly strong and overly weak. The fourth version says that if there is any possibility of an activity causing the slightest harm, then we should prohibit the activity. This version is plainly unreasonable. Conversely, the fifth version says that if the activity will destroy all life on Earth, and if we know this fact beyond reasonable doubt, then we should study the problem further. This version is useless, because it is so weak that it will fail to suggest any precautions. The problem for an advocate of the precautionary approach is to define a principle that is neither too strong nor too weak. We will examine the sixth version of a precautionary principle in the next section.

PRINCIPLE	DAMAGE CONDITION	KNOWLEDGE OF CONNECTION OF ACTIVITY TO CONSEQUENCE	POLICY RESPONSE
1. *Rio*	"Serious or irreversible damage"	"Lack of full scientific certainty"	"Cost-effective measures to prevent environmental degradation"
2. *Wingspread*	"Raises threats of harm to human health or the environment"	"Some cause and effect relationships are not established scientifically"	"Proponent of the activity, rather than the public, should bear the burden of proof"
3. *European Communities*	"Potentially dangerous effects on the environment, human, animal or plant health"	"Scientific evidence is insufficient, inconclusive or uncertain and there are indications through preliminary objective scientific evaluation that there are reasonable grounds for concern"	"Chosen level of protection"
4. *Too strong*	Any harm at all	Connection is merely possible	Absolute prohibition of activity
5. *Too weak*	Will destroy all life on Earth	Connection is known beyond reasonable doubt	Further study is required
6. *Limitation of CBA*	Will reduce incomes so as to make CBA unreliable	Reasonable grounds for concern, but connection is uncertain and probabilities are not known	Do not rely on CBA in deciding response

TABLE 21.4: Structure of some potential precautionary principles

PRECAUTIONARY PRINCIPLES AND
COST-BENEFIT ANALYSES

When we apply it in situations involving risk, situations where the probabilities of various outcomes are measurable, a cost-benefit analysis will calculate the expected values of the net benefits of the policies that we are comparing. When we apply it in situations involving uncertainty, situations where the probabilities of various outcomes are not measurable, a cost-benefit analysis does not work properly because, not knowing the probabilities, we cannot calculate the expected net benefits of at least one of the policies that we need to compare. A cost-benefit analysis does not work under conditions of uncertainty.

A cost-benefit analysis also will not work properly when applied to situations involving severe losses of income for people. When we do a cost-benefit analysis comparing policies that involve potential catastrophes, we presumably do the cost-benefit analysis before the catastrophe occurs. That means we measure costs and benefits in terms of willingness to pay for people at the income level that the people had before the catastrophe. The catastrophe, however, will change people's income levels for the worse. After the catastrophe, people will have a different ability to pay for economic goods and services than they had before the catastrophe. Consequently, their willingness to pay for the same economic goods and services will be very different before and after the catastrophe. A cost-benefit analysis will measure the cost of the catastrophe in terms of people's willingness to pay before the catastrophe occurs. Yet, what will matter to people after the catastrophe is the cost measured in terms of their willingness to pay after the catastrophe, not before. The cost of the catastrophe, as measured according to the willingness to pay of people when they were relatively well off before the catastrophe, will not be comparable to the cost of the catastrophe as measured according to the willingness to pay of the same people when they are relatively poorly off after the catastrophe. Willingness to pay before the catastrophe does not compare to willingness to pay after the catastrophe because ability to pay has changed so much.

This is a similar point to one we examined earlier. We cannot compare the willingness to pay of a billionaire with the willingness to pay of a pauper because of their differing abilities to pay. If a billionaire were to lose all of his money, then his willingness to pay after his loss would be different from his willingness to pay before his loss. We cannot compare the willingness to pay of the impoverished billionaire to the willingness to pay of the self-same flourishing billionaire because his ability to pay has changed so much. Analogously, we cannot compare the willingness to pay of people under regular conditions with the willingness to pay of the same people after they have experienced a severe income decline. Thus we cannot use a regular cost-benefit analysis in situations that involve the risk of severe damage to people's livelihoods. These are just the situations where policymakers take a precautionary approach.

SEVERE INCOME LOSSES AND UTILITY LEVELS

We can make the same point in a different way if we recall the diminishing marginal utility of income. Finding a way to measure utility has always been a difficult problem for utilitarians. One way, that employed by economic utilitarians, is to use willingness to pay for an extra increment of a good as a guide to the intensity of someone's preference for that good. Another way, which we looked at in the chapter on utilitarianism, is the von Neumann-Morgenstern method, which asks people to compare the intensity of their preference for a good with the intensity of their preference for a special sort of gamble. To apply the method, we first identify the worst possible outcome for a person and assign it a utility of o. Then we identify the best possible outcome for a person and arbitrarily assign it a utility of 100. We then construct a sort of lottery in which the prize is getting the best possible outcome. The lottery tickets each have different probabilities of winning the best outcome and they have no set price. The point at which someone is indifferent between receiving a particular economic good and a lottery ticket with a particular chance of winning is a measure, on a scale of o to 100, of the intensity of her preference for it.

Using von Neumann-Morgenstern utility as an independent measure of utility from that of willingness to pay, we can describe the declining marginal utility of income. We cannot do this without an independent measure of utility. If we use willingness to pay for income as a measure of the utility of that income, we will never see marginal utility decline. The maximum that someone is willing to pay for one dollar of extra income will always be one dollar. If we graph willingness to pay for income against income, then it will always be a straight line. Using an independent measure of utility, however, we can see the declining marginal utility of income. If we draw a graph of the total utility that people receive from their annual income, then we will see it rise quickly at first as people become better off. Then, later, we will see it rise less quickly as people become very wealthy.

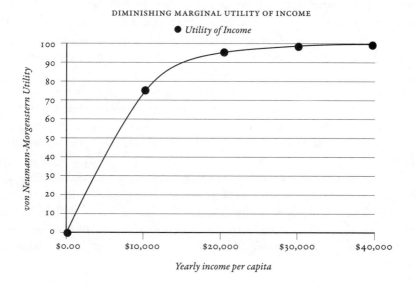

DIMINISHING MARGINAL UTILITY OF INCOME

FIGURE 21.1: Graph showing the total utility of a yearly income where the marginal utility of additional income diminishes with increasing yearly income

Figure 21.1 is a graph showing yearly income plotted on the horizontal axis and the total utility of that income, measured by the von Neumann-Morgenstern method, plotted on the vertical axis. The example is imaginary, but it illustrates how the marginal utility that people receive from additional income diminishes as their yearly income increases.

We can now see why a cost-benefit analysis carried out for people with middle-class incomes will give misleading results if a catastrophe reduces people's income to poverty levels. Figure 21.2 simplifies the last graph by showing the relationship between utility and income for poor, middle-class, and wealthy people. The graph shows that poor, middle-class, and wealthy people convert income into utility at different rates. Middle-class people, in this example, convert income into utility at the rate of one utile per $1000. Poor people receive more utility from increases in their income; they receive eight utiles per $1000 of increased income. Conversely, they lose utility more easily, losing eight units of utility for each $1000 decrease. Wealthy people, by contrast, receive zero extra utility for any increase in income.

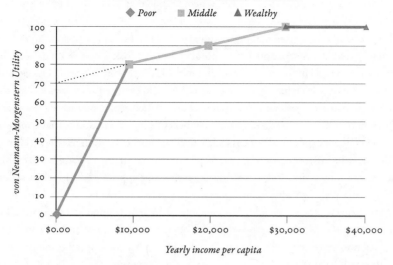

DIMINISHING MARGINAL UTILITY OF INCOME

◆ *Poor*　■ *Middle*　▲ *Wealthy*

FIGURE 21.2: Simplified graph showing utility vs. income for people with poor, middle class, and wealthy incomes, and the utility of a middle class income projected back to zero income

Suppose we have a middle-class person with an income of $20,000. For her, in financial terms the expected value of a 50% risk of losing $4,000 is −$2,000 and the expected value of a 10% risk of losing $20,000 is also −$2,000. Thinking purely as an economic utilitarian, she should be indifferent between the two situations. From the financial perspective, the two losses are the same. Thinking, though, as someone who is intuitively aware of the diminishing marginal utility of income, she will be very averse to the second situation. From the perspective of actual utility rather than income, she would be right to be averse to the second situation. At an income of $20,000, her utility is 90 units. If her income were to fall by $2000, from $20,000 to $18,000, her utility would fall by 2 units. However if her income were to fall from $20,000 to $0, her utility would not fall from 90 units down to 70 units, but from 90 units down to 0 units. In utility terms, her expected loss in the first case is 50% of 4 units which is −2 units, but her utility loss in the second case is 10% of 90 units which is −9 units. From the utility perspective, the second loss is much worse than the first.

POTENTIAL INCOME LOSS	PROBABILITY	EXPECTED INCOME LOSS	UTILITY LOSS	EXPECTED UTILITY LOSS
−$4,000	50%	−$2,000	−4 units	−2 units
−$20,000	10%	−$2,000	− 90 units	−9 units

TABLE 21.5: Comparing expected income losses to expected utility losses using Figure 21.2

She would be unreasonable not to recognize that a severe loss of income, which takes her from being middle class to being poor, is proportionately a much worse situation than is a smaller loss, which reduces her available income, but that keeps her in her usual range of income.

We have seen several examples of precautionary choice in earlier discussions. In the face of large and irreversible losses, reasonable people are frequently risk-averse. We have seen this in the reasoning of people in the original position in the justification of John Rawls's egalitarian theory of justice. Rawls claims that people who do not know their own personal attributes, and do not know their position in society, will choose a theory of justice for society that maximizes the income of the least advantaged members of society. He thinks that a reasonable person would take the precaution of ensuring herself against destitution. A reasonable person, thinks Rawls, will focus on avoiding catastrophe over maximizing expected gains. This reasonable person appears irrational in economic terms, but appears rational when we understand him to use realistic utility values that willingness to pay does not properly measure.

When they buy insurance, people are reasonable rather than economically rational. Buying insurance is a reasonable thing for people to do, but it is economically irrational in the sense that it does not maximize their economic self-interest. If people buy insurance for their houses, they will have to pay the insurance company a premium that will cover the risk of losing the house plus administrative costs and profit for the insurance company. People could maximize their expected financial benefit by not buying insurance. Yet, reasonable people buy insurance against catastrophic losses. Income and wealth, as we have seen, have declining marginal utility. Assuming that the householders are moderately well off, the utility loss of their yearly premiums may be relatively small, whereas the utility loss of losing their houses will be out of proportion to the financial loss. Buying insurance is actually rational in a non-economic sense, where householders use their intuitive understanding of their real utility, rather than financial measures, in their calculations. Analogously, a cost-benefit analysis does not give accurate results when applied to potentially severe damages that can impoverish people, or move them outside of their usual income range. People would be unreasonable to rely on cost-benefit analyses for guidance when severe loss of income is possible.

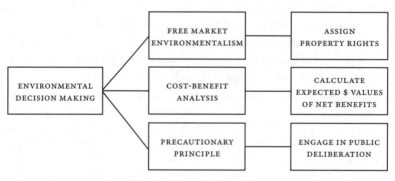

FIGURE 21.3: Some approaches to environmental decision making

We can conclude that the economic utilitarian method of cost-benefit analysis has limitations. The calculations of a cost-benefit analysis do not work either under conditions of uncertainty, when the probabilities of outcomes are unknown, or under severely damaging conditions, when the incomes of affected people are considerably diminished. This gives us version number 6 of the precautionary principle in Table 21.4:

> If either an activity or policy will potentially reduce incomes so as to make a cost-benefit analysis unreliable, or the connection between the activity and the damage is uncertain and probabilities are not known, then do not rely on a cost-benefit analysis in deciding a policy response.

The alternative to using an economic utilitarian cost-benefit analysis involving the calculation of financial costs and benefits is to use some process of public deliberation. In public deliberation, we present reasons, instead of numbers, for each policy response, and we debate the proper response. Whether to prohibit a potentially dangerous activity, to shift the burden of proof to proponents of the activity, to take cost-effective mitigation measures, or to make some other policy response is a matter for democratic decision making. Uncertain or catastrophic consequences call for a process of political deliberation, not economic number crunching. We see this notion at work in both the Wingspread and EC versions of the precautionary principle. The Wingspread Declaration says, "The process of applying the Precautionary Principle must be open, informed and democratic and must include potentially affected parties. It must also involve an examination of the full range of alternatives, including no action." The European Commission Communication talks of "the chosen level of protection," and refers to a political process among citizens. The public deliberation version of the precautionary principle warns us of the limitations of cost-benefit analysis, and offers an alternative decision making strategy for policies involving the uncertain chance of severe environmental problems.

SUMMARY

1. When we do not know the consequences of a policy for sure, then a cost-benefit analysis can use the technique of expected values. The expected value of a cost or benefit is the sum of the cost or benefit of each alternative outcome multiplied by the probability that that outcome will occur.
2. When dealing with potential outcomes, risk is a condition where we can measure the probabilities of alternative outcomes, and uncertainty is a condition where we cannot measure the probabilities of alternatives.
3. We cannot accurately perform an expected value cost-benefit analysis under conditions of uncertainty.
4. When potential losses are very severe, people are frequently averse to taking risks. Such an attitude is reasonable and highly prevalent, as is shown by a tendency for people to insure themselves against severe losses.
5. Different versions of a precautionary principle incorporate a damage condition, a knowledge condition, and a recommended policy response. The damage condition says that the precautionary principle applies when there are potential severe negative consequences. The knowledge condition

allows the principle to apply when outcomes are scientifically uncertain. The policy response may involve prohibition of a potentially dangerous activity, shifting the burden of proof to proponents of the activity, or cost-effective measures to mitigate the activity. The policy response is generally a political decision, not an economic decision.

6. A catastrophe, or severely damaging outcome, will reduce people's incomes and their ability to pay for economic goods and services. Since willingness to pay depends on ability to pay, this will make costs and benefits measured after a damaging event incommensurate with, or no longer comparable with, costs and benefits measured by a cost-benefit analysis before the damaging event.

7. Because income has diminishing marginal utility, an event that significantly lowers people's incomes will reduce their utilities by a disproportionately larger factor than their income loss. A cost-benefit analysis that measures costs by loss of income will not properly reflect utility loss when income losses are large.

8. For these reasons, we should not rely on cost-benefit analyses where we face conditions of uncertainty, or where outcomes involve significant loss of income. We should replace them by some form of political deliberation and democratic decision-making.

ONLINE READING QUESTIONS

The book's website contains reading questions on this chapter. Working through these questions will help you understand, remember, and apply important concepts from the chapter. Some of the questions supply useful hints for the study questions.

STUDY QUESTIONS

Using the text and hints from the online reading questions, write out, type, dictate to your computer, or at least formulate in your head answers to the following questions.

1. How can we do a cost-benefit analysis when we are not sure of the outcomes of a policy?
2. Why is a cost-benefit analysis inaccurate when applied to policies under conditions of uncertainty?
3. Why is a cost-benefit analysis inaccurate when applied to environmental catastrophes involving severe loss of income?
4. Why would a reasonable person buy insurance for her house, but an economically rational, risk-neutral person not do so?

Spend a few minutes thinking about the following questions, or, better yet, discuss them with fellow readers of this book.

1. How would the various precautionary principles that we have discussed apply to the issue of mitigating climate change?
2. Think critically about the precautionary principle recommended in this chapter, that a cost-benefit analysis should not be relied upon when either outcomes are uncertain or outcomes will lead to severe income loss. Is this a useful precautionary principle? Is it simply a vacuous tautology? Should it be weaker or stronger in some way?

Chapter 22

POLLUTION CONTROL

CARBON DIOXIDE AND OTHER GREENHOUSE GASES ARE POLLUTANTS. THEY ARE THE unintended, though foreseeable, by-products of production and consumption in the world's economies. They pose a multipoint accumulative harm both to those who produce them, and to other present and future living beings on the planet. By signing the Kyoto Protocol of 1997, most nations in the world committed themselves to decreasing their greenhouse gas emissions to 1990 levels. Several large emitters such as Russia, Canada, and Australia were slow to commit themselves, while the US has never signed the protocol. Many scientists and most environmentalists believe that the Kyoto commitments are inadequate for preventing dangerous climate change, and believe that much deeper cuts to greenhouse gas emissions will be required. Nations currently lack the political will to tighten, extend, or even enforce any international agreement on reducing greenhouse gas emissions.

How to make the required cuts in greenhouse gas emissions while allowing for sustainable economic development has become a pressing question. Governments recognized early on that leaving the issue to the free market was not going to work because the problem was an external cost and the solution is a public good. They also recognized that simply ordering firms to reduce their carbon emissions was not an efficient way to reduce emissions. Some jurisdictions have tried carbon taxes that shift the tax system so that citizens pay less tax on income and more tax on fossil fuel consumption. The European Union is experimenting with a system of tradable emission permits that investors can buy and sell on an exchange that is like a stock market. The trading of carbon emissions between countries is going on according to a system called the Clean Development Mechanism set up under the Kyoto Protocol. This international agreement allows industrialized countries, instead of cutting their own emissions, to invest in making equivalent reductions in carbon emissions in developing countries where it is less expensive to do so.

Whether we make policy decisions as economic utilitarians or as believers in a process of public ethical deliberation, we will still wish to solve environmental problems in the most cost-effective way possible. Here environmental economics has some useful advice. The least expensive way for a government to fix an environmental market failure is often not by directly commanding adherence to certain standards or regulations. Often, less expensive solutions will result from changing the incentives within the marketplace. In this chapter, we shall look at some cost-effective, market-based solutions to environmental problems, and examine the ethical issues that they raise.

Learning Objectives

1. To understand ethical issues regarding regulation as an approach to pollution control.
2. To understand ethical issues regarding emission charges as a market-based approach to pollution control.
3. To understand ethical issues regarding marketable permits as an approach to pollution control.

REDUCING POLLUTION

Based as it is in the utilitarian approach to ethics, market-based solutions to pollution problems will consider both the costs of pollution and the benefits of the economic activities of which pollution is a by-product. The socially optimal level of pollution is the point at which humans value the next consumer good more highly than they do the reduction in pollution that they could buy with the same money. The socially optimal level of pollution is not equal to zero pollution. The socially optimal level of pollution is the point at which the marginal benefit of cleaning up or preventing an additional increment of emissions equals the marginal cost of abatement. If the marginal benefit of cleaning up or preventing one more unit of emissions is higher than the marginal costs of abatement, then doing so will increase net benefits. If the marginal costs of cleaning up are higher than the marginal benefits, then pollution abatement will decrease net benefits. Hence, net benefits reach a maximum when the marginal benefits of pollution control are equal to the marginal costs of pollution abatement. The socially optimal level of pollution is the point at which the marginal benefit line intersects the marginal costs line on a graph of marginal benefits and marginal abatement costs.

Many environmentalists do not like the notion of a socially optimal level of pollution. They think that the only morally acceptable level of pollution is zero, or, at least, that less pollution is always better, and that polluters should always pay for any pollution that they produce. As we have seen, ethical criticisms of the economic utilitarian approach can come from any of several ethical approaches.

Criticisms may be character-based. People who pollute the environment are uncaring, thoughtless, and selfish. A community that says it is permissible to pollute to the socially optimal level is not a virtue promoting community. According to a teleological theory of value, pollution destroys the natural balance of the Earth and its ecosystems.

Criticisms may be duty based. Pollution is wrong, so people have a duty not to pollute the environment. What is the origin of this duty? One possible origin of this duty is a moral right. The external victims of pollution have rights not to be harmed by pollution. Any amount of pollution greater than zero is a violation of moral rights. Thus, everyone has a correlative duty not to create pollution that harms others. As we have seen, though, many pollution problems are multipoint in their sources, and many pollutants accumulate in the environment. When pollution is an accumulative harm, there is no direct causal link between emissions and harms to right-holders. It is then impossible to say on whom the duty not to pollute falls.

Other ethical criticisms of the socially optimal level of pollution are justice-based. People who are not benefiting from the activities causing pollution still suffer from the burdens of the harms caused by the pollution. The social optimum approach does not provide for compensation to the innocent victims of pollution.

Ethical criticisms can also concern issues of moral standing. The socially optimal level of pollution considers only the interests of those in a particular market. The interests of people outside the market, in distant countries or in the far future, and the interests of living beings incapable of market transactions are not represented properly in the calculation of a socially optimal level of pollution.

Finally, the socially optimal level of pollution approach rests on the use of willingness to pay in a market as a measure of preference satisfaction. We have seen several reasons to be concerned about WTP as a method for measuring degree of preference satisfaction or utility. Because the costs of pollution are external costs, economic utilitarians will require the methods of cost-benefit analysis to measure them.

NON-MARKET METHODS OF REDUCING POLLUTION

Several ways of controlling pollution do not use market-based techniques. Each has its limitations. One obvious way to reduce pollution is through the courts. Those who feel that pollution is harming them can sue those they believe to be causing the pollution, and use this litigation to either force the polluters to stop polluting, or force them to pay compensation. The litigation technique faces problems with the burden of proof and with its transaction costs. The burden of proof in civil litigation requires the plaintiff to show, first, that some particular pollutant has caused harm and, second, that the defendant emitted that particular pollutant. Neither of these is easy to show. The relationship between the level of a pollutant and the incidence of a particular disease or injury is often probabilistic and open to scientific dispute. The pollutant often comes from multiple sources and it is difficult to show that the defendant directly caused the pollutant in question. As well, the costs of litigation, such as research costs and legal fees, create large transaction costs that make the litigation method risky and often not cost effective.

Another technique is that of "moral suasion," which is what environmental economics calls environmental ethics. Moral suasion is often not very effective at the individual level. Ethical arguments sway some people, but not others. Those whom ethical reasons persuade to reduce, reuse, and recycle often end up feeling resentful toward those who continue with business as usual. More effective, perhaps, are advertising and educational campaigns to get people to internalize green virtues. The most effective place for ethical argument and moral suasion is likely in the political arena. In a process of democratic deliberation, where reasons are given and debated, the ethical assumptions behind different policies can be brought to light and assessed according to the ethical theories behind them.

Another obvious technique for reducing pollution is for the government to regulate emissions. In this method, sometimes called the command and control method, the government sets standards for polluting firms. The government may order firms to adopt a particular technology for pollution reduction, or may order each polluting firm to reduce its pollution by a specific amount. One large problem with the regulation method is that it offers firms no incentive to decrease pollution below the level that the government requires. Another problem is that it is not cost-effective. Unless every firm is identical in its cost structure, there will likely be a less expensive way to achieve the same result.

Cost-effectiveness analysis is a different notion than that of cost-benefit analysis. Cost-benefit analysis is a method of utilitarian economics for choosing between competing policies. COST-EFFECTIVENESS analysis is a method for deciding how to implement the chosen policy most efficiently or with least total social cost. Here we will construct an example to show how government regulation is often not cost effective (Frank et al. 2005: 370–74). Suppose there are two polluting firms, Acme Inc. and General Co., which, doing business as usual, each emit 400 tons of carbon dioxide per day. They face a choice of carbon dioxide emission control methods. Because it gets harder and harder to remove the carbon dioxide, the cost of additional reductions in carbon dioxide reduction increases. The two firms face different costs for carbon dioxide emission abatement methods as shown in Table 22.1. The government decides carbon dioxide must decrease by 400 tons in total. A government regulation orders each firm to cut its pollution in half. Each firm must cut its pollution from 400 tons per day to 200 tons per day. To do this each firm must use method B. The result, shown in dark gray, is that Acme's total costs will be $4000 and General's will be $2,900, for a total social cost of $6,900.

METHOD	BAU	A	B	C	D
Emissions (tons)	400	300	200	100	0
Acme's TC	$1,000	$2,000	$4,000	$7,000	$11,000
General's TC	$2,000	$2,300	$2,900	$3,900	$7,900

TABLE 22.1: Total costs (TC) of the two firms for different pollution control methods

This particular regulation is not cost-effective because there is a less expensive way of achieving the same 400-ton per day reduction in emissions. Because General's marginal cost for using a better pollution control method is lower, it would be more cost-effective if General reduces emissions by 300 tons by using method C while Acme reduces emissions by 100 tons by using method A. The result, shown in pale gray, is that Acme's total costs will be $2000 and General's will be $3,900, for a total of $5,900. The total social cost of this way of achieving the 400-ton per day reduction in emissions is $1000 less than using a regulation that requires each polluter to reduce its pollution by the same amount. Society could achieve the same carbon dioxide reduction more cheaply. How can policymakers achieve this result? Economists favour market-based solutions like pollution taxes or marketable permits.

MARKET-BASED METHODS OF REDUCING POLLUTION

Several market-based techniques for reducing pollution are economically more efficient than simple regulation. Though they are all cost-effective, they vary in their fairness and in their practicality.

One method, at which we have already looked, involves assigning a full set of transferable private property rights to the environment. According to the Coase theorem, members of the market society can then negotiate a socially optimal level of pollution without government intervention. From the economic utilitarian point of view, it does not matter who receives the private property rights. In practice, because of high transaction costs, the inability to define enforceable private property rights in the environment as a whole, and fairness issues, this method is of limited application.

A second method is for the government to charge for emissions of a pollutant. The government can impose a pollution tax that is proportional to emissions of the pollutant and set the level of the tax high enough to make polluting firms decide to cut pollution to the socially optimal level. Equivalently, from a market point of view, the government could offer a subsidy that had the same results as the tax.

A third method is for the government to create marketable permits. Each permit entitles a firm to emit a certain amount of pollutant. The government creates only that number of permits that will lead to the socially optimal level of pollution. In other words, the government puts a cap on the number of permits. Firms then trade the permits with one another. Firms that can reduce pollution at the lowest cost can then sell their permits to firms for whom pollution control is more expensive. This is a "cap-and-trade" system. The cap-and-trade system has two variants that are very important to distinguish. In one variant, the government *auctions* permits to emit a specific amount of the present pollution over a certain period to polluting firms. Firms may then sell or trade these permits with one another because they are effectively new property rights, bought from the government. In the second variant, the government *gives* permits to emit a specific amount of the present pollution to polluting firms, generally in proportion to their present emissions. Firms may then sell or trade these permits with one another because they are effectively new property rights, received as a gift from the government. Both variants can result in economically efficient pollution reduction. Which variant we choose has huge implications for the justice of the process.

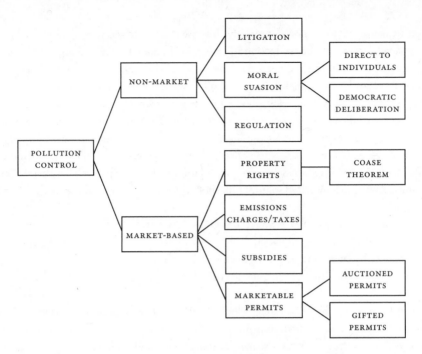

FIGURE 22.1: A taxonomy of pollution control methods

EMISSIONS CHARGES/POLLUTION TAXES

First, we will look at how emissions charges work, how they result in a cost effective reduction in pollution, and what their ethical issues are. Emissions charges, or pollution taxes, work through the self-interest of polluting firms; they do not require that the firms be public spirited or motivated by the greater good. Let us consider the effects of a carbon tax on the behaviour of the two firms in our previous example. Table 22.2 shows both the total costs of carbon capture and sequestration (CCS) for the two firms and shows the marginal costs of each additional degree of CCS capacity for each firm. Each firm will react to a particular level of taxation by considering whether it is less expensive to pay the tax and continue emitting, or to go to a higher level of carbon capture capacity and avoid the tax.

Suppose that the government imposes a tax of five dollars per ton, or $500 for each 100 tons of carbon dioxide emitted. As shown in Table 22.2, it would cost Acme $1000 to use method A and reduce its emissions from 400 to 300 tons. Since the cost of reducing emissions for Acme is higher than the cost of paying the tax, Acme will not reduce its carbon dioxide emissions. The marginal cost to General of reducing emissions by 100 tons is only $300. Since this cost is less than the cost of paying the $500 tax, General will reduce its carbon dioxide emissions by 100 tons. General will not use method B, however, because the marginal cost of going from method A to method B is $600, and this is higher than the tax of $500. If the government wishes to reduce carbon pollution by 400 tons in total to the socially optimal level, then the tax is not high enough.

METHOD	BAU		A		B		C		D
Emissions (tons)	*400*		*300*		*200*		*100*		*0*
Acme's TC	$1,000		$2,000		$4,000		$7,000		$11,000
Acme's MC		$1,000		$2,000		$3,000		$4,000	
General's TC	$2,000		$2,300		$2,900		$3,900		$7,900
General's MC		$300		$600		$1,000		$4,000	

TABLE 22.2: Total costs and marginal costs of the two firms for different pollution control methods

Suppose clever economic utilitarian policymakers set the tax at $10.01 per ton of carbon dioxide per day, or $1001 per 100 tons. The firms will reduce pollution as long as the additional cost of using a control method is below the tax that they would have to pay if they do not use it. Acme will use method A because the additional cost of doing so, $1000, is less than the cost of the tax it would have to pay if it did not do so ($1001). General will use method C because General's additional cost of $300 for method A, its additional cost of $600 to move from method A to method B, and its additional cost of $1000 to move from method B to method C are all lower than the tax of $1001. In each case, it is in General's self-interest to use better pollution control methods.

The emissions charges/pollution tax approach has advantages and disadvantages, both practical and ethical. From the economic utilitarian perspective, it maximizes net social benefits by minimizing social cost. It does this not by appealing to the benevolence of the emitters, but by giving them incentives that appeal to their self-interest. Better still, it gives emitters incentives to go on reducing pollution, where possible, in order to save paying the pollution tax. The taxes go initially to government. However, the tax revenue will transfer to everyone through reductions in other taxes or the establishment of new programs. The taxes that are collected are potentially available to compensate those on whom the external burdens of pollution fall. Tax revenue can even compensate those in distant countries, like those living in the river deltas of Bangladesh and Vietnam where climate change will lead to flooding due to rising sea levels, and who will bear the external cost of fossil fuel consumption in industrialized countries.

One practical disadvantage of all pollution control methods is that they require measurement of pollution emissions and enforcement of standards, and that measurement and enforcement are costly. For many emission-charges situations, the collection of pollution fees can be difficult. For example, if an authority imposes a fee per unit weight on curbside garbage, then it will need to weigh everyone's garbage, keep records, and send and collect bills. The collection of fees for the emission of carbon dioxide, however, is considerably more efficient. Authorities know the carbon content of fuels like coal, oil, and natural gas, and can levy a carbon tax based on how much carbon dioxide each unit of fossil fuel will produce when burned. Authorities can levy these taxes on fossil fuels when they are removed from the ground or brought into the country. These upstream emissions charges will then pass to consumers through the pricing decisions of the marketers of fossil fuels regarding the products that they create and sell. A carbon tax will apply efficiently to non-point source pollution, as well as to large stationary emitters of carbon dioxide. For example, a carbon tax applied to gasoline will affect all drivers, and will give all of them an incentive to drive less or buy more fuel-efficient cars. Because it works for accumulative, non-point source emitters of carbon dioxide, the carbon tax approach is potentially fairer than the other approaches, discussed below, because these approaches will only apply efficiently to large stationary emitters.

Another practical disadvantage of the tax approach is that policymakers do not know at what level to set the tax to achieve the desired degree of pollution control. Experimenting with the tax level to find the right level of pollution control may be wasteful because of the high capital costs to firms needed to meet the policy objectives. Note that unless taxes are set very high, emission charges and pollution taxes will not result in zero pollution.

We should note that a subsidy to cut pollution in the same amount as the pollution tax would have the same effect on the behaviour of the two firms. Let us suppose that authorities offer a subsidy of $1001 for each 100 tons per day of carbon dioxide emissions cut by the firms. Looking at Table 22.1, we can see that Acme will use method A, cutting 100 tons of emissions, because the subsidy of $1001 is higher than the marginal cost of moving from BAU to method A which is $1000. General will use method C, cutting 300 tons of emissions, because the subsidy is higher than the marginal costs of moving from BAU to A, from A to B, and from B to C. Though the subsidy is equally cost-effective, it has a severe ethical problem. The firms are the ones who are creating external costs for the rest of society, but the rest of society pays the polluters a subsidy to stop polluting. In the tax system, polluters pay compensation to the victims of pollution; in the subsidy system, the victims pay the polluters something akin to extortion payments to stop polluting. The economics is symmetric but the ethics is not.

CAP AND TRADE WITH AUCTIONED MARKETABLE PERMITS

Suppose government policymakers cap total pollution at 400 tons per day. The authorities then hold an auction between the two firms for the right to emit pollution in 100-ton lots. They put four permits up for auction. Without any permits, both firms will have to use emission control method D, and create no emissions. This will be very expensive for both firms.

Suppose that the auction for permits to emit 100 tons per day of carbon dioxide opens with a bid of $100. Both firms will want four permits because $100 is much less than the cost of using any methods of pollution control. Thus, both firms will be willing to go higher in their bids. Suppose the bidding reaches $500. Looking back at Table 22.2, we can see that now Acme will still want four permits, because Acme's cost of using even the cheapest method, A, is higher than $500. General, though, will now only want three permits because General's cost of using method A, $300, is less than the cost of bidding for a permit. Suppose the bidding now goes to $900. Acme will still wish to buy four permits, but now General will wish to buy only two. The total number of permits desired is six, but the number available is only four, so the auction will continue. Finally, when the bidding reaches $1001, Acme will wish to buy one permit and General will wish to buy three. At this point, all four permits will sell and the auction will end.

The auction will conclude with the two firms emitting a total of 400 tons per day of carbon dioxide in a way that is cost-effective. The total cost of pollution control for society as a whole will be at a minimum, as an economic utilitarian would wish. Auctioning marketable permits to pollute gives incentives to find better pollution control methods to save buying permits or to have permits to trade to other firms. For example, if General can lower its cost of moving from method C to method D to less than $1000, then it can sell its single emission permit to Acme for $1001 and keep the difference. Policymakers do not have to know firms' costs; they just set the emissions cap and hold the auction. They do not have to experiment with the tax level as they do in the emissions taxes method. Citizen's groups who disagree with the pollution level set by government policymakers can buy permits but not use them, and so reduce pollution. Auction proceeds go to the government. However, the proceeds will transfer to everyone through reductions in other taxes or through the implementation of new programs. In theory, the proceeds of the auction could compensate those parties external to the polluting activities on whom the burdens of pollution fall.

The principle practical disadvantage of this method is that it cannot easily apply to multiple sources of pollution (non-point source pollution). It might be practical for large coal-fired electric generators, concrete plants, or iron smelters to bid on permits to emit carbon dioxide, but it is not practical for individual drivers to bid on permits to buy fuel for cars. Relying only on a permit system for large point sources of carbon dioxide emissions, will fail to control non-point source emissions. For multiple sources of pollution, a carbon tax will work better. Both large cement plants and individual drivers of cars are creating carbon dioxide. It seems unfair that only the former should have to pay compensation for the external costs their activities create for society.

CAP AND TRADE WITH GIFTED MARKETABLE PERMITS

Suppose, again, that government policymakers cap total pollution at 400 tons per day. Instead of auctioning permits, the authorities *give* each firm two marketable permits each for the right to emit pollution in 100 ton per day lots. As long as the permits are marketable, the two firms will reach a cost-effective way of reducing pollution emissions by trading the permits between themselves.

METHOD	BAU		A		B		C		D
Emissions (tons)	400		300		200		100		0
Acme's TC	$1,000		$2,000		$4,000		$7,000		$11,000
Acme's MC		$1,000		$2,000		$3,000		$4,000	
General's TC	$2,000		$2,300		$2,900		$3,900		$7,900
General's MC		$300		$600		$1,000		$4,000	

TABLE 22.3: Total and marginal costs for two firms trading emission permits

Table 22.3 shows the starting point in light grey, with both firms receiving 2 permits that allow them each to emit 200 tons of carbon dioxide per day. It will be in the self-interest of both firms to buy and sell permits. If Acme offers General $1001 for one of its two permits, then General can accept because General's additional cost of implementing method C is only $1000. This trade will save firm Acme $2000, as it is now able to use method A at a cost of $2000 instead of method B at a cost of $4000. Table 22.3 shows the position of the two firms after the trade in dark grey. In fact, this permit can trade between the two firms at a price anywhere between $1001 and $1999, leave both firms better off after the transaction, and still minimize the social costs of pollution abatement.

The technique of gifted marketable permits can use the self-interest of polluters to reduce pollution just as cost-effectively as can the techniques of pollution charges and of auctioned marketable permits. It has the same practical advantage as the auctioned marketable permits technique in that it permits policymakers to decide on a level of pollution, the cap, without experimenting with tax rates. Implementing a system of gifted marketable permits to emit pollutants will meet with less political resistance from the polluting firms because, unlike the auction and tax systems, they will not have to pay for the legal right to emit pollutants. In effect, the gifted permits system grants a valuable new property right, the right to emit a certain amount of pollution legally, to the polluting firm, and allows the firm to sell that right to others and keep the proceeds.

The ethical disadvantages of the gifted permit system weigh against these technical advantages. Like compliance with the auctioned permits system, compliance with the gifted permit system can be enforced only for large emitters. It will not be practical to measure the emissions of cars, trucks, home heating systems, and recreational vehicles to verify their compliance with their permits to emit. Thus the gifted permit system, like the auctioned permit system, will be selective in its application. Unlike both the auctioned permit system and the tax system, any financial proceeds of the gifted permit system will go to the firm who sells the permit, and not, through income tax reductions or new government programs, to the citizens on whom the pollution damage falls. There will be no offsetting tax reductions or program increases for consumers and citizens. Thus, the gifted permit system is less fair than either the tax system or the auctioned permit system because it does not permit the possibility of using tax or auction proceeds to compensate the victims of pollution externalities. The gifted permit system also does not permit concerned citizens to bid for permits in order to reduce the general level of pollution.

The gifted permit system creates a new saleable property right, and generally gives it to firms who have been polluting in the past in proportion to their past emissions. Giving pollution permits on this basis rewards past polluting activity. Before the permit system comes into effect, firms and individuals are at liberty to use the assimilative capacity of the atmosphere and water of the Earth as a public good. After the permit system is in place, their liberty will be restricted. Polluting firms may argue that the gifted permits are compensation for this restriction to their liberty. Against this, environmentalists may respond that firms and individuals were never really at liberty to pollute as they saw fit because the harm principle limits their liberty, and their emissions were actually harming others by imposing external costs on them. In response, small polluters might argue that their emissions were too small to make any difference or that they were only part of an accumulative harm. This argument would be less plausible coming from large polluters.

Polluters might argue that the libertarian mechanism for the initial acquisition of property applies here. To make their valuable product (whatever it is), they have been "mixing their labour" with (that is using) some natural resources, including the environment's ability to assimilate pollution; they are entitled to do this, as long as they leave enough, and as good, of these resources for others. Environmentalists might reply that they create external costs for the rest of society, and do not leave others with enough, and as good, of the Earth's assimilative capacity for pollution.

Perhaps the largest problem with gifted marketable permits to pollute is that the system is easily confused with the auctioned marketable permits technique. From the point of view of environmental economics, both methods have the same results. They both result in a cost-effective equilibrium between polluters that reduces pollution to the required level. From the point of view of environmental ethics, however, the two systems are very different. There is potential for more unfairness and injustice in the gifted permit system than in either the auctioned permit system or the pollution tax system.

SUMMARY

1. Economic utilitarianism considers both the external costs of pollution and the economic benefits created by polluting activities. It balances the marginal benefits of less pollution with the marginal costs of preventing it or cleaning it up, including the costs of lost production. This results in a socially optimal level of pollution that is not equal to zero pollution.

2. Other ethical perspectives will criticize the idea of a non-zero socially optimal level of pollution. To virtue ethics, pollution is a vice that inhibits human flourishing. To rights theory, pollution is an interference with the moral rights of others that must be stopped, not minimized. To justice theory, the burdens of pollution usually fall on those who do not benefit from the productive activity that causes those burdens. To environmental ethics, the approach does not consider either damage to distant and future people or injury to non-human living beings. As well, we have reason to be suspicious of the use of willingness to pay to establish values.

3. One non-market method of pollution control is civil litigation. Litigation is expensive and difficult to apply to accumulative, non-point source pollution.

4. Another non-market method is moral suasion, or ethical persuasion. This is often not as effective as economic incentives at the individual level, but in a democracy, can be very effective at the political level.

5. Another non-market method is government regulation. This is not cost-effective when one polluting firm can make pollution reductions more cheaply than another can.

6. One market-based method is an emission charge or a pollution tax. Policymakers can set a tax on pollution emissions that will push firms, all acting in their own self-interest, to find the least expensive way of reducing pollution. The tax collected can compensate the victims of pollution. In the

case of a carbon tax, it is fairly simple and inexpensive to collect the tax and enforce compliance.

7. Another market-based method is for the government to cap pollution at a certain level, and auction transferable permits to pollute. In the auction, firms will reach the most cost-effective way of reducing pollution. Proceeds from the auction can compensate victims of pollution through reductions in other taxes or new programs. Enforcing compliance is difficult and expensive for non-point source polluters.

8. The government can also cap pollution and simply give away permits to pollute in proportion to past pollution emissions. While cost-effective, this method is unfair. There are no taxes or auction proceeds to use to compensate victims of pollution. A valuable saleable property right is created and given to those who in the past have created external costs for others. Gifted permits are easily confused with auctioned permits in popular discourse.

ONLINE READING QUESTIONS

The book's website contains reading questions on this chapter. Working through these questions will help you understand, remember, and apply important concepts from the chapter. Some of the questions supply useful hints for the study questions.

STUDY QUESTIONS

Using the text and hints from the online reading questions, write out, type, dictate to your computer, or at least formulate in your head answers to the following questions.

1. Describe some ethical criticisms of the social optimum approach to pollution used by economic utilitarians which implies that the best level of pollution is not zero pollution.
2. Why is a carbon tax potentially fairer and more just than the cap, auction, and trade approach to pollution abatement?
3. Why is the cap, auction, and trade approach potentially fairer and more just than the cap, give, and trade approach to pollution abatement?

QUESTIONS TO PONDER

Spend a few minutes thinking about the following questions, or, better yet, discuss them with fellow readers of this book.

1. Can you think of other ethical reasons for opposing the economic utilitarian notion of a non-zero socially optimal level of pollution besides those mentioned in the text?

2. How effective do you think that moral suasion can be at the individual level? At the political level?
3. Review the technical and ethical pros and cons of a pollution tax. Are there any more points that ethically informed policymakers should consider?
4. Review the technical and ethical pros and cons of a system of *auctioned* marketable permits to pollute. Are there any more points that ethically informed policymakers should consider?
5. Review the technical and ethical pros and cons of a system of *gifted* marketable permits to pollute. Are there any more points that ethically informed policymakers should consider?

Chapter 23

SUSTAINABLE DEVELOPMENT

HUMAN ECONOMIC ACTIVITY NOT ONLY CREATES ENVIRONMENTAL POLLUTION, BUT also depletes the Earth's natural resources. Human beings cannot avoid some economic activity; they need to produce and consume in order to live. The level at which they produce and consume, however, is an ethical issue. The accumulation of pollution and the depletion of natural resources have large effects on present and future others, both human and non-human.

Some natural resources are renewable over time. This is particularly true of biological resources like forests on land, water in rivers, and fish in the ocean. It is also true of energy from the sun and water from rain. It is possible, however, to use renewable resources at unsustainable rates, rates of use that are higher than the rate at which natural processes can replenish the resources. For example, the water in many of the world's rivers is sometimes totally used up for drinking water and for irrigation of crops by the time that the river reaches the sea. The rate at which the irrigation of crops uses many of the world's underground aquifers is higher than the rate at which rainfall replenishes these aquifers.

Other natural resources are non-renewable; there is no natural process working on a human timescale that will replenish the resource. Fossil fuels are an example. Natural processes replenish them on geological timescales, but not on human ones. It is an open question now whether we have reached the date of peak oil, after which oil production will inevitably decline. Mineral deposits are another example. The information economy is using up the rare elements used in electronic devices, and the lithium used in the batteries that power them.

The obvious ethical issue here is that of our obligations to future generations. How should our generation use the world's resources in a way that is fair to members of future generations? This is the issue of sustainable development.

A less obvious issue is that of how to assess our present environmental policies. Policymakers always define indicators that will measure the success of their policies. The success of our policies vis-à-vis the whole planet also needs an indicator. The commonest indicator of policy success at the macro level is the Gross Domestic Product. From an ethical perspective, however, the GDP has many weaknesses. It is a measure of economic activity, not a measure of human welfare, and it does not properly account for the costs of resource depletion or the costs of cleaning up pollution. We will look at the weaknesses of the GDP measure in more detail, and briefly examine attempts to replace it with an indicator better suited to assessing environmental policy.

Learning Objectives

1. To understand the notion of resource depletion and sustainable development.
2. To understand ethical criticisms of Gross Domestic Product (GDP) as a measure of sustainable human and non-human welfare.
3. To understand why people are trying to construct ethically better indicators of sustainable human and non-human welfare such as the Genuine Progress Indicator (GPI).

RESOURCE DEPLETION AND SUSTAINABLE DEVELOPMENT

Using natural resources now will eventually make them less available and more costly in the future. This future cost is a cost that does not figure in present-day market activities. It is not part of the cost of using the natural resources now, so it is an external cost of resource use. Hence, the future cost of depleted resources makes the economic market inefficient or non-maximizing over a long period. Nor does the future cost of depleted resources appear as a negative component of the Gross Domestic Product (GDP), which is the most common way of measuring total economic welfare. Therefore, using only the market to decide on resource use, and using only the GDP to measure welfare, will tend to make the economy unsustainable.

In physics, the First Law of Thermodynamics says that matter and energy can be neither created nor destroyed. The Second Law of Thermodynamics says that physical processes without external energy inputs (closed systems) always happen in ways that make energy less available for work. For example, useful forms of electrical energy often end up as useless heat. Ecological economists such as Herman Daly take the laws of thermodynamics to imply that the Earth is a closed system, and that we are using up its useful energy resources either directly or indirectly. Ecological economists believe that a growing market economy is not sustainable in the long term.

Sustainable development is itself a contested concept. There is dispute over what it should mean. It has something to do with the present generation's obligations to future generations, or obligations of intergenerational justice. It cannot mean that the present generation must bequeath to future generations a world that is precisely identical to the present world. This would be impossible, and since "ought implies can," that sort of sustainability cannot be an ethical obligation.

The most famous definition of sustainable development is contained in the Brundtland Report to the United Nations of 1987. SUSTAINABLE DEVELOPMENT is there defined as development that meets "the needs of the present without compromising the ability of future generations to meet their own needs" (World Commission 1987). The concept of what a present or future generation needs is somewhat vague. The economist, Robert Solow, tried to sharpen this definition. He proposed the following, based on considerations of intergenerational justice.

> The duty imposed by sustainability is to bequeath to posterity not any particular thing—with the sort of rare exception I have mentioned [he mentions Yosemite National Park and the Lincoln Memorial]—but rather to endow them with whatever it takes to achieve a standard of living at least as good as our own and to look after their next generation similarly. (Solow 1993: 168)

Sometimes human made substitutes can replace natural resources. For example, paper bags can be replaced by plastic bags, paper records by computer records, metals by plastics, perhaps fossil fuels by nuclear fusion, and so on. We can distinguish between strong and weak conceptions of sustainability. STRONG SUSTAINABILITY is a condition where stocks of natural resources do not decline. WEAK SUSTAINABILITY is a condition where human-made substitutes compensate for the depletion of natural resources. Solow thinks that the only reasonable form of sustainability is weak sustainability.

> A sustainable path for the economy is thus not necessarily one that conserves every single thing or any single thing. It is one that replaces whatever it takes from its inherited natural and produced endowment, its material and intellectual endowment. What matters is not the particular form that the replacement takes, but only its capacity to produce the things that posterity will enjoy. (Solow 1993: 168)

Each generation has no duty to bequeath particular things to the next, with the exception of an item like Yosemite National Park for which there is no human-made substitute.

Solow's definition of sustainable development is a recursive definition. When Solow says that it is the obligation of each generation to the next "to endow them with whatever it takes to achieve a standard of living at least as good as our own and to look after their next generation similarly," he defines the obligations of each generation (n) to the next generation (n + 1). Since generation (n) and the subsequent generation (n + 1) are, with very few exceptions, alive at the same time, there are no problems regarding a generation owing obligations to generations not yet born. We discussed the problems involved with obligations to nonexistent future generations in the chapter on Future Generations.

Solow states his definition a bit ambiguously, but he clearly means that generation n should endow generation n + 1 with whatever it takes to achieve a standard of living at least as good as that of generation n. Each future generation (n) attains a certain standard of living, which may be higher than ours, and then it (n) has the obligation to the next generation (n + 1) to endow them (n + 1) with whatever it takes to maintain a standard living at least as good as the one that it (n) achieved.

From the perspective of environmental ethics, the most obvious problem with these definitions is that they are thoroughly anthropocentric. The Brundtland report considers only the needs of present and future generations of human beings. Robert Solow considers only the standard of living of present and future generations of human beings. There is no direct consideration given here to the interests of animals, plants, or ecosystems. Nonhuman entities have only instrumental value; they get consideration only insofar as they meet the needs of human beings or contribute to the standard of living of human beings. For example, honeybees would be of value only because they produce honey and pollinate crops, and not because they have any intrinsic value themselves.

Conventional economists, such as Solow, disagree with ecological economists, such as Daly, regarding the depletion of natural resources. Conventional resource economics holds that when the supply of a natural resource diminishes, its price will rise, and this will call forth new efforts to discover more of the resource or to exploit previously uneconomic deposits. Technological innovation can make resource extraction more efficient and make it less expensive to extract resources from deposits previously thought too poor to use. Technological innovation and diminishing supplies can make recycling of scarce natural resources economically more attractive. Technological innovation and upward pressure on prices can also make it economically more attractive to use substitutes for scarce natural resources. The rising price of fossil fuels will push the economy into using alternative sources of energy like wind power and solar power as substitutes for fossil fuels. In conventional economic thinking, increasing technical knowledge replaces decreasing natural resources. Ecological economic thinking disagrees.

Ecological economists, but perhaps not conventional resource economists, would applaud the existence of a steady state economy, where growth at the expense of resource depletion had stopped, and all human beings had achieved a reasonable standard of living through the fair distribution of wealth and income. As long ago as 1848, John Stuart Mill, the English utilitarian philosopher and economist, wrote positively about what he called the "stationary state of capital and wealth." He disliked the competitive growth economy of his time, which he thought reduced human social life to "trampling, crushing, elbowing, and treading on each other's heels" (Mill 1848: IV.6.5). Mill did not believe, however, that a stationary state of resource-based capital and population would stop the growth of happiness in the world. If he thought a stationary state would lead to less than maximum happiness, then, as a utilitarian, he would reject it.

> It is scarcely necessary to remark that a stationary condition of capital and popu-
> lation implies no stationary state of human improvement. There would be as
> much scope as ever for all kinds of mental culture, and moral and social progress;
> as much room for improving the Art of Living, and much more likelihood of
> its being improved, when minds ceased to be engrossed by the art of getting on.
> (Mill 1848: IV.6.9)

Modern thinking on the same subject makes a distinction between growth and development. GROWTH is a condition of quantitative increase in the physical size of the economy including its use of natural resources and energy. DEVELOPMENT is a condition of qualitative improvements in the services and the physical artifacts and activities of the economy that are based on better knowledge and not on greater use of natural resources and energy. A steady state economy can continue to develop even if it stops growing. Growth can bring development, and does not necessarily bring environmental costs. The large economies of developed nations often consist of around 70% services. Services create less pollution and less resource depletion than do the production of goods by industry, mining, or farming. Service growth in the economy does not necessarily create the external costs of goods growth.

PROBLEMS WITH GROSS DOMESTIC PRODUCT AS AN INDICATOR OF SUSTAINABLE DEVELOPMENT

Economists distinguish between microeconomics and macroeconomics. Microeconomics is the study of how individuals make choices, and the implications of these choices for the quantities and prices of goods and services produced and consumed in a market. Macroeconomics is the study of the performance of the market as a whole and the effect of government policy on that performance. In our terms, microeconomics is an individualistic discipline, like biology, whereas macroeconomics is a holistic discipline, like ecology. With its assumption that the intensity of someone's preference is measured by her willingness to pay to have it satisfied, microeconomic utilitarianism tells us to maximize net economic benefit in the market for each individual good or service. The question then arises of how to measure net preference satisfaction for the economy as a whole.

The answer is suggested by macroeconomics. The most important concept in macroeconomics is that of the GROSS DOMESTIC PRODUCT (GDP), which is the market value of all final goods and services produced within the borders of a country during a given time period. Its originators intended GDP as a measure of total market activity, and not as an indicator of the aggregate welfare of all members of the market economy. However, people so often use it for the latter purpose, that it is worth examining some conceptual and ethical reasons why GDP is not a good measure of aggregate human welfare. If utilitarians were to take GDP as a measure of aggregate preference satisfaction, then they would have an obligation to aim for growth in the GDP in order to maximize the total amount of preference satisfaction. Macroeconomic utilitarianism implies GDP growth.

GDP is defined as the market value of all final goods and services produced in a country during a given time period. This definition contains two concepts that need clarification. The definition's use of market value implies that only goods and services actually sold are included in GDP. For example, the GDP does not include the value of unpaid housework. This is a value judgment. The definition's use of the notion of final goods and services implies that only the final product of a value chain is included. This is a conceptual issue and stops double counting. For example, GDP includes the value of the loaf of bread, but not of the flour, the wheat, the seed, or the tractor driver's labour. It does include the value *added by each step* in the production chain. It includes the value added by the retailer, the baker, the miller, the farmer, the seed producer, and the tractor driver. It does not count the total value passed on by each member of the value chain twice.

One way to increase the total GDP is to have a larger population, for example, by allowing more immigration. This may not increase the average GDP. The average GDP is the GDP per capita, which is the GDP divided by the population of the country. From a holistic, common good, ethical perspective, increasing the size of the total GDP might be most important because, for example, it would increase the power and prestige of the country as a whole. From the perspective of total utilitarianism, growing total GDP would also be the important issue. From an individualistic ethical perspective, where the welfare of each individual is the important issue, then the appropriate indicator would be average or per capita GDP.

GDP has many weaknesses as a measure of human welfare or utility. It has even more weaknesses as a measure of sustainable development. The idea of using GDP as a measure of utility depends on the idea that willingness to pay measures the intensity of preferences satisfied. As we have seen in previous chapters, there are many ethical and conceptual problems with this idea.

One problem with using GDP as a measure of human welfare is that it is too abstract. It does not distinguish between products and services that increase well-being and those that decrease well-being. All economic activity adds to GDP, even if it is destructive, regrettable, or unsustainable. GDP is a measure of total market activity. It lumps together economic goods and services that we should divide into either benefits or costs. Crime prevention, commuting costs, and auto accidents all generate economic activity and add to the GDP. On the one hand, these costs provide benefits to police officers, oil companies, and emergency room workers who receive pay to solve the problems that these costs generate. On the other hand, however, most people would prefer to avoid these costs.

A second problem with using GDP as a measure of human welfare is that it ignores the value of nonmarket transactions. It ignores the value of most child-care, household, and volunteer services. It ignores the value of subsistence production, and of production for home use. The value of nonmarket goods and services is especially high relative to the value of market goods and services in developing countries. The GDP will systematically understate human welfare in developing countries where much of what is good for people is not for sale. A related problem is that the GDP ignores the value of ecosystem services such as pollination by bees and insects, sequestration of carbon dioxide by oceans and plants, production of oxygen by plants, formation of soils, cleansing of water by filtration, and so on. Ecosystem services are not bought and sold in the marketplace, and, valuable as they are to human welfare, are not accounted in the GDP.

A third problem is that the GDP ignores some of the external costs of pollution. The pollution created as the by-product of an industrial economy is often both global and accumulative. The costs that pollution creates often fall on people outside the national boundaries of the industrial economy that is producing the pollution. The costs will also often fall on people many years in the future. For example, the climate change caused by the use of fossil fuels in industrial economies will create costs in distant, undeveloped economies 100 years from now. The GDP is the market value of final goods and services produced within a particular country and within a particular period. By definition, therefore, it will ignore external costs created in other countries at later periods.

A fourth, and related, problem with the GDP is that when it does take into account the external costs of pollution within a particular country's economy, it treats them as a positive benefit rather than a negative cost. The GDP includes costs of pollution clean-up. For example, the US GDP actually went up with the multi-billion dollar costs of the clean-up of the Exxon Valdez oil spill in 1989. The cleanup costs for the Deep Water Horizon oilrig explosion in 2010 are part of the final goods and services produced by the US economy. External costs within the country that produced them count as part of the economic activity within that country, and will add to, not subtract from, the Gross Domestic Product of the country.

A fifth problem with GDP as a measure of human welfare is that GDP ignores income inequalities. A country in which most of the value of the final goods and services produced in the country go to very few people could have the same GDP as a country that distributes goods and services evenly to everyone. Because of the declining marginal utility of income, it is clear that human welfare (utility) will be higher in the second country that distributes goods and services more equally. Using GDP as a measure of human welfare will not capture the welfare difference between these two economies. In a utilitarian ethical framework, we would be more interested in the growth of utility or human welfare than we would be in the growth of economic activity as measured by GDP.

In a deontological ethical framework, we would be interested in the fairness of the distribution of the value of goods and services. We would also be interested in how well the country prevented human rights abuse. GDP ignores the issue of a fair distribution and ignores both human rights abuses and the benefits of living in a free country. Suppose that two countries have the same per capita GDP. One country commits severe human rights abuses and curtails political liberties, while the other country protects human rights and encourages political liberty. The two countries would rank the same on a per capita GDP scale. Nevertheless, living in the second country would be preferable to living in the first.

Finally, using GDP or per capita GDP to measure the success of environmental policies will ignore the depletion of resources. The Earth's stock of non-renewable natural resources is like money in the bank. If we take money out of the bank now and spend it, there will be less money left for the future. Our decisions to use natural resources now will impose an external cost on future generations. The GDP, by definition, measures only economic activity during a period of a year at most; it does not consider the costs that our present decisions will impose on our future descendants.

OTHER INDICATORS OF SUSTAINABLE DEVELOPMENT

Policymakers have developed other indicators of human welfare and sustainable development. These include the UN's Human Development Index, the Happy Planet Index, the Index of Sustainable Economic Welfare, and the Genuine Progress Indicator (GPI). We will take a brief look at the GPI, to see how it deals with the problems of using the GDP as an indicator of sustainable human welfare.

A brief sketch of the procedure for constructing a Genuine Progress Indicator begins with first separating out from total GDP that portion of the GDP spent on personal consumption. GPI calculations accept the proposition that human welfare can be measured in financial terms, but GPI calculations only count those financial expenditures which are actually consumed, as opposed to being, say, invested in manufacturing equipment. The GPI adjusts personal consumption expenditure to take into account unequal distributions. High personal consumption by the rich together with low personal consumption by the poor will produce less human welfare than will moderate personal consumption by everyone. To the market's measurement of personal consumption, it then adds the estimated value of all those nonmarket activities that contribute to human welfare. From this total, it then deducts the costs of cleaning up pollution, paying for the medical expenses of pollution victims, and so on. (The GDP *adds* these costs.) Again from this total is deducted the estimated cost imposed on future generations through depletion of natural resources in the present period. The idea is that an indicator constructed like this will be a better measure of policy performance than the GDP.

Begin with estimates of personal consumption expenditures
↓
Adjust these for inequalities
↓
Add value of socially productive non-market activities
↓
Deduct costs of undesirable effects: pollution, crime, etc.
↓
Deduct costs for degradation and depletion of natural resources
↓
Use this "green GDP" index to guide policy

FIGURE 23.1: Steps in the Calculation of a Genuine Progress Indicator

Proponents of the GDP as an indicator of policy performance point out that calculating the GDP is a totally objective procedure, whereas calculation of other indicators such as the GPI is not objective. To calculate the GDP, economists simply follow a certain set of rules, defined by international agreements, and calculate the GDP from data about the national economy. On the other hand, since the GPI is more than just a tally of market expenditures, it will require the techniques of cost-benefit analysis to estimate some of the financial values that it employs. Cost-benefit analyses require contestable judgments, and these judgments lack the mechanical objectivity of the components of the GDP. Nevertheless, as we have seen before, because external costs are not in market prices, and because pollution and resource depletion impose external costs, environmental economists use techniques of cost-benefit analysis in order to estimate them. In other words, the decision to use only items that have market values in calculating the GDP amounts to a decision to disregard external costs. For example, the external costs of resource depletion will fall on future people, and so cannot count in the GDP by the very definition of the GDP as applying only to a particular period. The GDP purchases objectivity at the price of comprehensiveness.

A defender of the GDP as the appropriate indicator of policy performance might also claim that other measures make explicit value judgments in their construction, whereas the GDP is value free. It is true that the GPI, for example, makes the value judgment to count pollution costs in the indicator as costs and not benefits, and not to ignore the costs of resource depletion. These are value judgments. The GDP, however, implicitly makes the opposite of the value judgments embodied in the GPI. The GDP makes the implicit value judgment that the cost of cleaning up pollution makes a positive contribution to GDP. The GDP also makes the implicit value judgment that we should ignore the costs of resource depletion. These implicit value judgments rest on shakier foundations than the explicit value judgments of the GPI. Any policymaker using GDP as a measure of economic welfare is also making a value judgment about the appropriate indicator to maximize.

The GDP and the GPI are both thoroughly anthropocentric. Their calculations concern only the welfare and economic activity of human beings, and of those, only the ones who are resident in the country whose economy is measured. Other sustainability indicators are not restricted to just the welfare of humans. An Ecological Footprint measures the amount of biologically productive land needed to produce the resources and to get rid of the pollution required by a given lifestyle. Currently humans use 1.3 earths on average. A Carbon Footprint measures the total amount of GHG emissions produced by a person, country, industry, or other institution. Footprint calculators are available on the Internet.

SUMMARY

1. The depletion of non-renewable natural resources and the overuse of renewable natural resources by the present generation will make these resources more costly for future generations.
2. The present generation has an obligation to future generations to develop in a sustainable way. The economist's definition of sustainability does not involve preserving particular stocks of natural resources. Instead, it involves each generation bequeathing to the subsequent generation whatever it takes to maintain the standard of living prevalent in the bequeathing generation.

3. Ecological economists recommend a steady state economy where growth in the economy's use of natural resources stops while the qualitative improvement of people's lives, or development, continues.
4. Economists use growth in Gross Domestic Product as an indicator of policy success. GDP has many drawbacks as an indicator of the success of environmental policies, or as an indicator of sustainable human welfare.
5. Economists developed GDP as a measure of the total amount of economic activity in a country in a particular period. As such, it treats as positive contributions to GDP both consumer expenditures that contribute to human welfare and the medical and cleanup costs of pollution that detract from human welfare. GDP not only ignores the value of unwaged childcare and housework, but also ignores the services provided to people by the ecosystems in which they live. GDP is insensitive to income inequalities that decrease human welfare because of the diminishing marginal utility of income. Nor is it sensitive to issues of fairness and human rights. GDP is thoroughly and parochially anthropocentric. It considers only the interests of human beings living within a particular country in a particular period. It ignores the effects of market decisions on distant and future people, and on nonhuman living beings.
6. People have developed alternative indicators of sustainable development, like the Genuine Progress Indicator, that avoid some of the weaknesses of the GDP.

ONLINE READING QUESTIONS

The book's website contains reading questions on this chapter. Working through these questions will help you understand, remember, and apply important concepts from the chapter. Some of the questions supply useful hints for the study questions.

STUDY QUESTIONS

Using the text and hints from the online reading questions, write out, type, dictate to your computer, or at least formulate in your head answers to the following questions.

1. Explain how the GDP fails to account for the external costs of pollution properly.
2. Explain how the GDP fails to account for the costs of resource depletion properly.

QUESTIONS TO PONDER

Spend a few minutes thinking about the following questions, or, better yet, discuss them with fellow readers of this book.

1. Find an ecological footprint calculator on the web and calculate your own ecological footprint.
2. Find a carbon footprint calculator on the web and calculate your own carbon footprint.
3. Read about the construction of the Happy Planet Index on its website. Is this a more appropriate indicator of sustainable development than the GPI?

Chapter 24

THE
MARKET
WORLDVIEW

UNTIL A FEW CENTURIES AGO, SUBSISTENCE PRODUCTION AND SELF-SUFFICIENCY were the norm. Most families consumed what they produced themselves, and used market exchange only to acquire luxuries. Even before the development of money, people traded goods and services. After the development of widely accepted currencies, the exchange of goods and services became much easier. Industrialization changed this way of life. The accumulation of physical capital, the use of fossil fuels for energy, and the productivity gains from division of labour in the factory made it more efficient for people to specialize in the production of just one part of a good or service, and to buy whatever else they needed in the marketplace. Everything had a price. The new market society displaced the old feudal system where everyone had a place in the great hierarchy of being, a place to which they were tied by birth. People became mobile, moved to the cities, and started to depend on market exchanges with others for their livelihoods. The process accelerated in the second half of the twentieth century as development in mechanical and chemical agricultural techniques enabled a very small proportion of the population to feed the rest. The organization of industrial economies existed in two forms, centrally planned socialist economies, and decentralized capitalist economies. Since the last decade of the twentieth century, the capitalist decentralized planning has proved to be the more efficient of the two at allocating productive resources. Markets in capital as well as in consumer goods and services have spread around the globe. Many people now live in highly developed market societies.

An industrialized and urbanized market economy separates people from their natural environment and the land that previously supported them. These processes transform people both physically and mentally. Instead of being part of a community whose members have bonds of reciprocal cooperation, people are now mobile. They are isolated individuals whose only responsibility is to look after themselves and their families. Natural resources are commodities, priced according to what others were willing to pay for them. The obligations that people once owed to others have become services for which others now have to pay. The market economy has brought with it a worldview that seems normal to us now. It becomes visible to us only when we contrast it, for example, with the religious, hierarchical, feudal worldview of the Middle Ages.

In this last chapter, we will look at the worldview of market societies. Market societies bring with them a conceptual framework. We will review the ethical justifications for this conceptual framework and examine its ethical weaknesses. We will also look at the conception of the nature of ethics that underlies the market worldview. A market economy is an incredibly efficient mechanism for turning natural resources into both human welfare and pollution. The conceptual tools of environmental ethics provide a critical perspective on the widely accepted ways of thinking and valuing that underlie the market-based approach to environmental problems.

Learning Objectives

1. To consider whether the market-based approach to the environment is a conceptual framework.
2. To review the justification and critique of a market-based approach to environmental problems.
3. To understand the metaethical assumptions of the market-based approach to the environment.

THE CONCEPTUAL FRAMEWORK OF A MARKET SOCIETY

A conceptual framework is a self-reinforcing collection of basic ethical, natural, and sometimes supernatural beliefs that make certain ethical judgments seem natural and easy to justify, and makes dissenting ethical judgments difficult to justify or even understand. A conceptual framework contains core beliefs about what is valuable or virtuous and why, and beliefs about human nature. Typically, conceptual frameworks do not change in response to one argument, but instead require a revolution in thinking that is the culmination of extended critique. Metaphorically, a conceptual framework is like an ecosystem of ideas that modifies itself to remain stable in response to changes in its intellectual environment. The various species of ideas that make up the conceptual framework interact in ways that maintain the integrity of the whole system, and make it resilient in the face of external criticism.

In previous chapters, we have examined some examples of alternative conceptual frameworks. Paul Taylor recommended that we adopt the biocentric outlook on nature and offered us a rational justification for doing so. Karen Warren argued that there were important analogies between the oppressive conceptual framework of a patriarchal society and the logic of domination that structures our interaction with the environment. Arne Naess suggested that the conceptual framework within which we think about the nature of our selves is too narrow, and presented considerations favouring a wider notion of the self and a deeper connection to the environment. It may also be useful to think of market society as imposing a conceptual framework on how we think. The way of thinking necessary to getting on within a market economy seems both natural and normal to us. Most of the time, it is difficult for us to think outside the box imposed by participation in market society. Usually we buy the cheapest goods and services, not the ones most ethically produced.

The conceptual framework of a market economy provides us with a core ethical theory of value. Everything is a commodity, and how much people are willing to pay for a thing determines its value. It also provides a selection of core moral theories. How things should work is justified by contractarianism, libertarianism, or indirect economic utilitarianism. Proponents of the market-based conceptual framework often move between these various justifications, but the most powerful one is the last. Economic utilitarianism is the predominant ethical theory most applicable to environmental policy. The market worldview has a logic of domination embodied in its market-based anthropocentrism. Only humans beings can participate in markets, and, of these, only the ones in a particular market have moral standing within that market. Only the interests and preferences of human participants in a particular market receive consideration within the market mechanism. Others in distant countries and future generations, and all living beings and ecosystems not capable of buying and selling, have their interests ignored by market forces. In the absence of market failures, like the external costs of pollution and the public goods of cleaning it up, these market forces would otherwise supposedly maximize aggregate preference satisfaction for participants in the market.

The conceptual framework of market society accepts the understanding of nature given to us by modern science. It stresses, however, a particular idealization of human nature that permits the development of economics. Its core empirical theory of human nature, which is a version of psychological egoism, sees human beings as rational agents. Rational agents pursue their own self-interest. Each agent tries to maximize the expected value of her own utility. In doing so, she is risk neutral. She calculates the value of each option by multiplying how much she is willing to pay to have that option by the probability that her actions will bring it about, and then chooses the course of action that has the maximum expected payoff. She cooperates with others for mutual benefit according to the rules of the free market. This conception of human nature is the conception of economic man or *Homo economicus*—a word play on the name of our species, *Homo sapiens*. This view of human nature has a history. It did not exist in hunter-gatherer societies that emphasized the virtues of sharing over those of accumulation. It came into being with the growth of capitalism, and now seems natural to us.

It is perhaps easiest to see the conceptual framework of modern industrial economies by comparing it to a different one, the conceptual framework prevalent in Medieval Europe. People in Medieval European society had a shared worldview based on a biblical cosmology, a Ptolemaic and geocentric view of astronomy, and an Aristotelian and teleological notion of science. Its view of the nature of things and its view of the nature of human beings were both religious. Humans were immortal souls trapped in sinful, animal-like bodies. It had a divine command theory of ethics, based on priestly interpretation of the Bible. It had an obvious logic of domination embodied in a hierarchical chain of being, with God at the top, angels below God but above humans, and humans morally superior to animals, plants, and the rest of the environment.

	MARKET SOCIETY	MEDIEVAL EUROPE
View of nature	Modern science	Ptolemaic astronomy Aristotelian science Biblical cosmology
Metaphysics	Secular Physicalist Commoditised	Religious God's creation Heaven/Hell
Human nature	Psychological egoism Selfish Rational maximizer Risk neutral	Immortal soul in bestial body Fallen/Sinful
Ethics	Anthropocentric Economic utilitarianism Willingness to pay	Divine command
Logic of domination	Market-based anthropocentrism	Hierarchical chain of being

TABLE 24.1: Comparison of the worldviews of market and medieval societies

We have come to see the world through a lens provided by the market-based worldview. The task of making markets friendlier to the environment will not be easy. No one philosophical argument is likely to change the market-based worldview. Philosophy has a role in adding to a general ethical critique that can lead to large-scale attitude change.

JUSTIFICATION AND CRITIQUE

We have examined four different proposed ethical justifications for economic markets. Each attempts to justify a different approach to the interaction of a market economy and the environment. The contractarian approach sees state enforced market rules as a way for psychological egoists to avoid the dilemmas of cooperation. The libertarian approach sees the legal rules of the market as embodying natural rights to acquire and exchange goods and services. Both of these justifications lead to the *laissez-faire* approach to environmental problems of market fundamentalism. The indirect utilitarian approach sees the rules of the market place as a way for psychological egoists, each acting in their own self-interest, to produce the maximum possible amount of goods and services for everyone. Solving environmental problems within this approach leads to the methods of either free-market environmentalism or environmental economics. The social contract approach to justice sees the market as a means to maximize the amount of goods and services available to the least advantaged members of a society.

Figure 24.1 shows these different justifications for a market economy and the approaches to the environment to which they give rise.

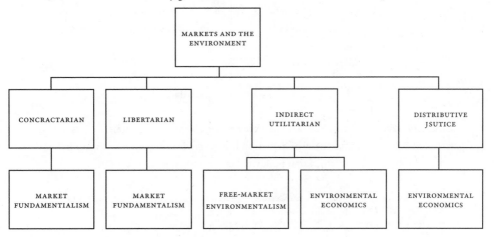

FIGURE 24.1: Justifications for economic markets and market-based approaches to the environment

The predominant justification for economic markets is the indirect utilitarian one. In this case, political reasoning bolsters ethical reasoning. Historically, the economic performance of market economies has been superior to that of command economies. Countries with large GDPs can afford to have large armed forces, and are important trading partners for other countries. The power of a country in world affairs depends largely on the size of its economy. National planners focus on the growth of GDP, which they see as a good thing both because it results in more consumption by individuals and because of its effect on the common good.

According to the indirect form of preference-satisfaction utilitarianism, policymakers should implement policies that cause the maximum aggregated satisfaction of preferences for all entities with moral standing. As we have seen, this approach to ethics raises many questions. Is preference satisfaction always ethically valuable? Is it the only thing that is ethically valuable? How do we measure preference satisfaction so that we can aggregate it? How do we aggregate preference satisfaction so that we can maximize it? What happens if maximizing preference satisfaction violates rights or ethical principles? What happens if maximizing preference satisfaction produces an unjust distribution of benefits and burdens? What ethical judgment do we make on the characters of utilitarian agents? Are the only entities that have moral standing those which have the mental capacity to have preferences?

With respect to economics and the environment, indirect preference-satisfaction utilitarianism exists in the form of economic utilitarianism. Economic utilitarianism holds that policymakers should implement market-based economic policies that maximize aggregate preference as measured by willingness to pay. Under certain conditions, conditions of perfect competition, a market economy will maximize preference satisfaction without any intervention by government policy. Table 24.2 lists some important conditions for market efficiency. Market failures occur when the conditions are not satisfied.

ECONOMIC	ENVIRONMENTAL
No monopoly buyers	No public goods
No monopoly sellers	No external costs
No economies of scale	No common property
No information problems	
No transaction costs	

TABLE 24.2: Conditions of market efficiency

The total social costs of economic activities are often greater than the internal costs to market participants. Pollution and resource depletion lead to environmental market failures and to intervention by economic utilitarian policymakers, as shown in Figure 24.2.

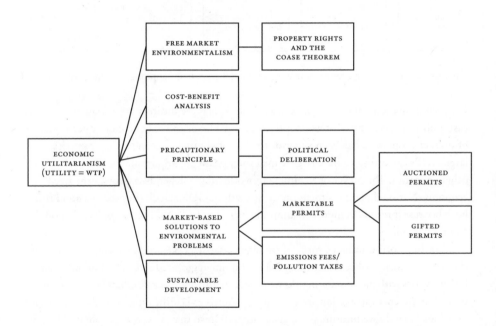

FIGURE 24.2: Taxonomy of economic utilitarian environmental policies

Economic utilitarianism has many weaknesses as an ethical theory. Willingness to pay is not a good measure of the intensity of preferences. It is distorted by wealth. It does not distinguish moral and immoral preferences. It is distorted by free-rider problems. Many valuable things do not have market values. The market economic system and utilitarian economics are compatible with human rights abuses. There are countries with flourishing market economies that do not permit political freedoms. Economic utilitarianism is insensitive to issues of distributive justice. In the model of two economies in Table 24.3, the lowest 20% of the population by income, or the bottom quintile, get 20 units of income in distribution A and only 5 units in distribution B.

QUINTILE	BOTTOM	2ND	3RD	4TH	TOP	TOTAL
A	20	20	20	20	20	100
B	5	5	5	5	81	101

TABLE 24.3: Fairness vs. maximization in income distribution

The economic utilitarian, market-based approach would favour distribution B over distribution A because B maximizes the number of units of income produced, even though A is much fairer. (Since economic utilitarians measure the utility of a good according to willingness to pay for that good, they cannot talk about the decreasing marginal utility of income. People's willingness to pay for a dollar is always a dollar. Consequently, economic utilitarians cannot use the declining marginal utility of income to say that an unequal distribution does not maximize utility, as traditional utilitarians can. Thus, economic utilitarians cannot reply to this objection by saying that inegalitarian distribution B has a lower utility than does egalitarian distribution A.) According to the indirect economic utilitarian justification of the market approach to the environment, people maximize utility by behaving as psychological egoists.

Economic utilitarianism is very tightly anthropocentric. Strictly speaking, it tells us to grant moral consideration only to possible participants in our own market, to ourselves, our friends and family, and other citizens of the same country and its close trading partners. It denies moral standing to foreigners who participate in different markets, future generations, animals, plants, natural objects, species, and ecosystems.

MARKETS AND METAETHICS

The market worldview contains a theory of human nature, which sees human beings as rational, risk neutral, calculators of self-interest. It contains a theory of ethics, predominantly indirect preference-satisfaction utilitarianism, and a theory of value, where willingness to pay measures value. The market worldview even contains a theory of the nature of ethics, simple metaethical expressivism. The simple expressivist metaethics of the market worldview has broad implications for the conceptual framework of the market.

Metaethical expressivism is the view that to say something is right or wrong is to express an attitude toward it. Such an expression of attitude is neither true nor false. For example, the ethical judgment that our country should implement a carbon tax means something like, "Hoorah for our country implementing a carbon tax!" Ethical argument is then about whether the attitude of approval or disapproval is appropriate. The preference satisfaction theory of value fits best with expressivism in metaethics. Wants and preferences are neither true nor false. We have a privileged status with regard to determining whether we want something. We do not usually argue with someone's expression of a preference. To the expression of preference, "I want vanilla ice cream," the response of "No, you don't," is seldom appropriate. We do not offer reasons for our wants and preferences. Instead, we express our preferences by our choices in an economic market. The preference-satisfaction theory of value employed by economics is a very simple form of expressivism, which takes preferences as brute facts and which has no need for a way of resolving differences about what preferences are best or most appropriate to have. We cannot say of our preferences that they are true or false, but we can say whether they are strong or weak. We cannot measure the truth-value of our preferences, but we can measure the intensity of preferences. We reveal the intensity of our preferences by our willingness to pay for goods and services in a market. The market is not concerned with any reasons that we might give for our preferences. It is concerned only with what we are willing to pay to have them satisfied. The market treats our choices as expressing preferences for goods and services that are more or less intense. It does not treat our choices as stemming from beliefs about value, beliefs whose truth or falsity is open to reasoning and debate.

Metaethical cognitivism, on the other hand, is the theory when we say that some policy is right (or wrong) we assert our belief that it is right (or wrong). Such an assertion of belief can be either true or false. Many philosophers claim that we do not make value judgments just by expressing our preferences, but that instead we have beliefs about what is valuable. They think we can offer reasons for our beliefs about value, and that such beliefs are subject to rational evaluation through argument and debate.

Resolving the disagreement between expressivism and cognitivism is beyond the scope of this book. Nevertheless, we can review the philosophical issue between them. A theory of the nature of ethics must explain both the action-guiding and the agreement-seeking nature of ethical judgments. The strength of expressivism is that it can explain why ethical judgments have action-guiding force: the attitudes that they express will motivate people to act in various ways. The weakness of the simple expressivism that is the metaethics of economic utilitarianism is that it cannot explain how people seek agreement in their ethical judgments. Seeking agreement requires argument and debate. This requires logical reasoning, and simple expressivism has difficulty accounting for logical reasoning about ethical judgments. The strength of cognitivism is that it explains how people seek agreement about ethical judgments. Ethical judgments are assertions of beliefs that can be true or false, and we can use them to construct arguments just as we use factual assertions. The weakness of cognitivism is that it has trouble explaining the action-guiding aspect of ethical judgments because beliefs, by themselves, do not motivate people. Some emotional component is needed as well.

The problem with the market worldview is not that it depends on expressivism in metaethics. Philosophers may be able to develop a form of expressivism that can account for the agreement-seeking aspect of ethical judgments, and this form of expressivism may well become the best philosophical theory of the nature of ethics. The problem with the market worldview is that it fails to recognize the need for the agreement-seeking aspect of ethical judgments. Because it fails even to recognize the need for deliberation and debate in the discovery of what is ethically required, the market worldview is an overly simplistic form of expressivism. The simplistic expressivism underlying the conceptual framework of market thinking leads to an ethic in which the intensity of preferences can be measured, but in which the reasons behind these preferences cannot be discussed. This fails to respect adequately the way in which people support their values by reasons. Mark Sagoff, who has written extensively on economics and the environment, describes the issue as follows:

The problem is this: An efficiency criterion, as it is used to evaluate public policy, assumes that the goals of our society are contained in the preferences individuals reveal or would reveal in markets. Such an approach may appear attractive, even just, because it treats everyone as equal, at least theoretically, by according to each person's preferences the same respect and concern. To treat a person with respect, however, is also to listen and respond intelligently to his or her views and opinions. This is not the same thing as to ask how much he or she is willing to pay for them. The cost-benefit analyst does not ask economists how much they are willing to pay for what they believe, that is, that the workplace and the environment should be made efficient. Why, then, does the analyst ask workers, environmentalists, and others how much they are willing to pay for what they believe is right? Are economists the only ones who can back their ideas with reasons while the rest of us can only pay a price? A cost-benefit approach treats people as of equal worth because it treats them as of no worth, but only as places or channels at which willingness to pay is found. (Sagoff 1981: 1290–91)

Sagoff points out that people who defend the market worldview are not even consistent. An economist who is defending a cost-benefit approach to environmental problems does not say that people should accept a cost-benefit approach because they are willing to pay more for that approach to be used than they are willing to pay for any alternative approach to be used. Instead, the defender of the cost-benefit approach presents reasons for accepting the approach, reasons that are open to critical evaluation through public deliberation.

A market-based approach to solving environmental problems fails to distinguish between a person's preference for chocolate over vanilla ice cream and a person's preference for the implementation of a carbon tax over the implementation of a system of gifted marketable carbon emission permits. In the first case, a simple expressivist theory of value is appropriate; in the second case, it is not. An adequate discussion of the latter issue requires more than a measurement of the costs and benefits of each proposal. Any adequate discussion of the latter requires public deliberation about issues of fairness and justice. We should not try to resolve complex ethical issues regarding the environment simply by measuring the intensity of people's preferences. We can see this more clearly by imagining how it would be to apply economic reasoning to other ethical issues, like that of the abortion debate. A 1970s era economics text makes the extreme suggestion that "... there is an optimal number of abortions, just as there is an optimal level of pollution, or purity.... Those who oppose abortion could eliminate abortions entirely, if their intensity of feeling were so strong as to lead to payments that were greater at the margin than the price anyone would pay to have an abortion" (Macaulay 1977: 120–21; quoted in Sagoff 1981: 1294). This market-based form of thinking seems absurd in the context of an ethical debate over abortion. Economic analysis confuses preferences to consume and beliefs about value.

People make judgments about what to buy according to their preferences to consume, but they make judgments about what policies to support as citizens with beliefs about what is valuable. Their consumption preferences and their political values are not necessarily even consistent, as illustrated in this tongue-in-cheek passage from Mark Sagoff.

> Are my preferences as a consumer consistent with my judgments as a citizen?
> They are not.... Last year, I fixed a couple of tickets and was happy to do so since
> I saved fifty dollars. Yet, at election time, I helped to vote the corrupt judge out
> of office. I speed on the highway; yet I want the police to enforce laws against
> speeding.... I love my car; I hate the bus. Yet I vote for candidates who promise
> to tax gasoline to pay for public transportation. And of course I applaud the
> Endangered Species Act, although I have no earthly use for the Colorado squaw
> fish or the Indiana bat.... I have an "Ecology Now" sticker on a car that leaks oil
> everywhere it's parked. (Sagoff 1981: 1286)

The market worldview understands people only as consumers and not as citizens, only as bundles of preferences and not as reasonable evaluators. Any adequate theory of human nature and any adequate theory of metaethics must take into account both of these sides to people.

Market metaethics uncritically takes people's preferences as it finds them. The market worldview's utilitarian ethical theory calls for the maximization of the preferences that people actually have, whether or not these preferences are good for the person. Actual-preference theories of value contrast with informed-preference theories. In an informed-preference theory, what is intrinsically valuable is satisfying the preferences that people would have if they had full information and made no mistakes in their reasoning. To recall an earlier example, a person would not want the chicken sandwich that she presently wants in a careless restaurant if she had full information about the sandwich's salmonella bacteria concentration. The preferences that a person would be disposed to have, if he or she were fully informed and rational, are not always the same as the preferences the person actually has. When we say that an outcome is valuable on an informed-preference theory, we are not expressing an actual want for it. We are making a hypothesis that, if we were fully rational and informed, then we would want that outcome. A hypothesis is not an expression of our wants or preferences, but is an assertion of belief about what we would be disposed to want under perfect conditions. That a person would prefer something if she were fully informed is an assertion which is either true or false, which can be reasoned about, and which she can discuss with other people. We treat actual preferences through calculations of intensity as revealed in a market economy. We treat informed preferences in a context of discussion, debate, and public deliberation.

The market worldview gives equal consideration to all preferences no matter what their nature. Yet, there seem to be many preferences whose satisfaction have no value, or worse, are immoral. Preferences can be silly, trivial, foolish, dangerous or harmful to others, vulgar, slothful, intemperate or decadent, selfish, greedy, thoughtless of others, jealous, masochistic or harmful to self, emotionally, physically, or sexually sadistic, criminal, racist, homophobic, sexist, pedophilic, and even psychopathic. Why should the satisfaction of such preferences be the goal of policymakers? Preferences should not be taken as given, but should themselves be open to critical reflection.

Certain sorts of character traits enable people to flourish in market societies. Virtue ethicists would say that these character traits are vices that make people selfish, greedy, self-centred, atomistic, individualistic, cold-hearted, mean-spirited, avaricious, money-grubbing, miserly, mercenary, ungenerous, and uncharitable. Communitarians would say that the economic power of maximizing market society destroys communities based on fellowship, reciprocity, fraternity and sorority, cooperation, community membership, communal feeling, loyalty, unity, solidarity, and the common good. One important type of community is a democracy. A healthy and sustainable democracy requires certain character traits. It requires that people think of themselves as concerned and participating citizens, and not just as individual consumers. Consumers merely seek out ways to satisfy their preferences with little regard for the environment. They treat the environment as a resource for satisfying their preferences and as having only instrumental value. Citizens actively debate the intrinsic value of conserving the environment. They participate in the formulation of government policy. Their beliefs about what is valuable lead them to take part in environmental actions to preserve the countryside, even though they might prefer to spend their time watching nature shows on a new wide-screen television bought at a great low price.

CONCLUSION

Our examination of environmental ethics has taken us full circle, from a discussion of the nature of ethics, through the variety of ethical theories and theories of moral standing, by way of the economic approach to the environment, and finally back to the nature of ethics and the critique of the conceptual framework of the market. We have found no definitive answers to any major environmental problems, but we have developed a range of conceptual tools that are useful for solving these problems in ethically acceptable ways. Environmental science and environmental economics alone cannot tell us what we should do. Only by also thinking about environmental problems from an ethical perspective can we find the solutions that we need, and give convincing reasons for them in the public forum of democratic deliberation.

SUMMARY

1. The core beliefs of the conceptual framework of the market worldview include the view of nature of modern science, and a highly idealized view of human nature. Human beings are rational calculators of economic advantage, each trying to maximize his or her self-interest.

2. The ethical theory that underlies the market worldview may be contractarian, libertarian, egalitarian, or indirect utilitarian, but is predominantly the last. Everyone acting in their own self-interest, while following the rules of the market, will maximize the aggregate good for everyone. Market failures, such as the external costs of pollution and resource depletion, require special treatment with the techniques of free-market environmentalism and environmental economics.

3. The theory of value that underlies the market worldview is that only the satisfaction of actual preferences is intrinsically valuable, where the intensity of a person's preference is measured by how much the person would be willing to pay to have that preference satisfied.
4. The metaethics that underlies the market worldview is a simple form of expressivism that makes no provision for the agreement-seeking aspect of ethical judgments.
5. The simplistic expressivism that underlies the market worldview does not give proper respect to the ethical side of human nature, where human beings assert beliefs about what is valuable, rather than merely expressing their preferences for consumer items. Beliefs about value can be true or false, and can be tested through reasoning and debate. Preferences only differ in intensity, which the market measures according to willingness to pay.
6. The dominance of the market worldview encourages people to think of themselves as consumers and not as citizens. Citizens participate in public deliberation and democratic decision-making regarding solutions to environmental problems.

ONLINE READING QUESTIONS

The book's website contains reading questions on this chapter. Working through these questions will help you understand, remember, and apply important concepts from the chapter. Some of the questions supply useful hints for the study questions.

STUDY QUESTIONS

Using the text and hints from the online reading questions, write out, type, dictate to your computer, or at least formulate in your head answers to the following questions.

1. What are the core beliefs of the conceptual framework of the market worldview?
2. Describe the weaknesses of the metaethics of the market worldview.
3. Explain how the economic utilitarian approach to the environment can conflict with the ideals of democratic citizenship.

QUESTIONS TO PONDER

Spend a few minutes thinking about the following questions, or, better yet, discuss them with fellow readers of this book.

1. The market worldview is just common sense. Modern economic science shows that all the core beliefs of its conceptual framework are true. The conceptual framework of economic science is not just one alternative

conceptual framework among many; it is the correct conceptual framework. Comment on this view.

2. The core idea of democracy is that everyone should have a vote. Voting provides a way of aggregating the political preferences of all citizens, and of making a decision about environmental policy. Whatever environmental policy this democratic process decides on is the correct one. Comment on this view.

3. How can abstract philosophical theories about the nature of ethics have anything to do with real world environmental policy? We should be interested in normative ethics, not metaethics. Comment on this view.

GLOSSARY

An ACCUMULATIVE HARM is a type of harm such that individual acts are not harmful (or produce vanishingly, immeasurably small harms), but when many individuals perform the acts, they accumulate into a serious harm to others.

ACTUAL-VALUE UTILITARIANISM judges an agent's action based on the utility the action actually produces instead of the utility the agent expected to produce.

ACT UTILITARIANISM is a form of direct utilitarianism that requires maximizing utility as a decision procedure for each action.

An ethical strategy involving ADAPTIVE PREFERENCES maximizes people's preference satisfaction by getting them to prefer less.

ANTHROPOCENTRIC, or human-centred, theories of environmental ethics consider only humans, members of the species *Homo sapiens*, to have moral standing.

AUTONOMY is the capacity to make competent, rational choices.

AVERAGE UTILITARIANISM maximizes the aggregate utility per person instead of the total utility of the group.

BIOCENTRIC theories of environmental ethics extend moral standing to all living things, including plants.

BIOCENTRIC EGALITARIANISM (Taylor) is the view that all living things have equal inherent worth and must be treated as moral equals in ethical reasoning.

BIODIVERSITY (or biological diversity) is the number or variety of species of organisms in a particular area.

The CARRYING CAPACITY of a species in an ecosystem is the number of individual organisms it can support indefinitely given its fixed resources.

The COASE THEOREM states that if private property rights are clearly defined and agents can negotiate, with no transaction costs, the buying and selling of rights to do activities that cause external costs, then bargaining can always find solutions that maximize preference satisfaction through minimizing total social costs. Counter-intuitively, the parties will be able to achieve a socially efficient outcome regardless of how the property rights are initially assigned.

COLLECTIVE GOODS are economic goods that people can be stopped from consuming, but whose use by one person does not diminish their availability to others (excludable and non-rival).

COMMONS GOODS are open-access economic goods that people cannot be stopped from using, but whose use by one person diminishes their value for others (non-excludable and rival).

The COMPENSATION test says that one situation is an improvement over another, even if some people in the old situation lose out, so long as, in the new situation, it is possible for those who are made better off to compensate those who are made worse off without themselves becoming worse off than they were in the old situation.

A CONCEPTUAL FRAMEWORK is a mutually supporting, seldom questioned, and resilient set of fundamental assumptions about the world, about human nature, and about ethical values, that affects how people think and act in the world.

A COMMON RESOURCE is a resource that is rival but non-excludable.

The COMMON GOOD APPROACH is a type of objective consequentialism in which each agent ought to act so as to contribute to the betterment of the community as a whole.

The role of COMPENSATORY JUSTICE is to ensure that people who harm others give their victims fair compensation for their injury.

CONSEQUENTIALISM is the ethical approach that assesses an action by considering how beneficial or harmful the consequences of that action are.

The CONTINGENT VALUATION METHOD uses carefully designed surveys to ask people directly how much they would be willing to pay for some benefit, or how much compensation they would expect for a cost.

CONTRACTARIANISM is the view that ethics is a state-enforced social contract that forces cooperation between ethical egoists.

If B has a right that A do X, then A has a CORRELATIVE DUTY to B to do X. A's duty is a direct duty owed to B.

A COST-BENEFIT ANALYSIS is a technique of environmental economics where the costs and benefits of different environmental policies are measured according to people's willingness to pay for them. The total net benefits of each policy are calculated and used either as a factual input to a policy decision, or as a way of making a policy decision.

COST-EFFECTIVENESS analysis is a method for deciding how to implement a chosen policy most efficiently or with least total social cost.

DEONTOLOGY is the ethical approach that focuses on the principles that guide the action, and assesses the action as right or wrong according to what duties the action complies with or according to what rights the action respects.

DESCRIPTIVE ETHICS is a branch of sociology whose goal is to describe the ethical beliefs of a community or culture.

DEVELOPMENT is a condition of qualitative improvements in the services and the physical artefacts and activities of the economy. It is based on better knowledge and not on greater use of natural resources and energy.

A DIRECT DUTY is a duty regarding a non-human entity that an agent owes to that non-human entity itself.

DIRECT UTILITARIANISM treats utilitarianism as a decision procedure, where each act must be judged according to a calculation of the utilities it causes.

The DISCOUNT RATE is the relevant percentage rate per year by which the value of a future cost or benefit is converted into a present value for comparison purposes.

According to the DISPOSITIONAL APPROACH to ethical value, each agent ought to act so as to best satisfy the wants that people would have if they were fully informed and were reasoning rationally.

DISTRIBUTIVE JUSTICE is concerned with how to distribute benefits and burdens in a fair way in society.

DIVINE COMMAND THEORIES are deontological ethical theories in which the moral principles that the agent should obey are the commands of God.

A DOMINANT STRATEGY in game theory is a strategy that yields a higher payoff regardless of the strategy chosen by the other player.

ECOCENTRIC theories of environmental ethics extend moral standing to ecosystems.

ECONOMIC UTILITARIANISM is an ethical theory that tells policymakers to implement policies that cause maximum aggregate net benefits, where net benefits are measured according to people's willingness to pay for economic goods and services.

An ECOSYSTEM is a biological community, together with its physical environment, functioning as a whole.

ENVIRONMENTAL CLASSISM occurs when environmental burdens fall unequally on poor people.

ENVIRONMENTAL ECONOMICS is an approach that recognizes market failures regarding the environment and studies how we can take collective action to fix environmental problems in a cost-effective manner.

ENVIRONMENTAL RACISM occurs when environmental burdens fall unequally on people of different racial or ethnic descent.

ETHICAL COGNITIVISM is the metaethical view that to say an action is right or wrong is to assert a belief about it, an assertion that can be either true or false.

ETHICAL EGOISM is the consequentialist ethical theory that people should always act in their own self-interest, or that they are morally obligated to do what is best for themselves.

ETHICAL EXPRESSIVISM is the metaethical view that to say an action is right or wrong is to express an attitude toward that action.

ETHICAL HOLISM is the view that wholes have moral standing either as well as, or instead of, their constituent parts.

ETHICAL NIHILISM is the metaethical view that there is no such thing as right or wrong.

ETHICAL RELATIVISM is the metaethical view that whether an action is right or wrong depends on the cultural membership of the person making a judgment on the action.

ETHICAL SCEPTICISM is the metaethical view that actions may be either right or wrong, but that we can never know which they are.

ETHICAL UNIVERSALISM is the metaethical view that if an action is the right action, then it is the right action for everyone in a similar situation.

An EXCLUDABLE GOOD is an economic good that it is possible to prevent individuals who do not pay for the good from consuming.

EXPECTED-VALUE UTILITARIANISM judges an agent's action based on the utility that the agent might reasonably have expected it to produce instead of the utility that the action actually produced.

An EXPERIENCING SUBJECT OF A LIFE (Regan) is a conscious creature with the capacity to want, prefer, believe, feel, recall, and expect things.

An EXTERNAL BENEFIT or positive externality is a benefit arising from the economic activity of an agent for which the agent is not compensated because the cost is not incorporated into the market price of the product.

An EXTERNAL COST or negative externality is a cost arising from the economic activity of an agent that is born by others because the cost is not incorporated into the market price of the product.

The FACT/VALUE DISTINCTION is the distinction between questions of scientific fact and questions of ethical value.

The FALLACY OF COMPOSITION says that it is incorrect to argue from the premise that a part has a certain property to the conclusion that the whole has that property.

The FALLACY OF DECOMPOSITION (or fallacy of division) says that it is incorrect to argue from the premise that a whole has a certain property to the conclusion that any of its parts have that property.

FREE-MARKET ENVIRONMENTALISM is the view that the bad environmental effects of market behaviour are not ethically permissible, but that the best solution to all environmental problems is to privatize the environment.

FREE-RIDERS enjoy the benefits of a public good without bearing the burdens of providing it because it is difficult or impossible to prevent non-contributors from enjoying a public good.

The GAIA HYPOTHESIS (Lovelock) is the hypothesis that Earth itself should be thought of as a self-regulating system that has stability as its goal.

A GENERAL RIGHT is a right whose correlative duty falls on everyone.

The GROSS DOMESTIC PRODUCT (GDP) is the market value of all final goods and services produced within the borders of a country during a given time period.

GROWTH is a condition of quantitative increase in the physical size of the economy including its use of natural resources and energy.

A population experiences GEOMETRIC GROWTH when the change in the size of the population in each generation is proportional to the size of the population in the preceding generation.

The HARM PRINCIPLE says that people (or the government) are permitted to interfere with someone's freedom, liberty, or exercise of their rights only in order to prevent harm to others.

According to HEDONISTIC UTILITARIANISM, each agent ought to cause the maximum balance of pleasure over pain for recipients with moral standing.

HOLISTIC theories of moral standing extend moral concern to organized wholes composed of individual entities.

IDENTIFICATION occurs when people have the same emotional attitudes toward the qualities of other persons or objects that they have toward those qualities in themselves.

An INCENTIVE is an additional property right, to something like more money, that motivates people to produce more.

An INDIRECT DUTY is a duty regarding a non-human entity that an agent owes to a person.

INDIRECT UTILITARIANISM treats utilitarianism as a standard of rightness for the application of the tools of non-utilitarian ethical theories. It advocates obedience to principles, respect for rights, inculcation of virtues, or other ethical tools in order to produce maximum aggregate utility.

INDIVIDUALISTIC theories of moral standing extend moral concern only to individual entities. Species and ecosystems are not individual entities.

A state of affairs is INSTRUMENTALLY VALUABLE if it brings about or causes another state of affairs that is valuable.

An INTENTION is a goal or plan that guides an action.

The INTEREST THEORY OF RIGHTS holds that the inherently valuable natural feature that justifies possession of a moral right is the interests of the right-holder.

A state of affairs is INTRINSICALLY VALUABLE if it is valuable for its own sake (though it might also be valuable because of some other state of affairs that it can bring about).

JUSTICE-BASED THEORIES are deontological ethical theories in which the moral principles that the agent should obey concern treating all morally considerable recipients fairly and as moral equals.

KINSHIP SELECTION is an evolutionary strategy that results in organisms having altruistic tendencies toward relatives who carry the same genes.

The LAW OF DIMINISHING MARGINAL UTILITY states that as the consumption of a given economic good increases, the marginal utility produced by the consumption of one additional unit of the good tends to decrease.

The LAW OF INCREASING MARGINAL COST is the assumption of economic reasoning that, in the short-term, the marginal cost of producing each additional item will tend to increase.

LEGAL RIGHTS are rights that people have that are justified according to legal standards.

LIBERTARIAN theories of justice justify a system of private property through the existence of natural moral rights to liberty and self-ownership.

LIBERAL FEMINISM denies there are morally relevant differences between men and women which prevent women having moral standing equal to that of men.

A LOGIC OF DOMINATION is a structure of argumentation that justifies relationships of domination and subordination.

The MARGINAL UTILITY of an economic good or service is the additional utility gained through the consumption of one additional unit of that good or service.

The conditions under which markets are not efficient are called MARKET FAILURES.

MARKET FUNDAMENTALISM is the view that, whatever the environmental effect of an economic market based on existing individual property rights, those effects are ethically permissible.

METAETHICS studies the meaning of ethical judgments.

METAPHYSICAL HOLISM is the claim that a whole has an independent existence that is just as real as that of its parts.

METHODOLOGICAL HOLISM is the philosophical view that we cannot have a complete understanding of a system just by knowing everything about is parts.

MORAL PATIENTS are individuals who do not have the capacity to act morally or immorally, but can still be acted on morally.

MORAL RIGHTS are rights that people have that are justified by moral standards.

An entity has MORAL STANDING if we must consider it (or its interests) for its (their) own sake when we are making an ethical judgment.

An entity is MORALLY CONSIDERABLE if the entity has moral standing.

A game has a NASH EQUILIBRIUM when there is a combination of strategies such that each player's strategy is the best he or she can choose given the other player's strategies.

According to theories of NATURAL RIGHTS, rights-bearers have rights because they have certain natural features.

The NATURALISTIC FALLACY is the fallacy of deriving ethical judgments from statements about the natural world.

A NEGATIVE RIGHT imposes a correlative duty on everyone else not to interfere with the right holder's activities.

A NEGATIVE EXTERNALITY (or external cost) is a cost arising from the economic activity of an agent that is born by others because the cost is not incorporated into the market price of the product.

NON-ANTHROPOCENTRIC theories of environmental ethics extend moral standing to non-human entities such as animals, plants, or ecosystems.

A NON-EXCLUDABLE GOOD, or an open-access resource, is a resource from which it is difficult to exclude other individuals.

A NON-RIVAL GOOD is an economic good whose consumption by one individual does not diminish its availability to others.

NON-POINT SOURCE POLLUTION happens when we cannot identify determinate individuals whose activity is causing the pollution.

NORMATIVE ECONOMICS is economic analysis that embodies ethical judgments about the right or best policy options.

NORMATIVE ETHICS identifies, justifies, and applies ethical judgments to the world we live in.

OBJECTIVE CONSEQUENTIALISM is a type of consequentialist ethical theory which holds that the intrinsic value which agents ought to cause is not constituted by any of the mental states of recipients.

An entity's OBJECTIVE GOOD is what is really good for it, whether or not it actually wants it.

In the OBJECTIVE INTERESTS approach to justifying natural rights, the inherently valuable feature that justifies rights is the non-mental benefit that will accrue to the rights-bearer.

An OPEN-ACCESS RESOURCE (or a non-excludable resource) is a resource from which it is difficult to exclude other individuals.

An OPPRESSIVE CONCEPTUAL FRAMEWORK is a conceptual framework that makes relationships of domination and subordination seem normal, natural, and unquestionable.

A market is PARETO EFFICIENT if no change can be made in the quantity produced that will make someone better off without also making someone worse off.

A change in the distribution of goods is a PARETO IMPROVEMENT if it makes at least one person better off without making any other person worse off.

A PAYOFF MATRIX for a game is a table that shows each player's payoff for every possible combination of strategies.

POINT SOURCE POLLUTION happens when we can easily identify determinate individuals whose activity is causing the harm done by the pollution.

A POLL TAX requires the same payment from each person regardless of his or her income.

A POPULATION of a species is a group (not a category) of individual organisms belonging to the same species living in a specified area or habitat.

POSITIVE ECONOMICS is economic analysis that offers scientific, cause-and-effect explanations of market behaviour that can, in principle, be confirmed or refuted by observational data.

A POSITIVE EXTERNALITY (or external benefit) is a benefit arising from the economic activity of an agent for which the agent is not compensated because the cost is not incorporated into the market price of the product.

A POSITIVE RIGHT imposes a correlative duty on others to assist the right bearer in some way.

According to PREFERENCE-SATISFACTION UTILITARIANISM, each agent ought to act to bring about the maximum amount of satisfied desires or preferences of recipients with moral standing.

A PROGRESSIVE TAX requires that those with more income pay a higher percentage of their income as tax than do those with less income.

A PROPORTIONAL TAX requires that all people pay an equal percentage of their income.

A game is called a PRISONER'S DILEMMA when both players have dominant strategies that, when played, result in an equilibrium with payoffs smaller than if each had played another strategy.

PRIVATE GOODS are economic goods from which it is possible to exclude others, and are such that their consumption by one person will prevent their consumption by others (excludable and rival).

PSYCHOLOGICAL EGOISM is the empirical theory that people always do act to maximize their own narrow self-interest.

PUBLIC GOODS are open-access goods whose use by one person does not diminish their availability to others (non-excludable and non-rival).

RADICAL FEMINISM affirms that there are morally relevant biological differences between men and women, and argues that these create, not different rights, but an alternative feminist perspective in ethics.

RECIPROCAL ALTRUISM is an evolutionary strategy in human populations that results in people being willing to bear a cost for others in situations in which they expect that they will receive a benefit back in the future.

A REGRESSIVE TAX requires that people with lower incomes pay a higher proportion of their income as tax.

The function of RETRIBUTIVE JUSTICE is to ensure that punishments are fair.

RIGHTS-BASED THEORIES are deontological ethical theories in which the moral principles that the agent should obey involve respecting the moral rights of ethically considerable recipients.

RISK is a condition where the outcome cannot be definitely predicted, but where the probabilities of different possible outcomes can be measured.

A policymaker who is RISK AVERSE will make a decision in a way that avoids seriously negative consequences, even if they have a low probability of happening, and even if this is contrary to expected-value rationality.

A policymaker who is RISK NEUTRAL will make a decision entirely on the basis of the expected values of the outcomes.

A RIVAL GOOD is a resource whose consumption by one individual diminishes its availability for others.

RULE UTILITARIANISM is a form of indirect utilitarianism that uses utilitarianism as a standard of rightness for which rules people should follow and which types of action they should perform.

SELF-REALIZATION, with a capital "S," is the Deep Ecology requirement that we seek a wide identification with both the human and non-human world.

A being has the capacity for SENTIENCE if it is conscious or capable of feeling.

A SIDE PAYMENT is a payment made from one party to the other to induce them to internalize an external cost.

The SOCIALLY OPTIMAL LEVEL OF POLLUTION is the point at which the human beings in a market place value the next consumer good more highly than they do the reduction in pollution that could be bought with the same money.

A SPECIES is a category defining a group of individual organisms that are capable of interbreeding.

SPECIESISM is the denial of equal moral standing based on species membership.

A SPECIFIC RIGHT is one whose correlative duty only falls on a determinate person or group.

STRONG ETHICAL EGOISM is theory that it is always morally required that people should act to maximize their own self-interest.

STRONG SUSTAINABILITY is a condition where stocks of natural resources do not decline.

SUBJECTIVE CONSEQUENTIALISM is a type of consequentialist ethical theory which says that the intrinsic value which agents ought to cause is constituted by certain mental states of recipients with moral standing.

An entity's SUBJECTIVE GOOD is what it wants for itself, or what it believes to be good for it.

In the SUBJECTIVE INTERESTS approach to justifying natural rights, the natural feature that justifies a right is the mental benefits that the rights-holder will experience.

SUSTAINABLE DEVELOPMENT is development that meets the needs of the present without compromising the ability of future generations to meet their own needs.

In the TELEOLOGICAL APPROACH to ethics, each agent ought to act so as to best enable the natural functioning of recipients with moral standing.

A TELEOLOGICAL CENTRE OF LIFE (Taylor) is a being that can be benefitted or harmed in ways that enhance or diminish its ability to flourish.

TOTAL UTILITARIANISM maximizes the aggregate utility added up for everyone, instead of maximizing the utility per person.

The TOTAL UTILITY of a stock of economic goods or services is the sum of all the utility produced by the consumption of those goods or services.

Garrett Hardin's TRAGEDY OF THE COMMONS is a particular type of external cost situation in which the external costs of any individual participant's actions are spread over all the participants in the situation. This gives each participant a positive net internal benefit and an incentive for doing the action, yet the result of similar actions by all participants is a worse situation for all.

TRANSACTION COSTS are the costs of reaching and enforcing an agreement between negotiating parties. They include the costs of researching information about the situation, negotiating the agreement, and legally enforcing the agreement.

The ULTIMATUM GAME is a behavioural economics experiment which demonstrates that people do not always behave as psychological egoists.

UNCERTAINTY is a condition where the outcome cannot be definitely predicted and where the probabilities of different outcomes cannot be measured.

UTILITARIANISM is a type of subjective consequentialist ethical theory which says that moral agents ought to cause the maximum aggregated amount of valuable mental states for recipients with moral standing.

UTILITY is an abstract measure of intensity for whatever mental states a utilitarian thinks should be aggregated and maximized.

VIRTUE ETHICS is the ethical approach that focuses on the character of the agent, and assesses the agent's character traits as virtuous or vicious.

WEAK ETHICAL EGOISM is the theory that it is always morally permissible for people to act to maximize their own self-interest.

WEAK SUSTAINABILITY is a condition where human-made substitutes compensate for depletion of natural resources.

According to the WILL THEORY OF RIGHTS, the natural feature that grounds a right is its holder's power either to insist that others follow their correlative duties, or not to so insist, according to the right-holder's will on the matter.

WILLINGNESS TO PAY (WTP) is the monetary value to an individual of enjoying the benefits of consuming a particular good or service.

ZOOCENTRIC theories of environmental ethics extend moral standing to other animals besides human beings.

REFERENCES

Aristotle. 350 BCE. *Politics*. Translated by Benjamin Jowett. Retrieved December 28, 2010 from the World Wide Web: <http://classics.mit.edu/Aristotle/politics.html>

Baxter, William. 1974. *People or Penguins: The Case for Optimal Pollution*. New York: Columbia.

The Bhagavad Gita. The Bhagavad-Gita Trust. Retrieved January 8, 2011 from the World Wide Web: <http://www.bhagavad-gita.org/index-english.html>

Bentham, Jeremy. 1823. *Introduction to the Principles of Morals and Legislation*. 2nd ed. Retrieved November 16, 2010 from the World Wide Web: <http://www.econlib.org/library/Bentham/bnthPML18.html>

Bookchin, Murray. 1987. "Social Ecology versus Deep Ecology." *Green Perspectives: Newsletter of the Green Program Project*. Nos. 4–5. Retrieved January 2, 2011 from the World Wide Web: <http://dwardmac.pitzer.edu/Anarchist_Archives/bookchin/soce-covdeepeco.html>

Broome, John. 2008. "The Ethics of Climate Change." *Scientific American*, Vol. 298. pp. 96–102.

Cahen, Harley. 1988. "Against the Moral Considerability of Ecosystems." *Environmental Ethics*. Vol. 10. pp. 195–216.

Coase, Ronald. 1960. "The Problem of Social Cost." *The Journal of law and Economics*. Vol. 3. pp. 1–44.

Commission of the European Communities. 2000. "Communication from the Commission on the Precautionary Principle." Brussels, 2.2.2000. COM(2000) 1 final. Retrieved March 28, 2011 from the World Wide Web: <http://eur-lex.europa.eu/LexUriServ/LexUriServ.do?uri=COM:2000:0001:FIN:EN:PDF>

Des Jardins, Joseph R. 1997. *Environmental Ethics: An Introduction to Environmental Philosophy*. 2nd ed. Belmont, CA: Wadsworth.

Devall, Bill and George Sessions. 2007. *Deep Ecology*. Salt Lake City: Gibbs Smith.

Feinberg, Joel. 1976. "Can Animals Have Rights?" In Peter Singer, ed., *Animal Rights and Human Obligations*. Englewood Cliffs, NJ: Prentice Hall. pp. 190–96.

Field, Barry C. and Nancy D. Olewiler. 2002. *Environmental Economics: Second Canadian Edition*. Toronto: McGraw-Hill Ryerson.

Frank, Robert H., Bens S. Bernanke, Lars Osberg, Melvin L. Cross, and Brian K. MacLean. 2005. *Principles of Microeconomics: Second Canadian Edition*. Toronto: McGraw-Hill Ryerson.

Guha, Ramachandra. 1989. "Radical American Environmentalism and Wilderness. Preservation: A Third World Critique." *Environmental Ethics*. Vol. 11. pp. 71–83.

Hardin, Garrett. 1974. "Living on a Lifeboat." *BioScience*. Vol. 24. pp. 561–68.

Hardin, Garrett. 1968. "The Tragedy of the Commons." *Science*. Vol. 162. pp. 1243–48.

Hobbes, Thomas. 1651. *Leviathan*. Retrieved August 10, 2010 from the World Wide Web: <http://www.gutenberg.org/ebooks/3207>

Hume, David. 1740. *A Treatise of Human Nature*. Retrieved August 10, 2010 from the World Wide Web: <http://www.gutenberg.org/ebooks/4705>

James, William. *The Principles of Psychology*. Retrieved January 8, 2011 from the World Wide Web: <http://psychclassics.asu.edu/James/Principles/>

Kant, Immanuel. 1976. "Duties to Animals." In Peter Singer, ed., *Animal Rights and Human Obligations*. Englewood Cliffs, NJ: Prentice Hall. pp. 122–23.

Kernohan, Andrew. 1995. "Rights against Polluters." *Environmental Ethics*. Vol. 17. pp. 245–57. Reprinted in D. Clowney and P. Mosto, eds., *Earthcare: Readings in Environmental Ethics*. Maryland: Rowman & Littlefield, 2009.

Kernohan, Andrew. 1993. "Accumulative Harms and the Interpretation of the Harm Principle." *Social Theory and Practice*. Vol. 19. pp. 51–72.

Kirchner, James. 1991. "The Gaia Hypotheses: Are They Testable? Are They Useful?" In S.H. Schneider and P.J. Boston, eds., *Scientists on Gaia*. Cambridge, MA: MIT Press. pp. 38–46.

Leopold, Aldo. 1949. *A Sand County Almanac*. New York: Ballantine, 1970.

Locke, John. 1689. *Second Treatise of Government*. Retrieved October 29, 2010 from the World Wide Web: <http://www.gutenberg.org/ebooks/7370>

Macaulay, Hugh and Bruce Yandle. 1977. *Environmental Use and the Market*. Lexington, MA: Lexington Books.

Manson, Neil A. 2002. "Formulating the Precautionary Principle." *Environmental Ethics*. Vol. 24. pp. 263–74.

Mill, John Stuart. 1863. *Utilitarianism*. Retrieved September 4, 2010 from the World Wide Web: <http://www.gutenberg.org/etext/11224>

Mill, John Stuart. 1848. "Of the Stationary State," from *Principles of Political Economy*, Book IV, Chapter VI. Retrieved April 11, 2011 from the World Wide Web: <http://www.econlib.org/library/Mill/mlP61.html>

Naess, Arne. 1985. "Identification as a Source of Deep Ecological Attitudes." In Michael Tobias, ed., *Deep Ecology*. San Diego: Avant Books. pp. 256–70.

Nozick, Robert. 1989. *The Examined Life*. New York: Simon and Shuster.

Parfit, Derek. 1984. *Reasons and Persons*. Oxford: Clarendon Press.

Pogge, Thomas. 2001. "Eradicating Systemic Poverty: Brief for a Global Resources Dividend." *The Journal of Human Development*. Vol. 2. pp. 59–77. Reprinted in Thom Brooks, ed., *The Global Justice Reader*. Oxford: Blackwell, 2008. pp. 439–53.

Rawls, John. 1971. *A Theory of Justice*. Cambridge, MA: Harvard University Press.

Regan, Tom. 1986. "The Case for Animal Rights." In Peter Singer, ed., *In Defense of Animals*. New York: Harper & Row.

Regan, Tom. 1983. *The Case for Animal Rights*. Berkeley: University of California Press.

Rowe, Jonathan. 2008. "The Parallel Economy of the Commons." *2008 State of the World: Innovations for a Sustainable Economy*. New York: Norton.

Sagoff, Mark. 1981. "At the Shrine of Our Lady of Fatima, or Why Political Questions Are Not All Economic." *Arizona Law Review*. Vol. 23. pp. 1283–98.

Schweitzer, Albert. 1923. *Civilization and Ethics*. Trans. C.T. Campion. London: Unwin Books.

Sen, Amartya. 1987. *On Ethics and Economics*. Oxford: Blackwell.

Singer, Peter. 1976. "All Animals Are Equal." In Peter Singer, ed., *Animal Rights and Human Obligations*. Englewood Cliffs, NJ: Prentice Hall.

Singer, Peter. 1972. "Famine, Affluence, and Morality." *Philosophy and Public Affairs*. Vol. 1. pp. 229–43.

Smith, Adam. 1776 (1904). *An Inquiry into the Nature and Causes of the Wealth of Nations*. Edwin Cannan, ed., Library of Economics and Liberty. Retrieved August 10, 2010 from the World Wide Web: <http://www.econlib.org/library/Smith/smWN1.html>

Solow, Robert. 2005. "Sustainability: An Economist's Perspective." In Robert Stavins, ed., *Economics of the Environment: Selected Readings*. 5th ed. New York: W.W. Norton & Company. pp. 505–13.

Solow, Robert. 1993. "An Almost Practical Step toward Sustainability." *Resources Policy*. September. pp. 162–72.

Summers, Lawrence. 1992. "Letter to the Editor." *The Economist*. February 15. Vol. 322. p. 4.

Taylor, Paul. 1986. *Respect for Nature: A Theory of Environmental Ethics*. Princeton: Princeton University Press.

Taylor, Paul. 1981. "The Ethics of Respect for Nature." *Environmental Ethics*. Vol. 3. pp. 203–18.

The Economist. 1992. "Let Them Eat Pollution." February 8. Vol. 322. p. 82.

United Nations Conference on Environment and Development. 1992. "Rio Declaration on Environment and Development." Rio de Janeiro, June 3–14, 1992. Retrieved March 28, 2011 from the World Wide Web: <http://www.un.org/documents/ga/conf151/aconf15126-1annex1.htm>

Warren, Karen. 1990. "The Power and Promise of Ecological Feminism." *Environmental Ethics*. Vol. 12, pp. 125–46.

White, Jr., Lynn. 1967. "The Historical Roots of Our Ecological Crisis." *Science*. Volume 155, Number 3767. pp. 1203–07.

Wingspread Conference on the Precautionary Principle. 1998. "The Wingspread Consensus Statement on the Precautionary Principle." Retrieved March 28, 2011 from the World Wide Web: <http://www.sehn.org/wing.html>

World Commission on Environment and Development. 1987. "Report of the World Commission on Environment and Development." 96th plenary meeting, December 11, 1987. Retrieved April 12, 2011 from the World Wide Web: <http://www.un.org/documents/ga/res/42/ares42–187.htm>

INDEX

from the publisher

A name never says it all, but the word "broadview" expresses a good deal of the philosophy behind our company. We are open to a broad range of academic approaches and political viewpoints. We pay attention to the broad impact book publishing and book printing has in the wider world; we began using recycled stock more than a decade ago, and for some years now we have used 100% recycled paper for most titles. As a Canadian-based company we naturally publish a number of titles with a Canadian emphasis, but our publishing program overall is internationally oriented and broad-ranging. Our individual titles often appeal to a broad readership too; many are of interest as much to general readers as to academics and students.

Founded in 1985, Broadview remains a fully independent company owned by its shareholders—not an imprint or subsidiary of a larger multinational.

***

If you would like to find out more about Broadview and about the books we publish, please visit us at **www.broadviewpress.com**. And if you'd like to place an order through the site, we'd like to show our appreciation by extending a special discount to you: by entering the code below you will receive a 20% discount on purchases made through the Broadview website.

Discount code: **broadview20%**

Thank you for choosing Broadview.

The interior of this book is printed on 100% recycled paper.